NURSING CARE
OF THE
PERSON WITH
AIDS/ARC

Edited by
Angie Lewis, RN, MS
Assistant Director of Nursing
Langley Porter Psychiatric Hospital
and
Assistant Clinical Professor
School of Nursing
University of California, San Francisco
San Francisco, California

Aspen Series in Medical Surgical Nursing,
Nancy Stotts, Series Editor

AN ASPEN PUBLICATION®
Aspen Publishers, Inc.

1988

Rockville, Maryland
Royal Tunbridge Wells

Library of Congress Cataloging-in-Publication Data

Nursing care of the person with AIDS/ARC / [edited by] Angie Lewis.
p. cm.
"An Aspen publication."
Includes bibliographies and index.
ISBN: 0-87189-774-1
1. AIDS (Disease)--Nursing. 2. AIDS-related complex--Nursing. I. Lewis, Angie.
[DNLM: 1. Aquired Immunodeficiency Syndrome--nursing.
2. AIDS-Related Complex--nursing. WY 150 N9715]
RC607.A26N87   1988   610.73'699--dc19
DNLM/DLC
for LIbrary of Congress
88-6353
CIP

Copyright © 1988 by Aspen Publishers, Inc.
All rights reserved.

Aspen Publishers, Inc., grants permission for photocopying for personal or internal use,
or for the personal or internal use of specific clients registered with the Copyright
Clearance Center (CCC). This consent is given on the condition that the copier pay a
$1.00 fee plus $.12 per page for each photocopy through the CCC for photocopying
beyond that permitted by the U.S. Copyright Law. The fee should be paid directly to the
CCC, 21 Congress St., Salem, Massachusetts 01970.
0-87189-774-1/88 $1.00 + .12.

This consent does not extend to other kinds of copying, such as copying for general
distribution, for advertising or promotional purposes, for creating new collective works,
or for resale. For information, address Aspen Publishers, Inc.,
1600 Research Boulevard, Rockville, Maryland 20850.

The authors have made every effort to ensure the accuracy of the information herein.
However, appropriate information sources should be consulted, especially for new or
unfamiliar procedures. It is the responsibility of every practitioner to evaluate the
appropriateness of a particular opinion in the context of actual clinical situations and with
due considerations to new developments. Authors, editors, and the publisher cannot be
held responsible for any typographical or other errors found in this book.

Editorial Services: Ruth Bloom

Library of Congress Catalog Card Number: 88-6353
ISBN: 0-87189-774-1

Printed in the United States of America

1 2 3 4 5

This book is dedicated to **Bobbi Campbell,** the "AIDS Poster Boy." I first met Bobbi, a graduate student in the School of Nursing at The Medical Center at the University of California, San Francisco, on the very day he was diagnosed (he was already wearing a button saying, "I Will Survive"), and I saw him last when I visited his bedside just a few hours before he died, almost two years later. He and I often joked about our "traveling road show" as we moved throughout northern California giving presentations on AIDS. Only a few months before he died, we gave a talk at the American Nurses' Association convention in New Orleans, and I remember saying, "I believe some folks with AIDS will make it through this, and Bobbi's going to be one." Bobbi *does* live in our memories and in the positive impact he had on many lives.

Table of Contents

Contributors

Isabel Auerbach, MPH
Community Health Worker II
San Francisco AIDS Foundation
San Francisco, California

Frances Blasque, MA
AIDS In-Home Services Coordinator
Alameda County AIDS Services
Oakland, California

Terri J. Brown, RN, BSN
Assistant Head Nurse—6 East
El Camino Hospital
Mountain View, California

Robin Candace, RN, BSN
Hospice Intake Nurse
Visiting Nurses and Hospice of San Francisco
San Francisco, California

Gary Carr, RN, MS, FNP
Nurse Practitioner
AIDS Clinic—Ward 86
San Francisco General Hospital
San Francisco, California

Elissa Chandler, RN, BSN
Executive Director
Community Hospice of the East Bay
Berkeley, California

Christina M.F. Clark, RN, MS, FNP
Case Manager
Visiting Nurses and Hospice of San Francisco
San Francisco, California

Susan D. Cochran, PhD
Associate Professor of Psychology
California State University
Northridge, California

Julia A. DeLisser, RN, BA
Coordinator, Continuing Care
El Camino Hospital
Mountain View, California

Dena Dickinson, RN, MS
Public Health Clinical Nurse Specialist
San Francisco Department of Public Health
San Francisco, California

Joan Dunkel, MSW, LCSW
Consultant/Lecturer
School of Social Welfare
University of California
Berkeley, California

Rita Fahrner, RN, MS, PNP
AIDS Clinical Nurse Specialist
San Francisco General Hospital
San Francisco, California

Barbara G. Faltz, RNC, MS
AIDS Services Coordinator
Santa Clara County Bureau of Drug Abuse
San Jose, California

Mary Lou Galantino, RPT
Director, Physical Therapy Department
Institute for Immunological Disorders
Houston, Texas

Shellie Hatfield, MSW, LCSW
Clinical Social Worker
Palo Alto Medical Clinic
Palo Alto, California

Suzanne F. Herbst, RN, MA
Founder and President
Bay Area Vascular Access Network
Redwood City, California

Anita Kline, MSW
Medical Social Worker—Ward 5A
San Francisco General Hospital
San Francisco, California

**Barbara A. Koenig, RN,
PhD Candidate**
Nursing School Coordinator
AIDS Professional Education Project
University of California
San Francisco, California

Marsha Lose, RN, MS, CIC
Infection Control Coordinator
Community Hospital
Santa Rosa, California

Grace Lusby, RN, MS
Infection Control Coordinator
San Francisco General Hospital
San Francisco, California

Judy Macks, LCSW
Director of Training
U.C.S.F. AIDS Health Project
San Francisco, California

Scott Madover, MFCC
Psychotherapist—Private Practice
San Francisco, California

Jeffrey S. Mandel, PhD, MPH
Psychotherapist—Private Practice
AIDS Professional Education Project
University of California
San Francisco, California

Vickie M. Mays, PhD
Associate Professor of Psychology
University of California
Los Angeles, California

Tolbert McCarroll
Author, *Morning Glory Babies: Children with
    AIDS and the Celebration of Life*
Starcross Community
Annapolis, California

Pat McCarthy, RN, MSN
Deputy Director
AIDS Education and Training
California Nurses Association
San Francisco, California

S. Christopher W. Mead, PhD
Psychologist—Private Practice
San Francisco, California

Alison Moed, RN, BSN
Head Nurse—Ward 5A
San Francisco General Hospital
San Francisco, California

**Cliff Morrison, MS, MN, RN, CS,
    CNA**
Deputy Director
AIDS Health Services Program
Institute for Health Policy Studies
University of California
San Francisco, California

Katherine Nelson, RN, MS
Maternal Child Clinical Nurse Specialist
San Francisco General Hospital
San Francisco, California

Patsy J. Oliver, RN, BS, CIC
Infection Control Coordinator
El Camino Hospital
Mountain View, California

Lyn Paleo
Director of Education
San Francisco AIDS Foundation
San Francisco, California

Tristano Palermino
Former Social Services Director
San Francisco AIDS Foundation
San Francisco, California

Elaine M. Peterman, RN, BS
Assistant Administrator, Nursing
El Camino Hospital
Mountain View, California

Joan Taber Pike, MA, RD
Senior Instructor/Nutritionist
School of Dentistry
Oregon Health Sciences University
Portland, Oregon
Former Clinical Nutritionist—Ward 5A
San Francisco General Hospital
San Francisco, California

Marcia Quackenbush, MS, MFCC
Coordinator
AIDS and Youth Education and Prevention
U.C.S.F. AIDS Health Project
San Francisco, California

Cynthia L. Reno, RN, BSN
Clinical Nurse III
The Medical Center at the University of
    California
San Francisco, California

Vinson Roberts, RN, BSN
Assistant Department Administrator—E R
Kaiser-Permanente
West Los Angeles, California

Marilyn S. Rodgers, RN, MS
Staff Development Instructor
El Camino Hospital
Mountain View, California

Helen Schietinger, MA, RN, MFCC
Director
AIDS Education and Training
California Nurses Association
San Francisco, California

Nancy Stoller Shaw, PhD
Associate Professor
University of California
Santa Cruz, California

George F. Solomon, MD
Professor of Psychiatry
University of California
Los Angeles, California

Dale W. Spence, EdD, FACSM
Professor
Department of Health and Physical Education
Rice University
Houston, Texas

Maria J. Gonzales Swafford, RN, MSN, CS
AIDS/ARC Home Care Case Manager
Ellipse Peninsula AIDS Services
Redwood City, California

Anita P. Walker, RN
Clinical Nurse III
The Medical Center at the University of California
San Francisco, California

Margaret Walter, RN
Hospice Intake Nurse
Visiting Nurses and Hospice of San Francisco
San Francisco, California

Foreword

At the beginning of the AIDS epidemic most health care providers, like the general public, were frightened, and many had reservations about caring for diagnosed persons. Regardless, significant numbers of nurses, doctors, and social workers volunteered to work with people with AIDS (PWAs). Over the past four years much has been learned and shared through innumerable professional articles and books. Today, as a result, thousands of nurses and other health care providers work with PWAs with relative ease. This has come about because these caring professionals became informed and involved.

Nurses are the single largest professional group in the United States. Almost everyone knows a nurse; when our profession comes to terms with the realities of AIDS, society as a whole will benefit greatly. By virtue of our professional education and training we are nurturers, educators, and advocates, which gives us an enormous public responsibility. We, along with other health care providers, are looked up to by the average person on the street; we often serve as role models for personal response. AIDS reinforces our need to keep our special position constantly in mind, whether we are working, entertaining friends or family, or riding on the bus. If we are not adequately informed or if we display negative behavior, those around us feel justified in reacting negatively. The single largest contribution nurses and nursing can make during this epidemic is to remember that our primary role is that of patient advocate. By keeping this role in mind, we have something tangible to guide us through daily situations.

The AIDS epidemic presents both new and recurring challenges to the nursing profession. For the first time we have an opportunity to demonstrate to the world what nursing is all about. To accomplish this task we must provide leadership within our profession. In order to advocate for PWAs as well as persons with other life-threatening illnesses, nurses are joining their local, state, and national professional organizations in increasing numbers.

AIDS also brings to the surface issues and problems that society, health care, and nursing in particular have avoided for decades. It forces us to deal with the

xvii

single most important issue for us all: not our rejection of particular lifestyles or fear of sexuality, but the fear of our own mortality. The more we come to terms with this basic reality and related issues, the better we will be as individuals and as professional caregivers, and our profession will develop the momentum for leadership. Our role as patient advocate will then become clear to all and nurses will achieve recognition as positive role models in the care of PWAs.

We will also become more actively involved in educating not only other health care providers but the general public.

This quest is especially important as AIDS is increasingly viewed as a nursing illness. With no cure in sight, it is the quality of care given by professional nurses that makes the difference to PWAs. Care and advocacy at every level of health care, whether in the home, clinic, hospital, nursing home, or hospice, is essential to these individuals. We must keep in mind that nursing is the only health care discipline that provides for the needs of the whole person, whether they are physical, emotional, or psychosocial.

To provide quality care for all patients we must first be in touch with the personal feelings and emotions that provision of care elicits from each of us. Nurses are human beings, and we bring our life experiences to our work. When we take those experiences and appropriately incorporate them into our professional role, we feel more satisfied with our work. Incorporating our experiences into our roles as nurses may often mean dealing objectively with our own issues surrounding morals, prejudices, death of a loved one, emotional or physical abuse, or our fear of rejection. We must each do our individual work to accomplish the collective goals of our profession.

Nursing has a responsibility to become involved in issues that are important to the health and welfare of society as a whole. We must commit ourselves to involvement at all political levels, constantly advocating to ensure that resources to provide quality care are available to everyone. This commitment means becoming involved in the financial issues of health care as well as taking a strong stand on specific health-related public policy issues. As we become more involved in these issues, we will feel a greater sense of control, gain self-confidence, and improve the overall morale within our profession.

Nursing is realizing many of these benefits as nurses become involved in AIDS issues and as leadership begins to respond appropriately and take a more vocal stand on the issues, and these changes are reflected in our professional literature. Nurses are becoming more supportive of each other and working collaboratively with other health care disciplines to accomplish our common goals. As a profession we must never lose sight of the importance of working with our colleagues. As our role enhances other health care professions, they in turn enhance our ability to provide quality care at every level within the health care continuum.

Never before in our history have we faced so many challenges. It is ironic that it has taken the AIDS epidemic for us to develop a vision for the future and realize our true potential as a profession. Out of the suffering of others always comes some good, and the AIDS epidemic, more than any other event in modern health care, is helping us see the flaws in our profession and in health care as a whole. For most of us the AIDS epidemic is the first time we have had to deal personally with death in a young population and with people we know. Eventually each of us will be touched by AIDS, and at that time we will begin to deal with all of these issues in a more humanistic way.

AIDS also offers us many opportunities for growth. Our tasks will continue to be difficult, and we may not receive the recognition that others do, but we can acknowledge the contributions we each make in working for the common good of all patients. Working with AIDS, as with other illnesses, can be extremely trying and stressful. Although it constantly tests our abilities as professionals and individuals, it does not have to be depressing. We can find unlimited fulfillment in our work with these patients, their families, and their significant others and walk away knowing that we have done our best. AIDS continues to test our society; those of us who accept the challenges and face the issues head-on will find a personal fulfillment and satisfaction that we have never known before.

In the environment created by AIDS and the challenges it presents for us, this book makes an important contribution to the care of affected persons. The expert clinicians who are the authors exemplify the accomplishments of health care providers who work directly with PWAs, their families and significant others, and affected communities. The information they share will be of great value to those of us providing care to persons with AIDS or AIDS-related complex (ARC).

Cliff Morrison, MS, MN, RN, CS, CNA
Deputy Director, AIDS Health Services Program
Institute for Health Policy Studies
University of California, San Francisco

Preface

My personal involvement with AIDS/ARC began on a sunny day in the summer of 1981; I attended a medical meeting and heard a presentation about an unusual occurrence of a disease I'd never heard of, Kaposi's sarcoma (KS). A virulent form of KS had recently been identified in a small group of young gay men in Los Angeles and New York. Some of these men also had a rare pneumonia, *Pneumocystis carinii*. The U.S. Centers for Disease Control (CDC) had been notified, a first report had been published in *Morbidity and Mortality Weekly Report* three weeks earlier, and a CDC task force had just been formed to investigate the new phenomenon. None of us, of course, had any idea that these events marked the beginning of a long-term problem that would eventually affect health care consumers and providers throughout the world.

As an educator in Nursing Education and Research at The Medical Center at the University of California, San Francisco, I was able to pursue my interest in this disease, and by early fall I was attending the formative meetings of the KS Study Group. During October, I began making daily visits to the first person we hospitalized with KS and offered to serve as a resource person for the staff on the oncology unit where he was located. During the following months, I visited most patients admitted and presented several short inservice programs for nursing and other ancillary staff. In June 1982 we presented what we believe to be the first all-day program designed specifically for nurses and other direct care providers. Entitled "Kaposi's Sarcoma and *Pneumocystis* Pneumonia: New Phenomena Among Gay Men," the program attracted almost 100 participants.

Over the years, I have watched the evolution of an AIDS/ARC industry, which often must straddle a thin line between creating panic in a community and generating resources to meet genuine educational and health care needs. Throughout these experiences, my early beliefs have been reinforced: at this writing AIDS/ARC is a disease in which caring—the kind of caring provided by nurses—is of primary importance to persons with AIDS/ARC, their significant others, and other family members and friends. With no cure presently known, maintenance of quality of life becomes their major concern, and the pivotal factors in maintaining that quality are often exactly those areas in which nurses have expertise. These include, but are not limited to:

- education of the patient, family, and significant others
- maintenance of nutrition
- assistance with activities of daily living
- pain management
- support in dealing with anticipatory grief and other psychosocial concerns
- maintenance of bowel function.

Further, nurses often serve as health educators for their families, friends, and communities, and in the epidemic they have also served a pivotal role in development of community resources.

Obviously, nurses function as members of the health care team, working with physicians and, when available, members of other professional disciplines, such as social workers, clinical nutritionists, and physical therapists, all of whom make invaluable contributions to the resolution of these issues of care.

This book is for nurses, other professionals, and laypersons who provide direct care to persons with AIDS/ARC. It is intended as a resource manual of practical advice not only for caregivers in the hospital and home but also for institutional administrators who might develop services for persons with AIDS/ARC and educators who are preparing inservices or continuing education programs. The authors are actively involved in provision of care and often present a highly personal view of the epidemic. In contrast to a highly technical presentation, this book focuses on AIDS/ARC in relation to the experiences of the people involved with the disease; it addresses not only the physiological and psychosocial needs of persons who have the disease but the feelings and responses of those who care for them.

Angie Lewis
June 1988

Acknowledgments

As the list of contributors shows, many individuals have donated their expertise to the development of this book. Because AIDS/ARC has evolved rapidly and the issues are so complex, no one individual is "the expert"; rather, we work collaboratively, each contributing that which we know and are learning. Over the past six years, it has been these professional colleagues—many of whom have become personal friends—who have often sustained me though difficult times. Through them I have expanded my horizons and been challenged to new heights of professional and personal creativity, and for that I thank them.

I also thank my life partner, Shirley Palmisano, for her continuing patience and loving support.

Introduction

The book is divided into five parts, each containing introductory comments by the editor and three or more chapters. Part I, AIDS in Perspective, provides background information on human immunodeficiency virus, discussions on the needs of six special populations, a chapter on the psychosocial responses of persons with AIDS/ARC, and an essay written by a person with AIDS. This information will be especially useful for providers with little or no experience caring for persons with AIDS, or for those whose experience is with a limited client population.

Part II, Care in the Hospital, is the longest section of the book, containing nine chapters. These cover care on an adult inpatient unit and implications for pediatric and obstetrical services. Also included are treatments and interventions provided by nursing, medicine, physical therapy, dietetics, and infection control. The emphasis is on nonmedical interventions provided by nurses and other professionals because many medical treatments are either experimental, unavailable outside of major research centers, or both. In addition to being useful for anyone providing direct care, this part provides essential, pragmatic information for supervisors and educators.

Part III moves into care in the community, covering discharge planning, care in the home, hospice care, and development of community resources. It is intended both for care providers in the community and nurses in the hospital who prepare patients and significant others for discharge. It is hoped that by raising awareness of discharge needs, institutions and communities can initiate anticipatory planning, thus avoiding potential problems related to discharge planning.

Part IV, which focuses on education and support of the care providers, opens with a discussion on understanding and working with the emotional reactions of staff. It then moves into staff education, self-awareness, and ethical and legal issues. These chapters will be especially useful for nurse educators and for clinical specialists who act as psychiatric liaisons.

The final part, The Community Provider Experience, presents the experiences of three community hospitals as they have faced the AIDS/ARC epidemic. Although all are in northern California, they were chosen specifically because they are community hospitals rather than teaching or research institutions, are outside the immediate San Francisco area, and have been required to develop their own resources. The closing chapter deals with techniques for developing community resources. This part will be of particular concern to providers who wish to become more involved in their community, and to administrators, who must become more involved.

AIDS in Perspective

In the early days of the AIDS epidemic, so little was known that the basics (commonly called AIDS 101) could be covered in a couple of hours. However, knowledge about AIDS has grown more rapidly than knowledge of just about any other disease in the history of the world. At this writing thousands of articles and numerous books describe every aspect of the disease.

In this book, the term human immunodeficiency virus (HIV) is used to refer to the AIDS retrovirus, the agent that causes infection. The disease that results from the infection may be referred to as acquired immune deficiency syndrome (AIDS), AIDS/AIDS-related complex (ARC), or HIV infection. The person or people with AIDS are often called PWAs rather than patients. This acronym, which was developed by the National Association of People with AIDS, is the preferred term for many of these individuals.

Part I answers the most basic questions:

- What is AIDS?
- Who gets AIDS?
- What is the psychosocial impact for the person with AIDS?
- What does it feel like to have AIDS?

To emphasize the impact of AIDS on people, six chapters in this part present the needs of special populations. This term is preferred rather than the term "risk groups" because belonging to a group doesn't place a person at risk—risk comes from the *behavior* of exchanging body fluids, specifically semen and blood.

The chapter on psychosocial impact and an article written by a man with AIDS are also placed in the first part to emphasize the importance of the personal psychological experience of the person with the disease.

Nurses play a vital role in providing support to persons with AIDS/ARC as well as those who are HIV-antibody-positive and the "worried well"—those who fear

1

they will get or may already have AIDS. When we demonstrate an attitude of understanding, caring, and acceptance, we not only help minimize some of the stressors on these individuals, but we also serve as positive role models for our colleagues and our society.

Chapter 1

HIV: The Basics

Angie Lewis

HISTORY OF AIDS/ARC

In the summer of 1981, the U.S. Centers for Disease Control (CDC) reported unusual outbreaks of *Pneumocystis carinii* pneumonia (PCP) and a virulent form of Kaposi's sarcoma (KS) among small numbers of young gay men in New York City and California.[1] This was unusual because KS had almost always been an indolent disease found in elderly Jewish and Italian men of Mediterranean descent and PCP was usually exclusively limited to severely immunosuppressed patients.[2] The cause of the outbreak was unknown, but an early hypothesis was the existence of a cellular immune dysfunction somehow related to sexual activity.

These early reports were a medical curiosity for most, but for the health care providers, including nurses, who were caring for the patients the reality was all too clear. These young men were rapidly dying, and nothing seemed to save them. While they were ill, their care needs were tremendous; physically they usually experienced profound diarrhea, weight loss, weakness, and fever, while psychologically they were often dealing with an unsupportive family and frightened, worried friends. Although most health care providers responded in an extraordinarily positive manner, a few reinforced this anxiety and fear with their nonsupportive attitude.

The number of cases increased rapidly, to 355 in June 1982. The next month cases were reported among persons with hemophilia A and in the Haitian community, and in September the disease acquired a name: acquired immune deficiency syndrome, or AIDS. For most persons aware of the problem, it had been "their" (the homosexuals') disease, and now it seemed to be spreading. The mortality was clear; the cause, treatment, and means of prevention were unknown; and the fear grew. That fall, the CDC published the first infection control precautions that encouraged the use of Hepatitis B precautions for clinical and laboratory staffs.

Beginning in 1982, the gay press frequently published information on AIDS as well as on ARC. Persons with ARC are not diagnosed with a disease that fits the CDC definition (prior to the 1987 revision), yet they experience significant health problems that are felt to be related to AIDS. Educational material on safe sex was developed and circulated in the gay community. Many gay men and lesbians responded to the crisis, either as direct care providers or as volunteers in the support and educational services that developed in affected cities. However, as the public media began to publicize the issues, hysteria grew among the general population. As the public began to experience a personal fear, articles detailing prejudice experienced by PWAs became common.

The number of cases continues to grow, not only in the United States but internationally. Every state in the nation and every major country in the world is dealing with what is clearly the major public health crisis of modern times.

WHAT IS AIDS?

AIDS is an extremely complex disease. As our knowledge and understanding have grown, the disease definition has been, and will continue to be, modified. In August 1987, the CDC issued the latest revision of the surveillance case definition, which was effective for case reporting as of September 1, 1987.[3] This definition, based on laboratory evidence for HIV, is more consistent with current diagnostic practices and should simplify reporting; importantly, it also allows inclusion of some individuals previously diagnosed with ARC.

For the nurse, the revised definition is rather cumbersome and awkward to use; education of patients and families presents a special challenge. Figure 1-1 provides a flow diagram for the new case definition; for a complete description of the definition, see Appendix A.

Perhaps more useful for the clinician is the classification system developed by the CDC in 1986 and shown in Exhibit 1-1.[4] This system, which has not yet been revised to reflect the new surveillance definition, classifies the clinical manifestations of persons diagnosed with HIV into four mutually exclusive groups. Because clinical improvement may not accurately reflect changes in the severity of the underlying disease, persons classified into a group should not be reclassified into a preceding group, even if clinical findings resolve. All groups and subgroups assume the absence of concurrent illness or a condition other than HIV infection to explain the findings.

WHAT CAUSES AIDS?

AIDS is caused by a retrovirus called HIV, which was first reported by a group from the Pasteur Institute in Paris in 1983. A virus is a piece of genetic informa-

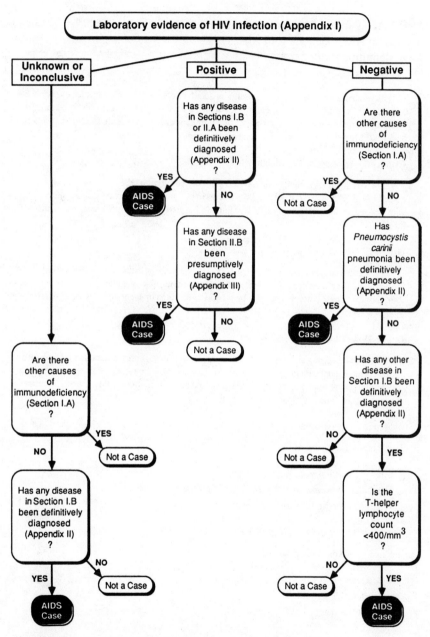

Note: Appendixes and sections mentioned in the figure are found in Appendix A.

Figure 1-1 Flow Diagram for Revised CDC Case Definition of AIDS, September 1, 1987. *Source*: Reprinted from *Morbidity and Mortality Weekly Report*, Vol. 36, No. 36, p. 8S, U.S. Centers for Disease Control, August 14, 1987.

Exhibit 1-1 CDC Classification System for Persons Diagnosed with HIV Infection

---

Group I—Acute Infection

These individuals experience transient signs and symptoms of a mononucleosis-like syndrome, with or without aseptic meningitis, which appears with acute HIV infection. Antibody seroconversion is required as evidence of initial infection. After the acute syndrome resolves, all Group I patients are reclassified to another group.

Group II—Asymptomatic Infection

This group includes patients who have no signs or symptoms of HIV infection and who have never been classified in Groups III or IV. Patients in this group may be subclassified into a group with normal or incomplete laboratory results and a group with results consistent with HIV infection.

Group III—Persistent Generalized Lymphadenopathy

These patients experience persistent generalized lymphadenopathy (PGL), defined as palpable lymph node enlargement of 1 cm or greater at two or more extra-inguinal sites persisting for three months. These patients may also be subclassified based on laboratory results as described in Group II.

Group IV—Other HIV Diseases

Patients in this group are assigned to one or more subgroups representing other HIV disease. Assignment is independent of the presence or absence of lymphadenopathy. Each subgroup may include individuals representing the illness spectrum, from the minimally symptomatic to the severely ill. These subgroups are not mutually exclusive.

Subgroup A.—Constitutional Disease

Defined as one or more of the following:

- fever persisting more than one month
- involuntary weight loss of greater than 10 percent of baseline
- diarrhea persisting more than one month.

Subgroup B.—Neurologic Disease

Defined as one or more of the following:

- dementia
- myelopathy
- peripheral neuropathy.

Subgroup C.—Secondary Infectious Diseases

This subgroup is reflective of "selected infectious diseases."* Prior to the August 1987 case definition revision, this subgroup was defined as the diagnosis of an infectious disease

---

Exhibit 1-1 continued

associated with HIV infection and/or at least moderately indicative of a defect in cell-mediated immunity. Patients in this subgroup were subdivided into two categories, C-1 and C-2. The C-1 group included any of the 12 diseases listed in the surveillance definition, while C-2 included 6 other specific diseases.

Subgroup D.—Secondary Cancers

The diagnosis of one or more kinds of cancer known to be associated with HIV infection, including:

- Kaposi's sarcoma
- non-Hodgkin's lymphoma (small, noncleaved lymphoma or immunoglastic sarcoma)
- primary lymphoma of the brain.

Subgroup E.—Other Conditions in HIV Infection

The presence of other clinical findings or diseases, not classifiable above, that may be attributed to HIV infection and/or may be indicative of a defect in cell-mediated immunity. Included in this group are persons whose signs or symptoms could be attributed either to HIV infection or to another coexisting disease not classified elsewhere and patients with other clinical illnesses, the course or management of which may be complicated or altered by HIV infection.

*Richard M. Selik, U.S. Centers for Disease Control, AIDS Office, personal communication, November 1987.

Source: Reprinted from *Morbidity and Mortality Weekly Report*, Vol. 35, No. 20, pp. 1–5, U.S. Centers for Disease Control, May 23, 1986.

tion, either RNA or DNA, protected by a protein coat. A retrovirus is a single piece of RNA also surrounded by an envelope or protein coat.[5] While the usual flow of genetic information is from DNA to RNA to protein, the retrovirus is able to reverse the process and make itself into a piece of DNA. This DNA is then inserted into the DNA in the nucleus of the infected cell, where it remains for the life of the cell. HIV is able to recognize a particular type of cell, called the T-lymphocyte helper cell, which normally coordinates the immune response.[6] HIV copies itself into the genetic material of the helper cell and eventually causes the death of the cell.[7] In a person with an intact immune system, there are twice as many helper cells as there are suppressor cells. The function of suppressor T-cells is to turn off the immune response when it is no longer needed. The person with AIDS has too few helper T-cells and an excess number of suppressor T-cells, often reversing the normal ratio; this individual is severely immunocompromised and susceptible to opportunistic infections and unusual malignancies.

HOW IS AIDS TRANSMITTED?

The HIV virus that causes AIDS is passed from person to person through body secretions. Although HIV is found in most body secretions, semen, blood, or both are generally implicated. The most common means of transmission are (1) sexual contact involving the exchange of body fluids and (2) blood-to-blood contact through shared needles. AIDS is not transmitted through casual contact.

WHO GETS AIDS?

As of November 9, 1987, the CDC had received reports of 45,436 cases of AIDS; 16,381 of these had been reported since January 1, 1987.[8] These numbers include the cumulative total of 641 cases reported in children. For adults, transmission categories include:

- Homosexual/bisexual male—66 percent of cumulative cases
- Intravenous (IV) drug abuser—16 percent of cumulative cases
- Homosexual male and IV drug abuser—8 percent of cumulative cases
- Hemophilia/coagulation disorder—1 percent of cumulative cases
- Heterosexual cases—4 percent of cumulative cases
- Transfusion, blood components—2 percent of cumulative cases
- Unknown—3 percent of cumulative cases

More specific epidemiological information is presented in Chapters 3 through 7.

HIV TESTING

The HIV antibody test shows whether a person has antibodies to HIV, thus indicating previous exposure. The test result (positive or negative) does not tell:[9]

- if someone has AIDS or ARC
- if someone will develop AIDS or ARC in the future
- if someone is immune to AIDS or ARC.

Almost 100 percent of patients with AIDS are found to have a positive antibody test, while the rate drops to 95 percent in persons with ARC.[10] The incidence of antibodies in the general population, as represented by blood donors, is believed to be about 0.04 percent. Someone who has a positive test is assumed to be contagious and capable of passing the virus on to others. HIV antibody testing raises many ethical and legal questions, which are discussed in Chapter 25.

NOTES

1. U.S. Centers for Disease Control (CDC), "Pneumocystis Pneumonia—Los Angeles," *Morbidity and Mortality Weekly Report (MMWR)* 30 (June 5, 1981): 250–52; and CDC, "Kaposi's Sarcoma and Pneumocystis Pneumonia Among Homosexual Men—New York and California," *MMWR* 30 (July 3, 1981):305–08.

2. P.D. Walzer et al., "*Pneumocystis carinii* Pneumonia in the United States: Epidemiologic, Diagnostic, and Clinical Features," *Annals of Internal Medicine* 80 (1974):83–93.

3. CDC, "Revision of the CDC Surveillance Case Definition for Acquired Immunodeficiency Syndrome," *MMWR* 36, no. 1S (August 14, 1987).

4. CDC, "Classification System for Human T-Lymphotropic Virus Type III/Lymphadenopathy-Associated Virus Infections," *MMWR* 35, no.TH20 (May 23, 1986):1–5.

5. Donald I. Abrams, "AIDS: Battling a Retroviral Enemy," *California Nursing Review* 8, no. 6 (November 1986):11.

6. Ibid.

7. Ibid.

8. CDC, *AIDS Weekly Surveillance Report, United States AIDS Activity*, November 9, 1987.

9. R. Baker et al., *AIDS Antibody Testing at Alternative Test Sites* (San Francisco, Calif.: San Francisco AIDS Foundation, revised 1987).

10. Abrams, "AIDS: Battling A Retroviral Enemy."

Chapter 2

The Gay and Bisexual Male

S. Christopher W. Mead, George F. Solomon,
and Jeffrey S. Mandel

The care of the typical oncology patient and that of the gay or bisexual client with AIDS/ARC are quite similar. In both situations, the nurse must attend to complex physical problems secondary to immune deficiency, at the same time confronting the issue of working with a life-threatening illness in a young or relatively young person. However, one significant difference between these patient populations is that the nurse caring for the gay or bisexual AIDS/ARC client must confront personal feelings about homosexuality and, sometimes, irrational fears of contagion.

THE GAY MALE

Throughout much of history, homosexuality has stirred conflict. Most often it has been regarded as a moral issue; gay people have been burned, hanged, and imprisoned for loving someone of their own sex. Individuals who engage in homosexual behavior have been seen as immature, immoral, or ill.[1] They have been victims of societal prejudices and attack.

Until this century, psychological theories treated homosexuality as a mental disorder. Some blamed the genesis of the disorder on parents.[2] As a consequence, some gay people perceive themselves as ill and parents often feel guilty. Finally, in 1973, after years of debate, the American Psychiatric Association removed homosexuality as an emotional disorder from the *Diagnostic and Statistical Manual of Mental Disorders* (*DSM-III*), except in the case of those individuals who cannot accept their homosexuality (ego dystonic homosexuality).

Feelings about homosexuality can be a source of emotional distress for the client and for health care providers. These feelings may be evoked by stereotypes about homosexuality and gays that focus primarily upon homosexuality as illness, false presumptions about effeminacy, and alleged widespread promiscuity.[3] As a consequence of these false assumptions, gay people have had to fight for their rights as human beings while also coming to terms with both their own and society's attitudes toward homosexuality. Frequently, gay people feel hurt and angry when others see them only in limited stereotypical ways. To be gay encompasses not only sexual behavior but also self-concept and affectional bonding. The nurse should not forget that the gay and bisexual population is just as diverse as the population at large.[4] "People are distinguished by a capacity for experience as well as by their behavior, and homosexuality is as much a matter of emotions as of genital manipulation."[5]

A diagnosis of AIDS/ARC raises many concerns. Many PWAs feel angry and frightened about having a communicable disease of highly variable course and, as yet, without curative treatment. Importantly, most HIV infections among gay men occurred prior to any knowledge that sexual activity carried a life-threatening risk. A diagnosis of AIDS/ARC may also reactivate a PWA's ambivalent feelings about his own homosexuality. He may be particularly vulnerable to the attitudes of those around him regarding his illness and his homosexuality, especially if his own feelings and attitudes are not secure. The gay person who accepts society's negative views about homosexuality can be said to have "internalized homophobia," which results in the fear and hatred of one's own homosexuality.

Social support is an important buffer against the psychological and physiological consequences of stress. Unfortunately, the spectrum of diseases associated with HIV can be isolating, both within the hospital and in the PWA's social world. Because of the fear of contagion, and discomfort induced by an illness that will probably be fatal, friends, lovers, and family may begin to spend less time with the patient. Even within a hospital setting, many PWAs report avoidance and withdrawal by the nursing and medical staff.[6] (For an in-depth discussion of isolation, see Chapter 8.)

Prior to diagnosis, many men will not have discussed their AIDS concerns with family or friends. For some individuals, a diagnosis of AIDS/ARC may also mean "coming out" as a gay man for the first time. He may now have to face the threat, and possibly the reality, of discrimination, loss of employment, and rejection by family, friends, and colleagues. The nurse can expect those individuals who are not openly gay with family or colleagues to have higher degrees of emotional distress than those who have not hidden their sexuality.[7]

Stigmatization can also be a contributing factor to the PWA's feelings of isolation. It may lead to shame, self-blame, and distress. (A discussion of stigma is included in Chapter 8.) When the illness is visually apparent, such as Kaposi's sarcoma lesions on the face or hands, the PWA may feel shunned or embarrassed in public settings, even in predominantly gay neighborhoods. Some see the hospital as a refuge from an alienating world, even though hospitalization may be isolating in itself. The PWA may struggle not only with his ambivalent feelings about his homosexuality and guilt about his prior life style but with feelings about the fact that his blood and semen are now infectious or "bad." Just when the PWA needs a stable sense of self-worth, his feelings may be translated into a belief that he himself is bad. Some individuals perceive their illness as a retribution or punishment for being gay, sexual, or sinful, particularly if their religious background was fundamentalist.[8] Support of this belief by care providers can exacerbate a PWA's distress.

The AIDS epidemic is altering the shape and form of the gay community. Many gay and bisexual men are experiencing great distress and protracted and repeated grief over the loss of friends and loved ones. Most urban gay men are practicing safer sex; they have stopped high-risk sexual behaviors.[9] Such change has been documented by the currently low seroconversion rate among gay men (unfortunately, in contrast to that among drug abusers). While distress is high among persons with AIDS and ARC, the HIV antibody–positive but asymptomatic gay male is also at psychosocial risk. He is likely to report greater distress, depression, and termination of more relationships than his seronegative counterpart.[10]

THE BISEXUAL MAN

Traditionally, the bisexual person has not been included in either the heterosexual or the gay worlds. Bisexuals have had less community support and acceptance and may feel isolated and alienated. The bisexual male is more likely to live within a traditional nuclear family structure and less likely to be open about his sexuality, especially if he is married. Frequently, to preserve the family structure, he engages in casual sex rather than having a primary outside partner.[11] After diagnosis, these men may have to "come out" to their wives and children. They may have infected their female sexual partners or put them at risk of having an infected child. The man's guilt and fear may be enormous.

THE ROLE OF THE NURSE

In the face of the AIDS epidemic, the role of the nurse is complex. The nurse must be an informed educator who is not only cognitively aware of current medical information, but also emotionally aware of personal attitudes, feelings, values, and biases. "There is no room in the care of AIDS patients for moral posturing."[12] The nurse must deal not only with the feelings, reactions, and multiple losses of the PWA but also, in many situations, with the reactions of the PWA's family, friends, and current and former sexual partners.[13] Parents may feel guilty and ask questions about the etiology of homosexuality. Appropriate and inappropriate anxieties may be raised about transmissibility and contagion.

Nurses must answer all questions in a nonjudgmental fashion. In order to do so, they must acknowledge personal feelings and attitudes about homosexuality (as described in Chapters 22 and 24), lest they interfere with good medical advice and education. Ethically, the nurse has a responsibility to provide services to all persons regardless of social, economic, or personal status and to overcome fear and prejudice. A nurse who has negative feelings (disgust, avoidance, exaggerated precautions, anger, moralizing) that cannot be resolved should make every effort to arrange for other staff members to care for the gay or bisexual client with AIDS/ARC.

The patient-nurse relationship is critical to healing. In the face of great adversity and stress, even among health care workers themselves, medical personnel must support their patients' struggles with their illness and their lives; the importance of the quality of life cannot be overemphasized. Although nothing can change the likely fatal outcome of this illness to date, many PWAs have discovered hidden personal resources and strengths they never knew possible. Sometimes, during moments of despair, PWAs and those around them begin to discover a deepening sense of wholeness, faith, and meaning in their lives. It is vital to support and encourage hope and the client's involvement in treatment. Hopelessness and helplessness, in a variety of illnesses, have long been recognized as prognostically devastating emotions.[14] Providing nursing care to the gay and bisexual man with AIDS/ARC is complex and challenging; it is also often a professionally and personally rewarding experience for the contemporary nurse.

NOTES

1. Mark Freedman, *Homosexuality and Psychological Functioning* (Belmont, Calif.: Brooks/Cole Publishing Company, 1971), pp. 1–4.

2. Charles Silverstein, *A Family Matter: A Parent's Guide to Homosexuality* (San Francisco: McGraw-Hill Book Co., 1977), p. 8.

3. Christopher W. Mead, *Men Loving Men: A Phenomenological Exploration of Committed Gay Relationships* (Ph.D. dissertation, California School of Professional Psychology, San Diego, 1979).

4. George F. Solomon and Christopher W. Mead, "Considerations in the Treatment of the Gay Patient with AIDS or ARC," *Humane Medicine* 3, no. 1 (May 1987):10–19.

5. Dennis Altman, *Homosexual Oppression and Liberation* (New York: Avon Books, 1971), p. 14.

6. Jay Baer, Kris Holm, and Susan Lewitter-Koehler, "Treatment of AIDS/ARC Patients on an Inpatient Psychiatric Unit," *Focus: A Review of AIDS Research*, January 1987, p. 1–3.

7. Jeff Mandel, "Affective Reactions to a Diagnosis of AIDS or ARC in Gay Men" (Ph.D. dissertation, Wright Institute, Los Angeles, 1985).

8. James W. Dilley, Herbert N. Ochitill, and Mark Perl, "Findings in Psychiatric Consultations with Patients with Acquired Immune Deficiency Syndrome," *American Journal of Psychiatry* 142 (1985): 82–86.

9. Leon McKusick et al., "Reported Changes in the Sexual Behavior of Men at Risk of AIDS, San Francisco, 1982–84, The AIDS Behavioral Research Project," *Public Health Report* 100 (6): 622–29.

10. Tom J. Coates, Stephen F. Morin, and Leon McKusick, "Consequences of AIDS Antibody Testing Among Gay Men: The AIDS Behavioral Research Project" (Paper delivered at the Third International Conference on AIDS, Washington, D.C., June 3, 1987).

11. F. Klin and J. J. Wolf, eds., *Bisexualities: Theory and Research* (New York: Haworth Press, 1985).

12. Jeff Mandel, J.M. Moulton, and Lydia Temoshok, "Psychological Reactions to Diagnosed AIDS or ARC in San Francisco," University of California Biopsychosocial AIDS Project (Lecture presented at the meeting of the American Psychological Association, Washington, D.C., August 1986).

13. Solomon and Mead, "Considerations in the Treatment of the Gay Patient with AIDS or ARC."

14. A.H. Schmale and H. Iker, "The Psychosocial Selling of Uterine Cervical Cancer," *Annals of the New York Academy of Science* 125 (1966):807.

Chapter 3

Ethnic Minorities and AIDS

Susan D. Cochran, Vickie M. Mays, and Vinson Roberts

WHO GETS AIDS?

Many people believe that AIDS affects only White gay men or IV drug abusers; they do not realize that AIDS has disproportionately affected ethnic minority communities, primarily Blacks and Hispanics. At present, 24 percent of reported AIDS cases have occurred among Blacks,[1] although Blacks constitute only 12 percent of the U.S. population[2] (see Table 3-1). It has been estimated that 1.0 to 1.4 percent of the Black population was infected with HIV as of January 1987.[3] In contrast, only 0.3 to 0.5 percent of the White population was estimated to be infected. Blacks are thus three times more likely than Whites to be infected with HIV. Hispanics are also at higher risk than Whites. Approximately 14 percent of reported AIDS cases occur among Hispanics, although they comprise only 6.3 percent of the U.S. population. Other ethnic minorities have been affected by AIDS, but not to the same devastating extent as Blacks and Hispanics. In total, these other groups, including Asian-Americans and Native Americans, constitute approximately 1.0 percent of AIDS cases and about 2.4 percent of the U.S. population.

Ethnic differences are even more pronounced among women affected by AIDS. While women represent only 7 percent of all AIDS cases, among women afflicted, Blacks account for 52 percent and Hispanics 19 percent as of October 5, 1987.

The CDC has calculated the chances of getting AIDS for several ethnic groups since 1981. As seen in Table 3-2, Blacks are at greatest risk for getting AIDS, followed by Hispanics, Whites, Asians, and Native Americans. Two cautionary points are relevant for ethnic minorities. First, while it is true that Blacks and Hispanics as communities are at higher risk for contracting the HIV virus, particular members within those communities are more at risk than others. Second, the present low number of cases among Asians and Native Americans should be viewed as an opportunity to provide appropriate AIDS health education

Table 3-1 Total Number of AIDS Cases by Risk Group and Gender for Each Ethnic/Race Group, United States, October 5, 1987

	Men					Women[b]				
	White	Black	Hispanic	Other	Total	White	Black	Hispanic	Other	Total
Homosexual/Bisexual										
Homosexual	17,810 (72%)[a]	2,842 (32%)	2,283 (43%)	220 (59%)	23,155 (59%)					
Bisexual	2,630 (11%)	1,221 (14%)	510 (10%)	62 (17%)	4,423 (11%)					
Homosexual + intravenous (IV) drug user	1,597 (6%)	431 (5%)	250 (5%)	16 (4%)	2,294 (6%)					
Bisexual + IV drug user	436 (2%)	269 (3%)	136 (2%)	3 (<1%)	844 (2%)					
Exclusively Heterosexual										
IV drug user	1,012 (4%)	2,674 (31%)	1,739 (33%)	25 (7%)	5,450 (14%)	323 (39%)	814 (49%)	284 (46%)	14 (44%)	1,435 (45%)
Heterosexual contact	74 (<1%)	680 (8%)	28 (<1%)	2 (<1%)	784 (2%)	192 (22%)	478 (29%)	200 (32%)	6 (19%)	876 (28%)
Hemophiliac	324 (1%)	17 (<1%)	25 (<1%)	8 (2%)	374 (<1%)	6 (<1%)	3 (<1%)	0 (0%)	0 (0%)	9 (<1%)
Blood transfusion	454 (2%)	69 (<1%)	40 (<1%)	12 (3%)	575 (1%)	223 (25%)	60 (4%)	23 (4%)	8 (25%)	314 (10%)
Other/unknown	393 (2%)	367 (4%)	180 (3%)	20 (5%)	960 (2%)	85 (10%)	145 (9%)	44 (7%)	2 (6%)	276 (9%)
Children (under age 13)	74 (<1%)	157 (2%)	76 (1%)	3 (<1%)	310 (<1%)	47 (5%)	160 (10%)	64 (10%)	2 (6%)	273 (8%)
Total male cases	24,804	8,727	5,267	371	39,169					
Total female cases						876	1,660	615	32	3,183

[a]Percentages are percent in each risk group calculated for each gender separately.

[b]No information is available on sexual orientation of female cases, but the number of cases among homosexual women is known to be extremely low.

Source: Adapted from Public Information Data Use Tape, U.S. Centers for Disease Control, October 5, 1987.

Table 3-2 Number of AIDS Cases and Cumulative Incidence Rates by Ethnic Group and Race, United States, August 3, 1987

	White	Black	Hispanic	Asian[a]	Native American[a]
Total cases	24,012	9,699	5,508	232	38
Cumulative incidence per 100,000	168.3	520.7	454.5	66.3	27.1

[a]Asian and Native American data are estimated from an analysis of data compiled by the U.S. Centers for Disease Control in May 1987.

Source: U.S. Centers for Disease Control, August 1987.

services to these communities in order to prevent the development of new cases in these subpopulations.

WHY DO CERTAIN ETHNIC MINORITIES GET AIDS?

Although among Whites AIDS is most frequently a disease of gay and bisexual men, Blacks and Hispanics show more widely dispersed epidemiologic infection patterns. The presumed primary routes of infection for cases reported as of October 5, 1987 are given in Table 3-1. As the table shows, IV drug use is an important additional infection vector for Blacks and Hispanics. Many of the heterosexual transmission cases are from sexual contact with IV drug users.[4] Similarly, pediatric cases most often occur among offspring born to women who are IV drug users themselves or the sexual partner of a man who is.

Thus, for Blacks and Hispanics, AIDS is a disease strongly associated with the sociological realities of poverty. Approximately 45 percent of AIDS cases among Blacks and Hispanics occur in the urbanized Northeast, including New York City. In poor, urban ethnic minority communities, IV drug use is much more common,[5] as is the sharing of needles or ''works'' (drug paraphernalia), the primary route for HIV transmission.[6] In addition, simply living in this environment is more likely to result in contact with HIV-infected individuals who may be potential sexual partners.

Other factors in poor ethnic minority environments may also contribute to the spread of HIV. For example, commonly practiced birth control methods may facilitate transmission. It has been suggested that males in Mexico may more frequently utilize anal intercourse with a woman as a birth control measure or as a means of maintaining vaginal virginity.[7] Data from gay men's studies indicate that receptive anal intercourse is the highest-risk sexual practice for contracting HIV infection.[8]

In both Black and Hispanic cultures there has always been a disdain for the use of condoms as a method of birth control.[9] While condoms may effectively fight the HIV virus, they are primarily associated with birth control. For some ethnic minorities, birth control is viewed as genocidal, depriving individuals as well as the community of the ethnic pride associated with parenthood.

Current risk reduction messages encourage condom use without consideration of their economic burden.[10] To suggest that a poor or ethnic woman living on a meager fixed income spend money on condoms, particularly when her partner is perhaps reluctant to use them, ignores the economic and social pressures in her life.

CARING FOR THE HIV-INFECTED INDIVIDUAL

Some special issues, including both medical and psychosocial concerns, arise in the care of ethnic minority clients with AIDS.

Medical Issues

First, there is evidence that Blacks and Hispanics are more likely to present with more severe acute opportunistic infections, necessitating more intensive medical and psychosocial care.[11] This is so because many of these individuals seek help late in the course of their illness or are IV drug users who were in poor health prior to HIV infection.[12]

Second, an increase in the incidence of tuberculosis infection has been noted among racial and ethnic minorities—a rate as high as six times greater than that among Whites.[13] Evidence suggests that much of the increase can be attributed to those individuals who are HIV-positive. Care should be taken to prevent transmission to adults or children who may be more vulnerable as a result of poor health status. In this regard, the prevention focus needs to encompass not only the PWA, but others in the social environment who may also be HIV-infected.

Third, educational, cultural, and language differences between health care providers and patients can hamper evaluation of the neurologic impairment seen in a significant percentage of AIDS patients.[14] The nurse must be especially sensitive to these differences before concluding that a client is neurologically impaired.

Psychosocial Issues

Cultural, ethnic, and racial barriers may create difficulties in communication that undermine the nurse-patient relationship. Some ethnic minorities, particularly

Hispanics and Asians, may find it culturally inconsistent to discuss or refer to specific body parts or sexual behaviors with a relative stranger, especially a woman. Equally true, nurses may refer to sexual behaviors and body parts in medical terms unfamiliar to some minorities. Cultural and ethnic barriers can compromise obtaining necessary information from clients as well as assurance that they understand risk reduction activities. For example, health educators have been encouraged by ethnic community AIDS workers to refer to condoms as "rubbers" or "protection." These language distinctions are important. Nursing personnel may find it helpful to discuss medical instructions for ethnic clients with a colleague of similar background to the clients' to ensure clear communication between nurse and client.

Other issues may be even more subtle. For example, among many Blacks a cultural norm is that one should behave more formally in the presence of non-Blacks to avoid the discriminations that occur unpredictably as a result of racist notions that Blacks are ignorant or poorly mannered. The need to maintain this formality in the hospital environment is underscored when family and significant others feel that hospital staff will perceive particular behaviors negatively, resulting in poor care for their loved one. This formality, however, is not always consistent with emotional needs or cultural norms for behavior when strangers are not present. For example, in a case related to us by one of our colleagues, a Black mother whose son was dying of AIDS in the hospital watched as he retreated in coma into a fetal position in the hours before his death. As a mother, she knew that what he needed (and what she needed also) was for her to crawl into bed with him and hold him as he died. But she was deterred by her fears that nursing personnel would not find this behavior acceptable and would reprimand her. To this day, she berates herself for sacrificing her son's dying needs in order to maintain their family's ethnic dignity in the face of the predominantly non-Black world of the hospital.

This conflict between maintaining formality and facing the reality of hospital life, with its frequent violations of personal or family privacy, does not always have to be so dramatic. Some Blacks may experience discomfort or embarrassment when White or Asian nursing staff perform the more intimate nursing behaviors, such as removing fungi from under toes or washing up after an episode of incontinence. The sociological realities of racism and interethnic group prejudices, translated into everyday life, mean that many Blacks do not normally have such intimate encounters with members from these groups. Culturally, Blacks, particularly from the lower socioeconomic groups, are proscripted to avoid these moments of vulnerability as a protection against possible discrimination. Some acknowledgment from the staff—a smile, a fragment of conversation—some attempt to lessen the sharp pain to the client's ethnic pride may be comforting. Indirectly, this may assist in diffusing any possible perceptions by the client's family that nursing staff are not adequately caring for a particular patient out of perceived racist motivations.

Finally, in providing care for IV drug users, nurses need to realize that clients may, if the opportunity is present, steal drug-related paraphernalia, such as needles, to be resold on the streets. Precautions are recommended.

PSYCHOLOGICAL IMPACT ON PATIENTS, FAMILIES, AND SIGNIFICANT OTHERS

Little information has been published addressing the specific psychological needs of ethnic minority clients with AIDS. PWAs, irrespective of their ethnic status, may experience severe psychosocial disruptions, including, but not limited to, affective distress, loss of or severe strain on their systems of emotional and tangible support, and financial distress.[15] Ethnic minorities affected with AIDS differ from Whites in their family and friendship networks and in the role ethnic and cultural norms play in their health care behaviors.

As an example, homosexuality is viewed differently in ethnic minority cultures.[16] The gay ethnic minority man with AIDS may have chosen never to reveal or discuss his sexual orientation with his friends or family. In many instances such behavior has been well hidden by occasional heterosexual liaisons or is a known "secret" not talked about by his family and friendship network. It is important that nursing staff respect the possible role of this family secret in maintaining sources of social support.

For White gay men, the loss of family support can frequently be compensated for by support from the gay community, a primarily White social structure. For ethnic men, however, ethnic barriers in the gay community may inhibit the receipt of adequate and culturally relevant support. Thus maintenance of the family system may be even more critical. In settings with dedicated AIDS wards where PWAs and visitors are openly gay, the pressure may be for gay men to be "out." The individual from an ethnic minority, however, may suddenly become "closeted" while his family or friends are around. This behavior, should it occur, is understandable, given that cultural and racial identity of some gay ethnic minorities is even more fundamental to their self-image than their sexual orientation.[17] Emotional, familial, and economic ties may be to the ethnic community first and the gay community second. Since families may find it easier to accept drug abuse or prostitution as the source of their son's infection than sexual activities with another male, this may be the client's story line. Such a client would find it comforting to know that nursing staff will not openly or unintentionally reveal his guarded secret.

While hospital rules limiting immediate family to visitation in critical care units serve an important function for the nursing staff, they are sometimes problematic for ethnic minorities. As an example, an ethnic male chronic drug abuser separated from his wife but currently living with a companion may have very few emotional ties to his family of origin or to his wife. Where possible, nursing staff may lessen the conflicts that could occur by asking that only visitors *close* to the patient visit, as opposed to legally sanctioned individuals (i.e., married or blood relatives). This type of discrimination has been most salient for ethnic gay men whose lovers were unknown to family members or barred by hospital staff because of a nonkin status. Emotionally, the man may have been closer to his lover than his family, from whom he has been estranged because of his hidden gay status. Sensitivity on the part of nursing staff to the importance of extended family, gay family, or health care family (buddies) may prove to be a source of comfort for the client.

SUMMARY

1. Ethnic minorities, primarily Blacks and Hispanics, are disproportionately more likely to contract AIDS or an HIV infection than Whites.
2. Risk factors for HIV transmission in ethnic minority populations are more dispersed than among Whites. IV drug use and heterosexual sexual contact with infected individuals assume a more important role in HIV transmission than among Whites.
3. Care of ethnic minority PWAs requires a sensitivity to subtle, as well as obvious, ways in which cultural differences influence medical expression of HIV infection and psychosocial sequelae.

NOTES

1. U.S. Centers for Disease Control, *AIDS Weekly Surveillance Report, United States AIDS Activity,* October 5, 1987.

2. U.S. Department of Commerce, Bureau of the Census, *Characteristics of the Population. General Population Characteristics, Part 1* (Washington, D.C.: U.S. Government Printing Office, 1983).

3. V.M. Mays and S.D. Cochran, "Acquired Immunodeficiency Syndrome and Black Americans: Special Psychosocial Issues," *Public Health Reports* 102 (1987):226–31.

4. D.C. DesJarlais, C. Casriel, and S. Friedman, "The New Death Among IV Drug Users," in I.B. Corless and M. Pittman-Lindeman, eds., *AIDS: Principles, Practices, and Politics* (Washington, D.C.: Hemisphere Publishing, 1987), pp. 135–50.

5. L.E. Gary and G.L. Berry, "Predicting Attitudes Toward Substance Use in a Black Community: Implications for Prevention," *Community Mental Health Journal* 21 (1985):112–18.

6. S.R. Friedman, D.C. DesJarlais, and J.L. Sotheran, "AIDS Health Education for Intravenous Drug Users," *Health Education Quarterly* 13, no. 4 (1986):383–93.

7. J.M. Carrier, "Sexual Behavior and the Spread of AIDS in Mexico," *Medical Anthropology* (in press).

8. H.W. Jaffee, et al., "The Acquired Immunodeficiency Syndrome in Gay Men," *Annals of Internal Medicine* 103 (1985):662–64.

9. M.E. Taylor and D.D. Adame, "Male and Female Sexuality Attitudes: Differences and Similarities," *Health Education* 17 (1986):8–12.

10. V.M. Mays and S.D. Cochran, "Interpretation of AIDS Risk and AIDS Risk Reduction Activities by Black and Hispanic Women," *American Psychologist* (in press).

11. B. Safai et al., "The Natural History of Kaposi's Sarcoma in the Acquired Immunodeficiency Syndrome," *Annals of Internal Medicine* 103 (1985):744–50.

12. W. Greaves, "The Epidemiology of AIDS in the Black Community" (Paper presented at the Conference on AIDS in the Black Community, Washington D.C., 1986).

13. U.S. Centers for Disease Control, "Tuberculosis as Related to AIDS and HIV Infection Among Minorities" (Paper presented at the National Conference on AIDS in Minority Populations in the United States, Atlanta, Georgia, 1987).

14. Mays and Cochran, "Acquired Immunodeficiency Syndrome and Black Americans."

15. Ibid.

16. Ibid.

17. Carrier, "Sexual Behavior and the Spread of AIDS in Mexico"; Cochran and Mays, "Sources of Support in the Black Lesbian Community" (Paper presented at the meetings of the American Psychological Association, Washington, D.C., August 1986); Mays and Cochran, "Relationship Experiences and the Perception of Discrimination" (Paper presented at the meetings of the American Psychological Association, Washington, D.C., August 1986); J. Peterson and E. Andrews, "AIDS and Blacks: Gay Identity, Racial Poverty and Racial Discrimination" (Paper presented at the meetings of the American Psychological Association, Washington, D.C., August 1986); and L. Icard, "Black Gay Men and Conflicting Social Identities: Sexual Orientation versus Racial Identity," *Journal of Social Work and Human Sexuality* 4 (1986):83–93.

Chapter 4

Substance Abuse in Persons with HIV Infection

Barbara G. Faltz, and Scott Madover

As the AIDS epidemic unfolds, an awareness of the connections between HIV infection and drug and alcohol abuse is emerging. The connections include:

- sexual transmission of HIV to partners of IV drug users
- neonatal transmission by infected mothers who are IV drug users or partners of IV drug users
- increased risk due to disinhibition under the influence of drugs or alcohol
- increased risk due to immunosuppression caused by drug or alcohol use
- inability to utilize resources (social, financial, or health) because of substance abuse.

ASSESSMENT

Substance abuse assessment for persons with HIV is an essential part of a psychosocial assessment. It includes an assessment of the amount, frequency of use, duration of use, and last use of all classifications of illicit drugs, mind-altering prescription medication, and alcohol. Assessment of the following factors is helpful in determining if a client has a substance abuse problem:

1. emotional, social, relationship, employment, legal, or other difficulties that can be linked to the use of alcohol or drugs
2. loss of control over the frequency or amount of alcohol or drug use
3. preoccupation with drug(s) of choice or alcohol
4. self-medication for anxiety or sadness
5. use of drugs or alcohol while alone
6. rapid initial intake of drugs or alcohol

7. protection of drug or alcohol supply—stocking up or hiding supply
8. tolerance to large quantities of alcohol or drugs
9. withdrawal symptoms
10. blackouts.

BARRIERS TO TREATMENT

Substance abuse in a person with HIV infection or a diagnosis of AIDS or ARC can have profound consequences. The individual and loved ones are often traumatized by the diagnosis and loved ones may be reluctant to confront the client's substance abuse. Physicians and other health care workers, too, may overlook substance abuse in persons diagnosed as having AIDS or ARC. They may perceive the disease to be their most immediate concern and the substance abuse an ancillary issue for which they may offer a referral.

The combined problem of AIDS and substance abuse raises critical clinical, ethical, and personal dilemmas for clients, loved ones, and health care providers. The perplexities of this situation often lead to barriers to effective substance abuse treatment. Because of the overwhelming nature of an HIV-related diagnosis, treatment providers as well as clients often feel a sense of hopelessness that precludes the possibility of major positive life changes. Rationales for ignoring drug or alcohol abuse and the possibility of successful treatment for it include: (1) the PWA will die anyway, (2) substance abuse treatment will take away a "coping mechanism," and (3) substance abuse treatment is stressful. These rationales imply the question, "Why bother treating substance abuse in PWAs?" Health care providers can play a positive role in facilitating conscious choices and in making avenues of treatment available to the individual who may choose to "die high" or to improve the quality of what may be a chaotic life style.

Often substance abuse is viewed as a weakness or a choice, not as a disease. A person with this view may feel that treatment should consist of a lecture on "right" or "wrong" behavior, an exhortation to control one's impulses, or both. Substance abuse is not a weakness but a chronic and progressive disease for which there is treatment and hope. Viewing substance abuse otherwise can result in failure to refer the client for appropriate treatment.

Additionally, many obvious and some more subtle anxieties are associated with confronting substance abuse problems in PWAs. There is a concern that confronting clients may alienate them in a time of need, that they are fragile in all areas of life, and that confrontation may increase stress. A careful look at one's own anxieties in connection with the complex problems associated with the diagnosis of both AIDS/ARC and substance abuse is essential.

Finally, so many other physical, emotional, financial, and legal concerns are associated with AIDS that often substance abuse problems are not seen as a priority to address as aggressively as other needs. Minimizing this aspect of treatment can impede progress in other areas as the client experiences exacerbated emotional, legal, medical, and other problems.

SPECIFIC PSYCHOSOCIAL CONCERNS

Specific psychosocial concerns arise from the dual diagnosis of AIDS/ARC and substance abuse disorder. One of these is confusion concerning appropriate interventions for denial. A person grieving a life-threatening diagnosis may appropriately deny its reality. This type of denial is usually supported until the person can begin to absorb the impact of the diagnosis. In the case of substance abuse, however, denial is the chief defense against seeing the extent of the problem and the consequences of the addiction. Substance abuse evaluation and intervention are most effective when a client is becoming more accepting of the substance abuse diagnosis.

Dealing with behavioral manifestations of addiction such as flattery, intrusiveness, intimidation, or inflammatory remarks can be frustrating for the care provider. Often, clients attempt to turn one staff member or agency against another. These behaviors protect continued abuse by avoiding confrontation, by deflecting attention, and by justifying use. Care providers must avoid expressing anger, blame, or disappointment toward the continual abuser, but should encourage the constructive expression of feelings, hold clients responsible for their actions, and maintain a sense of values, quality care, and professional practice standards. These actions will help prevent a feeling of helplessness in coping with addictive behaviors.

Motivation for treatment is often missing in clients who are actively pursuing their addiction—especially if they have not felt the continued painful consequences of years of drinking or drug use. They and health care workers may feel that the problem "is not bad enough yet" to seek treatment. Even if clients have limited motivation for treatment, it is important to educate them about sexual practices, needle use, and immunosuppressant drug use and to support behavioral change in these areas. (Appendixes 4-A and 4-B contain further educational information.)

SUMMARY

Current epidemiological data confirm the connections between substance abuse and AIDS. Projections for the future suggest that substance abuse will command even more attention from health care providers and educators, as well as health policy officials. While many problems are associated with dual diagnoses of substance abuse and AIDS, health care providers can intervene effectively by first recognizing how their own values and anxieties affect treatment. Next, they can accept substance abuse as a problem that can be ameliorated by treatment interventions. Finally, the health care provider must remain aware of community resources that provide accurate assessment and effective treatment to the substance abuse client.

Appendix 4-A

Example of a Community Campaign

A number of agencies in San Francisco are participating in a campaign to help stop the spread of AIDS among IV drug users. One part of the campaign is distribution of a comic book (*The Works—Drugs, Sex & AIDS*) and a bright yellow card in English and Spanish, both of which use pictures to give instructions on how users can clean their works:

1. Pour full-strength bleach into a glass.
2. Fill the needle and syringe with bleach.
3. Squirt out the bleach.
4. Repeat steps 2 and 3.
5. Wash the glass with water.
6. Fill the glass with clean water.
7. Fill the needle and syringe with water.
8. Squirt out the water.
9. Repeat steps 7 and 8.

Community street workers distribute small bottles of bleach to users on the street. Although it is too early to evaluate the program, results are being seen and the rate of transmission seems to be dropping. Materials are being distributed on the streets, in jails, and at homeless shelters.

Community workers believe that nurses, especially those in urban centers working in emergency rooms, obstetrics, and other areas where substance abusers might be seen, are in a key position to educate the IV drug-using public.

Appendix 4-B

AIDS Substance Abuse Program (ASAP) Guide to AIDS Prevention

Needle Safety

- Remember that people who look healthy can carry the AIDS virus
- Don't shoot-up drugs
- Don't share needles
- Clean "Works": flush twice with bleach (Clorox) and with water
- Don't shoot-up or reuse bleach

Prevent Sexual Transmission

- Use condoms
- Remember people who look healthy can carry the AIDS virus

Use of Drugs

- Alcohol, pot, speed, coke and poppers can lower your resistance to diseases

If You Want To Have Children, Get Medical Advice If You

- Shared needles
- May have been exposed to AIDS through sexual contact

Keep Healthy

- Get rest, exercise, eat a healthy diet and reduce stress

Want More Information?

- AIDS Hotline (800) 863-AIDS
- Drug Hotline (415) 752-3400

Source: Reprinted from *AIDS and Substance Abuse: A Training Manual for Health Care Professionals* by B.G. Faltz and J. Rinaldi, p. 14, AIDS Health Project, 1987.

Chapter 5

Heterosexuals and AIDS

Vickie M. Mays, Susan D. Cochran,
and Vinson Roberts

One of the greatest concerns of the general public today is whether AIDS will spread among the heterosexual community in a parallel fashion to that witnessed among gay men and IV drug users. This question has been widely debated.[1] Data indicate that as of July 6, 1987, 26 percent of all adult cases of AIDS were thought to involve exclusively heterosexual individuals. Using reported AIDS cases from 1981 to 1986, Dr. James Curran, director of the AIDS Program for the Center for Infectious Disease of the CDC, found the greatest acceleration from 1985 to 1986 among bisexual men (82 percent more cases reported in 1986 than in 1985) and among women (77 percent more cases) (see Figure 5-1).[2] The largest increase occurred among heterosexual men, and the lowest among gay men. Figures 5-2 and 5-3 show percentage increases for women and heterosexual men differentiated by ethnic background.[3] For both men and women, the largest percentage increase occurred among Whites. However, these data evaluate only changes in cases reported across a one-year period. Blacks and Hispanics already constitute a higher than expected risk group, as discussed in Chapter 3.

Debates continue regarding the extent to which the general population of heterosexuals should be concerned about AIDS if they lack the obvious risk factors of past IV drug abuse or sexual contact with an IV drug abuser (IVDA) or homosexual or bisexual male contact. The search for sources of transmission in the White heterosexual community has focused on (1) gay or bisexual males and (2) female, and in some cases male, prostitutes. In the Black community attention has centered on the male drug abuser and the female prostitute. While the actual risk to heterosexuals is certainly a source of worry for many individuals, they would be wise to remember that other factors influence what level of actual risk exists. Ethnicity is an important variable. For example, the most probable primary transmission vector into the White heterosexual population is sexual contact with a previously infected individual. In the Black and Hispanic ethnic minority communities, IV drug use is an additional important transmission vector.

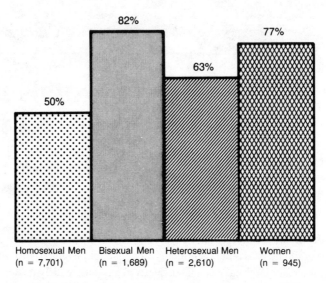

Figure 5-1 Reported Cases of AIDS in the U.S. Sex and Sexual Orientation, 1986 Percentage Increase Over 1985. *Source:* Reprinted from J. Curran, "Mayor's Task Force Addresses Heterosexual Transmission, Youth Education," *AIDS Information Exchange*, Vol. 4, No. 2, pp. 5–6, U.S. Centers for Disease Control, 1987.

A sensible approach to understanding levels of risk for heterosexuals involves assessing both the *risk activities* and the *proximity* to an infectious agent (source) of transmission as a function of contacts with blood or bodily fluid from potentially positive or seropositive individuals. One way to perform this assessment is to examine all the potential sources and their degree of risk for heterosexuals. For example, heterosexual men who received blood transfusions during 1977–85, who have visited male or female prostitutes in particular geographic regions, or who were IVDAs might consider themselves at relatively high risk for infection. On the other hand, if these same heterosexual men engaged only in masturbation with the prostitutes and never shared works while abusing drugs, the risk might be considered low. Thus not all heterosexuals are at equal risk. Rather, those individuals who have come into direct contact with known seropositive populations or have a high vulnerability to direct introduction of the HIV virus into their bloodstreams are most at risk.[4] Also potentially at risk in the heterosexual group are those individuals who lack knowledge about how AIDS is transmitted and who are actually at risk. These individuals may be unaware that they have exposed themselves to the virus, and while they may not appear to have any major risk factors, their inability to assess unsafe sexual practices and to assess adequately the history of their past partners places them in a potential risk category. The degree of risk, of course, is modified by the age of the person as it relates to

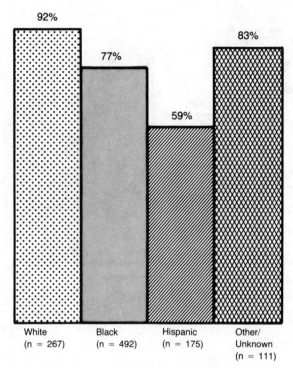

Figure 5-2 Reported Cases of AIDS in the U.S. Women by Race, 1986 Percentage Increase Over 1985. *Source:* Reprinted from J. Curran, ''Mayor's Task Force Addresses Heterosexual Transmission, Youth Education,'' *AIDS Information Exchange*, Vol. 4, No. 2, pp. 5–6, U.S. Centers for Disease Control, 1987.

exposure, sexual history, and the types of contacts the person has had with blood and bodily fluids.

CHARACTERISTICS OF HETEROSEXUAL AIDS CASES

The epidemiologic pattern of AIDS in heterosexual groups indicates distinct racial, ethnic, and gender differences. As indicated in Table 3-1, heterosexual men account for a negligible proportion of the AIDS cases among Whites. Among these men, the largest risk group identified by risk category is IVDAs, but heterosexual IVDAs still account for only 4 percent of all of AIDS cases in White men. On the other hand, Black and Hispanic heterosexual male IVDAs account for approximately one-third of AIDS cases in their respective ethnic groups. In addition, Black heterosexual men are more likely to contract HIV through hetero-sexual sexual contact than are either White or Hispanic men.

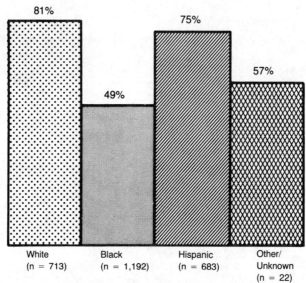

Figure 5-3 Reported Cases of AIDS in the U.S. Heterosexual Men by Race, 1986 Percentage Increase Over 1985. *Source:* Reprinted from J. Curran, "Mayor's Task Force Addresses Heterosexual Transmission, Youth Education," *AIDS Information Exchange*, Vol. 4, No. 2, pp. 5–6, U.S. Centers for Disease Control, 1987.

Blacks and Hispanics comprise the largest number of the cases of AIDS in women, 51 percent and 20 percent respectively. Examining the number of cases of AIDS in ethnic women as a function of their percentage in the population reveals that a Black woman is 13 times more likely than a White woman to contract the AIDS virus. For Hispanics, the risk ratio is approximately 9 times greater.[5] While the actual number of cases for ethnic minority women is lower than for ethnic minority men, minority women in comparison with White women are more affected by AIDS than ethnic minority men compared with White men.[6] For women the primary routes of viral transmission are first, IV drug use and second, heterosexual contact with a person at risk for AIDS.[7] It is in this latter category of heterosexual contact that women outnumber men. In many of the cases, the women may not have known about their partner's history of drug abuse or bisexuality, they may have not asked, they may have asked but been deceived, or they may have known but not realized that they were at risk.[8]

PSYCHOSOCIAL ISSUES IN CARING FOR THE HIV-INFECTED HETEROSEXUAL

In male heterosexual AIDS cases the activities that led to the infection may have involved previously hidden behaviors. For some heterosexual men sexual encounters with men or women in the sex industry, sexual encounters with gay or bisexual men, or occasional recreational use of IV drugs may have been well hidden or merely suspected but never discussed with family members. Upon discovery of HIV seropositivity the heterosexual man may worry not only about his diagnosis but about the impact of his secret activities on his relationships with his family of origin, his significant others, and, in some instances, his children. He may also be upset that people suspect he is gay or bisexual. Nursing personnel may find in some clients a reluctance to or a decision not to inform their spouse or significant other of their HIV status. In some cases clients may be reluctant to admit to a spouse or family member the activities that are suspected as the cause of the infection. The client may explain the HIV status in a manner that seems vague or implausible to family or significant others. Nursing staff may find themselves facing questions from the family about the origins of their loved one's infection or merely a desire to ask questions to clarify their understanding of how a person becomes infected with HIV. In these situations, it is important to protect client confidentiality.

Nursing staff may face an emotional and ethical conflict as a result of either the client's request not to reveal the HIV status to the significant other or a statement of intention to continue to engage in high-risk behaviors. Such statements represent a potential duty to warn and protect. The nurse who might be faced with this situation should try to request consultation *prior to* the occurrence. A sound policy coupled with an implementation plan will result in better services for clients and lessen nursing staff anxieties. The training and education department may wish to address not only the legal and professional responsibilities for nurses (see Chapter 25) but methods for coping with personal reactions to this situation (see Chapter 22).

Heterosexual men and women, particularly if both members of a couple have become infected (as happens with IVDAs), experience a great emotional trauma related to their responsibilities to their own families and children. Many parents are afraid they will infect their children. Accurate information regarding transmission of the virus, as well as specific examples of intimate activities, such as kissing or hugging, that can be continued, may be helpful. While difficult, it is important for parents to plan for the future of their children both as the parents become progressively sicker and after their death.

Families of persons with AIDS experience tremendous emotional upheaval at the impending loss of their child, parent, spouse, or significant other. Nursing staff may serve a useful function to the family and children of the HIV-infected individual by informing them of services such as support groups, bereavement groups, or places where they can volunteer their time to help others with ARC or AIDS.

For the HIV-infected individual who wishes to remain sexually active, nursing staff may be called upon to discuss frankly the projected risk associated with particular sexual behaviors (see Chapter 24 and Appendix B). Some clients may need information on behaviors that can be substituted for behaviors previously used for sexual gratification as well as behaviors that may result in emotional closeness.

A particularly difficult problem for people with AIDS in the hospital is regulations that prevent visits by their children who are under age 13. Nursing staff may wish to discuss with hospital administration ways to handle this problem that do not disrupt care on the unit but facilitate meeting the needs of the individual patient.

When hospitalized, some women with AIDS feel isolated because they do not encounter any other females with AIDS. They have no source for comparison, no role model for hope, nor any source of practical advice. In this situation, nursing staff may find it helpful to arrange for a "buddy" from an AIDS support agency. Many women with AIDS also lack basic information specific to their needs. Women quite often ask how to dispose of tampons or sanitary napkins soiled from their menstrual flow. Female nursing staff may be the only source that some women will ask because of their embarrassment in asking a male physician.

Some heterosexuals with AIDS may feel uncomfortable in the presence of gay men, which is a particular concern on dedicated AIDS units with large numbers of gay men. Some heterosexuals may be reluctant to have particular family members or religious advisers visit because of the presence of openly gay men on the ward. Nursing personnel should intervene early in the client's stay if this appears to be a problem. Social support is an important element in coping with major life illnesses and, therefore, comforting clients and visitors is a priority. It may be useful to point out to such individuals the courageous role that gay men have played in advancing knowledge of AIDS through their volunteer efforts.

SUMMARY

1. Heterosexuals are likely to be concerned, and in some instances confused, about their actual risk for contracting the HIV infection.
2. The epidemiologic pattern and risk for infection differ among Whites and ethnic group members. Black and Hispanic heterosexuals are disproportionately more likely to contract AIDS or an HIV infection than are Whites.
3. Heterosexual AIDS patients may require basic information about AIDS and HIV infection.
4. Care of the heterosexual person with AIDS requires attention to the needs of spouses/significant others and children. These two groups may also rely on nursing staff as their source of information and comfort.

NOTES

1. R.R. Redfield et al., "Heterosexually Acquired HTLV-III/LAV Disease (AIDS-Related Complex and AIDS)," *Journal of the American Medical Association (JAMA)* 254, no. 15 (October 18, 1985):2094–96; U.S. Centers for Disease Control, "Human T-Lymphotropic Virus Type III/Lymphadenopathy Associated Virus Antibody Prevalence in U.S. Military Recruit Applicants," *Morbidity and Mortality Weekly Report (MMWR)* 35, no. 26 (July 4, 1986):421–23; M.M. Lederman, "Transmission of the Acquired Immunodeficiency Syndrome Through Heterosexual Activity," *Annals of Internal Medicine* 104, no. 1 (1986):115–17; M.A. Fischl et al., "Evaluation of Heterosexual Partners, Children, and Household Contacts of Adults with AIDS," *JAMA* 257, no. 5 (1987):640–44; and K. Leishman, "Heterosexuals and AIDS," *The Atlantic* 259, no. 2 (1987):39–58.

2. J. Curran, "Mayor's Task Force Addresses Heterosexual Transmission, Youth Education," *AIDS Information Exchange* 4:2 (1987):5–6.

3. Ibid.

4. Polaris Research and Development, "A Baseline Survey of AIDS Risk Behaviors and Attitudes in San Francisco's Black Communities" (San Francisco, Calif.:1987).

5. V. Mays and S. Cochran, "Interpretation of AIDS Risk and AIDS Risk Reduction by Black and Hispanic Women," *American Psychologist* (in press).

6. R. Bakeman, J.R. Lamb, R.E. Jackson, and P.N. Whitney, "The Incidence of AIDS Among Blacks and Hispanics," *JAMA* 257, no. 5 (1987).

7. M.E. Guinan and A. Hardy, "Epidemiology of AIDS in Women in the United States: 1981 through 1986," *JAMA* 257 (April 17, 1987):2039–42.

8. V. Mays, "Women and AIDS: The Forgotten Women," (paper presented at the 95th Annual Convention of the American Psychological Association, New York, August 1987).

Chapter 6

Women

Nancy Stoller Shaw

Women of every age, ethnic background, class, and sexual orientation have contracted HIV, but HIV infection occurs with greater frequency in the Black and Hispanic populations than among Whites, as described in Chapters 3 and 5.

The primary AIDS risk factors for women are IV drug use (52 percent), heterosexual contact (21 percent), and blood or blood products (9 percent). A few women have contracted the virus from artificial insemination, and several, via sexual contact with other women. Approximately 12 percent of women with AIDS have not had the precise mode of transmission documented. In all documented cases, however, the same body fluids are implicated: blood, semen, or vaginal secretions. Women may also pass on the virus through vaginal secretions or breast milk. If an initial assessment indicates that even one risk factor is present for a client, AIDS education should be initiated during that visit. Because IV drug use (IVDU) is such an important aspect of HIV transmission in women, practitioners who work in communities with high rates of IVDU should be especially sensitive to the possibility of HIV infection and should be trained to identify early symptoms of drug use.[1]

PREVENTIVE EDUCATION

Women may be poorly educated concerning the virus or the illness that can result from infection.[2] Education in the clinic or office setting can thus be a crucial factor in reducing HIV transmission among women. Current research indicates that women prefer to receive information about AIDS from a health care professional and that family planning clinics and physicians' offices are primary locations for such education.[3] Appropriate educational literature should be accessible in waiting and examining rooms. Because AIDS is a stigmatizing illness, women should be able to pick up the material without drawing attention to themselves.

Information about HIV transmission and prevention can be integrated into discussions of other aspects of health. For example, in discussing family planning, the nurse might recommend the use of condoms, possibly in addition to other measures, for clients who have multiple sex partners or who are uncertain about the viral status of their steady partners. The topic of AIDS can also be raised in discussions of drugs or pregnancy. Information obtained from the intake and history forms, or as a result of the physical examination or laboratory results, can indicate when to bring up the subject.

Information on reducing the risks of IVDU should be provided in a supportive manner. Specialists in the field can more appropriately provide long-term treatment and counseling for drug users.

Because women with HIV infection or disease have many and diverse needs, referral lists are important. These lists should be discreetly available in the same locations as the educational material concerning AIDS.

Teenage women are an especially important group to reach. Pregnancies, sexually transmitted disease rates, and data on drug use all indicate that teenage behavior patterns put young women at high risk for infection if the virus is found in their social communities. Black teenagers are at especially high risk for sexually transmitted diseases. (For further discussion, see Chapter 3.)

ISSUES FOR HIV-POSITIVE WOMEN

Like men, women who discover an HIV infection often experience heightened anxiety, denial, and preoccupation with maintaining health.[4] In clinic settings they also express concerns in the following five areas:[5]

1. transmission (drug use, sexual practices, negotiating sexual encounters)
2. disclosure of antibody status to immediate family as well as in work or other settings
3. childbearing and child rearing
4. access to social and emotional support services
5. isolation exacerbated by the small number of women with similar infections.

Most women who are HIV-positive are of childbearing age; many have children. Almost always, the care of women with HIV and HIV disease requires a family perspective. In the first place, the reproductive role of women and the risk of maternal transmission are ever-present issues for infected women. Clients need counseling concerning pregnancy, the possibility of abortion, breast feeding, contraception, and if pregnancy is pursued, preparation for uncertainty concerning the infant's status and future. Although the pregnancy should be classified as high-risk, the additional complications of confidentiality and medical uncertainty about the course of HIV infections in pregnant women may result in challenges to adequate management and support of the patient.

The overwhelming majority of children with AIDS have contracted the virus perinatally, as described in Chapter 11. In cases where an asymptomatic, HIV-positive mother has been identified through a child's diagnosis, further tracking sometimes uncovers additional infections in older children, as well as in male partners, such as the child's father. An entire family may be affected. The woman is faced with many issues, ranging from her own ill health and possible death to arrangements for her child (or children), and for approximately half, an ongoing struggle with needle use. In addition, most of the women are living at poverty levels, are in generally bad health, have a history of inadequate health and nutrition, and are suffering the multiple consequences of racism.[6]

ISSUES FOR WOMEN WITH HIV DISEASE

For the woman who has physical symptoms of HIV disease, additional concerns emerge:[7]

1. physical health and appearance, including changes in body image and chronic infections, such as vaginitis and other gynecological complications
2. economic stress
3. child custody planning, including adoption or guardianship after the death of the mother
4. emotional issues associated with the death and dying (herself, her partner, and her child).

When a woman becomes ill with HIV disease, her role as a primary caregiver to a child or children or to other adults in the household is immediately affected. The family is severely disrupted, and she herself has to make many adjustments. Even if her children are healthy and uninfected, they may be indirectly affected by her diagnosis because of prejudice and fear.

With AIDS, as with other sicknesses, it is ordinarily the mother who is expected to care for or manage the care of a child or spouse. But since most pediatric AIDS cases are the result of maternal transmission, the mother herself may be ill. Her ability to care for her child or lover may be further impaired by illegal survival activity, incarceration, loss of housing, or the threat of foster care, child abuse, or neglect proceedings associated with her drug use.

Women represent a special challenge to nurses caring for people with HIV disease. But for the nurse who is aware of and responds to the multiple roles these women fulfill, such work can be uniquely rewarding as a form of family-oriented nursing.

NOTES

1. Peter Selwyn, "AIDS: What Is Now Known," *Hospital Practice*, June 15, 1986.

2. Harold M. Ginsburg et al., "Health Education and Knowledge Assessment of HTLV-III Diseases Among Intravenous Drug Users," *Health Education Quarterly* 14, no. 4 (Winter 1986):373–82.

3. Research and Decisions Corp., *Designing an Effective AIDS Risk Reduction Program for San Francisco: Results from the First Probability Sample of Multiple/High Risk Partners of Heterosexual Adults* (San Francisco: San Francisco AIDS Foundation, 1986), p. 18.

4. Stephan Buckingham and Susan J. Rehm, "AIDS and Women at Risk," *Health and Social Work Journal* 12, no. 1 (Winter 1986):5–11.

5. Adapted from guidelines developed by Lauren Poole, AWARE Research Project, San Francisco General Hospital, 1986.

6. Health status and social-psychological backgrounds of women IVDUs are explored in Carolyn McCall et al., *Pregnancy in Prison: A Needs Assessment of Perinatal Outcome in Three California Penal Institutions* (California Department of Health Services, Maternal Child Health Division, June 1985).

7. Adapted from guidelines developed by Lauren Poole, AWARE Research Project.

RECOMMENDED READINGS

Houston-Hamilton, Amanda. "A Constant Increase: AIDS in Ethnic Communities." AIDS Health Project, University of California, San Francisco, *FOCUS* 1, no. 11 (October 1986):1–2.

Shaw, Nancy. "Serving Your Patient in the Age of AIDS." *Contemporary OB/GYN* 28, no. 4 (October 1986):141–49.

Stewart, G.J. et al. "Transmission of Human T-Lymphotropic Virus Type III (HTLV-III) Virus by Artificial Insemination by Donor." *Lancet* 2 (1985):581–84.

Women's Program. *Women and AIDS Clinical Resource Guide, 2nd Edition.* San Francisco AIDS Foundation, 1987.

Chapter 7

Children and Youths—Special Needs

Marcia Quackenbush

HIV infection and AIDS present many special concerns for children and adolescents in the areas of modes of transmission, prevention strategies, treatment, and public health policy issues. In addition, the emotional issues may differ from those in adult cases (see also Chapter 11).

CHILDREN (NEWBORN TO APPROXIMATELY TEN YEARS OLD)

Modes of Transmission

Three general routes of HIV transmission should be considered for young children:

1. exposure to blood or blood products
2. maternal transmission
3. sexual molestation by an HIV-infected perpetrator.

Prevention

Effective measures to prevent exposure to HIV-contaminated blood, including testing of all blood products for HIV, are already in place in the United States. Maternal transmission is best prevented through interventions directed at women of childbearing age, as discussed in the previous chapter.

In some instances HIV has been transmitted to children through sexual molestation by infected adults. In cases where sexual molestation is suspected, interventions should be aggressive and investigations thorough. Good programs to prevent sexual abuse must be supported, including those that teach children assertiveness skills, concepts of privacy, and the right to self-determination about their bodies.

Special concerns arise for children living with an addicted parent. Their homes are often chaotic, and the children may be poorly tended. The actively addicted parent has few resources available that allow effective protection or advocacy for a child. In the event of molestation, perpetrators might be more likely to be HIV-infected in these settings, so effective interventions to stop sexual abuse are essential.

Treatment Issues

Caring for infected children places special demands on nursing providers as well as family members. The children are often severely ill, and neurologic complications are common. Infection control precautions demand greater time and effort in care. Families or foster care providers need careful and thorough instructions on guidelines to prevent exposure of the child to infectious diseases, as well as to prevent the transmission of HIV. For example, simply telling parents (or nurses) to wear gloves when changing diapers is not adequate; the process of taping and untaping disposable diapers while wearing gloves is challenging, and hands-on instruction is essential. Further, families may hesitate to follow routines they feel will draw attention to and stigmatize themselves or their child.

Nurses play an essential role in educating and counseling these families, for whom the process of making health care decisions may be thoroughly confusing. Home nursing assistance or social work intervention may be necessary, especially if the child's mother is actively addicted. In some instances, foster placement is chosen. Unfortunately, many children with HIV infection are not accepted into foster placements and are unnecessarily living out their lives in inpatient settings. (For discussion of an alternative solution to this problem, see Chapter 28.)

Public Health and Public Policy Issues

In general, children with HIV infection should be offered the most normal life possible. When practical, home care is preferable; attendance at normal day care or elementary schools is encouraged, health permitting. The role of the school nurse as educator, patient advocate, and role model may be crucial to acceptance of the children.

Foster placements for HIV-infected children raise further concerns:

- Who should know the child's infection status?
- Should all children referred to foster care be tested for the AIDS antibody?
- Can HIV-positive children be placed in homes with children who are not infected?
- What is to be done with the large numbers of children at risk for HIV infection who will have difficulty being placed?

Questions can also be raised about the ethics of performing AIDS antibody tests on children in the foster care system:

- Who is eligible to provide informed consent?
- On what basis should children be tested?
- What kinds of caretaking decisions may ethically be made based on antibody test results, the accuracy of which is nebulous for infants?
- Who should determine policy on these issues?

These complex questions contribute to the uncertain status of the HIV-infected child and place great demands on health care providers.

Emotional Issues

The tragedy of children whose lives are filled with the suffering of chronic, severe illness is familiar to most nursing providers; HIV-infected children do not bring a new struggle in this realm. The greater difficulty may lie in the knowledge that the disease is preventable.

AIDS *is* a different sort of disease, because of its stigma and because of its preventability. In addition to the usual issues raised when working with children with life-threatening or terminal illness, many providers experience fear of contagion and resentment directed at the parents for "causing" this suffering in their child. Some feel anger toward the treatment system (the foster care system, the social-political system) for neglecting the needs of these children. Most experience frustration compounded by a sense of helplessness at an epidemic that continues to expand at an alarming rate and whose casualties will continue to be children in ever greater numbers.

ADOLESCENTS (APPROXIMATELY 11–20 YEARS OLD)

Modes of Transmission

There are three general routes of HIV transmission for adolescents:

1. exposure to blood or blood products
2. unsafe sexual practices
3. shared needle use.

In addition, the possibility of transmission through sexual molestation should be considered.

Prevention

As previously discussed, prevention of HIV infection associated with blood or blood products is currently in place.

Many teenagers engage in unsafe sexual practices. Of the 29 million adolescents over the age of 12 in this country, approximately 12 million have engaged in sexual intercourse. The mean age of first intercourse is under 15. Sixteen percent of women enrolled in high school report having had four or more partners. Sexually transmitted diseases in this population are at epidemic proportions and continue to rise.

Concern is also growing over the amount of needle use among adolescents. Though no specific national statistics exist on teen use of IV drugs, it is estimated that over 200,000 enrolled high school students have used heroin, and millions more have used other drugs that can be and are injected. Out-of-school youths have even higher rates of drug use.

Considering the high levels of high-risk activities among teenagers, the potential for significant penetration of HIV into this population is frightening. While teenagers represent a small number of diagnosed AIDS cases, a significant proportion of 20-to-29-year-old individuals diagnosed with AIDS (about 21 percent of total U.S. cases) were infected in their teens. Despite our lack of data on seroprevalence in the teenage population, the virus seems to be present and circulating among that group.

Adolescents need careful and thorough education about AIDS risks, transmission, and prevention. To be effective, this education must include explicit information about which sexual acts are risky, what body fluids are implicated, and *how* one can protect oneself from exposure. (See Chapter 24 and Appendix B for related information.)

Major programs to prevent teen pregnancy, sexually transmitted disease, and drug abuse have been in place for years, with varying levels of success. AIDS education alone cannot change long-established behaviors. However, school and community HIV education programs that not only provide specific HIV education but integrate information that enhances teen self-esteem, provide techniques for values clarification, and teach decision-making skills can be more effective than information offered in isolation. The information about AIDS will also be more accepted if it is repeated over the course of a student's school career. This repetition emphasizes the importance of the information and allows for broader understanding of the disease.

Nurses and other care providers may have significant opportunities to promote AIDS prevention with teens. Contacts with young adults in health clinics or medical offices can review AIDS prevention techniques and receive an update of the patient's sexual history. This update is important both for sexually active teenagers and those who are not yet active—presumably most youths will engage in sexual activity at some future time. Posters, brochures, and condoms can be made available in waiting rooms.

Treatment

Clinical manifestations of AIDS among adolescents appear to be similar to those among adults. However, the young person with HIV infection quite possibly is an individual already dealing with chronic illness, such as hemophilia, or a street youth who began engaging in risk behaviors, such as prostitution or IV drug use, at an early age. The latter group tends to have multiple and often severe social and psychological problems, with higher than normal incidences of:

- sexual and physical abuse
- suicide attempts
- sexually transmitted diseases
- drug use
- involvement with the criminal justice system.

Medical treatment may be hindered by noncompliance, acting out, and loss of contact.

Families of adolescents with HIV infection have needs as varied as the adolescents themselves. Parents of children with chronic illness may feel totally defeated by the disclosure of HIV infection. (For a discussion of parental response to HIV contracted through homosexual activity, see Chapter 2.) Perhaps most distressing of all, parents of many street youths do not appear to care at all about the welfare of their children or the meaning of such a diagnosis.

Public Health and Public Policy Issues

The comments previously made about children also apply to adolescents. Once again, controversy arises over the placement of HIV-infected adolescents in foster care, particularly in group home settings. Many young people in the foster care system have a history of sexual acting out, so the concern is not entirely unfounded. Evaluation of these youths on a case-by-case basis is encouraged, and thorough and repeated AIDS education should be a regular part of the program in any adolescent group home setting.

Placement of HIV-infected youths in juvenile detention facilities has raised policy questions. Isolation of these youths is not recommended. Again, providers should evaluate these young people case by case based on personal history and a realistic appraisal of the likelihood of risk activities occurring in a particular setting.

Many youths at highest risk, and therefore most likely to come into the HIV testing system, are psychologically fragile. In general, antibody testing for adolescents is not recommended unless medically indicated to clarify diagnosis, and involuntary testing of adolescents in foster, correctional, or school settings is discouraged.

Emotional Issues

Nurses have been meeting the challenges posed by adolescents for some time. In AIDS-related work, there is grieving and perhaps despair in anticipation of debilitation or death of young patients. When working with high-risk street youths, nurses may feel resentment, anger, or distrust in reaction to acting-out behaviors or noncompliance, along with occasional envy of their apparent freedoms. Care providers also feel compassion for the psychological and physical injuries such youths have usually experienced.

In prevention work with adolescents, providers often feel frustration and self-blame for their inability to change risk behaviors. Here, providers must practice compassion for themselves. AIDS prevention education is never the task of a single individual. Nurses who provide young people with even a small piece of information that might support their motivation to care well for themselves have succeeded better than many in their task. This thought may encourage care providers to continue these efforts as the demand grows and the circumstances become more grave in the years ahead.

Chapter 8

Psychosocial Responses of People with HIV

Judy Macks

People with HIV face a complex set of psychosocial needs and issues as they confront the impact of their diagnosis on their lives.[1] Various models of psychological responses to AIDS diagnosis have been proposed, such as the situational distress model of crisis [2] and adaptive responses by stage and task.[3] Many of the psychological responses to and coping mechanisms for dealing with a life-threatening illness are similar to those of people with illnesses such as cancer and heart disease.[4] However, the social and political nature of AIDS, combined with the fear of contagion, sets it apart from other diseases. The fact that HIV affects disenfranchised populations disproportionately and evokes strong cultural taboos about homosexuality, sex, death, and drugs accounts for the stigma attached to the illness. The complexity of psychosocial responses to the diagnosis is complicated by the young age of most people with HIV. Any comprehensive biopsychosocial program must address the psychological as well as the sociocultural impact of AIDS on those affected by the disease.

While HIV has been described as a spectrum disorder, people with ARC experience unique psychosocial stressors related to the uncertainty associated with the diagnosis and the lack of a consistent medical definition. Most significantly, higher levels of distress, depression, and anxiety have been documented among people with ARC.[5] Commonly feeling as though they are living in a state of limbo, people with ARC may become preoccupied with symptoms, immobilized, and functionally impaired. Paradoxically, while they fear an AIDS diagnosis, some people feel relieved when AIDS is diagnosed because somatic complaints can finally be defined. Most people with ARC have limited access to financial, emotional, and social support, and many, even those with disabling conditions, have been unable to obtain the benefits accessible to people with AIDS. The CDC's August 1987 redefinition of AIDS to include conditions formerly classified as ARC will assist some of these individuals.

The most profound psychosocial stressors for people with HIV fall into five areas:

1. stigma
2. informational needs
3. economic impact and concrete needs
4. psychological and emotional responses
5. social support.

STIGMA

Society attaches a severe stigma to HIV because the epidemic is associated with culturally unacceptable behavior, that is, homosexuality and drug use. Furthermore, the fact that HIV can be transmitted raises fears of contagion, both reasonable and irrational. This fear of contagion, coupled with negative attitudes toward the populations most affected, often results in irrational fear of and response to people with HIV. Furthermore, a climate of blame, usually targeted at gay communities, prostitutes, or other disenfranchised groups, surrounds the epidemic. This stigma affects individuals with HIV in two ways. First, people with HIV must contend with the attitudes and values of their families, friends, community, health care practitioners, employers, the media, and the culture at large. Negative attitudes, judgments, rejection, or discrimination may be directed at the individual with HIV. Second, people with HIV often internalize these negative messages, complicating the psychological process of adapting to a diagnosis.

As a result of the stigma associated with diagnosis, many people with HIV choose not to disclose their diagnosis to their most intimate support networks, including family members, colleagues, and friends. At the time when clients most need familial and community support, they may isolate themselves in an attempt to avoid the stigmatization of themselves or their families. Since many people with HIV have been rejected by family members and have been the target of discriminatory reprisals and violence, fears of disclosure may be very realistic.

Stigma affects people with HIV in a variety of ways depending upon different variables. Risk factors, socioeconomic status, ethnic background, sexual orientation, sex, and psychological functioning affect the unique concerns of individuals in different risk groups. For example, gay and bisexual men who define themselves as such may belong to culturally, economically, racially, politically, and socially diverse communities. However, they share some experiences in dealing with the stigma associated with both HIV and homosexuality. Gay partners of people with HIV experience the stigma associated with AIDS and homosexuality as well. Legally, gay couples cannot marry, nor can they benefit from the same civil and legal guarantees afforded heterosexual couples. As a result, gay partners may not be granted hospital visiting rights as family members, may not be granted bereavement leave by employers, and may face challenges by biological family members to their designated position as holder of power of attorney, parent of a child, or recipient of assets left in a will. (Additional information on gay and bisexual men is found in Chapter 2.)

Women experience the stigma associated with HIV in other ways. Being diagnosed with a disease that has been identified as affecting primarily men contributes to an extreme sense of isolation. Women with HIV belong to diverse communities in which there is often no context to discuss HIV, which heightens the women's sense of isolation, secrecy, and potential rejection. The AIDS epidemic highlights and exacerbates the financial inequities and the general lack of comprehensive health care, mental health, and substance abuse services that address the particular needs of women and families. (For further information, see Chapter 6.)

INFORMATIONAL NEEDS

Throughout the course of the illness, people with HIV must sort through rapidly changing medical and epidemiologic information in order to make informed choices about their health care. This task can be overwhelming given the amount of information regularly reported in the media and medical journals. Additionally, many important medical questions regarding treatment, prognosis, and course of illness remain unanswered, engendering confusion and anxiety for many. Clients often feel frustrated with the lack of consistent answers and the degree of uncertainty with which they are faced. They need accurate information whenever possible to maximize their sense of control over their lives.

Educational interventions, whether individual or group, can be crucial for people with AIDS. In particular, people with HIV need information about the medical aspects of AIDS, ongoing treatment options and their side effects, infection control, the course of the illness, neuropsychiatric complications, transmission, and risk reduction guidelines addressing sexual transmission as well as needle sharing. Clients also need information about available resources, including medical, mental health, legal, and social services. All practitioners can play a vital role in providing this information. Particularly at a time of crisis such as diagnosis, most people will not retain the information given them. Repetition over a period of time is required before clients integrate the information. Compiling this information in written form, therefore, is extremely useful.

Information regarding the neurologic complications associated with HIV is extremely important for clients and their families, since researchers estimate that 30 percent to 75 percent of people diagnosed with AIDS may experience some degree of cognitive impairment.[6] Clients and their caretakers need to know that symptoms such as short-term memory loss, confusion, disorientation, depressive symptoms, or behavioral changes may be associated with HIV. It is most important that practitioners provide medical and neuropsychiatric referrals to ascertain etiology and potential treatment of the presenting symptoms. Clients and family members need to be educated about the cognitive, behavioral, and emotional aspects of dementia, as well as what can be expected both prognostically and on a day-to-day basis. Family members need both practical assistance in the care of their loved one and instruction in developing interventions to help the person who is confused, disoriented, and experiencing short-term memory loss. For example, large calendars, lists of activities for the day, verbal reminders and cues, and utilization of simple language can all help the client with dementia. Family members may also need assistance in assessing the intentionality of and responding to the client's problematic behavior.

Many clients need to be educated regarding adaptive emotional responses they may experience throughout the course of the illness. Knowing what to expect and being reassured that certain responses are normal and extremely common can allay fears and anxieties about decompensation and losing control.

ECONOMIC IMPACT AND CONCRETE NEEDS

For many people with HIV, the immediate financial concerns of survival are of foremost importance. In addition, many individuals need housing, child care, transportation, home care, and legal services. Obtaining financial benefits quickly is essential given the rapid progression of the disease and the continued need for expensive medical services. For the majority of people, the economic impact on the individual and family is devastating. For people with ARC, who do not presumptively qualify for disability benefits, obtaining financial assistance is even more burdensome.

Housing concerns may be critical for a person who suddenly cannot meet rent or mortgage payments, has been evicted from a living situation because of diagnosis, has moved suddenly to a new area seeking better medical attention, or has a history of unstable living situations. Lack of housing contributes to longer hospital stays, adds unnecessarily to high health care costs, and deprives people who are not in need of acute care of the option of being home with loved ones. Women with HIV who have children have an even more difficult time securing housing and are often forced to live in situations that are overcrowded, chaotic, and unsafe for themselves and their children.

Women with children need child care services, not only for the times they are too ill to care for their children, but for the time-consuming task of dealing with a life-threatening illness. To comply with medical care and treatment protocols, keep social service appointments, and seek mental health and support services, mothers with HIV must have access to child care services.

Important and complex legal issues arise for the person with HIV. Wills, powers of attorney, funeral arrangements, and decisions regarding life support need to be documented legally. Given the progressive and debilitating nature of the illness, it is imperative to attend to this future planning early in the illness when clients are clearly competent to make their wishes known. For gay clients, whose relationships are not protected by law, and who wish a partner to retain power of attorney and other primary decision-making roles for them, legal documentation becomes particularly significant. Without this safeguard, biological families can intervene and are not legally required to act according to clients' wishes. Also, all parents with HIV must address custody arrangements. This decision usually creates great stress and anxiety for the parent, often compounded by complex familial situations.

People with HIV who do not require acute hospitalization but need some assistance in living need home care services (described in Part III), which are not readily available and can be costly. However, economic analyses have documented the cost effectiveness of outpatient and home care services as compared with inpatient care.[7]

PSYCHOLOGICAL RESPONSES

Because AIDS is a life-threatening disease involving progressive physiologic and often cognitive deterioration, practitioners must simultaneously attend to the physiological, psychological, and sociocultural aspects of AIDS for each client. It is particularly important to assess the individual in relation to:

- premorbid personality style
- coping skills
- strengths and weaknesses
- risk for psychological decompensation as evidenced by psychiatric history, as well as occupational and social functioning
- family history
- substance use
- self-esteem
- feelings about HIV and the individual's risk factors.

Attention to particular cultural, religious, and spiritual values and attitudes as they relate to communication styles, homosexuality, drugs, and death, dying, and grief is also critical. These factors may be the best indicators of the client's ability to cope with this catastrophic illness.

Stage of Illness

The psychosocial concerns of people with HIV may vary considerably depending on the state of illness. Three stages of psychological responses to an AIDS diagnosis have been identified, each characterized by specific issues and tasks.[8] The beginning stage, in which a person is diagnosed with HIV, is a period of crisis. Emotional responses range from affective numbing to affective discharge. Often, the individual experiences shock and denial and is unable to absorb information beyond learning of the diagnosis. Others feel overwhelmed and flooded with emotion; fear and anxiety feel uncontained and out of control. Whether or not the individual's health status is immediately life threatening, a sense of urgency and impending death usually accompanies this crisis. At this point in the illness, the psychological task for the client is to resolve the initial crisis; that is, to return to the previous level of psychological and social functioning.

After the initial crisis resolves, people with HIV enter a middle phase that involves three distinct tasks. The first is that of getting on with life; that is, learning to live with a life-threatening illness as opposed to waiting to die. The second task is that of facing immediate and anticipated losses, requiring the ability to manage fluctuating emotions associated with grief, such as sadness, anger, despair, guilt, and hopelessness. Losses may range from loss of mobility, independence, and self-esteem to anticipated death. Ongoing tasks and processes such as reviewing one's life and taking care of unfinished emotional and practical business can contribute to the ability to continue living. Individuals may attempt to resolve conflicts or resentments with loved ones as well as deal with concrete matters such as wills, powers of attorney, and directives to physicians. The third task in the middle phase is that of coping with the fluctuating or deteriorating physical state associated with the disease.

Throughout this middle stage, periods of crisis emerge as a result of such events as:

- onset or recurrence of symptoms or infections
- sudden or profound loss of mobility
- weight loss and other changes in physical appearance
- treatment failure
- rejection by a family member
- changes in sexual and intimate relationships
- loss of financial or housing security
- custody battles.

People with HIV continually engage in a psychological process in which they vacillate between crisis and adaptation to the crisis, integrating the new turn of events into their lives. This process can leave clients emotionally exhausted and feeling a profound sense of hopelessness.

In the end stage, when a client is close to death, the focus of issues and tasks shifts. Both people with HIV and their loved ones can experience great fear of death, pain, and abandonment. Practitioners must provide adequate pain management along with reassurance that the client need not die in pain. Interventions must be designed to work with the entire support system by honoring the clients' wishes and facilitating the dying process for all involved.

Grief Reactions

The psychological responses of people with HIV are similar to the responses of patients diagnosed with cancer. Kubler-Ross identified stages associated with the grief process including denial, anger, bargaining, depression, and acceptance.[9] People with HIV experience these stages, usually described as "a roller coaster of emotions," as they face their mortality and death, the anticipated loss of loved ones, and other losses incurred during the illness, including loss of previous sources of self-esteem. Feelings of fear related to death and dying accompany grief. As one client stated, "I am not afraid of dying, but I am terrified of the dying process." While some clients are terrified of death itself, others most fear a prolonged process of dying in which they anticipate physical debilitation, dependence on others, cognitive impairment, and pain. The young age of people with HIV (close to 50 percent are between the ages of 30 and 39) compounds the difficulty of facing a life-threatening illness. Not only is the death premature, but many people have had little experience dealing with death previous to their illness. Existential and spiritual concerns are common themes throughout the diagnosis.

The grief process is often complicated by the fact that people with HIV not only must deal with their own diagnosis, but may simultaneously be grieving the loss of a partner, child, or other friends lost to AIDS. Similarly, community grief resulting from massive loss of its members complicates the grieving process even further.

Managing Distressing Feelings and Reactions

People with HIV may request assistance in managing their fluctuating emotional and psychological reactions. Common feelings are anger, helplessness, loss of control, fear, guilt, sadness, despair, and hopelessness. The medical realities of HIV, the lack of an effective treatment and cure, and the uncertainty and ambiguity associated with earlier stages of the illness contribute to these feelings. Many people with HIV, young and at the beginning or peak of their careers, are forced to abandon their sources of income, social support, and self-esteem. For others, feelings of failure accompany disappointment in that they will never realize dreams, plans for the future, and intentions of creating a more stable life. Chronic fatigue, physical deterioration, loss of mobility, and loss of bodily functions, while devastating for anyone, can be especially difficult for a young client.

Self-esteem can be seriously impaired as the disease begins to affect clients' sense of identity, productivity, and status in the world. Physical appearance, attractiveness, loss of image as a healthy person, and loss of the role of financial provider or parent can all be associated with feelings of self-worth. For example, many women with HIV have been mothers and caretakers their entire lives, relying on these roles as their source of self-esteem. As they get sicker, their ability to maintain these roles diminishes, precipitating a distressing identity crisis.

Guilt and self-reproach for having contracted HIV are commonly expressed. These feelings may be associated with an individual's unresolved or restimulated conflicts about homosexuality or sexuality in general. They can also reflect internalized manifestations of societal condemnation of homosexuality and other attitudes related to race and sex role expectations. It is most helpful for practitioners to reframe this thinking by discussing with the self-blaming client the actual causes of HIV.

Although strong emotional reactions to living with a life-threatening illness are appropriate and expected, they can grow into severe and incapacitating anxiety or depression. Anxiety reactions are quite common with clients complaining of intrusive or ruminative thoughts about HIV, symptoms, death, etc. These thoughts can be accompanied by panic attacks, sleep disturbance, and somatic complaints. When depression becomes more severe, clients may present with:

- feelings of extreme despair
- lack of motivation
- lethargy
- sleep disturbance
- poor appetite
- difficulty concentrating
- suicidal ideation
- other symptoms associated with depression.

Some of these symptoms associated with anxiety and depression may also be caused by the medical condition, medications, or neurologic manifestations of the disease. When the anxiety or depression begins to interfere seriously with the client's functioning, the practitioner should refer the client for psychological assessment and treatment.

Most people with HIV have thought about suicide. Suicidal ideation is associated with depression; attempts to manage feelings of despair, loss of control, and helplessness; and an immediate crisis and/or fear of or knowledge about future events. It is important to assess the risk of the client's committing suicide and to explore in depth the associated thoughts and feelings. Actively suicidal clients frequently have a clinical history of depression, anxiety, previous suicide attempts, substance abuse, or characterological disorder. When clients consider suicide during the final stage of the illness, complex legal, ethical, and emotional concerns are raised for the practitioner.

HOPE AND DENIAL

Maintaining hope is a primary task for every person with HIV, and it is one of the most difficult. The feeling of hope fluctuates for everyone, and the source of hope differs from person to person. Some examples of decisions and situations that have helped clients feel hopeful include:

- participating in experimental treatment protocols
- actively pursuing alternative treatments and therapies
- making significant and desired life changes
- making plans for the future, such as vacations or returning to school
- getting involved in a relationship
- joining a support group
- becoming politically active
- developing a spiritual practice.

The most important factor in maintaining hope is active participation in decision making, health care, and life activities.

Denial, an important and protective defense mechanism, is integrally linked with maintaining hope. As one client stated, "I need a vacation from AIDS. I don't want to live and breathe it from the time I wake up until the time I go to sleep." Constructive denial allows for these much-needed breaks and cushions the impact and intensity of emotional reactions. Practitioners, on the other hand, need to confront this denial if it results in destructive behavior such as avoiding medical care, discounting serious physical or psychological symptoms, continuing to engage in high-risk behavior, or increasing substance use. Ultimately, any intervention that helps a person with HIV to feel empowered and maintain control serves to strengthen feelings of hope.

SOCIAL SUPPORT

The literature documents the importance of social support for its ameliorative effect on depression and coping with medical illness.[10] Adequate social support systems are of primary importance for people with HIV. Because of the stigma and secrecy associated with HIV, maintaining or strengthening clients' support systems can be complex and difficult. Some clients have experienced rejection by family members, partners, friends, and coworkers, while others anticipate potential rejection and fear it. Clients commonly associate their isolating behavior with (1) rejection or discrimination, (2) the desire to protect loved ones, (3) feelings of contamination, (4) fear of contagion, and (5) physical and emotional exhaustion. Although people with HIV and their families who reach out for support run the risk of being rejected, most have found that people respond with caring, love, and courage.

The emotional responses of couples dealing with HIV are similar to family responses in other patient groups. For instance, partners of people with HIV similarly have a difficult time setting limits and managing their own needs as they take on the role of caretaker. However, the sexually transmissible nature of HIV raises unique concerns for couples. The diagnosis of HIV demands drastic changes in couples' intimate and sexual lives. Couples may need to change their sexual behaviors to incorporate safer sex practices. Some people with HIV feel contaminated and dirty and withdraw from sexual as well as physical and affectional closeness. These feelings, although not uncommon for people facing life-threatening illnesses, may be exacerbated by the nature of HIV. Many couples describe sexual difficulties resulting from diminished sexual interest and desire. Most commonly it is the person with HIV whose sexual interest decreases as a result of physical exhaustion, medications, and emotional factors. For some couples, the association of sex, HIV, and death becomes so strong that any sexual contact becomes threatening and emotionally painful. Feelings of guilt or self-recrimination may arise if one partner feels responsible for infecting the other. Impotence is not uncommon. Partners may feel dissatisfied with not having their sexual and intimacy needs met but often feel guilty about feeling or expressing this need. Most likely, the partner has been exposed and possibly infected with HIV through sexual contact. The couple must contend simultaneously with the impact of the HIV diagnosis on the relationship and the uncertainty of the partner's future health.

Family systems, despite their configuration, risk fracture as they attempt to manage the enormous impact of this illness on their lives. Lack of social and financial support, as well as the possible presence of substance-abusing adults in the family, increases this risk of fracture. Families in which a parent was abusing drugs or alcohol prior to the diagnosis may have already been chaotic and fragile. These families need to find drug treatment options, which is often difficult for women with children. For the partner and other members of the abuser's family, codependency patterns need to be identified and confronted. Often, in families where one person is sick, others are infected. Women, especially, feel profoundly guilty and responsible if their child has been infected with HIV, whether or not the mother knew her health status during pregnancy. Immediate caretaking concerns, particularly as the disease progresses, only increase mothers' anxiety and guilt about leaving their children motherless when they die. To complicate matters further, many women live with the fear that their children will be taken away from them either through custody challenges by family members or the courts. The mother must decide what, when, and how to tell children about the diagnosis, as well as how to prepare them for and support them through feelings of grief and the reactions of their peers and community.

Parents and siblings of people with HIV have still other crises to contend with. Parents, of course, have to face the possibility of losing a child, while simultaneously they may be learning that their child is gay. Parents are not prepared for their child to die before them, nor are they generally prepared to face their child's homosexuality. Their child may have moved away from the family, seeking out a safer and more supportive environment for gay people. Parents and siblings may have to travel great distances to visit with and care for the person with HIV, requiring flexibility in schedules and financial resources. Parents and siblings may find little support in their own communities, often keeping the diagnosis and their grief secret.

Group interventions have been documented as useful for people facing life-threatening illnesses.[11] Groups enhance social support and provide clients with the opportunity to discuss issues and problems related to the illness with others experiencing similar problems. Separate groups for (1) people with HIV, (2) couples in which one or both partners are diagnosed, (3) families, (4) children, and (5) parents and/or siblings help address the unique concerns of those most affected by the disease.

CONCLUSION

The AIDS epidemic undoubtedly requires a multidisciplinary approach to the care of HIV clients and a consistent collaboration among medical, mental health, social service, substance abuse, and community-based organizations. Clearly, no single service or intervention can meet the complex biopsychosocial needs of people with HIV.

Models of care will differ geographically to reflect the social, economic, and political characteristics of the communities most affected by AIDS, the local community at large, and the organization and structure of the health care delivery system.[12]   However, an effective approach will link hospital-based services both with public health, mental health, and substance abuse systems and with private practitioners, community-based groups, AIDS agencies, volunteers, and representatives from the communities most heavily affected by HIV. (Refer to Chapter 22 for a discussion of the development of community resources.) The availability of outpatient and home-based services is of particular importance, both in terms of quality of care and cost effectiveness.[13]

Useful psychological interventions for people with HIV should be designed to enhance adaptive and integrative functioning by (1) encouraging emotional expression, (2) maximizing coping skills, (3) assisting clients in managing fluctuating moods and physical states, and (4) assisting clients in maintaining control and mastery in their lives. A full range of psychosocial services should be available for people with HIV, including case management, benefits counseling, crisis intervention, individual and family therapy, and group interventions.

Finally, the key to successful work with people with HIV lies ultimately in the willingness of providers to look at their own attitudes, beliefs, and fears stimulated by the AIDS epidemic and work with clients. In this way, and in this way only, can practitioners provide the most effective and humane services to people with HIV.

NOTES

1. D.L. Wolcott, F.I. Fawzy, and R.O. Pasnau, "Acquired Immune Deficiency Syndrome (AIDS) and Consultation-Liaison Psychiatry," *General Hospital Psychiatry* 7 (1985):280–92; G. Christ, L. Wiener, and R. Moynihan, "Psychosocial Issues in AIDS," *Psychiatric Annals* 16 (1986):173–79; K. Siegel, "AIDS: The Social Dimension," *Psychiatric Annals* 16 (1986):168–72; M. Cohen and H. Weisman, "A Biopsychosocial Approach to AIDS," *Psychosomatics* 27 (1986):245–49; D.J. Lopez and G.S. Getzel, "Helping Gay AIDS Patients in Crisis," *Social Casework*, September 1984; J. Mandel, "The Psychosocial Challenge of AIDS and ARC," *Focus* 2(January 1986):1–2; and J.W. Dilley et al., "Findings in Psychiatric Consultations with Patients with Acquired Immune-Deficiency Syndrome," *American Journal of Psychiatry* 142 (1985):82–86.

2. S.E. Nichols, "Psychosocial Reactions of Persons with Acquired Immunodeficiency Syndrome," *Annals of Internal Medicine* 103 (1985):765–69.

3. J.W. Dilley, "Treatment Interventions and Approaches to Care of Patients with Acquired Immune Deficiency Syndrome," in Nichols and Astrow, eds., *Psychiatric Implications of Acquired Immune Deficiency Syndrome* (Washington, D.C.: American Psychiatric Press, Inc., 1984), pp. 62–70.

4. Wolcott, Fawzy, and Pasnau, "Acquired Immune Deficiency Syndrome (AIDS) and Consultation-Liaison Psychiatry"; M. Forstein, "The Psychosocial Impact of the Acquired Immunodeficiency Syndrome," *Seminars in Oncology* 11 (1984):77–82; S. Morin, K. Charles, and A. Mahyon, "The Psychological Impact of AIDS on Gay Men," *American Psychologist* 39 (1984):1288–93; and Nichols, "Psychosocial Reactions."

5. Mandel, "The Psychosocial Challenge."

6. Wolcott, Fawzy, and Pasnau, "Acquired Immune Deficiency Syndrome (AIDS) and Consultation-Liaison Psychiatry"; R.J. Loewenstein and S.S. Shartstein,"Neuropsychiatric Aspects of Acquired Immune Deficiency Syndrome," *International Journal of Psychiatry in Medicine* 13 (1983–84): 255–60; B.G. Gazzard et al., "Clinical Findings and Serological Evidence of HTLV III Infection in Homosexual Contacts of Patients with AIDS and Persistent Generalized Lymphadenopathy in

London,'' *Lancet* (1984):480–83; J. Holland and S. Tross, ''The Psychosocial and Neuropsychiatric Sequelae of the Acquired Immunodeficiency Syndrome and Related Disorders,'' *Annals of Internal Medicine* 103 (1985):760–64; W.D. Snider et al., ''Neurological Complications of Acquired Immune Deficiency Syndrome: Analysis of 50 Patients,'' *Annals of Neurology* 14 (1983):403–18; D.E. Bresden and R. Messing, ''Neurological Syndromes Heralding the Acquired Immune Deficiency Syndrome,'' (abstract) *Annals of Neurology* 14 (1983):141; and S. Perry and S. Tross, ''Psychiatric Problems of AIDS Inpatients at the New York Hospital: Preliminary Report,'' *Public Health Reports* 99 (1984):200–05.

7. P.S. Arno, ''The Nonprofit Sector's Response to the AIDS Epidemic: Community Based Services in San Francisco'' (University of California, San Francisco, Institute for Health Policy Studies, Institute for Health and Aging, February 1986); and D.J. Sencer and V.E. Botnick, ''Report to the Mayor: New York City's Response to the AIDS Crisis'' (City of New York, Office of the Mayor, December 1985).

8. Dilley, ''Treatment Interventions and Approaches.''

9. E. Kubler-Ross, *On Death and Dying* (New York: Macmillan Publishing Co., 1969).

10. S. Cavanaugh, D. Clark, and R. Gibbons, ''Diagnosing Depression in the Hospitalized Medically Ill,'' *Psychosomatics* 24 (1983):809–15; R. Moos, ed., *Coping With Physical Illness* (New York: Plenum Medical Book Co., 1977); and S. Cobb, ''Social Support as a Moderator of Life Stress,'' *Psychosomatic Medicine* 38 (1976):300–14.

11. R.H. Rahe, H.W. Ward, and V. Hayes, ''Brief Group Therapy in Myocardial Infarction Rehabilitation: Three to Four Year Follow-up of a Controlled Trial,'' *Psychosomatic Medicine* 41 (1979):229–42; T.P. Hacket, ''The Use of Groups in the Rehabilitation of the Post-Coronary Patient,'' *Advances in Cardiology* 24 (1978):127–35; and D. Spiegel and I.D. Yalom, ''A Support Group for Dying Patients,'' *International Journal of Group Psychotherapy* 28 (1978):233–35.

12. P.S. Arno and R.G. Hughes, ''Local Policy Response to the AIDS Epidemic: New York and San Francisco'' (University of California, San Francisco, Institute for Health Policy Studies, Institute for Health and Aging, June 1986).

13. Ibid.

Chapter 9

Psychosocial Issues: One Man's Experience

Tristano Palermino

My personal and professional lives have been entwined since 1981 with the realities of the AIDS epidemic. I was diagnosed with AIDS on October 15, 1986, as a result of *Pneumocystis carinii* pneumonia (PCP) being found in my lungs. I was deeply relieved to get the news. I had been sick a long time.

My first experience with a person with AIDS was to become friends with Bobbi Campbell, the nurse to whom this book is dedicated. I was having medical problems of my own when Bobbi was diagnosed. I had extreme fatigue and some unexplained neurological symptoms such as photophobia and a numbing in my right leg. I knew something was terribly wrong but no one could tell me what. I have chronic Hepatitis B, and some symptoms were attributed to it. Some could not be explained and different doctors had differing opinions. I wanted to believe that it was psychosomatic.

I moved to Provincetown in June 1982. That fall, I experienced shortness of breath, increased short-term memory loss, and gastrointestinal problems. I panicked. I went to the doctor I had seen over the summer in Provincetown. His office personnel acted strangely the day I went to see him. He frankly admitted he had no idea what was going on and just said, " Go to Boston right away." I left for evaluation.

Fenway Community Health Center, a community health clinic sensitive to the health care needs of gay people, provided me with excellent care. Diagnostic evaluations were conducted and mental health counseling arranged. My fatigue was immobilizing. I felt like I was dying. Living with the unknown was a frightening experience. My faith, and the support of my brother and friends, made all the difference.

Evaluations were not turning up anything conclusive. I thought, maybe much of this is psychosomatic. I wanted to believe that but deep in my heart I knew my body was doing some bizarre things. Knowing someone with AIDS was important to me. At the time, Bobbi Campbell was the only person I could call. I telephoned

Bobbi and told him I just knew I had AIDS. "You do not have AIDS until they prove it to you," he said. This advice permitted me to remain hopeful; not to engage in the trap of doom and gloom, of feeling like I was a goner. I told him I did not trust the medical expertise of the Boston doctors, since at the time Boston had had only 12 known cases.

Bobbi reassured me that I was receiving the best available care. To have someone who knew what I was going through was the best medicine of all. In 1982 there was no test for the HIV antibody. I insisted on a neurological consult. An EEG revealed slightly abnormal brain activity, and a lumbar puncture revealed nothing. However, the neurologist who evaluated me told me, "I believe you have a viral infection in the brain. I cannot say for sure. Sometimes these things come and go." He spoke to me for 20 minutes but all I heard over and over in my head was, "A viral infection in the brain."

I appreciated the neurologist's directness. I was in shock but preferred to know the honest truth. I felt empowered with provision of the real picture.

PROFESSIONAL INVOLVEMENT

I returned to San Francisco in January 1983. My health steadily improved. I worked part time. I pursued some of my life dreams. My brush with the possibility of dying triggered me to evaluate what I enjoyed doing. If I was to accomplish some of those dreams, I could not wait any longer. I took voice lessons and acting lessons. I began vocational counseling through the community college. The counselor became sick with AIDS. Another friend was sick with AIDS. AIDS seemed all around me.

My professional work history includes over ten years in human services. I decided I wanted to take my knowledge and experience and work with people with AIDS, their families, and their friends. I was hired by the San Francisco AIDS Foundation in March 1984 as a social worker. I liaisoned with several San Francisco hospitals to improve care and understanding of the disease. The city was doing its best to meet the challenges. Health care providers from around the country phoned our office for help. As busy as our office was, I always took the time to speak with callers. I could not forget the isolation I had felt in Provincetown, when no one seemed to understand. My own health remained good. The HIV test became available. I did not get tested. I did not want to jeopardize insurance possibilities and had certainly seen enough abuse of confidentiality to be concerned.

I became the director of the Social Services Department in April 1985. This position was more stressful than the case work position. Classic AIDS symptoms returned. In December I developed bronchitis and asthma, which took three months to clear up. I resigned as director but wanted to keep working at the

Foundation. I was afraid to go out on disability leave, since it may have jeopardized future employment. I used up my vacation time and returned to work in the Education Department, but my ability to work was compromised by my AIDS symptoms. I knew in my heart that it was probably just a matter of time before I got a more severe opportunistic infection.

GETTING DIAGNOSED

In October 1986 I developed a dry cough. No other symptoms appeared for a few weeks. Breathing got more difficult. I became frightened. Within 24 hours I went from panting after walking a block to panting after walking *down* a flight of stairs. I assumed it was PCP, but kept Bobbi's words in mind, "You do not have AIDS until they prove it to you." A bronchoscopy was scheduled. As the operating room technician wheeled me to OR on a gurney, I began to cry. I knew what the verdict would be.

Later that day, I awakened drowsily from the operation. Two friends sat at the end of my bed. Both my doctor, Steven Mehalko, and the surgeon who had performed the bronch, Jan Bossart, were in the room. My doctor gave me the news. My first reaction was one of relief. The years of uncertainty had ended. The myriad of symptoms could all be explained. No more worries about if I would develop AIDS. I now had it.

Fortunately I was able to be treated with Bactrim at home. I requested my friends take me to lunch, which they did. I was still in a fog. The next day, I lay in bed exhausted and began to realize the full meaning of the diagnosis. What may lie ahead?

I had moments of denying it was really happening; I wanted to believe I would be well in a few days. I phoned my supervisor at work and told her I would be back in two days. I only briefly wondered if there had been some mistake. Maybe I had been misdiagnosed. My mind was racing. I could not concentrate on anything for more than a few seconds. Ninety percent of my thoughts were death related or reflections on what life choices I had made. Mistakes, broken dreams, what . . . . What would my funeral be like? My obituaries? What infection would finally kill me?

Suffering and grief were what I felt. Not just for me, but for memories of others I had worked with, whether they had AIDS, or rubella, or leukemia. I do not think you can truly appreciate facing a crisis like this unless you have had your life so threatened. Imagine losing your job, your love relationship, your home, and all of your friends. On top of that you feel you have no future; you will not feel the wind against your skin, or watch snow fall. You will not hear music or go sailing with friends. And you will not love or be loved.

I had crossed the line. The line between the living and the dead. I feared being alone and yet needed to be alone. I was atheistic as a child but in my 20s I grew to believe in God, or my higher power, as I prefer to call him. Had he betrayed me? I felt ripped off. Yet I also had a sense of universal truths, of my own connection with all that I feared losing. And I do believe that on some level I have always been a part of this world and always will be.

I was selective in who visited me. I have many friends and colleagues who wanted to visit. As lucky as that may seem, to face each and every one of them so soon was too much to bear. As it turned out, many were in shock and did not want to see or talk to me right away. I did not want to feel obligated to anyone or have anyone obligated to me. I requested no phone calls, but I encouraged people to send cards. It worked beautifully. I reached out to those I felt I could and knew that eventually I would be in touch with everyone who mattered to me and vice versa.

One friend sent a card with the following note: "I know there is nothing I can say or do to change your diagnosis. My heart is with you. I love you. If you need anything, call. I am here for you if and when you're ready. Take things slowly, be gentle with yourself, meditate, scream, cry, laugh. Be yourself." In the height of the crisis of being diagnosed these words were of great comfort—particularly the reminder to "be yourself" and permission to contact her "if and when" I wanted to. I received other cards that simply said "I care" or "I don't know what to say." I cherished these notes as well, for they were honest.

My sexual identity was shaken by the diagnosis. I was impotent for the first few weeks. I had feelings that since I had this disease, no one would ever love me again. I was not in a long-term lover relationship at the time. Fortunately I do have male friends with whom I have been physically involved. They treated me with kindness and affirmed that I was still an attractive man.

I had begun to date a man just the month before. We had a date planned the week I was diagnosed. I called him intending to cancel; I felt diseased and wanted to reject him before he rejected me. He insisted on keeping the date. He held me as I cried for hours. I tried to explain what I was feeling. He simply said, "Don't try to 'process' that which cannot be processed. Leave yourself alone. Just let your mind do what it needs to do." This was good advice for me. I felt so out of control and wanted so much to be in control. We made love that night. I was still attractive and was not rejected, although I felt, "What can he see in me now?"

Shortly after my diagnosis I began dating my current lover, David. He has AIDS-related complex. This relationship has been healing, as love of any kind truly is. At times our illnesses impact on the relationship but I truly believe each of us has gained so much from loving the other—most of all, optimism about our prognosis and the sense that whatever we face, we will do it together and with the support of many friends and family.

Through the first week, my biggest concern was telling my parents. They are both in their 70s. My family has suffered from the disease of alcoholism. My parents divorced when I was ten but have done their best to raise eight children. I felt a tremendous sense of forgiveness and appreciation for what they had done. I knew the news of my diagnosis would hurt them both deeply. I also knew they would not be able to support me in the ways that some parents can. I invited my mother and my brother Chris to visit me. I wanted my mother to meet my doctor and my many friends. I feel it is crucial that families who wish to be involved do so, but on the terms of the person who is ill.

Both my parents have known of my gayness for years. Neither has been able really to accept it, both preferring to not talk about it at all. I have "adopted" a few men as my fathers and a few women friends as my mothers. These people rushed to my aid beautifully. I braced myself for telling my six brothers and one sister. My sister lives in San Jose, just an hour away. My brother Chris in Boston would be devastated. I wanted to protect him and Lori from the suffering I knew they would face. One cannot know for sure the reactions of friends and loved ones. I didn't expect it, but my oldest brother Paul has become one of my main sources of support since my diagnosis.

My sister and I meet monthly with four of my closest friends who have agreed to support me through my illness. They have agreed to accept areas of responsibility such as cooking, cleaning, finances, and medical decisions should I become disabled in any of these areas. It is great relief to know that all will be taken care of by people who want to help and can.

The early weeks of my diagnosis were the most challenging so far. The week after I was diagnosised with *Pneumocystis*, the doctor found a KS lesion in my mouth. I was afraid to see my doctor. What else might he find? I was terrified I would die if he did not keep a close watch, and yet I feared he would continue to find other infections. He and his staff were excellent when I needed them the most. He is a model doctor because when I need things explained, he always takes the time to do so. One day his office staff needed to take several tubes of blood. One drew blood while another massaged my belly. A personal touch is so important when you are being assaulted by so many needles and so much machinery.

I have experienced varying periods of depression, grandiosity, rage, and gratefulness. I had thoughts of suicide several times during the first few weeks. Looking back, I see it as an attempt to control what was happening to me. "If I am going to die, I want to say when and how." I had seen all the horrible possibilities of the disease and wondered what would befall me. I started to bargain: "I can accept weight loss and chills, but not fevers. Skin lesions? Yes, but not constant vomiting or diarrhea." And I was most terrified about going insane due to neurological infections.

I reestablished my relationship with Bobbi Campbell. I was grateful to have lived past 1984; he did not. I became grateful for new treatments, such as azidothymidine (AZT), and the experience of San Francisco's care providers. The spirit of Bobbi and many other men with AIDS who lived with dignity and grace boosted my spirits.

One friend who had been diagnosed the year before told me, "Things will fall into place, it gets easier." He was right. Eight months have passed since my diagnosis. I continue to experience the roller coaster effects of having a life-threatening illness, but the peaks and valleys are less dramatic. For now my health is relatively good and I can go on with living.

At age 33, I watched my salary drop to 60 percent of what it had been. Second to facing death, I believe financial concerns are the major issue for most people with AIDS. The bureaucracy and intricacies of disability and medical coverage are astounding and infuriating. Loss of career status has also been a difficult transition. Fortunately, I am able to write, do public speaking, and participate in most life activities. At times I am jealous of friends who are able to maintain a "normal" life. I have grown to accept what I can and cannot do each day, to enjoy that which I can do and appreciate the mere fact that I am alive today. I try to do something joyous every day.

SOME POINTERS TO CAREGIVERS

I have learned many lessons from my AIDS diagnosis. I feel my faith has been strengthened and my understanding of universal truths has magnified. Much of that which we think is important in our daily lives really is not. Truth, integrity, and a willingness to listen, as well as speak out, are qualities that matter. In working with your patients, be aware that many have a heightened sense of a spiritual nature. I advise you to examine your own values concerning AIDS and, more importantly, the meaning of life itself.

People with AIDS are people, not unlike your other patients. As a professional you have developed skills. Your experience on the "front lines" with other ill or disabled people is invaluable; do not let the diagnosis of AIDS panic you. You will not have all the answers, and if patients expect that of you, don't let them get away with it. Many people who are sick want everything made easier, even in the most difficult situations. Health care providers bend over backward, and then some, to try to please. My advice to you is to be yourself. Be human and caring, and expect the same in return.

AIDS does present some unusual problems because of people's fear of the disease. A common complaint of people with AIDS in hospital settings is overhearing their diagnosis being discussed freely at nursing stations. Remember, the subject is not a person who is admitted for a "routine" disease such as a coronary.

Neighboring patients and their family members have become incensed and hysterical upon learning there is an AIDS patient on the floor. Confidentiality is crucial and a right for all patients. The possible ramifications of breaking that confidentiality can mean havoc.

As in life, people facing death have a right to do it their own way. Do not pry or force patients to feel feelings or "face" death. It's a disservice to force patients to give up their denial or to give cheery false hopes. Sometimes I just want someone to listen. Sometimes I do not want to talk about my medical treatments. Sometimes I do not want to talk at all. If you stay in the moment, contribute what you can, and permit the patient to do the same, you cannot fail.

Bobbi Campbell strove to educate everyone about the then rare and bizarre disease known as AIDS. As a nurse he understood medical aspects, as a patient he understood the isolation and fear of the unknown, and in both roles he confronted the stigma of AIDS. He worked to increase everyone's understanding of this disease, even those who believed he "deserved" the disease for his homosexuality. He advanced the status of people with AIDS everywhere. To know Bobbi personally was to be challenged, confronted and "nursed" into accepting him as a person of equal worth, not a victim, not someone to be pitied.

You can be an advocate. You, too, can make a difference. Pressures from those who do not understand, including coworkers, family members, and the families of other patients, have led to massive discrimination against people with the disease. The quality of care has been compromised. More than any other disease, AIDS is talked about as a moral issue and a tax burden. People with the disease are seen as villains, somehow responsible for the disease and its spread. People with AIDS deserve fair treatment. I thank you for your commitment to helping all sick people. So does Bobbi Campbell. I just know it!

RECOMMENDED READINGS

Corless, Inge B., and Pittman-Lindeman, Mary. *AIDS: Principles, Practices, & Politics*. Washington, D.C.: Hemisphere Publishing Corp., 1987.

Corr, C., and Corr, D. *Hospice Care; Principles and Practice*. New York: Springer Publishing Co., 1983.

De Vita, V., Hellman, S., and Rosenberg, S. *AIDS: Etiology, Diagnosis, Treatment and Prevention*. New York: J.B. Lippincott Co., 1985.

Durham, Jerry, and Cohen, Felissa. *The Person with AIDS: Nursing Perspectives*. New York: Springer Publishing Co., 1987.

Epstein, C. *Nursing the Dying Patient*. Reston, Va.: Reston Publishing Co., 1975.

Flaskerud, Jacquelyn H. "AIDS: The Psychosocial Dimension," *Psychosocial Nursing* (special issue) 25, no. 12, December 1987.

Glaser, B., and Strauss, A. *Awareness of Dying*. Chicago: Aldine Publishing Co., 1965.

Kubler-Ross, E. *On Death and Dying*. New York: Macmillan Publishing Co., 1969.

McKusick, Leon. *What To Do About AIDS: Physicians and Mental Health Professionals Discuss the Issues*. Berkeley, Ca.: University of California Press, 1986.

Rubin, T. *Compassion and Self-Hate: An Alternative to Despair*. New York: Ballantine Books, 1975.

Selye, Hans. *The Stress of Life*. New York: McGraw-Hill Book Co., 1956.

Shelp, E.E., Sunderland, R.H., and Mansell, P.W. *AIDS: Personal Stories in Pastoral Perspective*. New York: The Pilgrim Press, 1986.

Wilcox, S.G. and Sutton, M. *Approaching Death and Dying: An Interdisciplinary Approach*. Dominguez Hills, Calif.: California State College, 1977.

Part II

Care in the Hospital

Care for the person with AIDS or ARC in the hospital is challenging and complex. The technical skills required, however, are primarily those caregivers always use with patients, as the following chapters illustrate. The primary difference in this situation is the effect of the psychosocial dimension on both patient and caregiver. Other differences may include the age of the patient, the severity of symptoms, and the terminal diagnosis. Most of the care for the hospitalized patient occurs on either the oncology unit or the general medical unit. Fewer patients are choosing to pursue aggressive treatment in ICUs, although this trend may be modified by the availability of azidothymidine (AZT) and other drugs being developed. With the hope of prolonged life from the drugs, more PWAs may elect aggressive management of their disease, especially the respiratory complications resulting from infections.

In the following chapters the person with AIDS/ARC is occasionally referred to as a "patient." Many individuals with HIV feel very negatively about the term, preferring to be called PWAs. They feel the term patient denotes dependency and powerlessness, and they are working very hard to empower themselves. The empowerment of patients and their involvement, along with their significant others, in making decisions about their care is a recurring theme throughout this book. Assuming other groups of patients follow this model and view empowerment as a goal, this emphasis by both consumers and health care providers may be one of the ways in which the health care system will feel a long-term positive impact from the AIDS epidemic.

The following chapters also illustrate another positive trend—the true collaborative relationships developing among a variety of disciplines and departments. Staff nurses, clinical nurse specialists, nurse practitioners, physical therapists and a nutritionist have all contributed to Part II. Other parts include chapters by social workers, psychologists, substance abuse counselors, and community health workers, all of whom also make significant contributions. One important contributor who is not represented is the chaplain or spiritual counselor. Based on the wish of the PWA and significant others, this individual is often a very important member of the health care team.

Chapter 10

Providing Direct Nursing Care in the Adult Inpatient Setting

Cynthia L. Reno, and Anita P. Walker

FEELINGS OF A NURSE

The first feelings I can remember in regard to caring for AIDS patients were ones of dread—not of the disease, but of the fact that the first AIDS patients I cared for required an extraordinary amount of emotional support since they were among the first cases of a disease for which we had few answers and no solution. At that time I was not afraid because I still considered it a homosexual disease.

As my awareness increased, I realized I did have some fears. They were complicated by an incident in which I received a puncture from a needle used for one of my AIDS patients. I enrolled in the CDC study on parenteral exposure in health care workers (see Chapter 18). I was relieved to learn that there had been no seroconversions, but I became quite afraid upon the admission of one of the physicians with whom I had worked. She was diagnosed with PCP. There were no obvious clues as to how she acquired it, but the attending physician assured us it was not from casual contact. At staff's request, the medical director of the Adult Immunodeficiency Clinic reviewed the most recent research conclusions. He eased my fears and I relaxed again.

Meanwhile, the patients being admitted were critically ill and made extreme physical and emotional demands. Most had families and friends who reacted in a variety of ways. I had great admiration and respect for many of the patients and their loved ones, which made it all the more difficult to watch young, previously healthy people deteriorate so rapidly. I reached a point of wanting and needing a break; I was drained and exhausted. I took a vacation to relax and recuperate.

When three health care workers later seroconverted, my awareness and concern mounted. Infection control established new guidelines, and the general consensus became "consider the secretions of all patients infected." This policy gives me the opportunity to be protected all the time as well as to let patients know they are protected, too.

My feelings have run the gamut of emotions. Despite waxing and waning fears, I have tried to remain a calm educator and care provider. Although I accept the presence of AIDS, I still have hope and faith that science can and will find a way to control it, if not eliminate it.

CARE ON THE UNIT

It's 8:00 A.M. and report has just been given on 20 patients. Typically, five of these are known HIV patients suffering from opportunistic infections. The five patients vary widely in acuity, as typified by two patients. The patient in the corner room is a man who is only slightly short of breath, ambulatory, and performing his own activities of daily living. He has just started discussing his fears about his diagnosis. At the end of the hallway, another male patient uses 100 percent oxygen, yet his PaO_2 is still only 60, his lips are cyanotic, and his respirations labored. He has frequent diarrhea stools, over which he has minimal control. In addition, his mental status fluctuates from alert and oriented to confused and delirious. His temperature of 39°C will not return to normal despite Tylenol every four hours. He requires total care for every need. His close friend stays with him on a cot in the room.

Though they sound different, these patients both have the diagnosis of AIDS. In the hospital, the nurse devotes a significant amount of time and energy to dealing with the multiple needs of this patient population, functioning not only as a primary caregiver but also as a provider of emotional support, an educator, a resource utilizer, and a discharge planner.

The key to addressing the multiple problems encountered with the HIV patient is a thorough baseline assessment. An effective way to conduct it is to obtain a nursing history on admission. An example follows, along with specific points to consider for this patient group.

General Appearance (Functional Category: Rest/Sleep)

- Is the patient healthy looking?
- Is the patient gaunt or cachectic?
- What is the patient's baseline disposition?

Possible Nursing Diagnosis

- Disturbances in Self-Concept

Neurological (Functional Category: Cognitive/Perceptual)

- Is the patient awake and alert?
- Is the patient's speech clear?
- Is the patient initially oriented, and is the orientation maintained throughout the interview?
- Is the patient able to recall events that led to admission?
- Is there nuchal rigidity?
- Is there sensation or numbness peripherally?
- Does the patient have pain?

Possible Nursing Diagnoses

- Alteration in Mental Status
- Alteration in Thought Processes
- Alteration in Sensory Stimulation
- Potential for Harm
- Alteration in Comfort

Head, Eyes, Ears, Nose, Throat (HEENT)

- Is the patient having headaches?
- Is the patient's vision clear and accurate?
- Are the pupils equal and reactive to light?
- Are there white plaques on the oral mucous membranes?
- Is the patient complaining of a dry mouth?
- Is the patient having difficulty swallowing?
- Are there enlarged lymph nodes?

Possible Nursing Diagnoses

- Alteration in Comfort
- Alteration in Sensory Stimulation
- Alteration in Oral Mucous Membranes

Musculoskeletal (Functional Category: Activity/Exercise)

- Is the patient able to move all extremities?
- Is the patient ambulatory? If assistance is required, what device is used?
- Has the distance the patient can ambulate increased or decreased over the past year? Over the past month?
- Does the patient have edema?

Possible Nursing Diagnoses

- Activity Intolerance
- Alteration in Comfort
- Alteration in Fluid Balance

Cardiovascular

- Is the heart rate between 60 and 100 bpm or tachycardiac?
- Is the blood pressure hypotensive or hypertensive?
- Are the peripheral pulses present?

Possible Nursing Diagnoses

- Alterations in Fluid Balance
- Alterations in Electrolytes

Pulmonary

- Is the patient short of breath at rest?
- Is the patient dyspneic on exertion?
- Is the patient coughing? Is the cough productive?
- Are the breath sounds clear, distant, or decreased?
- Is or was the patient a smoker?

Possible Nursing Diagnoses

- Gas Exchange, Impaired
- Breathing Pattern, Ineffective

Gastrointestinal (Functional Categories: Nutritional/Metabolic; Elimination)

- Does the patient have an appetite?
- Is the patient able to eat?
- What is a typical meal?
- Is the patient nauseated? Vomiting?
- Has the patient lost or gained weight over the past year? Over the past month?
- What is the patient's alcohol usage?
- Is the patient's abdomen soft and flat, or firm and distended? Are bowel sounds present? Is there tenderness on palpation?
- What is the frequency of stools? Does the patient have trouble with constipation or diarrhea? Is the patient continent of stool?
- Are there hemorrhoids or blisters present on the anus?

Possible Nursing Diagnoses

- Alteration in Nutrition
- Alteration in Elimination
- Alteration in Comfort
- Self-Care Deficit: Toileting

Genito-urinary (Functional Category: Elimination)

- Are there blisters or sores on the genitalia?
- Is there abnormal discharge?
- Is the patient urinating regularly? Is there hesitancy or retention of urine? Is the patient continent of urine?
- Does the patient report any signs or symptoms of infection?

Possible Nursing Diagnoses

- Alteration in Comfort
- Potential for Infection
- Alteration in Fluid Balance
- Self-Care Deficit: Toileting

Integumentary

- Is the patient's skin temperature cool or warm?
- Is the patient febrile?
- Does the patient report night sweats?
- Is the skin integrity intact? Is the skin color pale or flushed? Is the skin turgor supple, or dry and cracking?
- Is there any rash, especially on the face?
- Are there any red-violet raised lesions?

Possible Nursing Diagnoses

- Alteration in Skin Integrity
- Alteration in Comfort
- Alteration in Tissue Perfusion

Medications/Allergies

- What currently prescribed medications are taken?
- What over-the-counter medications does the patient take? What alternative medicine preparations, i.e., herbs?
- What recreational drugs does the patient use, if any?
- Does the patient have any allergies?

Past Medical History

- Has the patient had hepatitis?
- Has the patient had any viral infections?
- Has the patient had any fevers of unknown origin?
- Has the patient had any sexually transmitted diseases?
- Has the patient had lymphadenopathy?
- Does the patient have a history of parasitic infections?

Psychosocial History (Functional Categories: Self-Perception/Self-Concept; Sexuality; Coping/Stress; Value/Belief)

Residence

- Does the patient live alone or with friends or family?
- Does the patient own or rent?

Occupation

- Is the patient currently employed or on disability?
- If currently employed, is the employer aware of the illness?

Other Responsibilities/Recreation

- Does the patient have dependents?
- Does the patient have pets?
- Does the patient have a garden, yard, or house plants?
- What recreational activities does the patient enjoy?

Support System

- Whom does the patient consider support people?
- Are they aware of the patient's illness?
- Does the patient have a religious affiliation? If so, does a particular person need to be called?
- Would the patient prefer a hospital chaplain?

Sexuality

- Does the patient have a partner?
- What questions does the patient or partner have about safe sex?

Insurance

- What type of health insurance, if any, does the patient have?
- Does the patient need to apply for state or federal medical aid?
- Does the patient need social work follow-up?

Possible Nursing Diagnoses

- Anxiety
- Fear
- Coping
- Disturbance in Self-Concept

CASE STUDY

This case study illustrates a patient situation that requires meticulous nursing care, creative problem solving, and excellence in health teaching and psychological care.

History

Bob is a 38-year-old bisexual man with a six-month history of difficulty walking due to bilateral lower extremity weakness. He reports a two-month history of frontal headache and stiff neck, and poor memory for the past three months. During the past three weeks he has had urinary retention requiring frequent catheterization, and currently he has an indwelling urinary catheter. Bob also suffers from constipation, requiring daily laxatives and weekly enemas. A lesion on the perianal area has been diagnosed as herpes.

Past medical history includes syphilis in 1983 and Hepatitis B in 1981. A previous work-up with lumbar puncture, magnetic resonance imaging (MRI), and myelogram was negative. HIV is positive. He usually smokes one pack of cigarettes per day but has recently increased his consumption due to the stress of his illness.

Bob moved in with his mother when he became too weak to take care of himself. She was unaware of his sexual orientation or his diagnosis at the time of admission. Recently, Bob has spent most days in bed or in a wheelchair and has been able to walk only with the assistance of two people. His mother has to work, so he is alone most of the day. He has some friends locally, and neighbors come in to help his mother. Visiting nurses have been teaching Bob and his mother how to deal with his bowel and bladder problems.

Bob states he is feeling very depressed by his illness, especially by the constant headaches. Now that he cannot work, he feels not only useless but a burden to his mother, who goes to work and then comes home to cook and take care of him. He was very fit but now is thin and weak; he lies in bed and watches TV all day. Bob hopes that during this hospitalization his headaches will be treated and he will be able to walk again.

Physical Examination

Vital Signs

Temperature, 36.7°C; blood pressure, 120/70; heart rate, 100; respiratory rate, 20.

General Appearance

White male lying in bed. Thin and pale, unshaven. Alert and oriented times 3.

HEENT

Pupils equal and reactive to light. Complains of photophobia and headache. Tongue midline, coated and brown. White plaques on oral mucous membranes. Neck reveals shotty nodes.

Neurological

Speech clear. Slight stiffness to flexion of neck.

Musculoskeletal

Bilateral lower extremity weakness. Unable to stand unassisted. Needs two-person assist to get from wheelchair to bed. Joints stiff to range of motion (ROM). No edema. No foot drop.

Cardiovascular

Heart tones normal. Sl S2 regular rhythm.

Pulmonary

Lungs clear. Cough with clear sputum early in the morning, unchanged in the past few months. Smoker as described in history.

Gastrointestinal

Abdomen flat, no scars. Bowel sounds present in all four quadrants. No bowel movement (BM) for three days. Digital exam reveals stool in rectum. Guiac negative.

Genito-urinary

Unable to void. #16 fr. Foley catheter in place. Draining amber urine with foul odor. Specimen obtained and sent to lab. No discharge from meatus.

Integumentary

Many bony prominences. Coccyx area reddened, but skin intact. Open lesion to left of anus, red with some white exudate—approximately 3 cm in diameter.

Allergies

None known.

Functional Categories

Nutritional/Metabolic

Has lost 20 lbs. in the past few months. Does not feel like eating because nothing tastes good.

Elimination

Chronic constipation. Unable to have BM without laxatives or enema. Takes Milk of Magnesia daily and a Fleet's enema three times a week. Does not know much about fiber or need for increased fluid intake.

Unable to void. Sometimes is incontinent. Has needed to be straight-cathed three times a day, and has had an indwelling Foley catheter for the past two weeks; he prefers the Foley as it is easier to deal with when he is alone all day.

Activity/Exercise

Bedbound due to weakness of lower extremities. Can sit in a wheelchair for an hour if his mother can get help to assist getting him up and down. Needs help to bathe and dress.

Rest/Sleep

Does not sleep very well. Headaches are worse at night. Usually ends up taking a pain pill. Lies in bed and watches TV.

Cognitive/Perceptual

Has photophobia most of the time, and likes to keep the house dark. Has never had trouble with his eyes before, and does not wear glasses or contacts. Has had some memory loss, which seems to be getting worse. Cannot always remember what his mother told him earlier in the day, which he finds very frustrating. Pain is his biggest problem, a headache that never seems to go away. Also, shooting pains up his shins are very troublesome. Tylenol with Codeine helps to take the edge off his pain, but it makes his constipation worse and further impairs his memory.

Self-Perception/Self-Concept

Asked, "What is wrong with me?" and "Will I ever be able to walk again?" Being confined to the house, he feels helpless and hopeless and a burden to his mother. Sometimes feels angry about all the things that have happened to him in the past six months. "It has all happened so fast."

Sexuality

Has not had sexual relations since his illness started. Before that he was quite active but did not have a steady partner.

Coping/Stress

Bob is unable to work, so he has very little money to live on and has to rely on his mother. He has been filling out forms to apply for financial assistance and state or federal medical aid. He tries to do some positive thinking but finds it difficult.

Value/Belief

Bob was raised a Catholic and has been thinking more about the church lately. He would like to talk to a priest while he is in the hospital.

Medical Work-Up

- Chest x-ray—within normal limits
- Urinalysis with micro, culture and sensitivity
- EKG—normal
- Lumbar puncture—spinal fluid filled with cryptococcus
- MRI—some abnormal lesions
- Blood chemistries—electrolytes, BUN, creatinine, glucose.

Medical Diagnoses

- Cryptococcal meningitis
- Radicular myopathy

- Anemia
- Urinary tract infection
- Urinary retention
- Constipation
- Rectal herpes
- Oral candidiasis

Nursing Diagnoses

- Activity Intolerance
- Knowledge Deficit
- Alteration in Nutrition; less than body requirements
- Alterations in Comfort; headache and bilateral leg pain
- Alterations in Urine Volume
- Alterations in Oral Mucous Membranes
- Impaired Skin Integrity
- Alterations in Elimination
- Home Maintenance Management

Individualized Patient Care Plan

(See Appendix 10-A for a standardized care plan that can be used as the basis for an individualized care plan.)

Activity Intolerance

1. Get patient up in chair three times a day for a half hour, then increase as tolerated. Eggcrate square in wheelchair/armchair for comfort and skin protection.
2. Arrange physical therapy (PT) consult to evaluate status and thereafter to see patient daily for progressive ambulation. Nurses to do ROM to legs 2 times daily.

Knowledge Deficit

1. Teach Bob about disease process, reason for headache and leg pains. Include mother in teaching when she visits.

2. Teach Bob about medications and side effects.
3. Gradually teach central line care, stressing the need for sterile technique and the potential for infection.
4. Incorporate urinary catheter care into everyday bathing and hygiene.

Alterations in Nutrition; Less Than Body Requirements

1. Arrange nutritionist consultation as soon as possible after admission.
2. Allow Bob to choose his food. Provide frequent small meals.
3. Give Bob high-protein milkshakes between meals. Maintain adequate fluid intake to combat symptoms of urinary tract infection (UTI) and constipation.
4. Have mother bring in favorite foods from home on weekends if Bob desires.
5. Weigh on Monday, Wednesday, Friday.
6. Assess skin turgor and integrity daily.
7. Assess oral mucosa daily.

Alterations in Comfort; Headache and Bilateral Leg Pain

1. Keep Bob in position of comfort. Turn side to side and position with pillows.
2. Keep room dark if photophobia persists.
3. Give adequate analgesia for pain.
4. Massage legs as alternative therapy for comfort and pain relief.
5. Maintain a quiet and restful environment, use relaxation techniques, play music of choice.
6. Limit visitors, and medical personnel if possible, so Bob may have rest periods during day.
7. Give adequate sedation at night to promote sleep. Limit interventions during night as much as possible.

Alterations in Urine Volume

1. Foley catheter to straight drainage; intake and output.
2. Urology consult done; Bob will need permanent indwelling catheter.
3. Foley catheter to be changed q three weeks. Drainage bag to be changed q Friday. Date bag and document all change dates in nurses notes and on nursing kardex.
4. Meatus to be cleaned q day at bath time and prn. Note discharge/redness and c/o pain or burning.
5. Adequate fluid intake to be maintained to decrease urine concentration.
6. Bob to be taught to care for catheter in preparation for discharge.

Alterations in Oral Mucous Membranes

1. Inspect oral cavity q day before breakfast.
2. Maintain adequate fluid intake to prevent dehydration.
3. Have Bob use soft toothbrush to lessen trauma. Give mouthwashes after meals.
4. Give Mycelex troches to suck q six hours.
5. Give soft bland foods if discomfort is a problem.

Skin Integrity

1. Inspect skin thoroughly every A.M. and P.M.
2. Provide eggcrate mattress for bed and square for chairs.
3. Encourage Bob to turn in bed every two hours.
4. Get Bob out of bed as much as tolerance allows.
5. Maintain good nutrition and fluid intake.
6. Redress central line site using aseptic technique every Tuesday and Friday. Observe for signs of redness or discharge.

Alterations in Elimination

1. Ensure adequate fluid intake.
2. Give high-fiber foods, including bran, with breakfast if tolerated.
3. Give laxative of choice if no BM for two days, enemas if no effect from laxatives.
4. Check stools for blood.
5. Have Bob use bedside commode or bathroom for BMs.

Home Maintenance Management

1. Investigate agencies in Bob's home town. See if agency will do home IV therapy with amphotericin B.
2. When above is determined, discuss needs with Bob and mother. Also involve nurses, MDs, PT, and social worker.
3. Complete referral form (see Exhibit 10-1). Call in referral to agency.
4. Order equipment for home. Finalize teaching and assess further needs to be continued at home.
5. Order transportation to home if Bob is not able to travel by car for three hours. Have mother bring in clothes at next visit.
6. MD to arrange for medical follow-up in home town.

Exhibit 10-1 Public Health Referral Form

602-75 2/86

1 - AGENCY COPY   2 - MEDICAL RECORD COPY   3 - UNIT/CLINIC COPY

ADDRESS	AGE
CITY	PHONE
NEAREST RELATIVE / FRIEND	PHONE
ADDRESS	
LANGUAGE Spoken/Understood	SEX	MARITAL STATUS	Religion
ADMISSION DATE	DISCHARGE DATE
MEDICARE NO.	SOCIAL SECURITY NO.
MEDI-CAL NO.	INSURANCE NO.

UNIT NUMBER

PT. NAME

BIRTHDATE

LOCATION   DATE

REFERRED TO Name of Agency   PHONE

ADDRESS

MEDICAL Primary, Secondary Diagnoses (Onset Dates).
       Surgical Procedures, Major Complications (Dates)

Cryptococcal Meningitis -
Radicular Myopathy
Oral candidiasis - resolved
Rectal herpes - resolved
Urinary retention
Constipation

ALLERGIES none known

REHAB POTENTIAL   PATIENT KNOWS DIAG./PROG. ☒YES ☐NO

MEDICAL ORDERS Home Health Services, Treatments, Medications, Diet, Activities

CHECK SERVICE INDICATE FREQUENCY AND SPECIFIC SERVICES REQUIRED

☒RN   ☒PT   ☐OT   ☐ST   ☒MSW   ☒HHA

Change dressing over central line site 2x wk.
Pt. has been taught to do this, but still needs
some supervision. (Tues & Fri.)

Foley Catheter - can wear leg bag during day,
and drainage bag at night. Pt. able to clean
around meatus daily. Knows s&s symptoms of UTI.

Needs to have PT cont. to work with him on
increasing ambulation with walker, tends to
still be nervous about getting up by himself.
Amphotericin B to be given via central line
Q. Fri.

MEDICATIONS (Indicate New)   DIET Reg, hi calorie

Amphotericin B. 40mg. in 500 cc D5W over 4 hrs.
Q. Fri.
Percocet tabs. 2 q4hrs prn for leg pain.
Mycelex troche 1 q6hrs to suck.

FUNCTIONAL PATTERNS

	WNL	DYSFUNCTION		WNL	DYSFUNCTION
BATHE		X	ABLE TO COMMUNICATE	X	
DRESS		X	MOTIVATED TO SELF CARE	X	
EATING	X		FOLLOWS DIRECTIONS	X	
PERSONAL HYGIENE		X	BOWEL CONTROL LAST BM 6/15	X	
TRANSFERS		X	BLADDER CONTROL		X
AMBULATE		X	DATE - CATHETER INSERTED 6/15		

☐CANE ☐CRUTCH ☒WALKER ☒ALERT ☐CONFUSED ☐RESTRAINTS

EQUIPMENT AND SUPPLIES Sent with patient, Date Ordered, Company

Eggcrate mattress
wheelchair, walker, catheter bags x3.

OTHER THERAPIST, SOCIAL SERVICE DIETICIAN

P.T. to visit daily for 2 wks. to work on
increasing ambulation with walker. Exercises
to strenghen leg muscles.
MSW to work with pt. and mother on psych.
support and financial assistance.

PRESSURE AREAS - DECUBITUS ULCERS Describe

Sacral area tends to be reddened. Pt. instructed
to change position frequently, and be up and
about during the day.

NURSES REPORT: Observations, Instructions, Continuing Teaching Needed,
Unresolved Problems, Nursing Goals.

T 37°C P 82 R 18   BP 120/60 WT 70kg

Goal for pt. is to be able to walk with walker
for short distances. To be able to perform
ADLs as much as poss. Needs to be reminded
of details of his care due to some cognitive
impairment which is part of disease process.
Watch for fever, and increase in headache, as
signs for further infection. Also, decrease
in mental status or set back in lower extremity
strength as signs that disease is progressing.
Pt. may need to be hospitalized again if the
above occur.

At future date long-term care facility or
hospice will be needed.

		PHONE	
ATTENDING MD (Hosp)			
PHYSICIAN FOR CONTINUING CARE		CLINIC APPT. DATE	
ADDRESS		PHONE	
PHYSICIAN SIGNATURE		DATE	
REFERRAL CALLED IN	DATE	TIME	DATE SENT
NURSE SIGNATURE		UNIT	UNIT PHONE

UCSF
The Medical Center
at the University of California, San Francisco
San Francisco, California 94143

DEPARTMENT OF NURSING
PATIENT TRANSFER AND REFERRAL-ADULT

Source: Courtesy of Nursing Department, The Medical Center at the University of California, San Francisco.

7. Social worker from local agency to follow up at home for psychological support and financial assistance counseling. Try to find AIDS/ARC support group in local area.

Hospital Course

After diagnosis, treatment for cryptococcal meningitis was started with amphotericin B, infused via a right subclavian central line catheter. (See Chapters 14 and 15 for discussion of this drug and its administration.) Also administered was flucytosine (ANCOBON), a drug often used in conjunction with amphotericin B for the treatment of cryptococcal meningitis because it crosses the blood-brain barrier. Side effects of this drug include decreased renal function and bone marrow suppression, and therefore it cannot always be used for long periods of time in this compromised patient population.

After a few days of increased headache and nausea, the drug therapy was well tolerated. During the hospital stay of approximately one month, activity tolerance improved with daily PT, and Bob was able to walk in the halls with a walker and one person assist. (For a discussion of PT, refer to Chapter 17.) Skin integrity was maintained with the use of an eggcrate mattress, frequent turning and positioning, and increased time spent in the chair. The rectal area herpes lesion progressed to complete healing after treatment first with oral acyclovir and then with topical acyclovir. Appetite and calorie intake improved as Bob's general condition improved.

Bob's mother visited on weekends, and staff spent time answering her questions and preparing her for the care that Bob would need at home. Bob revealed his sexual orientation to her, and also his diagnosis. She found these revelations overwhelming at first but did accept them with the help of her religious counselor.

With slow and steady progress in his physical condition, Bob's psychological state also improved. Despite lessening of his headaches, which soon enabled him to watch TV and read, the pains in his legs continued to be a problem. He needed frequent analgesia to enable him to withstand daily PT but by the time of discharge this problem was lessening. Prior to discharge, arrangements were made for necessary equipment and IV therapy. Bob was discharged home with a visiting nurse referral.

REFERENCES

Abrams, Donald I. "AIDS: Clinical Update, Part I." *California Nursing Review* 8, no. 5 (1987):4–7, 26–29.

Abrams, Donald I. "AIDS: Battling a Retroviral Enemy." *California Nursing Review* 8, no. 6 (1987):1, 10–16, 36–37, 44.

Abrams, Donald I. "AIDS: A New Direction in Therapy." *California Nursing Review* 9, no. 1 (1987):1, 4–7, 11–13, 38–40.

Barnhardt, Edward R. *Physician's Desk Reference*. Oradell, N.J.: Medical Economics Co., Inc., 1987.

Bennett, JoAnne. "What We Know About AIDS." *American Journal of Nursing* 86, no. 9 (1986):1015–20.

Macher, A.M., Masur, H., Lane, C.H., and Faci, A.S. *AIDS Diagnosis and Management*. Research Triangle Park, N.C.: Burroughs Wellcome Company, 1983.

Schietinger, Helen. "A Home Care Plan for AIDS." *American Journal of Nursing* 86, no. 9 (1986):1021–28.

Scitovsky, Anne A. and Rice, Dorothy P. "Estimates of the Direct and Indirect Costs of Acquired Immunodeficiency Syndrome in the United States, 1985, 1986, and 1991." *Public Health Reports* 102, no. 1 (1987):5–17.

Wyngaarden, James B. and Smith, Lloyd H., Jr. eds. *Cecil Textbook of Medicine*, 17th ed. Philadelphia: W.B. Saunders Company.

Appendix 10-A

Care of the Patient with Acquired Immune Deficiency Syndrome

To activate: Circle the number of each item. Date and sign additional entries.

| GAS EXCHANGE, IMPAIRED | Related to: ineffective breathing patterns, increased respiratory secretions, inability to move secretions |

_____ RN: _____   Expected Outcomes: ____
Date Activated   Signature   _____

_____ RN: _____   _____
Date Resolved   Signature

As evidenced by _____

NURSING ORDERS:

1. Assess pulmonary status at appropriate frequency.
2. Pace activities and treatments to allow comfort. Position for comfort.
3. Assess need for pulmonary toilet.
4. Assess effectiveness of delivery method of prescribed oxygen.
5. Spend time with patient for reassurance during times of acute dyspnea.

Source: Courtesy of Nursing Department, The Medical Center at the University of California, San Francisco.

6. _____
7. _____
8. _____

POTENTIAL FOR INFECTION

Related to: impaired immune system, environmental pathogens, invasive procedures

_____ RN: _____
Date Activated   Signature

_____ RN: _____
Date Resolved   Signature

As evidenced by _____

Expected Outcomes: _____
_____
_____

NURSING ORDERS:

1. Follow appropriate infection control guidelines (see manual).
2. Hadnwashing before and after all patient contact.
3. Strict aseptic technique for all invasive procedures and therapies.
4. Observe for impairment of skin and oral mucous membrane integrity.
5. Monitor CBC and vital signs for signs of infection.
6. Counsel patient and visitors about infection control procedures.
7. Consider immune status of patient when making nursing assignments.
8. _____
9. _____
10. _____

COPING, INEFFECTIVE, INDIVIDUAL

Related to: crisis due to disease, new or exacerbated

_____ RN _____
Date Activated   Signature

_____ RN: _____
Date Resolved   Signature

As evidenced by _____

Expected Outcomes: _____
_____
_____

NURSING ORDERS:

1. Provide atmosphere of acceptance, encourage expression of feelings.
2. Assist patient in identifying effects of his behavior on others.
3. Assist patient in identifying own most positive and effective methods of coping.
4. Provide emotional support for persons significant to the patient.
5. _____
6. _____
7. _____

ANXIETY

Related to: diagnosis, hospital environment, changes in lifestyle

_____ RN: _____   Expected Outcomes: _____
Date Activated   Signature   _____
                                         _____
_____ RN: _____
Date Resolved   Signature

As evidenced by _____

_____

NURSING ORDERS:

1. Determine and document level of anxiety in terms of behavioral statements.
2. Increase simplicity, concreteness, and repetition in communication if patient is very anxious.
3. Explain features of immediate environment.
4. Frequent nongoal-directed visits by nurse—use touch as appropriate.
5. Assist patient in identifying signs and symptoms of anxiety, and identify ways to control anxiety.
5. _____
6. _____
7. _____
8. _____

| NUTRITION, ALTERATION IN: LESS THAN BODY REQUIREMENTS | Related to: anorexia, nausea, vomiting, fever, alteration in oral mucosa, ineffective breathing patterns |

_____ RN: _____   Expected Outcomes: ____
Date Activated   Signature   _____

_____ RN: _____   _____
Date Resolved   Signature
As evidenced by _____

NURSING ORDERS:

1. Assess and document height, weight, age, body build, muscle strength, activity tolerance, patient report of recent food, fluid intake.
2. Assess etiology of current nutritional state by patient account, nutritionist consultation. Assess bowel elimination. Assess oral mucosa.
3. Monitor intake and output, daily weight, laboratory values, skin integrity.
4. Provide feedings sized and timed to patient's tolerance; encourage food to be brought from home.
5. _____
6. _____
7. _____

| HOME MAINTENANCE MANAGEMENT DEFICIT | Related to: knowledge deficit concerning local resources, activity intolerance, inadequate finances, and/or support system |

_____ RN: _____   Expected Outcomes: ____
Dated Activated   Signature   _____

_____ RN: _____   _____
Date Resolved   Signature

As evidenced by _____

NURSING ORDERS:

1. Assess and document patient's knowledge level concerning own needs for care and assistance at home, and personal support available.
2. Maintain ongoing documentation of progress of discharge plans.
3. Refer to social worker for advice on applying for financial assistance.
4. Advise patient about support groups such as Shanti.
5. Assess need for equipment at home, i.e., oxygen, bedside commode, walker, etc.
6. Make referral to nursing agency near patient's home.
7. Assess need for transport to home.
8. _____
9. _____
10. _____

Chapter 11

Care on the Pediatric Service

Rita Fahrner

The incidence of children infected with HIV was well established as early as 1983.[1] Children under the age of 13 years comprise about 1.5 percent of all reported AIDS cases in the United States. Because the spectrum of HIV infection ranges from indeterminate to asymptomatic to symptomatic infection, undoubtedly at least four times as many children infected with HIV did not fit the strict CDC surveillance criteria for AIDS prior to the revision in August 1987 and therefore have not yet been counted. It is estimated that by 1991 over 10,000 children will be infected with HIV. As with adults, it is not known what proportion of these children will progress to clinical disease. Information regarding epidemiology, natural history, clinical manifestations, health care management, and psychosocial issues of children with HIV infection is evolving.

EPIDEMIOLOGY OF CHILDREN WITH AIDS

Demographics

Because the vast majority of children with AIDS have been born to HIV-infected mothers, the epidemiology of this group closely parallels that of women with AIDS. Three-quarters of the documented pediatric cases have been reported in the four states with the highest numbers of AIDS cases: New York, New Jersey, Florida, and California. The parenteral cases, however, represent a broader geographic distribution. As with women, children with AIDS have been primarily from ethnic minority communities. Over half, or 56 percent, are Black, while 24 percent are Latino. White children comprise only 20 percent of all pediatric AIDS cases. Again, the parenteral cases have a wider ethnic distribution, more congruent with the ethnic populations in this country.

HIV Transmission

The primary modes of transmission of HIV to children have been perinatal and parenteral. About 80 percent of the children with AIDS have been born to mothers who are themselves infected. Seropositive women who have already delivered an infected child have the highest risk of transmission in subsequent pregnancies.[2] (Further discussion of perinatal transmission is found in Chapter 12.)

The second most significant mode of transmission has been parenteral, accounting for 17 percent of pediatric AIDS cases. Transfusions of blood and blood products have been implicated in 12 percent. Although antibody testing of the blood supply is now routine, a very small risk of HIV infection through transfusion remains because of the window of time between exposure and antibody production. Therefore, most newborn nurseries and pediatric units have changed their previous practice of small-aliquot frequent transfusions from multiple donors to less frequent larger aliquots from single-donor quadpacks. Children with hemophilia or other coagulation disorders requiring factor concentrates who were infused prior to the initiation of heat treatment in 1985 are probably infected with HIV and are at risk for development of AIDS. This group accounts for about 5 percent of all reported cases.

The modes of transmission for the remaining 3 percent of pediatric AIDS cases are either unknown, unreported, or undetermined.

DEFINITION OF PEDIATRIC AIDS

The August 1987 revision of the CDC Surveillance Case Definition for Acquired Immunodeficiency Syndrome superseded the 1985 provisional case definition for pediatric AIDS.[3] As described in Appendix 11-A, the revision addresses both adults and children with AIDS but notes two distinct differences. First, multiple or recurrent serious bacterial infections and lymphoid interstitial pneumonia and/or pulmonary lymphoid hyperplasia (LIP/PLH complex) are diagnostic of AIDS in children but not in adults. Second, the laboratory criteria for HIV infection are more severe for children under 15 months of age whose mothers are thought to have been HIV-infected during their prenatal period because the presence of HIV antibody alone does not necessarily indicate the child's HIV status; passive maternal antibody may be present in the infant up to 15 months old. The numbers of pediatric cases will no doubt increase significantly in view of this revision.

A classification system for HIV infection in children under 13 years old has been developed.[4] This system provides a simple design for categorizing those children with asymptomatic versus symptomatic infection. (See Appendix 11-A for a system summary.)

NATURAL HISTORY OF THE DISEASE

Documentation of HIV infection in infants born to infected mothers is essentially impossible because of an inability to distinguish transplacentally acquired maternal antibody. Neither antigen titers nor HIV cultures are easily available, and their results are difficult to interpret. Many groups attempting to document natural history are performing serial antibody testing beginning with cord blood in order to document the time passive maternal antibody is lost and infected infants begin to manufacture their own antibody. These studies are also attempting to correlate antigen and viremia with antibody status.

DIFFERENCES BETWEEN CHILDREN AND ADULTS

The risk of progression to AIDS following neonatal HIV infection is estimated at 50 percent over a two- to three-year period, higher than the current estimates for older children and adults. The higher rate may reflect the relative immaturity of the neonatal immune system. An additional postulation is that repeated activation of T4 helper lymphocytes, which occurs during acquisition of the normal immune system in early infancy, may actually enhance viral replication.[5]

The time from viral exposure to development of symptoms appears to be shorter in children than in adults.[6] Infants infected perinatally who develop AIDS first develop symptoms at a median age of 4 months, and half are diagnosed with AIDS before their 1st birthday. Only a few of these children (5 percent) are diagnosed after 5 years of age. Children who are infected parenterally generally develop symptoms at a median time of one year from exposure. Hemophiliacs, however, tend to present with symptoms during their early teens, at a median age of 14 years. The mortality rate in pediatric AIDS is 65 percent, compared with 55 percent in adults. Children who survive beyond 3 years generally have a better prognosis.[7]

Children tend to develop serious recurrent or chronic bacterial infections because of poor antibody production. HIV in children destroys not only the T4 helper lymphocytes but also the B lymphocytes that manufacture antibodies to fight bacteria. The resultant abnormalities in humoral as well as cell-mediated immunity result in poor specific antibody formation. These children fail to respond to antigens to which they have no prior history of exposure.[8] Infected adults, because of their prior exposure, may be able to mount a secondary response. The high mortality rate in children is in large part due to these overwhelming bacterial infections, which are manifested by sepsis, pneumonia, meningitis, and chronic otitis media, and are often caused by encapsulated pyogenic pathogens. Prompt aggressive treatment is necessary.

Polyclonal hypergammaglobulinemia is common in HIV-infected children, presumably secondary to stimulation of B cells, decreased suppression of T lymphocytes, or both.[9] Hypergammaglobulinemia is usually a sign of B-cell dysfunction and results in an inability to respond specifically to new B-cell dependent antigens to stimulate specific immunoglobulin synthesis. Lymphopenia is noted rarely, but thrombocytopenia is commonly seen in these children.

The noninfectious pulmonary LIP/PLH complex is diagnostic for AIDS in children. The natural history of LIP appears to depend on the initial clinical presentation, and the mortality rate is relatively low, approximately 15 percent.[10] LIP tends to present later than pulmonary opportunistic infections, with a mean age of onset of 14 months as compared with 6 months for PCP. It is unclear why some children develop LIP, but it may reflect a specific host immune response. Lymphadenopathy, including hepatosplenomegaly and parotitis, is frequently noted in conjunction with this pulmonary complex.

AIDS-related malignancies are rare in children but do occasionally occur. Cutaneous KS is extremely unusual, but lymph node biopsies and post-mortem examinations have demonstrated extensive nodal KS in some series of children with AIDS.[11]

Neurologic complications are more frequent in children and are noted in well over 50 percent of those diagnosed with AIDS/ARC. Some studies have documented neurologic abnormalities in up to 90 percent of children studied. Static and progressive encephalopathy have been documented, both presumably caused by direct HIV infection of the brain. The presence of progressive neurologic disease is correlated with a poor outcome. Progressive encephalopathy appears to occur in a stepwise fashion, rather than a rapid downhill course, but there has been no documentation of substantial improvement or recovery. The most common neurological findings include developmental delay, loss of developmental milestones, or both, impaired brain growth with acquired microcephaly, cortical atrophy on computed tomography (CT)/MRI, and generalized weakness with pyramidal signs. In addition, many children show delayed language skills with more expressive, rather than receptive, abnormalities.[12]

SIGNS AND SYMPTOMS

Infants and children with HIV infection present with a wide range of signs and symptoms. Often the clinical manifestations that occur early in infection are general and can be seen in healthy children, as shown in Exhibit 11-1. However, in HIV-infected children these signs and symptoms are usually chronic and severe, and fail to respond to appropriate treatment.

Children also develop opportunistic infections with the same protozoal, viral, fungal, and bacterial pathogens as do adults. PCP is the most frequently diagnosed

Exhibit 11-1 Clinical Features of HIV Infection in Infancy and Childhood

---

General Manifestations That Tend to Occur Early in the Spectrum of Infection:

- Failure to thrive (FTT)
- Wasting syndrome
- Diarrhea—chronic or recurrent
- Small for gestational age (SGA)
- Fever of unknown origin (FUO)
- Lymphadenopathy

- Salivary gland enlargement; parotitis
- Hepatosplenomegaly
- Oral thrush—persistent or recurrent
- Thrombocytopenia
- Developmental delay; loss of milestones
- Encephalopathy

---

opportunistic infection, with disseminated cytomegalovirus (CMV), *Candida*, *Mycobacterium avium intracellulare* (MAI), cryptosporidiosis, and chronic herpes simplex virus noted far less frequently.

In addition, other clinical manifestations such as cardiomyopathy, nephropathy, and hepatitis are seen with greater frequency in pediatric HIV infection.

CLINICAL MANAGEMENT

Pediatric HIV infection is a chronic, life-threatening disease with frequent exacerbations and remissions. The model of care is based on other chronic childhood illnesses, including leukemia, hemophilia, and cystic fibrosis. However, it differs from these other models because it usually is a family disease that has also infected one or both parents as well as siblings. The social stigma of AIDS also causes reactions in the community that necessitate intervention with community agencies, day care, and schools. The need for a multidisciplinary team approach among all who collaborate in or coordinate any phase of care is apparent.

Because current therapy is supportive rather than curative, the major focus is on symptom control as well as prophylaxis and prompt aggressive treatment of diagnosed infections. The goal of treatment is to limit the degree to which the disease process and its therapy interfere with the child's development and education and disrupt the family unit.

Newborn nursery and pediatric inpatient care of the potentially HIV-infected child should follow regular hospital guidelines and procedures for care of the immunosuppressed patient. To prevent possible infection, circumcision should be strongly discouraged and umbilical cord stumps must be cleaned with alcohol at each diaper change. Many providers suggest the use of CMV-negative, irradiated blood for transfusion to decrease the risk of both disseminated CMV and graft-versus-host (GVH) disease.

Follow-up care of these children should be regular and frequent, focusing on presumed immunodeficiency and growth and development, as well as on psychosocial and family issues. Live virus vaccines should be avoided, but the inactivated vaccines, including pertussis, diphtheria, and tetanus, as well as *Hemophilus influenzae* and polyvalent pneumococcus, should be given as regularly scheduled.[13] Although asymptomatic HIV-infected children have not been shown to experience serious adverse reactions to the live virus vaccines of the Sabin oral polio (OPV) and measles-mumps-rubella (MMR), it makes sense to avoid these. OPV may be excreted and transmitted to close contacts, which may expose immunodeficient adults in the child's environment, thus causing them an increased risk of vaccine-associated poliomyelitis. Killed Salk polio vaccine is an appropriate substitute for OPV.

Because of the high risk of PCP in these children, many treatment centers use daily oral low-dose trimethoprim-sulfamethoxazole as prophylaxis. This combination is well tolerated and appears to be efficacious in children. Monthly IV or intramuscular gamma globulin is sometimes administered to prevent bacterial infection but continues to be a controversial issue. As yet there are no data to support its efficacy. The postulation for its use is that because gamma globulin contains antibodies to a variety of bacteria to which the child may not have yet been exposed or developed antibody, it might decrease the severity and/or frequency of bacterial infection. Most centers that use gamma globulin begin treatment after the child has experienced one or two serious infections. The cost of this treatment is high, averaging about $18,000 yearly.

Only recently have antiviral clinical trials been opened to the pediatric population. It is hoped that such treatment for the underlying HIV infection may be more effective when administered to neonates and young children who have low concentrations of virus.

CONSIDERATIONS FOR HOME CARE, FOSTER CARE, AND ADOPTION

Home discharge, either to the nuclear or the extended biologic family, is strongly encouraged if at all possible for neonates who are potentially HIV-infected through maternal transmission of the virus. Because of the myriad of social and psychological problems of IV drug–using parents, as well as the problems associated with maternal and familial HIV infection, the urban centers of high AIDS populations have seen an ever-increasing number of children who become ''boarder babies''—children who continue to live in acute pediatric units long after they are ready for hospital discharge.

Few states have proactively developed policies and guidelines to address the issues of foster care and adoptive placement. Approximately one-third of all children with AIDS have been orphaned or abandoned, and many of these children die without ever leaving the hospital. Some innovative programs have been developed, such as the home for children with AIDS developed by the city of Boston, and Starcross Community, which is described in Chapter 28. Foster home placement has in some areas been built on the model of the medically fragile child, which ensures that the foster parents are capable of caring for children with chronic medical problems and are given a larger stipend to provide for the complex needs of these children. Adoption of children who might be HIV-infected has been generally unsuccessful. Most adoptive parents want healthy White infants, and historically children who are non-White, ill, or both have rarely been adopted.

Regardless of where the child is discharged, the care providers need to be taught appropriate home care. This includes specifics of feeding, infection control, and signs and symptoms of infection, as well as intensive counseling services focusing on issues such as confidentiality, needs of the chronically ill child, and what to tell family, friends, and neighbors. Families and care providers need referrals to appropriate community resources, including support networks, home nursing agencies, financial resource agencies, and ongoing medical follow-up. Ideally, each child and family should have a nurse–case manager who coordinates all aspects of care.

CONSIDERATIONS FOR DAY CARE, SCHOOL

Because day care is not a legal requirement for children, individual providers may develop their own policies in accordance with local, state, and federal regulations. Currently, the vast majority of children with AIDS are under five years of age. Historically, day care centers have had a relatively high rate of transmission of contagious diseases. This transmission is associated with such factors as close physical contact, inadequate toilet and handwashing facilities, and object-mouthing behaviors characteristic of this age group, as well as the general increased risk for community-acquired infections with large groups of children. Because of these factors, the American Academy of Pediatrics has recommended the following:[14]

1. Decisions are to be made on an individual basis, looking at the developmental determinants, including control of body secretions, hand-object-mouthing behaviors, biting, and encephalopathy.
2. Universal blood and body fluid precautions need to be developed and utilized for each day care center.
3. Because HIV-infected children are presumed to be immunodeficient and are therefore at risk for severe complications of viral diseases such as varicella, CMV, HSV, and measles, consider passive immunoprophylaxis after

exposure to decrease the possibility of severe bacterial disease, and consider the utility of monthly prophylaxis with gamma globulin.

4. Immunize appropriately as mentioned previously.

It is imperative that someone at the day care center be knowledgeable about the child's immunosuppression—though perhaps not the specific cause of the immunosuppression—so that the family will be notified regarding exposure to specific infections.

Some areas with high rates of pediatric HIV infection have begun to develop and run day care centers specific to this population. These types of programs are particularly useful for children who are too sick to attend regular day care. In this setting, health care providers work closely in a collaborative practice with the day care personnel. Obviously, both types of day care services should be available to HIV-infected children.

As more and more HIV-infected children survive longer, an increasing number will attend school. If the schools apply criteria similar to those for day care, HIV-infected children can attend public school. Communities and school boards need to be proactive in developing a comprehensive plan that not only addresses the need for appropriate support services but also gives particular consideration to the needs of children who have HIV neurologic disease with resultant developmental delay. Both communities and school boards respond in a myriad of ways when HIV-infected children have tried to attend public school. The children do not put their fellow classmates at risk, but communities need to deal proactively with the hysteria of parents surrounding their fears of their children becoming infected through casual contact. HIV-infected children deserve the same educational opportunities provided their noninfected counterparts.

PSYCHOSOCIAL ISSUES

HIV infection is a family disease, and when a child is diagnosed, a family crisis ensues.   The nurse, with the entire health care team, has the opportunity to assist the family throughout this crisis by providing excellent care, accurate information, and appropriate referrals, as well as by helping the family to identify its own coping styles, strengths, weaknesses, and personal resources. Because AIDS has such a heavy social stigma attached to it, many families feel isolated and unable to call on their normal support systems for help, for fear of social rejection and retaliation. Since many of these families have experienced repercussions, these fears are not unfounded.

The fact that 80 percent of the documented pediatric AIDS cases are Black and Hispanic children makes it imperative for health care workers to be aware of and provide for the cultural needs of minority AIDS cases. Perceptions of illness and contagion, as well as the meanings of life and death, differ in various ethnic cultures. Providing optimum psychosocial care requires an understanding of these issues. The health care system needs to recruit health care team members who are culturally sensitive and who can work with the predominantly White middle class health care providers to increase their understanding of the issues.

The nurse who follows these children and families consistently can often become a source of support and develop close relationships. The role of nurse advocate may be pivotal in assisting a family to receive optimal care. In addition, networking with other families who have HIV-infected children can provide a support system that cannot be paralleled by health care team members. Peer counseling can decrease the social isolation and deal with the special concerns of this group. In addition, families need to know that the health care system is working to develop a comprehensive, holistic program to deal with the physical, social, psychological, and educational needs of their children.

CONCLUSION

HIV infection in children is a challenge to our society as well as to the health care system. The nurse, as both a direct care provider and as an advocate for the child and family, has a responsibility to promote comprehensive care for the HIV-infected child both in the health care system and in the community at large.

NOTES

1. P.A. Thomas et al., "Unexplained Immunodeficiency in Childhood: A Surveillance Report," *Journal of the American Medical Association (JAMA)* 252 (1984):639; and M.F. Rogers, "AIDS in Children: A Review of the Clinical, Epidemiologic, and Public Health Aspects," *Pediatric Infectious Disease* 4 (1985):230–36.

2. G.B. Scott et al., "Mothers of Infants with the Acquired Immunodeficiency Syndrome—Evidence for Both Symptomatic and Asymptomatic Carriers," *JAMA* 253 (1985):363–66.

3. U.S. Centers for Disease Control (CDC), "Revision of the CDC Surveillance Case Definition for Acquired Immunodeficiency Syndrome," *Morbidity and Mortality Weekly Report (MMWR)* 36 (1987):1s–15s.

4. CDC, "Classification System for Human T-Lymphotropic Virus Type III/Lymphadenopathy Associated Virus Infections," *MMWR* 35, no. 20 (1986):334–39.

5. A.J. Pinching, "The Spectrum of HIV Infection: Routes of Infection, Natural History, Prevention, and Treatment," *Clinics in Immunology and Allergy* 6(1986):467–88.

6. City and County of San Francisco, Department of Public Health, Perinatal and Pediatric AIDS Advisory Committee, "Education of Children Infected with Human Immunodeficiency Virus," *San Francisco Epidemiologic Bulletin* 3 (1987):25–65.

7. W.P. Parks and G.B. Scott, "An Overview of Pediatric AIDS: Approaches to Diagnosis and Outcome Assessment," in S. Broder, ed., *AIDS: Modern Concepts and Therapeutic Challenges* (New York: Marcel Dekker, 1982), pp. 245–62.

8. S.D. Barbour, "Acquired Immunodeficiency Syndrome of Childhood," *Intensive Care* 31 (1987): 247–68.

9. Parks and Scott, "An Overview of Pediatric AIDS."

10. Ibid.

11. Ibid.

12. L.G. Epstein et al., "Neurologic Manifestations of Human Immunodeficiency Virus Infection in Children," *Pediatrics* 78 (1986):678–87.

13. G.W. Rutherford et al., "Guidelines for the Control of Perinatally Transmitted Human Immunodeficiency Virus Infection and Care of Infected Mothers, Infants, and Children," *Western Journal of Medicine* 147 (1987):104–08.

14. American Academy of Pediatrics, Committee on Infectious Diseases, "Health Guidelines for the Attendance in Day-Care and Foster Care Settings of Children Infected with Human Immunodeficiency Virus," *Pediatrics* 79 (1987):466–69.

Appendix 11-A

Pediatric Classification of HIV Infection

Class		Subclass		Category	
P-0	Indeterminate infection				
P-1	Asymptomatic infection	A.	Normal immune function		
		B.	Abnormal immune function		
		C.	Immune function not tested		
P-2	Symptomatic infection	A.	Nonspecific findings		
		B.	Progressive neurologic disease		
		C.	Lymphoid interstitial pneumonitis		
		D.	Secondary infectious diseases	D-1	Specified CDC AIDS-defining infectious diseases
				D-2	Recurrent serious bacterial infections
				D-3	Other secondary infectious diseases
		E.	Secondary cancers	E-1	Specified CDC AIDS-defining cancers
				E-2	Other cancers possibly due to HIV infection
		F.	Other diseases possibly due to HIV infection		

Source: Adapted from *Morbidity and Mortality Weekly Report,* Vol. 35, No. 20, U.S. Centers for Disease Control, 1986.

Chapter 12

Perinatal HIV Infection

Katherine Nelson

The potential transmission of HIV virus from infected women to infants during the perinatal period is a very serious problem. Prevention of transmission to offspring is crucial, yet very little is known about it. Current rates of virus transmission around the world range anywhere from zero to 65 percent.[1] The most recent prediction of virus transmission is about 40 percent.[2] Certainly, with increasing numbers of heterosexuals infected with HIV, more women of child-bearing age are becoming infected and potentially jeopardizing their unborn infants.

The HIV virus has been cultured from:

- fetal tissue[3]
- the placenta[4]
- amniotic fluid
- female genital secretions[5]
- breast milk.[6]

Infants are thought to become infected during the perinatal period either by acquiring the virus while in utero or by receiving it from the placenta during the birth process. The method of delivery is being scrutinized, but caesarean section has not yet proven to be a method for preventing transmission from mother to infant.[7] Mothers of infants with AIDS have an increased likelihood of virus transmission to future unborn children.[8] One infant has become infected from breast milk; thus, breast feeding by known HIV-positive mothers is discouraged.[9]

Because of decreased immunity, one of the physiological processes of pregnancy, mothers of infants with AIDS are at high risk of subsequently developing AIDS or ARC themselves.[10] Early reports of maternal deaths due to acceleration of HIV symptoms related to pregnancy are very worrisome; the prognosis for women who bear HIV-positive infants is an area where more information is needed.

EPIDEMIOLOGY

In the United States, approximately 7 percent of the adult cases of AIDS are women. Of these cases, 80 percent of the women are of childbearing age, between 20 and 49 years old. These women are predominantly of ethnic minorities: 52 percent are Black and 20 percent are Latino.[11] The geographical distribution of these women is skewed toward large urban areas in New York, New Jersey, and Florida, although recently increased numbers of cases are being reported in Texas, California, and other states.[12] Women who are unaware of their own HIV status until the birth of an infected child face a very unfortunate and painful experience. Women considering pregnancy, particularly those from high-risk groups, are encouraged to seek antibody testing with appropriate counseling. (For further discussion of women and HIV, refer to Chapter 6.)

RISK REDUCTION

Education of all sexually active adults is a major focus as we attempt to reduce the risk of HIV transmission. The long latency of the virus, known to be up to nine years, extends the period of undefinable risk for childbearing women. In addition, public efforts to modify the behavior of women considering pregnancy raise issues about reproductive freedom. Access to HIV screening prior to pregnancy is very important, but particular solutions, including abortion for HIV-positive pregnant women, have not been well received. Women are distrustful of public control of women's bodies during pregnancy for the sake of the unborn child.

Ideally, pregnant women need support and guidance to make informed decisions about their behavior in the context of the rest of their lives. However, concern about continued transmission of HIV virus from women to their offspring has provoked some to call for states, courts, and legislators to restrict reproductive rights and the autonomy of pregnant women. Women need to be educated so they may make informed choices, not punished or deprived of choices altogether. Pressure in this area has increased, with recent cases of children suing their mothers for actions while pregnant that may have adversely affected the child's development before birth.[13]

All women should be offered HIV screening prior to pregnancy. High-risk women who are initially seronegative should be retested in the late third trimester to rule out HIV infection. Anonymous testing is encouraged to protect the client's confidentiality; however, all testing should be done with informed consent.

CARE OF INFANTS

Infants born to women who are known to be HIV-positive should be treated as other newborns. These infants need to be picked up, held, and cuddled, as do other infants. As previously noted, breast feeding is discouraged. Evidence of casual transmission of HIV has been disproven in households sharing such common items as toothbrushes, razor blades, and dishes.[14] (See Chapter 11 for elaboration on these issues.)

INFECTION CONTROL

Protective measures are important in the perinatal area for prevention not only of HIV transmission but of other blood-borne communicable diseases such as Hepatitis B, Hepatitis nonA nonB, and CMV. Universal precautions should be practiced for all patients, not only those known to have the disease.

Special areas of concern for maternal child health care workers include labor, delivery, and any specialized procedure that might increase exposure to blood and body fluids. Precautions taken for invasive procedures may include masks for protection of mucous membranes and protective eyewear to prevent splashes. Suctioning and resuscitation of the newborn in the delivery room require mechanical suctioning with the collection of meconium.

All units in the perinatal area are strongly encouraged to develop a high level of awareness of infection control practices. Both comprehensive education about virus transmission and adequate provision and utilization of appropriate barrier protectors are crucial. Recommendations for maternal-child infection control guidelines are found in Appendix 12-A.

CONCLUSION

With the increase in heterosexual HIV infections, more women of childbearing age are at risk of transmitting HIV perinatally to their offspring. Education regarding safe sex and condom usage is an important issue for all sexually active adults to prevent further transmission of HIV. Women who are infected and bear children need to avail themselves of medical and pediatric follow-up. As with other specialized areas, health care workers in the maternal-child area need to be aware of the risks of contracting the virus from exposure to infectious blood and body fluids so that workers can use appropriate barrier methods.

NOTES

1. G.B. Scott et al., "Mothers of Infants with Acquired Immunodeficiency Syndrome: Evidence for Both Symptomatic and Asymptomatic Carriers," *Journal of the American Medical Association (JAMA)* 253 (1985):363–66.

2. S. Blonche et al., "Prospective Study in Newborns of HIV Seropositive Women in Paris, France" (Paper delivered at the Third International Conference on Acquired Immunodeficiency Syndrome (AIDS), Washington, D.C., June 1–5, 1987).

3. E. Jovaisas et al., "LAV/HTLV III in 20 Week Fetus" (letter), *Lancet* 2 (1985):1129.

4. Washington Hill, Veronica Bolton, and James R. Carlson, "Isolation of Acquired Immunodeficiency Syndrome Virus from the Placenta," *American Journal of Obstetrics and Gynecology* 157 (1987):10–11.

5. Connie Wofsy et al., "Isolation of AIDS Associated Retrovirus from Genital Secretions of Women with Antibodies to the Virus," *Lancet* 1 (1986):527–29.

6. J. Zeigler et al., "Postnatal Transmission of AIDS-Associated Retrovirus from Mother to Infant," *Lancet* 1 (1986):896–98.

7. Alan Lifson and Martha Rogers, "Vertical Transmission of Human Immunodeficiency Virus," *Lancet* 2 (1986):337.

8. Scott et al., "Mothers of Infants with Acquired Immunodeficiency Syndrome."

9. Zeigler et al., "Postnatal Transmission of AIDS-Associated Retrovirus."

10. Scott et al., "Mothers of Infants with Acquired Immunodeficiency Syndrome."

11. A.M. Hardy and Mary E. Gunn, "AIDS in Women in the United States" (Paper presented at the Third International Conference on Acquired Immunodeficiency Syndrome (AIDS), Washington, D.C., June 1–5, 1987).

12. Ibid.

13. Joan Robertson and Joseph Schalnon, "Pregnancy and Prenatal Harm to Offspring: The Case of Mother with PKU," *Hastings Center Report* (August 1987):23–32.

14. Gerald Friedland et al., "Lack of Transmission of HTLV-III/LAV Infections to Household Contacts of Patients with AIDS or AIDS-Related Complex with Oral Candidiasis," *New England Journal of Medicine* 314, no. 6 (February 6, 1986):344–49.

Appendix 12-A

Maternal-Child Infection Control

HANDWASHING

Handwashing is the single most important precaution. It is MANDATORY before and after all procedures caring for a woman, child, or infant.

- Wash between touching infants in the nursery.
- Wash after diaper changes.
- Wash after changing Chux, sanitary napkin, or linen.
- Wash immediately after any skin contact with blood or other body fluids.

IF HANDS ARE RAW, CHAPPED, OR HAVE OPEN CUTS, GLOVES SHOULD BE WORN.

GLOVES

Gloves are to be worn when procedures may involve contact with body fluids:

- starting IVs
- drawing blood
- drawing or running cord blood gases
- weighing or handling placenta or umbilical cord
- handling baby prior to first bath
- changing bloody or soiled dressings and linens
- coming into contact with wound drainage

- changing meconium diapers or diarrheal diaper
- coming into contact with feces.

GLOVES ARE NOT NECESSARY FOR CONTACT WITH UNSOILED ARTICLES OR INTACT SKIN.

GOWN, SCRUBS, SHORT DISPOSABLE PLASTIC APRONS

Gowns, scrubs, and/or short disposable plastic aprons should be worn in situations where blood or body fluids may splash on personal clothing.

Sterile gowning technique should be maintained, or "jump suits" used, for:

- C-sections
- delivery room resuscitations.

Health care workers should CHANGE their scrub clothing as soon as possible if soiled with blood or body fluids.

MASKS AND EYE PROTECTION

Use when there is a possibility that mucous membranes may be splashed with blood or other body secretions, including:

- artificial rupturing of membranes
- drawing cord blood gases
- caring for patients with undiagnosed respiratory conditions who are coughing or sneezing extensively.

Safety glasses with prescription or clear glass lenses are preferable to goggles.

NURSERY PROCEDURES

- Wear gloves and gown when handling newborns prior to first bath.
- Bathe all infants with Neutrogena or similar soap as soon as temperature is stable.
- Provide cord care with alcohol at each diaper change.
- Discourage circumcision if there is any doubt about infection status.

- Discourage breast feeding for HIV-positive mothers.
- Provide normal nurturing and stimulation when caring for all infants.

PEDIATRIC CARE

- Encourage normal home placement and care.
- Defer immunizations with live vaccines (oral polio, MMR) until HIV infection status is clear, and do not give if HIV infection is present.
- Give inactivated polio vaccine (IPV) as scheduled.
- Give IPV for routine immunization for uninfected children living in a household where a member is infected.
- Teach home care providers exposed to body fluids and excrement of exposed infants and infected children about the potential for transmission and the importance of good handwashing and other sanitary practices.

Chapter 13

Nursing Interventions

Rita Fahrner

Approximately 10 percent of AIDS patients require acute hospitalization at any one time with a variety of common infections. (See Appendix 13-A.) HIV-infected patients may also be hospitalized for problems unrelated to their HIV infection. In addition, as a result of the ever-increasing need for subacute, skilled nursing and hospice care, and the lack of such 24-hour care facilities, more and more PWAs experience prolonged acute-care hospitalizations even when they do not require (or perhaps benefit from) that level of care. (For additional discussion of inpatient care, refer to Chapter 10.)

Nursing care of acutely ill patients with AIDS does not require a new body of knowledge. Rather, it has become a model of holistic, patient-centered care that can be used for all acutely ill patients. In the acute hospital setting, nurses provide 24-hour continuity of care and thus become the coordinators of care.

Holistic care demands a multidisciplinary collaborative practice model that places the patient, family, and friends in the center. The various care providers then form concentric circles moving out from the core team of nurses, doctors, and social workers, through the extended team, to community agencies that provide services at home and extended care facilities. Using a collaborative practice model, rather than the traditional medical model, the appropriate team member provides leadership for each particular issue or problem. This type of teamwork is a dynamic, ever-changing process, with communication as its central focus. Nurses, with their round-the-clock assessment, intervention, and responsibility, naturally assume the role of coordinator of care in the acute hospital setting.

Because AIDS is a chronic life-threatening illness that has no cure, it is essentially a nursing disease—that is, the essence is caring rather than curing. Acute inpatient care, then, is actually nursing care. Nurses are experts at providing symptom control in a supportive nurturing environment, the basis of care for acutely ill PWAs.

RESPIRATORY DISTRESS

The major reason for hospitalization of AIDS patients continues to be respiratory distress, as PCP is the most common opportunistic infection. Other causes of respiratory distress include:

1. pneumonias caused by CMV, cryptococcus, *Mycobacterium tuberculosis* (MTB), pneumococcus, and other community-acquired bacteria (See Appendix 13-A)
2. pulmonary KS, which can be accompanied by pleural effusion
3. LIP/PLH in children
4. pneumothoraces caused by procedures such as transbronchial biopsy and percutaneous central line placement, or by infection
5. severe anemia with resultant hypoxemia.

Nursing intervention for the patient with impaired gas exchange is crucial in dealing with the physical as well as the psychosocial aspects of severe respiratory distress. It is necessary to assess the patient frequently for signs and symptoms of hypoxemia:

- tachycardia
- tachypnea
- cyanosis
- altered mental status
- irritability
- anxiety.

Monitoring arterial blood gas measurements and/or O_2 saturation by pulse oximetry, as well as blood counts for anemia, gives objective data. These data help the nurse assess the patient's degree of comfort with and tolerance to the current mode of oxygen administration and respiratory therapy, and provide a basis for discussion of alternatives with both the patient and the medical staff.

Many patients who are severely hypoxic tend to feel more air-hungry and frightened with a tight-fitting oxygen mask. Because fear increases both oxygen consumption and air hunger, it often makes sense to use nasal cannulae in addition to a loose-fitting face tent—both at high flow—even if the oxygen concentration is lower than with the tight nonrebreather mask. Restraining the hands of patients who are severely hypoxic and subsequently become confused sometimes becomes necessary to prevent accidental removal of oxygen masks and cannulae. Having a nurse or sitter with such patients is strongly advisable at all times.

Patients need frequent observation for tachypnea, anxiety, and air hunger, as well as appropriate narcotic analgesia to promote comfort. Following opiate administration, observation for signs of respiratory depression and irregularity is imperative. Morphine sulfate appears to be the drug of choice for (acute) air hunger, preferably administered by IV push or by continuous IV infusion. Resuscitation status must be determined prior to regular use, as it may be more appropriate to consider endotracheal intubation and mechanical ventilation for those severely hypoxic patients who desire full resuscitation attempts.

Optimal nursing care of patients with respiratory distress also includes administration of medications, including antibiotics, chemotherapy agents, and steroids to treat the underlying causes of the distress, and support for patients experiencing such frightening signs and symptoms. The goals are to minimize symptoms and to maintain appropriate oxygenation, pulmonary function, and optimal breathing pattern.

PAIN CONTROL

Patients with AIDS can experience a variety of pain symptoms. The specific causes include:

1. peripheral neuropathy, particularly in the lower extremities, which seems to be caused primarily by direct HIV infection of nervous system cells
2. pressure on nerve endings secondary to KS lesions, most often in the deeper lymph nodes, as well as by tumors caused by non-Hodgkin's lymphomas
3. severe headaches caused by CNS involvement due to cryptococcal meningitis, toxoplasmosis encephalitis, progressive multifocal leukoencephalopathy (PML), lymphomas, or stress
4. excoriation of mucous membranes (oral, rectal, vaginal) secondary to opportunistic infection (i.e., Candida, herpes simplex virus [HSV] or urinary or fecal incontinence
5. muscle aches due to immobility
6. other infiltrates, ulcerations, infections, and surgical wounds.

After assessing the character and intensity of the pain, the nurse can assess the need for and type of intervention required. Obviously, treatments aimed at eliminating the cause of pain are primary. Analgesia administered with the intention of relieving pain can often be more effective when the nurse stimulates the patient's placebo response by suggesting that the medication *will* be effective. Chronic pain is best relieved by administering analgesics on a routine basis, rather than as needed.

In addition to pharmacological intervention, alternative pain relief measures can be provided by the nurse. These techniques include:

- massage
- therapeutic touch
- distraction
- guided imagery
- visualization
- active listening
- verbal support.

Effective pain management requires innovative, creative approaches by nursing. The goal is to assist the patient to be maximally pain free and to tolerate pain at an acceptable level.

FALL RISK

Unlike most other acutely ill hospitalized patients in the same youthful age group, AIDS patients exhibit a high risk for falls. This population sees itself as independent and able to care for itself, and individuals often do not recognize the factors contributing to their increased risk. Nurses need to help patients identify factors that put them at increased risk and institute a care plan that integrates these factors. Initial, as well as ongoing, assessment of the patient must include a falls risk assessment and intervention plan.

Five factors associated with increased risk for falls are:

1. weakness
2. sedation
3. mental confusion
4. orthostatic hypotension
5. severe diarrhea.

For patients with extreme weakness, the nurse must ensure that necessary items are within easy reach to decrease the need for unnecessary movement around the room. In addition, patients need to be encouraged to use the call light to ask for assistance in ambulation.

Patients who have received sedative medications need frequent monitoring to evaluate their safety in independent actions. Drowsy or unsteady patients should have bed siderails up and be assisted with ambulation.

The high incidence of HIV encephalopathy as well as CNS disease in this population means that many acutely ill AIDS patients experience mental confusion. These patients benefit from frequent reorientation, which can include:

- calendars
- clocks
- photographs
- familiar objects
- signs identifying their room and bathroom
- message boards identifying the names of their nurses, day of the week, date, names, and phone numbers of friends and family
- verbal reorienting as to day, time, location, etc.

Often a sign reminding them to call the nurse for assistance in ambulating helps. Occasionally such patients require restraints to ensure their safety; this is often a difficult procedure for nurses. Emotionally, nurses find it hard to tie patients down against their will, even if it is for their own best interests.

Patients with severe diarrhea can become dehydrated, which exacerbates their weakness. Again, in an effort to maintain independence, most patients want to use the toilet, but some are physically unable to get out of bed and ambulate into the bathroom in a timely manner. Bedside commodes can make it possible for patients to maintain some degree of independence in toileting, while still providing for their safety. For patients who are bedbound, a bedpan needs to be discreetly within reach at all times.

Orthostatic hypotension, the last risk factor, occurs most frequently as a side effect of IV pentamidine. Often, this hypotension occurs unexpectedly after patients have recovered sufficiently from PCP to allow them to ambulate independently and freely. The nurse needs to inform the patient of this possibility, particularly as blood pressure decreases are noted. Again, the use of the call light for assistance in standing and ambulating is encouraged.

Certainly nurses want to help patients to maintain their self-sufficiency and independence and support them in their quest for empowerment. Nurses can do that and still ensure patients' safety.

ACTIVITY INTOLERANCE

Patients with AIDS who are acutely ill usually experience some activity intolerance related to weakness and fatigue, alteration in normal sleep patterns, decreased nutritional intake, hypotension, side effects of medications, and emotional responses. Nurses can play a large part in controlling the hospital environment in a way that supports the patient's needs for sleep, rest, and activity by planning nursing activities around these needs. Patients frequently have difficulty in limiting visitors and phone calls, and nurses can assist by suggesting limits. The nurse can assess the patient's increases in tolerance and encourage increased activity. Physical and occupational therapy can be included in the plan of care. The goal is for the patient to achieve optimal levels of activity, thus remaining as independent as possible while getting an adequate balance of sleep, rest, nutrition, and activity.

ALTERATIONS IN NUTRITION

Most acutely ill AIDS patients experience gastrointestinal (GI) problems, including anorexia, nausea, vomiting, and diarrhea, at some time during their hospitalization. These symptoms can result from infections, masses, side effects of medications, or from HIV infection of the gut itself.

Many of the antibiotics used to treat opportunistic infections, as well as chemotherapeutic agents used to treat the AIDS-associated malignancies, cause significant nausea and vomiting. (See Appendix 13-B.) The regular use of anti-emetics—often in combinations of drugs with different modes of action—can often minimize these uncomfortable side effects. Favorite foods from home are usually tolerated much better than hospital food.

Diarrhea is a frequent problem for AIDS patients. Antidiarrheals, often in combination, can provide relief at times. In general, however, patients need to learn to live with the diarrhea and adjust their food and fluid intake as appropriate.

Nursing interventions for patients experiencing these GI problems include monitoring weight, intake and output, signs of dehydration, and lab values including serum protein, albumin, and electrolytes. IV fluids are frequently necessary during times of acute nausea, vomiting, and/or diarrhea. The goal is to maintain optimal nutritional support. (For further discussion of these issues, refer to Chapter 16.)

SKIN INTEGRITY

AIDS has long been characterized by a wasting syndrome, and altered nutrition is one factor related to impairment of skin integrity. The other factors include (1) the effects of immobility producing prolonged unrelieved pressure and (2) the presence of excretions, secretions, or both. The nurse needs to assess the patient's skin surfaces at least every shift for redness, breakdown, excessive moisture, and lesions. The bath is both an excellent time to perform this head-to-foot assessment and an opportunity for range of motion exercises and for skin massage to increase tissue perfusion. Patients with severe hypoxia are often reluctant to change position from a semi-Fowler's as it gives the most room for bilateral lung expansion. Since turning these patients according to an established schedule is impossible, it may be prudent to provide appropriate pressure-relieving mattresses or beds early in hospitalization to reduce the risk of pressure sores. Skin should be kept clean and dry. Mobility should be encouraged within functional limits.

Patients who are incontinent and bedbound have a double threat to skin integrity. Diarrhea stool can be extremely caustic to the skin surrounding the rectal area, and the presence of poor tissue perfusion in that area increases the risk of skin breakdown and ulceration. Rectal tubes can be used when the stool is liquid; fecal incontinence collectors may be useful with thicker stool but are often difficult to place well. Urinary incontinence can be effectively dealt with in males by using condom catheters but is difficult to manage in women. Meticulous nursing care is necessary to prevent skin breakdown.

PREVENTING NOSOCOMIAL INFECTION

Although the opportunistic infections that AIDS patients develop are generally believed to be reactivations of latent infections, acutely ill AIDS patients are at risk for hospital-acquired infections. Also, because many of the drugs used to treat patients with AIDS cause bone marrow suppression, these patients frequently become neutropenic.

The best and most effective way to prevent nosocomial infection is to wash hands well before and after any patient contact. Families and friends need to be taught why handwashing is so important.

Controversy continues regarding the usefulness of neutropenic precautions, which commonly include the use of masks, eliminating milk products and fresh, unpeeled fruits and vegetables from the patient's diet, and eliminating plants and flowers from patient rooms.

All invasive procedures and treatments, including use of IV catheters, require strict aseptic technique to reduce the risk of introduction of pathogens.

PSYCHOSOCIAL ISSUES

Psychosocial issues for people with AIDS have been thoroughly discussed in other chapters. The important point here is that nursing care of the acutely ill patient with AIDS hinges directly on the nurses caring for the patient. As coordinators of care, and as the 24-hour care providers, nurses set the stage. Compassionate holistic care is predicated on the idea of individual acceptance of all patients, whoever they may be. Cultural, ethnic, and religious beliefs and values need to be integrated into the plan as well. Primary nursing, or modified versions thereof that provide consistent caretakers, can benefit the patient by ensuring a system that values relationship development and safety for the patient. One major goal is to provide opportunities for patients to express feelings and feel accepted.

SUMMARY

All nurses who work in acute care hospitals will undoubtedly be called upon to care for patients with AIDS or HIV infection. Caring for these patients demands that the nurse be compassionate, caring, and skilled. Pain and symptom management, as well as strong skills in assessment, are the keys to optimum nursing care of acutely ill patients with AIDS.

Appendix 13-A

Opportunistic Infections in AIDS/HIV Infection

Protozoal Infections	Diagnosis	Treatment
1. *Pneumocystis carinii* pneumonia (PCP)	Sputum induction; bronchoscopy. Organism identified under light microscopy. May be presumptively diagnosed in HIV+ with CXR and ABGs.	Sulfamethoxazole/trimethoprim (Bactrim/Septra) PO, IV, pentamidine IM, IV, aerosolized dapsone/trimethoprim PO. Duration of treatment: 14–21 days.
2. *Toxoplasma gondii* encephalitis	Presumptive diagnosis based on CT/MRI scanning in HIV+. May require open brain biopsy for tissue confirmation.	Pyrimethamine/sulfadiazine PO. Clindamycin PO, IV for those unable to tolerate sulfa. Duration of treatment: lifelong.
3. *Cryptosporidium enteritis* This protozoan can be transmitted to immunocompetent as well as immunosuppressed hosts. Healthy hosts usually have a mild self-limited diarrhea.	Stool sample; direct visualization of parasite on acid-fast stain of stool.	No effective treatment known. Routine symptomatic treatment for diarrhea, dehydration.

continues

Fungal Infections	Diagnosis	Treatment
1. Candida		
Oral thrush	Visual identification; potassium hydroxide prep (KOH) of yeast.	Mycelex troches; nystatin swish and swallow. Duration of treatment: ongoing.
Esophagitis	Barium swallow; esophagoscopy may be presumptively diagnosed in HIV + with presence of oral thrush and appropriate symptoms.	Ketoconazole PO; amphotericin B IV (low-dose short course). Duration of treatment: may need to be ongoing.
2. Cryptococcus		
Meningitis	Cryptococcal antigen titer: serum, CSF.	Amphotericin B IV 6-week course, approximately 1.5 gm total dose; then less frequent dosing.
Pneumonia	Sputum induction; bronchoscopy.	If WBC adequate: 5-FC (flucytosine) PO in conjunction with amphotericin B.
	Culture blood, CSF, sputum.	Experimental: ketoconazole PO (high dose). Duration of treatment: may need to be ongoing.
3. Histoplasmosis disseminated (pulmonary, bone marrow)	Bone marrow biopsy; culture of blood, bone marrow; bronchoscopy; culture sputum.	Amphotericin B. Duration of treatment: may need to be ongoing.

Viral Infections

1. Disseminated cytomegalovirus (CMV):

   Retinal

   GI

2. Mucocutaneous herpes simplex

3. Progressive multifocal leukoencephalopathy-papovavirus

Bacterial Infections

1. *Mycobacterium tuberculosis* (MTB): disseminated (This bacterium can be transmitted to immunocompetent as well as immunosuppressed

---

Direct opthalmologic examination.

Endoscopy with tissue biopsy showing intracellular inclusions.

Visual identification; culture + HSV.

Open brain biopsy—tissue diagnosis.

AFB stain
- In sputum
- Positive culture.

DHPG (Gangcyclovir) IV.
Foscarnet IV—experimental.
Duration of treatment: lifelong.

Acyclovir PO, IV.
Duration of treatment: may need to be ongoing.

No available treatment.

Various combinations of INH, rifampin, ethambutol, pyrazinamide.

continues

	Diagnosis	Treatment
Bacterial Infections (*continued*)		
hosts.) Respiratory isolation required for minimum of 7 days after tx started.		
2. *Mycobacterium avium intracellulare* (MAI)	Bone marrow biopsy—AFB culture.	Treatment with above agents may reduce symptoms. Experimental agents include clofazimine and ansamycin.

Appendix 13-B

Drugs Used in AIDS/HIV Infection and Their Side Effects

	Usual Dose	Side Effects
Drugs for Thrush/Candida		
1. Nystatin: liquid for swish and swallow	5 cc QID	*Frequent:* none *Occasional:* diarrhea, GI distress, nausea and vomiting
2. UC swish and swallow (Mycostatin Suspension, Hydrocortisone, Benadryl)	5-10 cc 4-5 ×/day	Same as for Nystatin
3. Clotrimazole (Mycelex) troches	1 troche 5 × daily	Same as for Nystatin
4. Ketoconazole: tablets	200-400 mg/daily	*Frequent:* nausea, vomiting, elevated liver enzymes *Occasional:* abdominal pain, constipation, GI bleeding, headaches, diarrhea, rash, pruritis

continues

	Usual Dose	Side Effects
Drugs for Cryptococcus		
1. Amphotericin B: IV infusion given usually over 4 hours mixed with hydrocortisone and heparin and given via central line to decrease phlebitis. Benadryl and Tylenol given prior to infusion to decrease reaction.	Begin w/ test dose, and increase up to full dose gradually. 0.6–0.8 mg/kg daily to total dose of 1.5 gms then 1–3 × weekly.	*Frequent:* nausea and vomiting, fever, chills, headache, diarrhea, abdominal cramping, body aches, decreased renal function w/ elevated creatinine and BUN, hypokalemia. *Occasional:* peripheral neuropathy, anaphylaxis arrhythmias, bone marrow suppression, rash, blurred vision.
2. 5-Flucytosine (5-FC) tablets—may be given with ampho.	75-100 mg/kg/d in 4 divided doses	*Frequent:* elevations of liver enzymes, BUN, and creatinine, nausea, vomiting, diarrhea, bone marrow suppression. *Occasional:* headache, sedation vertigo, confusion.
3. Ketoconazole: high doses used experimentally for suppressive therapy.	1 gm/daily	Same as above for ketoconazole.
Drugs for Pneumocystis (PCP)		
1. Trimethoprim/Sulfamethoxazole (Bactrim or Septra) tablets, IV preparation.	15 mg/kg daily in 3–4 divided doses	*Frequent:* nausea and vomiting, anorexia, diarrhea, fever, bone marrow suppression, rash, headache. *Occasional:* elevations in liver enzymes, insomnia, stomatitis, depression, hallucinations.

2. Dapsone/Trimethoprim tablets. Need normal G6PD before starting and methemoglobin levels weekly.	Dapsone: 100 mg daily Trimethoprim: 15 mg/kg daily in 3–4 divided doses	Similar to Trimethoprim/sulfa with addition of hemolysis in patients who are G6PD deficient or methemoglobin reductase-deficient. Generally less toxic than TMP/SMX.
3. Pentamidine: IV infusion given over at least one hour	4 mg/kg daily	*Frequent:* anorexia, nausea and vomiting, decreased renal function with elevated BUN and creatinine, bone marrow suppression. *Occasional:* hypoglycemia, hypotension, elevated liver enzymes, arrhythmias.
IM injection	4 mg/kg daily	Same as IV, with addition of high incidence of sterile abscess formation at injection sites.
Aerosolized	600 mg/6 cc sterile H_2O (probably 10% is absorbed)	Virtually no systemic effects. May cause irritation of bronchial tree and, therefore, cough.
Drugs for Toxoplasmosis		
1. Pyrimethamine tablets Folinic acid is usually given simultaneously as pyrimethamine inhibits folinic acid metabolism.	100 mg initially, then 25 mg daily PO	*Frequent:* anorexia, nausea and vomiting, diarrhea, rash, headache. *Occasional:* atrophic glossitis, adverse nervous system effects, photophobia.
2. Sulfadiazine tablets Generally given in combination with pyrimethamine as the two work synergistically	1 gm PO 4 × daily	*Frequent:* anorexia, nausea and vomiting, diarrhea, rash, headache. *Occasional:* elevated liver enzymes, drug fever, neuropathy, decreased renal function.

continues

	Usual Dose	Side Effects
Drugs for Toxoplasmosis (*continued*)		
3. Clindamycin tablets, IV infusion Used when patients unable to tolerate sulfadiazine. Experimental in CNS toxo, but has been used extensively for retinal toxoplasmosis.	PO: 600–1200 mg q6° IV: 900 mg q8°	*Frequent:* nausea, vomiting and diarrhea, abdominal pain, rash, elevated liver enzymes. *Occasional:* neutropenia, jaundice.
Drugs for Herpes Simplex/Herpes Zoster		
1. Acyclovir tablets, IV infusion	HSV: 200 mg PO 5 ×/d HZV: 10–15 mg/kg/q6° IV/PO in divided doses	*Frequent:* nausea, headache, rash, bone marrow suppression. *Occasional:* decreased renal function with increased BUN and creatinine particularly in patients with pre-existing renal disease or concurrent use of other nephrotoxic drugs.

Chapter 14

Medical Treatment of Persons with AIDS/ ARC

Gary Carr

Development of the actual diseases labeled AIDS and ARC is a two-step process. First, infection with HIV leads to a depletion of peripheral helper/inducer (T4) lymphocytes, which allows the second step, infection with opportunistic diseases that may proliferate only in the absence of these cells. Therefore, medical treatment for AIDS is considered in two separate areas: treatment of the HIV infection itself and treatment of the infections and malignant diseases arising as a result of the HIV infection.

TREATMENT OF HIV INFECTION

In the area of HIV infection, the primary problem is that no treatment has yet been demonstrated effective in either halting or reversing the destruction of T4 lymphocytes. Strategies thus far attempted fall into two areas: immune modulation and antiviral activity.

Immune Modulation

Immune modulation proposes the use of chemical agents to restimulate the host immune system into producing T4 lymphocytes despite the HIV infection, thereby attempting to fight HIV in the body and resist opportunistic diseases as well. Substances known to occur naturally in the human body and possess immune-stimulating and antiviral activity have been synthesized by recombinant gene technology and administered in clinical trials to patients infected with HIV. These include alpha-interferon, interleukin-2, and gamma-interferon.

Alpha-interferon, the first drug tried for immune system modulation, showed no useful activity for restimulating the immune system. However, the drug has

131

demonstrated efficacy against KS in about 40 percent of patients, presumably due at least partially to the same immune-modulating effect. In doses large enough to be effective, alpha-interferon causes toxicity described as "flu-like," with symptoms including fatigue, malaise, fever, and headache. The drug is still used in KS therapy for limited numbers of patients; patients are taught to self-administer the drug at home by injection. Interleukin-2 and gamma-interferon failed to show any benefit in clinical trials.

Isoprinosine is an oral immune-modulating drug with an unknown mechanism of action; it has not been demonstrated effective in controlled clinical trials. Many individuals are believed to be taking isoprinosine, which must be obtained from Mexico since it is not authorized for use in the United States. In this group, no consistent benefit has been seen, but evaluation is difficult as the drug is used in varying dosages and durations, and without controls.

Diethyldithiocarbamate (DTC) is an oral drug that has been shown to increase the numbers of circulating T4 cells. It is a metabolite of disulfuram (Antabuse, used in anti-alcoholism therapy) and therefore may not be used in actively alcoholic patients. Its side effects include nausea and vomiting, behavior changes, and, when administered via IV infusion, chest pain. In the presence of alcohol, "Antabuse reaction" may occur: flushing, shortness of breath, nausea, and headache. The ability of the drug to restore immune function and stop the progression of HIV in patients is not yet known; clinical trials with placebo control are under way.

Antiviral Activity

The antiviral approach to HIV infection is based on some basic facts about the biology of the AIDS virus. This virus is of a type called retrovirus, which, in order to convert its RNA into DNA, must use an enzyme called reverse-transcriptase. This enzyme is the weak point at which most antiviral drugs attempt to disrupt the destructive activity of the virus, although these drugs may have other anti-metabolic actions as well.

One of the first antivirals tried on patients was Suramin, a drug that has been used for many years in treating trypanosomiasis (a parasitic protozoal disease). Suramin demonstrated such high toxicity in human subjects that research with it has been terminated. HPA-23 is a reverse-transcriptase-inhibiting drug developed in France that was found ineffective and toxic to platelets in clinical trials. Riboviron is a viral antimetabolite of unknown mechanism that, like isoprinosine, is unapproved by the U.S. Food and Drug Administration (FDA) but widely obtained from sources in Mexico. Recent clinically controlled trials with riboviron have led to controversial data, but they have shown no effectiveness in stemming HIV infection.

AZT

The most promising drug yet tried in anti-HIV therapy, azidothymidine (AZT), lies within the antiviral part of the spectrum. This drug, initially referred to as Compound S, is now called zidovudine and marketed under the brand name Retrovir. Initial placebo-controlled clinical trials, begun nationally in January 1986, demonstrated significantly decreased mortality associated with the use of this drug. It became available to post-PCP patients in a nonplacebo "Investigational New Drug" (IND) protocol in October 1986. In March 1987, it was licensed for limited use for all post-PCP patients and for patients with ARC or other AIDS diagnoses who have less than 200 T4 cells/mm^3 in peripheral blood (greater than 450 T4 cells/mm^3 is generally considered normal). Because of the urgency of the situation, AZT was released early in the investigational process, so clinical trials are continuing even as the drug is available openly to a limited group of patients. Present trials include persons now eligible to receive the drug in nonplacebo trials and placebo-controlled trials with HIV-infected persons who would not be eligible for open-label drug under present indications. The process of learning what must be known about AZT, especially in long-term use, is ongoing.

AZT has several major advantages as a therapeutic agent. Its oral form makes it easy to administer. It is known to penetrate the CNS by crossing the blood-brain barrier, an important therapeutic implication since HIV is known to infect the brain.

AZT is also associated with certain toxicities, which must carefully be monitored. The majority of patients initially experience headache, fever, and nausea. These often tolerable symptoms frequently cease after several weeks. More serious is the anemia associated with AZT. In up to 20 percent of patients, hemoglobin levels fall to a point where transfusion has been necessary; many patients on the drug may become dependent on periodic transfusions. White blood cell counts may also decrease. There seems to be no way to predict which patients will have adverse reactions.

Because of the high risk of hematologic toxicity, patients on AZT must be monitored closely. Weekly complete blood counts (CBCs) for the first two months, then biweekly to monthly CBCs are recommended. Both the manufacture of the drug and the need to monitor it with laboratory studies are associated with another serious drawback: high cost.

Despite problems of toxicity, availability, and cost, AZT is the focus of the greatest optimism regarding anti-HIV therapy at this time. Most experts believe the answer lies in developing effective drugs for both immune modulation and antiviral activity. Using such drugs concurrently would promote the replacement of peripheral T4 lymphocytes while allowing the new cells to remain uninfected. Use of new drugs must await demonstration of a reasonable certainty of safety through individual clinical trials.

TREATMENT OF INFECTIONS AND MALIGNANT DISEASES

While medical treatment of HIV infection remains at the theoretical stage, treatment of the specific infectious diseases and malignancies suffered by patients is the main medical means of attempting to prolong life. Although AIDS is associated with a high rate of mortality, diagnosis and treatment of disease have clearly been of great significance.

Pneumocystis carinii Pneumonia

The most common infectious disease in AIDS is PCP, caused by an opportunistic protozoan organism. Much has been learned about this disease, and now more than 75 percent of cases may survive treatment. The first choice for drug treatment in PCP remains sulfamethoxazole/trimethoprim (Septra, Bactrim). Although more than 50 percent of HIV-infected patients experience adverse reactions to this drug, they are easily reversible when therapy is discontinued or another drug is substituted. Administered intravenously or orally, toxic effects commonly include nausea, vomiting, fever, chills, and rash. Laboratory evaluation may show leukopenia and thrombocytopenia.

Pentamidine isethionate has been known to be effective against PCP since before the AIDS epidemic. The sudden increase in requests for this previously unlicensed drug at the CDC in 1981 helped bring initial attention to the onset of the AIDS epidemic. Its toxicities include metallic taste, flushing, tachycardia, and sudden hypoglycemia or sudden hypotension. These emergent events are unpredictable in onset, not necessarily directly following administration of the drug. Renal toxicity is common and BUN and creatinine must be monitored for elevation. This drug is usually administered intravenously, making hospitalization necessary. It is not available in oral form. Intramuscular use is not advisable as painful sterile abscesses usually form at the site of injection and may last for many months. Recent trials of the drug in inhalation form delivered directly to the lung via nebulizer have been promising—this route, when authorized by the FDA, may decrease internal organ toxicity and be more readily available on an outpatient basis.

Dapsone, a drug previously used in treating human leprosy, is effective against PCP. It is used orally in combination with trimethoprim; in combination, they may be used for outpatient treatment. Toxicities may include abdominal pain, nausea, vomiting, and peripheral neuropathy. Bone marrow suppression may occur. Dapsone causes a decreased erythrocyte life span; and as a consequence it becomes important to monitor the levels of methemoglobin, an immature, ineffective form of hemoglobin that may be released into the circulation.

Trimethoprim is an antimalarial agent used in combination with sulfamethoxazole (Septra) or dapsone. It is synergistic with both but may be responsible for some adverse reactions, particularly of the skin, so caution is advised in switching between the two combination regimens that include trimethoprim.

In patients who have survived PCP, prophylaxis against subsequent cases has been tried with sulfamethoxazole/trimethoprim and pentamidine at less frequent doses than those given for acute treatment, and with dapsone at the same dose as is given for acute treatment. Fansidar, a sulfatrimethoprim combination with a long half-life, has also been tried. Pentamidine by the inhalation route may play a role in prophylaxis as well. None of these regimens has proven to be a certain way of preventing recurrence of PCP, but all may have some value.

Toxoplasmosis

Toxoplasmosis is infection of the brain by *Toxoplasma gondii*, a protozoan that causes space-occupying brain lesions, which may be seen on a CT scan of the head. Neurologic symptoms may include headache, changing mental status, and seizures. Fever is common. The treatment of choice is a combination of sulfadiazine and pyrimethamine, used orally and usually continued for the remainder of the patient's life in order to prevent relapse. Sulfadiazine may cause fever and chills, and frequently causes rash (as do other sulfa drugs). Leukopenia and thrombocytopenia may be seen. Pyrimethamine may lead to nausea and vomiting and also to bone marrow suppression. In these patients, frequent laboratory monitoring for toxicity is important, as well as additional neurological evaluation and brain CT scans to monitor resolution of disease with treatment.

Cryptococcosis

Cryptococcosis is infection with the opportunistic fungus *Cryptococcus neoformans*. The most common manifestation is a meningitis, caused when the organism infects the cerebrospinal fluid. Pneumonitis, as well as blood sepsis without organ focus, is also possible. Diagnosis is by detection of the organism in tissue by a serologic antigen test or by culture. Treatment of cryptococcal disease is with amphotericin B, administered intravenously. Frequently an indwelling central line is inserted for this treatment. Therapy is usually daily until a total dose of 1.5 grams is delivered over about six weeks. Maintenance may then follow. Oral maintenance with ketoconazole (see "Candidiasis" below) may be effective at high doses (800 to 1000 mg/day).

Amphotericin B is notorious for its side effects, and many nurses have heard it called "amphoterrible." Very common are:

- severe fevers and chills
- headache
- anorexia leading to weight loss
- nausea
- vomiting
- malaise
- diarrhea
- dyspepsia.

Phlebitis may occur. Patients on this drug are frequently premedicated with Tylenol, Benadryl, and Demerol to decrease the discomfort associated with infusions. In the laboratory evaluation, patients on amphotericin B must be monitored for anemia, bone marrow suppression, abnormal renal function, and decreased serum potassium level. Flucytosine may be used in combination with amphotericin B in cryptococcal meningitis. This drug may be the cause of anemia, leukocytopenia, thrombocytopenia, and increased hepatic enzyme levels, BUN, and creatinine. (For further information on amphotericin B and central lines, refer to Chapter 15.)

Cryptosporidiosis

Cryptosporidiosis is an infection of the lining of the gastrointestinal tract with *Cryptosporidium enteritis*, a protozoal agent that prior to the AIDS epidemic was thought to be only a veterinary pathogen, but is now known to be opportunistic in humans. No antibiotic agent has been shown effective against this infection, although many have been tried.

Clinical trials are now underway with a drug called spiromycin. Its toxicities may include nausea, vomiting, diarrhea, gastrointestinal pain, and colitis, very much the same symptoms caused by the infection itself. With no available therapy against the agent, symptom control is very important. Bowel control with agents known to slow gastrointestinal motility may be successful. Lomotil and Imodium may be titrated by the patient to achieve control, but overuse of these and other antidiarrheal agents may lead to painful constipation. If stronger agents are needed, tincture of opium and paregoric are available. For patients with persistent diarrhea due to cryptosporidiosis or any etiology, dehydration is a danger. Patients should be encouraged to maintain oral fluid intake; vital signs should be monitored for orthostasis. Intravenous fluid replacement may be indicated. Serum potassium levels should be monitored as much potassium is lost with diarrhea. Skin care of the perianal area is important, as it is in all patients with stool incontinence.

Cytomegalovirus

CMV is a virus that may affect many organs in the immune-compromised host. The most common manifestations in AIDS are retinitis (eye infection with accompanying blindness), pneumonitis, and colitis. Treatment is available with intravenous administration of an anti-CMV agent called dihydroxy phenoxymethyl guanine (DHPG) [Gancyclovir]. Initial induction includes ten days of administering the drug every eight hours, usually followed by maintenance on a lesser dose given three to five times weekly. Some patients with CMV retinitis respond well enough to the initial induction that maintenance is not necessary. In these patients, maintenance usually prevents further visual loss. CMV colitis responds to DHPG treatment about 50 percent of the time; pneumonitis does not usually respond to treatment.

Patients on DHPG may experience nausea, anorexia, diarrhea, muscle aches, headache, or disorientation due to the drug. In the laboratory, patients must be monitored for neutropenia, granulocytopenia, and elevation of liver function tests. Testicular atrophy may occur. (Further discussion of this drug is found in Chapter 15.)

Herpes Simplex

Herpes simplex virus may cause acute, very painful outbreaks in patients with AIDS. Oral, genital, and perianal outbreaks are common. Herpes is treatable with the drug acyclovir (Zovirax), available topically for localized outbreaks or orally for more widespread or severe infection. Used orally, the drug is usually very well tolerated, but it may cause nausea, vomiting, rash, fatigue, or metallic taste. Routine laboratory tests are used to monitor for the occurrence of nephrotoxicity. Used topically, the drug is quite benign although not effective perianally; to avoid spreading the virus, patients are advised to wash their hands very well after application. Careful handwashing is encouraged even when the patient has followed advice and used gloves for application. Herpes zoster caused by varicella virus ("shingles") occurs more frequently than in the general population and is also treated with oral acyclovir, usually at higher doses than in herpes simplex therapy. During the acute phase of zoster, nonsteroidal, anti-inflammatory, or narcotic pain medications may be indicated; antipruritics such as Benadryl may be helpful while the skin lesions are healing.

Candidiasis

Candidiasis, or superinfection with the yeast *Candida albicans*, which is normal flora in humans, is also common in HIV-infected persons and is, in fact, probably one of the most common infections in AIDS and ARC. The most common sites are in the gastrointestinal tract, especially the oral, esophageal, and anal areas. Skin and vaginal infections may also occur. Treatment of oral candidiasis, "thrush," is frequently accomplished with nystatin, in oral suspension, or with clotrimazole in troche form (Mycelex), which is slowly dissolved in the mouth; both these drugs may cause nausea, vomiting, and diarrhea. Clotrimazole may also cause elevation in liver function tests (LFTs), especially SGOT, and when applied topically as a cream, may lead to blistering erythema. Ketoconazole is administered orally both for esophageal Candida, because the drugs mentioned above are locally acting and may not reach the site, or for candidiasis for which the above-mentioned drugs fail as therapy. Ketoconazole may cause rash, nausea and vomiting, insomnia, anorexia, and headache as well as elevated LFTs. It is toxic to the adrenal glands and may cause an adrenal hormone insufficiency, which leads to fatigue, malaise, and weight loss and may profoundly affect how the patient feels. Oral corticosteroid therapy may be indicated in adrenal insufficiency.

Mycobacterial Infections

Mycobacterial infections in AIDS also occur with greater incidence than in the general population, both *Mycobacterium tuberculosis* and atypical mycobacterial infections, especially with the ubiquitous *Mycobacterium avium intracellulare* complex (MAI). Nonpulmonary presentation of these infections is also greater in HIV-infected patients. Tuberculosis in AIDS patients fortunately responds to the same drugs used in the general population. Multidrug therapy is used due to organism resistance to antibiotics. In MAI infection, drug resistance is greater than that seen in most tuberculosis strains, so treatment with antituberculosis medications may be only partially effective, or even ineffective. In many patients, symptoms of the infection, such as fever, drenching sweats, fatigue, and anorexia, are somewhat relieved by treatment, but the patients remain infected and cultures remain positive while patients are on therapy.

Isoniazid, widely used in antituberculosis therapy, may cause fever, skin rash, hepatitis, or peripheral neuritis (this occurs in 20 percent of patients on the drug and is avoided by the concurrent use of the vitamin pyridoxine). Ethambutal may cause decreased visual acuity with decreased ability to see the color green (reversible when the drug is discontinued). Rifampin may cause an orange discoloration of urine and other body fluids. Ansamycin is a derivative of rifampin that is used in treatment of MAI because MAI is highly resistant to rifampin. Ansamycin may cause thrombocytopenia or transaminase elevations. MAI infection itself may cause these signs, so monitoring of patients can be difficult. Nonsteroidal anti-inflammatory medications may be useful for symptom control in patients with MAI. These medications should be taken on a full stomach or with food.

TREATMENT OF MALIGNANT DISEASES

Since the onset of the AIDS epidemic, the two types of malignancy associated with HIV infection have been cancers previously identified as related to immune suppression: Kaposi's sarcoma and lymphomas.

Kaposi's Sarcoma

KS is a diffuse malignancy consisting of multiple tumors of the wall of blood vessels throughout the body. Cutaneous tumors (lesions) are visible and may be a cosmetic problem; tumors within lymph nodes may block lymphatic drainage and cause edema of extremities or of the face; pulmonary lesions may impede oxygen exchange and cause death. The variability of dissemination and progression of KS in AIDS patients has been so enormous that no single pattern is recognized, and monitoring and treatment of each patient is highly individualized.

Since the disease is diffuse in the body, chemotherapeutic interventions have been systemic. Most commonly used are the vinca alkaloids vinblastine (Velban) and vincristine (Oncovin), administered intravenously. Vinblastine may cause nausea, leukocytopenia, and alopecia (fortunately, this is very rare). Vincristine may cause peripheral neuritis. Frequently these two drugs are given in an alternating weekly schedule to maintain the antitumor activity but decrease the possibility of side effects. Etoposide (VP-16) is also used intravenously in 3-day cycles every 21 days. This therapy has resulted in a high rate of alopecia. Alpha-interferon, described previously in the section on immune modulation of this chapter, is also used.

Radiation therapy administered locally in brief courses and intralesional injection of Velban have been used, but these are treatments for individual obstructive or cosmetically undesirable lesions; they are not treatments for the systemic disease.

Lymphomas

AIDS-related lymphomas tend to be B-cell non-Hodgkin's lymphomas of very high grade and rapid growth. They occur most frequently in the CNS and in bone marrow. Even with aggressive chemotherapy, lymphoma is the most dismal diagnosis in AIDS, associated with very high and rapid rates of mortality due both to the poor response of the tumors to treatment and to the frequent presence of other AIDS diseases, especially opportunistic infections. No standard chemotherapeutic regimens exist for AIDS-related lymphomas; these patients are individually evaluated and treated by oncologists experienced in this field.

Chapter 15

Care of the HIV Patient with a Vascular Access Device

Suzanne F. Herbst

Drug protocols for HIV often require daily IV infusions until the patient either can no longer tolerate them or dies. Multiple venipunctures put patients at risk for infection, peripheral vein damage, or extravasation; subject patients to painful searches for a vein; induce fear of injections; and place stress on the nurse.

There are many alternatives to multiple venipunctures. Long-term placement of silicone rubber (Broviac/Hickman) catheters, introduced in the early 1970s, has proven safe, reliable, and comfortable for immunosuppressed patients. Made by a variety of manufacturers, each vascular access device (VAD) has unique features. Staying abreast of evolving technology requires communication between persons using the devices in order to share experiences and enhance patient care. In the San Francisco Bay Area, the Bay Area Vascular Access Network (BAVAN) was established in 1985 to help meet this need. (For further information on this group, see Appendix 15-A.)

The widespread nature of AIDS and the nursing shortage means that nurses must expand their role as educators. Ironically, although many nurses are barely comfortable using VADs, their use is already being turned over to patients and nonprofessional caregivers. Nurses play a key role in developing patient and caregiver educational materials that include clear illustrations and understandable terminology.

SAFETY GUIDELINES FOR CAREGIVERS

The HIV virus is transmitted via blood, and VADs are placed in the circulatory system. All persons handling these devices must be trained to follow recommended precautions, as described in Chapter 18. Agency guidelines need to be established, implemented, continuously updated, and practiced by all caregivers.

CLASSIFICATION OF DEVICES

VADs provide venous access for blood sampling and for administration of fluids, drugs, and blood products. The devices described below, constructed of silicone rubber unless otherwise stated, may be divided into three major classifications: tunneled catheters, nontunneled catheters, and implanted ports.

Tunneled Catheters

In the early 1970s, Broviac introduced a tunneled silicone catheter for delivery of total parenteral nutrition (TPN) to patients.[1] Later, Hickman increased the inner diameter and showed that these catheters were safe and reliable to use in bone-marrow transplant patients.[2]

A cuff is attached to the catheter where it is tunneled into the subcutaneous tissue, as shown in Figure 15-1. This cuff, generally of Dacron, anchors the catheter and provides a mechanical barrier against ascending infection.

The newest tunneled catheter is the Groshong, made of thin-walled, translucent silicone with a radiopaque strip and a three-way valve along the side of the distal tip. The valve remains closed when the catheter is not in use, creating the following advantages:

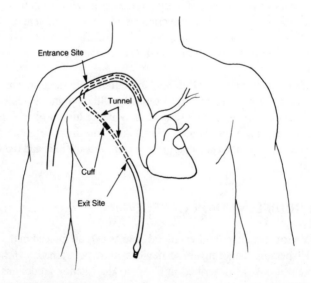

Entrance Site

Tunnel

Cuff

Exit Site

Figure 15-1 Tunneled Catheter

- minimizes the potential for air embolism
- reduces the risks of blood backflow or hemorrhage
- decreases maintenance by eliminating heparin flushes
- decreases saline flushes to once a week.

At the distal end of the catheter is a push-fit blunt needle adapter of appropriate gauge, which facilitates repair should the catheter become damaged.

Points to consider when selecting or using an external access device include the following:

- Most require daily heparin flushes; the Groshong uses weekly saline flushes.
- All require meticulous site care and frequent dressing changes.
- The tunnel may be a problem for persons with extensive Kaposi's sarcoma on the chest.

Nontunneled Catheters

This type of catheter has been used traditionally as a routine central venous pressure (CVP) line. Incidence of complications among 16,000 catheters included infection, less than 2 percent; thrombosis, less than 2 percent; and phlebitis, less than 3 percent.[3]

Nontunneled catheters are of a smaller gauge polymer and are percutaneously inserted as follows:

1. Centrally: a physician inserts the catheter over a guidewire or through a peelaway sheath via the internal jugular or subclavian veins.

   - Risks: hemorrhage, pneumothorax
   - Examples: Baxter (Centrasil), Arrow, Cook, Davol

2. Peripherally: a nurse or physician inserts the catheter through a slotted needle, breakaway needle, or peelaway sheath via the basilic or cephalic vein.

   - Risks: minimal
   - Examples: Baxter (Intrasil), Gesco (Per-Q-Cath), Becton-Dickinson (VIA-PIC—made of Vialon, a unique polyurethane material)

A nurse may insert a nontunneled catheter peripherally at the bedside, in outpatient clinics, or in the home at less cost and with less risk and trauma to the patient than in inpatient units. Infected or damaged catheters may be replaced by an overwire exchange technique.

The Per-Q-Cath has been used for several years in neonates, with a low incidence of complications. Recently, fine-gauge catheters have been used successfully in adults requiring continuous short-term therapy (i.e., two to four weeks of antibiotics; end-stage symptom management). The catheter is inserted about four to six inches into the basilic or cephalic vein, remains in place 30 to 180 days, and may provide an excellent short-term alternative to multiple venipunctures.

Decisions regarding the use of nontunneled catheters must take into account the following requirements: external access; daily heparin flush and site evaluation; and dressing changes, for which patients with peripherally inserted catheters may need assistance. Moreover, peripheral insertions may limit patient mobility.

Implanted Ports

Introduced in 1984, implanted ports—totally implanted VADs—have gained popularity and are made in adult and pediatric sizes by many manufacturers (see Figure 15-2). They have low maintenance requirements when not being used and are desirable for patients interested in body image. Although each port has its own unique features, all share four main components:

1. a resealable septum of silicone rubber or other material
2. a metal or plastic housing

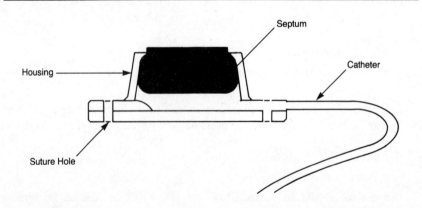

Figure 15-2 Implanted Port

3. a catheter of silicone rubber or other polymer
4. suture holes or method for securing.

When preparing the site for insertion, many people use alcohol or alcohol/acetone to de-fat the skin; however, BAVAN has eliminated this step from its recommended implanted port procedure. Site preparation is an area where further studies need to be conducted. Regardless, the next step is application of povidone-iodine, left on the skin no less than two minutes. Venous access is achieved by aseptically inserting, with or without the use of gloves, a noncoring/Huber needle through the silicone rubber septum into the fluid path.[4] Any other needle may damage the septum, requiring removal of the port. Straight needles are used for bolus injection or blood sampling and then removed. Ninety degree bent needles, for continuous infusions, are left in place and secured well. The use of a short extension tube with a clamp or a needle with tubing already attached is recommended.

As the need for venous access increases, the port requires either an increased number of needle punctures or permanent placement of the bent needle. Both increase patient discomfort and the potential for infection, which providers should take into consideration when selecting this device.

SELECTION, INSERTION, AND MAINTENANCE OF A DEVICE

Selection

Improvements and variations in all VADs continue. (See Table 15-1.) Many are available with double, triple, and quadruple lumens, which increases the risk of complications; providers should carefully consider the necessity of selecting these devices. Assisting the patient to select a device requires thoughtful planning, especially considering the progressive dementia that often accompanies HIV disease. The single-lumen (tunneled) catheter appears to be most frequently selected for home care.

Nurse As Advocate

Patients tolerate insertion of a VAD best when they are stronger, so they should be encouraged to think about a VAD early in treatment. As the need for therapy becomes imminent, the patient and significant others should be reminded of the benefits and risks and, as feasible, included as active participants in a discussion of the following issues:

- physical status of patient

  —visual acuity (CMV retinitis creates degrees of blindness)
  —manual dexterity
  —level of fatigue and weakness

- psychological status of patient and support persons
- frequency of access and duration of therapy
- intellectual ability of patient or caregiver
- home environment and family support
- assistance required and available

Insertion

All VADs are placed in patients under local or general anesthesia. Improvements in insertion techniques have simplified procedures and decreased trauma. When possible, the surgeon, nurse, and patient need to discuss the procedure and patient preference for location of exit site or port pocket.

Successful catheter function depends on proper placement. Catheter tip position must be confirmed by x-ray prior to any use; the most common position is in the

Table 15-1 Catheter Size

		Approximate Equivalencies	
French Size	O.D.*	Gauge	Catheter
10.0	3.30 mm	10	Hickman
8.0	2.70 mm	12–13	Groshong
7.0	2.20 mm	13–14	Groshong
6.5	2.15 mm	15	Broviac
5.5	1.80 mm	16	Groshong
5.0	1.70 mm	16	Intrasil/Centrasil/VIA-PIC
4.8	1.50 mm	16	Per-Q-Cath
3.5	1.10 mm	19–20	Pediatric Broviac/Groshong/VIA-PIC
2.8	0.75 mm	20	Per-Q-Cath
1.9	0.50	23	Per-Q-Cath

*Outer Diameter

superior vena cava. A catheter tip in the right atrium may put the patient at greater risk for arrhythmias or heart perforation.[5] During this early post-insertion period, care varies widely. Some prefer that a port not be used until the skin pocket incision has healed and any swelling or redness has been resolved, about five days after insertion. When using a tunneled catheter, providers should take care not to pull the catheter out until the cuff has a chance to adhere to subcutaneous tissue, which usually takes seven to ten days.

Maintenance

Maintenance begins when insertion and exit sites have healed well, usually 10 to 14 days after insertion. All sites must be assessed at least once a day as infections can progress rapidly. Sites are usually cared for with alcohol followed by povidone-iodine, and swabsticks rather than swabs are recommended to decrease contamination. Prefilled syringes are available for heparin and saline flushes and are especially convenient for use in the home. Maintenance procedures are similar for all VADs, but nontunneled catheters and ports are cared for according to sterile technique, while clean technique suffices for tunneled catheters. The lack of standardization in maintenance procedures is demonstrated in the table of common procedures found in Appendix 15-B.

Procedure Example for Tunneled Catheters

After exit site is healed:

- Use clean technique.
- Wash hands.
- Remove old dressing.
- Examine skin around catheter.
- Report any pain, swelling, redness, or drainage.
- Wash hands.
- Clean skin area around catheter exit site with alcohol swabs, using circular motion from insertion site outward.
- Repeat previous step using povidone-iodine.
- Allow povidone-iodine to remain on the skin for two minutes.
- Remove excess povidone-iodine with sterile 2 × 2 swabs.
- Apply dressing of choice.

Note: If povidone-iodine ointment is used, the dressing should not be left on longer than 48 to 72 hours.

Dressings

Occlusive dressings may be unsuitable for tunneled catheters, since a large percentage of patients experience sweats. A large flesh-colored Bandaid (Johnson & Johnson^R), changed daily to keep the exit site dry, works well. Some patients wear no dressing.

Nontunneled catheters are generally felt to require *sterile* dressing changes, but there is controversy over the issue. Occlusive dressings are changed once a week or when necessary; other dressings are changed three times a week.

Ports need dressings only when a needle is in place. The Cormed Port-Gard^R stabilizes the needle very well while providing a window to monitor the needle insertion site.

Blood Sampling

The following procedure simplifies blood sampling procedures, minimizes the risk of coming into contact with blood, and works with all VADs with an injection cap at the distal end.

- Wear gloves.
- Use vacutainer needle and holder to enter injection cap.
- Insert first tube into vacutainer, fill, then discard.
- Insert and fill as many tubes as necessary for sampling.
- Remove needle and vacutainer.
- Flush with 20 ml of saline.
- Heparinize as usual.

COMPLICATION TROUBLESHOOTING

Providers should make every effort to prevent complications that would require removal of the VAD. A troubleshooting guide to managing common complications is found in Appendix 15-C.

Thrombophlebitis

Thrombophlebitis is clot formation with inflammation of the intima, a complication reported in the early use of nonsilicone central venous catheters. Silicone rubber catheters have decreased the incidence, which is now at 4 percent.[6] Repeated inability to draw blood may be a harbinger of this problem.

Infection and Sepsis

Armstrong reports that heavy colonization of Candida puts patients with HIV at higher risk for IV catheter–associated fungemia.[7] Thus far, this has not been the case in the author's practice. Catheter-related sepsis may be confirmed only by culturing the catheter tip, which requires removal of the catheter. The most common organisms associated with catheters are the nosocomial pathogens that usually originate from the caregiver or the patient's own bacterial flora. As more patients are treated at home, the incidence of nosocomial infections has declined. Reported incidence of central line infections in other patient populations ranges from 2 percent[8] to 27 percent[9]. Taking temperatures daily is critical, as is meticulous daily site care.

Rare Complications

Other possible complications occur rarely. Backflow or hemorrhage usually results from disconnection or misconnection of Luer fittings. To prevent this problem, *all fittings* should be Luer-lok and all tubing connections must be taped.

Air embolism is caused when there are openings in the system (i.e., Luer-lok misconnections or disconnections) and cyclical negative pressure in the thoracic cavity during respirations facilitates the entry of air into the venous system. When opening any connection (i.e., changing a cap), providers should use a plastic clamp (not necessary with Groshong) and have the patient lie down and hold his or her breath. Symptoms of air embolism include:

- cyanosis
- chest pain
- decreased BP
- increased venous pressure
- weak rapid pulse
- loss of consciousness.

To treat patients, providers should place them on the left side in Trendelenburg's position, administer oxygen, and notify the physician.

Damage to the catheter can be prevented by using clamps made of plastic rather than metal and by using the kits and instructions provided by the manufacturer for

VAD repair. The Groshong is easily repaired by aseptically cutting the catheter and inserting the blunt needle adapter. External catheters may be repaired in emergencies with a short plastic peripheral cannula until permanent repair is achievable. If the catheter is damaged inside the patient, the device must be removed.

Extravasation may be caused by:

- a displaced Huber needle
- disconnection of the catheter from an implanted port
- a damaged catheter in tunneled area
- extensive clot formation along the catheter.

Before infusing extravasating drugs, the provider should check for blood return and flush with 20–50 ml of normal saline to assure position of the catheter. If any question arises, the provider should arrange for an x-ray and venogram.

HOME INFUSION OF AMPHOTERICIN B AND DHPG

Amphotericin B and DHPG therapies require frequent infusions for an indefinite period of time. (See also discussion in Chapter 14.) Since both of these medications are known to cause phlebitis, they should be administered through a VAD, and the therapy should be initiated in the hospital prior to home use.

Amphotericin B

The dosage of amphotericin B is 0.25 to 1.5 mg/kg/day, given two to five times per week, depending on kidney function and patient response. Patient safety and comfort are paramount. If a patient reacts to amphotericin, the provider may take several measures to decrease the complications or side effects. The drug should be given in the late afternoon to early evening so that sedative drugs will not interfere with patients' daytime activity. The patient is often medicated 30 minutes prior to the infusion with some or all of the following:

- Tylenol tablets, ii PO
- Benadryl, 25–50 mg IV
- Demerol, 25–50 mg IV.

Amphotericin should be infused in 250 or 500 ml D5W via a pump, controller, or dial-a-flow over two to six hours (a shorter or longer infusion may decrease side effects). An in-line filter should not be used. Usually about one hour into the infusion, chills with or without fever begin; premedications (except Tylenol) should be repeated, and the patient covered with blankets. If side effects continue, the provider should reevaluate the dose and the need for therapy. Demerol, Benadryl, and hydrocortisone added directly to the infusion have decreased side effects for some patients.

As the patient and caregiver become more familiar with administering the medications, reactions can be anticipated and premedications given before the side effects occur. Patients should be monitored weekly for weight, renal function, CBC, and blood chemistries.

Concentrated amphotericin is stable in a 5-mg/ml syringe or vial for seven days, but when diluted in 250–500 ml D5W it is stable only for 24 hours. Amphotericin is compatible with heparin, but not with potassium salt or saline.

DHPG (Gancyclovir)

Unlike amphotericin, DHPG is tolerated very well. The most common adverse reaction reported is neutropenia. Other side effects include pruritic rash and thrombocytopenia.

The dose is dependent on renal function and patient response. Initial induction begins with a dosage in the range of 2.5–7.5 mg/kg/q8–24h for 10 or 11 days.

Maintenance is on an outpatient basis with a usual dose of 5 mg/kg/day. DHPG is infused via gravity with Dial-a-flow over one hour. Patients need to be monitored twice a week for weight, renal function, blood chemistries, and CBC (if neutrophil count is 800 or below, DHPG should not be given).

When diluted in 100 ml normal saline, DHPG is stable for 48 hours. It is compatible with heparin. DHPG should not be refrigerated.

NEW TECHNOLOGY

Two additional developments are of interest:

- New catheter materials are being developed from complex polymers that are more biocompatible and less thrombogenic than silicone.
- Ports with side entries are being introduced. These may eliminate the problem of keeping bent needles in place.

NOTES

1. J.W. Broviac et al., ''A Silicone Rubber Atrial Catheter for Prolonged Parenteral Alimentation,'' *Surg. Gynecol. Obstet.* 136 (1973):602.

2. Robert O. Hickman et al., "A Modified Right Atrial Catheter for Access to the Venous System in Marrow Transplant Recipients," *Surg. Gynecol. Obstet.* 148 (1979):871–75.

3. Milly Lawson et al., "The Infusion Therapy Team" (Houston, Texas: M. D. Anderson Hospital and Tumor Institute, 1985).

4. Lisa Schulmeister, "A Comparison of Skin Preparation Procedures for Accessing Implanted Ports," *NITA* 10 (Jan./Feb. 1987):45–47.

5. B.S. Ducatman et al., "Catheter-Induced Lesions of the Right Side of the Heart," *Journal of the American Medical Association* 253, no. 6 (February 8, 1985):791–95.

6. A.H. McLean Ross et al., "Thromboembolic Complications with Silicone Elastomer Subclavian Catheters," *Journal of Parenteral and Enteral Nutrition* 6 (1982):61–63.

7. Donald Armstrong et al., "Treatment of Infections in Patients with the Acquired Immunodeficiency Syndrome," *Annals of Internal Medicine* 103 (1985):738–43.

8. M. Lawson et al., "The Use of Urokinase to Restore the Patency of Occluded Central Venous Catheters," *American Journal of Intravenous Therapy and Clinical Nutrition*, Abstract, 1982.

9. W.W. Clenedenen and M.E. Ryan, "Infection in the Pediatric Intensive Care Unit: How to Minimize Risk," *Postgraduate Medicine* 77 (1985):1399–1408.

Appendix 15-A

Bay Area Vascular Access Network (BAVAN)

BAVAN was established to ensure collaboration in education, standardization, and research in order to benefit patients and caregivers using VADs.

BAVAN has the following objectives:

1. assess current VAD utilization
2. develop a core Bay Area group with VAD expertise and establish its credibility
3. develop policies and procedures for standardization
4. participate in VAD research and product evaluations
5. disseminate information related to state-of-the-art VAD utilization (news releases, newsletters, workshops, etc.).

BAVAN now has over 100 members representing all major hospitals, home care agencies, home IV services, and device manufacturing representatives in the Bay Area. The network is beginning studies on VADs and persons with HIV.

For further information write:

BAVAN
P.O. Box 1394
Pleasanton, CA 94566

Appendix 15-B

Maintenance Summary of Vascular Access Devices*

Classification	Maintenance		
Tunneled Catheters	Most Popular ⟶		Least Popular
Hickman/Broviac			
Heparin strength used	100 u/ml	10 u/ml	1,000 u/ml
Amount of heparin flush	3 ml or >	2.5 ml	< 2.5 ml
Frequency of irrigation	QD	BID	QOD
Frequency of cap change	weekly		as needed
Dressing	occlusive	gauze/tape	none
Frequency of dressing change	weekly	QOD	daily
Clamping when not in use	never		always
Groshong			
No heparin flush required			
Normal saline flush	5 ml		
Frequency of irrigation	weekly and after each use		
Frequency of cap change	weekly		as needed
Dressing	occlusive	gauze/tape	none
Frequency of dressing change[a]	weekly	QOD	daily
Clamping when not in use	never		
Implanted Ports			
Heparin strength used	100 u/ml	1,000 u/ml	10 u/ml
Amount of heparin flush	5 ml	< 5 ml	> 5 ml

*Sources: NITA, Vol. 7, pp. 287–289, J. B. Lippincott Company, © July/August 1984; BAVAN, Nursing surveys conducted at Oncology Nursing Society, 1987 Congress and Vascular Access Device Workshop.

Frequency of irrigation when not in use	after each use monthly	> 1 month	weekly
No dressing necessary when not in use			
Noncoring needle insertion	with sterile gloves		no gloves
Frequency of needle change (continuous infusion)	weekly 5 days	< 1 week	> 1 week up to 30 days

Nontunneled Catheters

Heparin strength used	100 u/ml		
Amount of heparin flush	1 ml	2 ml	> 2.5 ml
Frequency of irrigation	QD	BID	QOD
Frequency of cap change	weekly		as needed
Dressing	occlusive	gauze/tape	
Frequency of dressing change[a]	weekly	QOD	daily

[a]Depends on dressing used.

Appendix 15-C

Complication Management and Troubleshooting

Complication or Problem	Troubleshooting	Possible Cause
Unable to withdraw blood, able to infuse "one-way valve" (most common problem reported)	Change patient position, have patient take deep breath, cough, stand up, walk around.	Migration of catheter into smaller vessel catheter tip against vessel wall
	Check position of Huber needle.	Huber needle not fully advanced through septum
	Flush gently with 10–20 ml NS to assure catheter function.	Fractured catheter between clavicle and first rib
		Damaged catheter in subcutaneous tunnel
	If unsure, consider chest x-ray. Venogram catheter may need to be repositioned under fluoroscopy.	
	Flush in push/pull manner with 10–20 ml NS to dislodge fibrin sleeve or intralumen clot.	Temporary fibrin sleeve or intralumen clot
	Use fibrinolytic agent (urokinase 5000 u)* in a volume slightly greater than that of catheter. Follow instructions carefully.	
	Chest x-ray/venogram.	Thrombophlebitis with clot formation along catheter

Signs/Symptoms	Intervention	Possible Cause
Unable to infuse or withdraw	Consider continuous infusion of fibrinolytic agent.	Extensive thrombosis
	Remove catheter or device.	
	Check position of Huber needle.	Huber needle not fully advanced through septum
	Use fibrinolytic agent (as above). Use push/pull motion.	Intralumen clot
		Drug precipitation (i.e., heparin and noncompatible drug)
		Catheter kinked or in knot
	Take chest x-ray/venogram.	
	Remove catheter/device.	
Arm edema, swelling of neck		Extensive thrombosis
Enlarged superficial veins of chest		Superior vena cava syndrome
INFECTION		
Local		
Tunnel ⎫ tenderness	Reevaluate site care.	Poor technique used for site care
Port site ⎬ erythema		Patient may be sensitive to Betadine
Suture site ⎭ site induration slight drainage		
	If drainage present—take culture.	
	Ensure daily meticulous site care.	
	Use no occlusive dressings until infection resolves.	
	Use topical antibiotics as indicated.	
	Remove port needle.	Needle in too long or not secured well
	Do not use port until symptoms resolve.	

continues

Complication or Problem	Troubleshooting	Possible Cause
	If sutures involved—remove. Secure catheter end—resuture when symptoms resolve.	
	If symptoms do not resolve, device may have to be removed.	
Systemic		
Fever, chills, gastric symptoms	D/C infusion/change infusate.	Contaminated infusate—gram negative
Headache	Take blood culture—from catheter	Contaminated hub—gram positive
Hyperventilation	—from peripheral vein	(*S. aureus, S. epidermidis*)
Shock		Non-catheter-related sepsis
	Initiate course of IV antibiotics through device.	
	Perform overwire exchange of catheter if possible.	
	If infection recurs, device may need to be removed.	

*M. Lawson et al. reports 98 percent success in clearing over 1,600 catheters with the use of urokinase.

Chapter 16

Nutritional Support

Joan Taber Pike

NUTRITION AND IMMUNITY

There is a strong correlation between malnutrition and immunosuppression. Malnutrition most profoundly influences cell-mediated immune response.[1] In addition, the ability to withstand the consequences of infection is decreased greatly by protein-calorie malnutrition (PCM) and deficiencies in vitamins A, B complex, C, iron, iron-binding proteins, and zinc.[2] Similarities exist in the prevalence, severity, and patterns of infections in individuals who are malnourished and in those with immunodeficiency disorders.[3] *Pneumocystis carinii* has been found in patients with conditions other than AIDS, including the malnourished and those with an underlying disease that compromises their immune status. Also, *Pneumocystis carinii* infection was easily introduced to rats on a protein-deprived diet.[4]

Similar symptoms are found in HIV and graft-versus-host (GVH) disease.[5] GVH disease occurs in bone marrow transplant patients and results in problems of the skin, liver, and gastrointestinal (GI) tract. *Pneumocystis carinii* and CMV have been found in patients with GVH disease. Patients with either HIV infection or GVH disease may develop diarrhea and malabsorption, tissue wasting, fever, skin rash, and abnormal liver function, and patients with both conditions can develop pneumonia caused by similar infectious organisms. Malabsorption, in both conditions, compromises nutritional status, leading to depression of immune function.

Cell-mediated immunity and T-cell–dependent antibody responses are impaired by deficiencies of folic acid, pyridoxine, and vitamin A. An extreme deficiency of vitamin C may also compromise cell-mediated immunity.[6] Selenium levels were significantly reduced in a group of HIV patients.[7] Selenium deficiency has resulted in increased risk of oral candidiasis in animals, and a relative lack of selenium may increase the risk of KS in man and impair helper T-cell numbers, which improve during selenium repletion. There was a correlation between low plasma selenium levels and decreased serum albumin in HIV patients.[8]

Low and borderline zinc concentrations were found in a group of HIV patients with chronic diarrhea.[9] Since zinc plays a major role in various immune functions, and is specifically linked to T-lymphocyte function, chronic diarrhea in immunosuppressed patients may further impair immune function by inducing zinc deficiency.

An intake of 15 mg of zinc per day has been recommended for adults. If serum zinc levels are low, supplemental zinc may be helpful, but daily intake of large amounts for a long period can be harmful and can impair lymphocyte and polymorphonuclear leukocyte functions. When taken in amounts exceeding two grams, zinc produces vomiting, abdominal cramps, and diarrhea.[10]

Cholesterol and high density lipoproteins are important for lymphocyte function, but excessive amounts may suppress the immune system.[11]

NUTRITIONAL STATUS OF HIV PATIENTS

Infectious illnesses have a profound effect on nutritional status. Metabolic changes lead to nutritional deficiencies, and infection and malnutrition can develop into a vicious cycle, with each new infection leading to more severe nutritional deficits.[12] The muscle catabolism noted in AIDS patients may be a result of impairment in carbohydrate, protein, and fat metabolism; infections that increase metabolism; and the inability to meet those energy and protein needs.[13]

Two studies of body composition and nutritional status in HIV patients found a moderate to severe depletion of skeletal muscle mass[14] and body cell mass, as measured by total body potassium.[15] Tissue depletion was similar to that of a person in a stressed or injured condition rather than one suffering from simple starvation.[16] Increased extracellular water resulted in a less apparent reduction in body weight, body cell mass was significantly lower in patients with diarrhea than in those without diarrhea, and fat stores were not severely depleted in either study. Protein degradation for energy increased in relation to fat degradation.

A combination of both kwashiorkor (protein malnutrition) and marasmus (PCM) has been seen in AIDS patients. Normal body weight and nearly normal creatinine-height index, as in kwashiorkor, and depletion in midarm circumference and midarm muscle area, as in marasmus, occurred concurrently. Albumin and transferrin levels were depressed, suggesting reduction of visceral protein stores.[17] This depression may be due to an underlying disease, decreased protein intake, or a combination of these two factors. Anemia is also common, as reflected by low hemoglobin levels.[18]

Replenishing body cell mass is difficult even when the patient is clinically stable. One study found severe progressive malnutrition in adult AIDS patients.[19]

Patients in early stages of the disease, before diagnosis, have been found to increase total body potassium as a result of therapy.[20] It has also been suggested that malnutrition affects the course of the disease.[21] The degree of tissue wasting correlates with the time of death.

COMPLICATIONS THAT AFFECT NUTRITIONAL STATUS

Poor nutrient intake among HIV-infected individuals may be caused by:

- anorexia
- nausea
- vomiting
- fever
- shortness of breath
- oral and esophageal thrush
- oral KS lesions.

The disease process, medications, and infections contribute to anorexia and GI problems. Decreased nutrient absorption may result from diarrhea, GI infections, decreased enzyme secretions, and disruption of intestinal absorptive area.[22]

Anorexia, Nausea, and Vomiting

Nausea and vomiting may be caused by some medications and treatments as well as infection. KS lesions in the oropharyngeal and oral-esophageal areas may cause vomiting, which is aggravated by gastritis or esophagitis.[23] Medications, including antibiotics, antiviral and immune modulators, and chemotherapy, may contribute to anorexia, nausea, and vomiting.[24] Taste changes may occur with the use of antiviral and immune modulators.[25] Mycelex, used in the treatment of candidiasis, leaves a chalky or sawdust flavor in the mouth, affecting appetite.

Health care professionals may suggest the following to patients suffering from nausea and vomiting:[26]

1. Eat small, frequent meals, and avoid greasy foods if fat is a problem.
2. Avoid overly sweet foods, especially if vomiting is a problem. Salty foods may be better tolerated.
3. Eat dry foods, such as toast or crackers.
4. Try rice, soft-boiled or poached eggs, apple juice, apricot and pear nectars, custards, and other soft bland foods that may be easier to tolerate.

5. During specific times you know that nausea or vomiting may occur, avoid favorite foods so that you do not get "turned off" by them.
6. Sip cool, clear liquids slowly through a straw to avoid gulping air. Any liquids you can tolerate are recommended, such as clear soups, flavored gelatin, carbonated beverages, and Popsicles®.
7. Drink liquids 30 to 60 minutes before eating, and not with meals.
8. Try cold foods, which have less odor and may be better tolerated than hot foods; entrée suggestions include cottage cheese and fruit, meat salad sandwiches, and yogurt.
9. Rest after eating, with your upper body elevated. Don't lie flat.
10. Eat more at your favorite meal of the day.
11. Take antinausea medicine one-half to one hour before eating, according to directions.

Fever

In one study, HIV patients with diarrhea were found to spike fevers to about 39°C.[27] Fever increases energy needs, since the basal metabolic rate increases 11 to 13 percent for each degree centigrade the temperature is elevated.[28] In addition, protein needs increase approximately 10 percent for each one-degree-centigrade elevation.[29] Anorexia may decrease oral intake at a time when metabolism is increased and the need for calories and protein is great. Since anorexia and fever encourage more weight loss and muscle wasting, and since little body fat may be available, the nutritional cost of fever further increases. If energy intake is inadequate, amino acids are diverted to meet energy needs rather than to create new proteins.

Dyspnea

Shortness of breath results in a low energy level, which may lead to insufficient food intake. Eating may be more difficult because an oxygen mask interferes with intake.

The following suggestions may help patients with dyspnea improve their intake of food:[30]

1. Eat small, frequent meals throughout the day.
2. Eat high-calorie, high-protein snacks, such as milkshakes, ice cream, sandwiches, fortified milk and juices, and palatable commercial enteral supplements.

3. Concentrate on nutrient-dense foods and drinks, and avoid filling up on low- or no-calorie foods.
4. Prepare meals ahead of time that can be divided into individual servings and frozen until ready for use.
5. Keep easy-to-prepare foods on hand (frozen dinners, canned foods, and eggs).
6. Eat by the clock, having a small meal or snack every one or two hours.
7. Enjoy your favorite foods in pleasant surroundings with friends or family.

Candidiasis

Common mucosal lesions in immunosuppressed patients include candidiasis, herpes simplex, hairy leukoplakia, and KS lesions of the oral cavity. Untreated oral Candida may descend into the esophagus, causing plaque lesions, resulting in significant pain and dysphagia, and contributing to weight loss. Candida may also affect the gut, causing infections that may contribute to malabsorption, leading to malnutrition and further immunosuppression.[31]

The following ideas may help patients with thrush to increase their tolerance to food:

1. Try soft, nonirritating foods, such as eggs, cream soups, ice cream, puddings, ground meats, baked fish, soft cheeses, cooked fruits, and noodle dishes.
2. Avoid spicy and acidic foods, such as citrus fruits and juices.
3. Try cold and room temperature foods; avoid very hot foods.

Diarrhea and Malabsorption

Diarrhea occurred in 55 percent of HIV patients in one study.[32] Diarrhea and malabsorption were found more often in patients with GI infections (90 percent) than in those without infections (25 percent).

Diarrhea and weight loss occurred at the onset of complications of HIV infections in some patients and later in the course of the disease in other patients; some patients had no symptoms at all.[33] Diarrhea may cause significant losses of fluid, electrolytes, and minerals and contribute to fever and malaise, thus exacerbating an already compromised nutritional status. Carbohydrate and fat malabsorption are frequently seen in HIV patients and are confirmed by fecal fat and D-xylose absorption tests.[34]

Cryptosporidium, CMV, MAI, *Giardia lamblia*, and widespread intestinal involvement with KS may cause diarrhea and malabsorption.[35] Medications and some foods may promote diarrhea. In one study 75 percent of HIV patients had diarrhea, malabsorption, and mucosal abnormalities without detectable bacterial or parasitic origin,[36] a condition known as AIDS enteropathy.[37] Hypoalbuminemia may cause diarrhea in HIV patients in whom no viral, bacterial, or parasitic infections have been identified[38] and result in edema of the intestinal mucosa that impairs intestinal absorption.[39] Critically ill patients with no explanation for their diarrhea have been studied. While all of the patients with serum albumin below 2.6 gm/dl developed diarrhea, none who maintained a serum albumin level greater than 2.6 gm/dl developed diarrhea.[40] The diarrhea resolved and serum albumin increased during institution of a peptide-based enteral formula.

Chronic or recurrent diarrhea with malabsorption greatly affects nutrition status. *Cryptosporidium* infections may cause secretory diarrhea. Currently, there is no effective treatment for this protozoa infection. Nutritional complications include significant weight loss and loss of nitrogen, electrolytes, fluid, trace minerals, and fat- and water-soluble vitamins. With extensive gut impairment, effective nutrition treatment requires proper hydration and may involve total parenteral nutrition (TPN).

Most HIV patients have a functioning GI system and can tolerate oral feedings. Diet and medications may require adjustment when diarrhea is a problem. Health care professionals may instruct patients with diarrhea as follows[41]:

1. Tolerance to different sources of lactose varies. Alterations in the gut may cause lack of the enzyme that breaks down lactose in dairy products for digestion. Lactaid®, a commercially manufactured enzyme that can be added to milk to break down lactose, may help you tolerate milk better. If lactose intolerance is a problem, you may need to decrease consumption of or avoid dairy products. However, you may be able to tolerate yogurt and cheeses in small amounts.
2. Increase your intake of liquids such as water, broth, fruit juices, Jello®, Popsicles®, etc., to replace fluids and electrolytes.
3. Take a trace mineral supplement to replace minerals that have been lost. A multimineral supplement is suggested of less than or equal to 100 percent of the Recommended Dietary Allowances (RDA) published by the Food and Nutritional Board of the National Academy of Sciences—National Research Council.
4. Eat high-potassium foods, such as bananas, apricot or peach nectar, meat, and potatoes, to replace potassium lost with diarrhea.
5. Eat small, frequent meals.
6. If you have discomfort after eating fatty foods, try eating some foods lower in fat such as lean meat, starches, sherbet, and Jello®.
7. Foods at room temperature may be better tolerated.

8. If you have cramps, avoid foods that produce gas or cramps, such as cabbage, broccoli, cauliflower, spicy foods, carbonated drinks, beer, beans, excess sweets, and chewing gum.
9. Avoid caffeine-containing foods and beverages, such as coffee, chocolate, and some carbonated beverages.
10. Oatmeal, dried beans, apples, pears, potatoes, and other foods from the fruit-vegetable and cereal-grain groups are good sources of certain types of fiber (pectin and gums) that may help to alleviate diarrhea.[42] Limit bran-types of fiber, seeds, and tough skins on grains.

NUTRITIONAL ASSESSMENT

Nutritional care of hospitalized HIV patients should include the following:

1. Nutritional assessment early in patient contact to detect patients at nutritional risk. Criteria used to identify high-risk patients include weight loss greater that 10 percent within the past six months, low serum albumin or transferrin, and inability to eat enough to meet energy needs.
2. Nutrition education and support to encourage improved food intake in the early stages of the disease. Maintenance of weight and body cell mass enhances resistance to infections and to side effects of therapy. If nutritional problems are not evident, a nutrient-dense, balanced diet with high-calorie, high-protein commercial food supplements may be encouraged to maintain optimal weight. If intake is inadequate, or if malabsorption or diarrhea is apparent, a daily multivitamin and mineral supplement not to exceed 100 percent of the RDA may be recommended.
3. Recommendation of tube feedings or TPN in patients with extreme complications, such as long-term inadequate intake or severe diarrhea and malabsorption. Tube feedings may be necessary when oral intake is inadequate. TPN may be indicated when severe malabsorption is present.
4. Information about community resources, such as feeding programs and food banks, that are available to support the nutrition care of the patient.
5. Information about alternative nutrition therapies, objectively evaluated for effectiveness and possible harmful effects. Patients can then be equipped to make intelligent choices about their course of treatment.

Anthropometric Measurements

Weight

Height and weight measurements are useful in evaluating the nutrition status of HIV patients. However, immunodeficient patients were found to have a higher percentage of body weight as water than healthy adult controls.[43] This may result in an underestimation of the severity of malnutrition in immunosuppressed patients. Usual body weight (UBW), or pre-illness weight, is a more meaningful standard of weight status than ideal body weight (IBW) for HIV patients. As previously noted, a recent 10 percent weight loss is an indicator of compromised nutritional status.

A study of weight status in hospitalized HIV patients revealed that 62 percent lost more than 10 percent of their UBW.[44] During hospitalization, the patients lost an average of 16 percent following admission. Figure 16-1 compares three different standards for evaluating weight status. In the study, weight status varied according to the standard used. Blackburn's standards (Metropolitan Life Insurance Company, 1959) use IBW and show that 59 percent of HIV patients were depleted.[45] The National Health and Nutrition Examination Survey (NHANES) standards considers patients below the 15th percentile of reasonable body weight

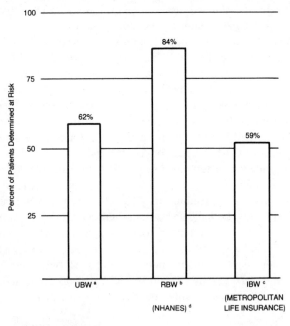

a. Usual body weight
b. Reasonable body weight
c. Ideal body weight
d. National Health and Nutrition Examination Surveys

Figure 16-1 Results of Comparing Three Standards for Weight Status (n = 50). *Source:* P. O'Sullivan et al.: "Evaluation of Body Weight and Nutritional Status among AIDS Patients." Copyright The American Dietetic Association. Reprinted by permission from *Journal of the American Dietetic Association*, Vol. 85:1483, 1985.

to be at nutritional risk; 84 percent of patients studied fell below this benchmark. According to the UBW standard, 62 percent of patients lost at least 10 percent of UBW and were therefore considered to be at nutritional risk. All three methods indicated weight loss in HIV patients during hospitalization. Another study showed significant weight loss among HIV patients who averaged 80 percent of IBW, versus 101 percent for controls.[46]

In some patients, weight loss may precede the development of the end-stage complications of HIV infection. A study of hospitalized HIV patients discovered no significant weight loss throughout admission. However, approximately half of them lost weight prior to admission.[47] In this study, every patient who lost weight also developed PCP and gained weight after treatment. It is unclear whether the patients lost weight prior to the PCP infection or whether it occurred as a result of the infection.

Body Composition

In skinfold measurement, which indirectly estimates body fat or calorie stores, skinfold calipers are used to measure a double layer of skin and subcutaneous fat over the tricep muscle, because the triceps area usually shows little edema, even in PCM.[48] Skinfold measurements should be interpreted cautiously since measurement accuracy is questionable.[49]

Midarm circumference and creatinine excretion may be used as a measure of the muscle component of the fat-free body mass. Midarm muscle circumference correlates with serum albumin, percentage of weight lost, plasma prealbumin, and hemoglobin.[50]

The decreased midarm muscle circumference and midarm muscle area seen in AIDS patients may indicate decreased muscle or somatic protein stores.[51] Urinary creatinine excretion slightly below normal levels reflected depleted muscle protein stores. Triceps skinfold measurements indicated that fat stores were not depleted. In another study, immunodeficient men had a relatively greater depletion of body potassium than of fat, and body fat exceeded 100 percent of normal values.[52] This type of wasting is typical of stressed conditions, such as sepsis, trauma, or surgery, in which "protein degradation for energy increases in relation to fat catabolism."[53]

Laboratory Measurements

Visceral or transport protein stores may be measured by serum albumin and transferrin. Transferrin is a more sensitive indicator of PCM than albumin because of its shorter half-life.[54] Serum retinol-binding protein (RBP) is a sensitive indicator of developing protein deficiency. Total iron-binding capacity (TIBC) measures the amount of iron that can be carried in the blood by transferrin.[55] Significantly lower values of RBP and TIBC were found in immunodeficient patients (Table 16-1), indicating decreased synthesis, rapid breakdown of these proteins, or both. Decreased levels of albumin and transferrin were found in immunodeficient patients, reflecting the decreased protein intake, the underlying disease, and/or an increase in extracellular water volume.[56] Albumin levels were lower in patients with diarrhea than in controls without diarrhea.[57]

Since amino acids are nitrogen-based, amino acid or protein utilization is determined by nitrogen retention as measured in nitrogen balance. Nitrogen balance uses the difference between nitrogen intake and output to measure protein anabolism. The urinary urea nitrogen (UUN) indicates nitrogen output, and negative nitrogen balance occurs when nitrogen excretion exceeds intake. Patients in the later stages of AIDS often develop negative nitrogen balance as a result of inadequate intake of protein and calories along with increased protein catabolism. Because nitrogen is lost in diarrhea, accurate estimation of nitrogen excretion may be difficult when diarrhea occurs.

Hemoglobin may be an indicator of iron deficiency anemia, along with serum iron values, and is significantly lower in AIDS patients.[58] Low protein intake, as well as chronic infection, may help to explain this anemia.

It is important to monitor laboratory serum and urine values and be aware of various drug-nutrient interactions to tailor a diet appropriately to meet each patient's needs. Treatments such as Septra, pentamidine, and amphotericin B may result in increased BUN and creatinine because of nephrotoxic and hepatotoxic effects.[59] Since the patient's intake may be poor during this time, it may not be necessary to restrict dietary protein. However, hyperkalemia, which often occurs in patients treated with pentamidine, may require restricted potassium intake until renal function is stabilized. Amphotericin B therapy may depress serum potassium and magnesium levels, so these levels should be monitored and appro-

Table 16-1 Serum Studies

	AIDS	Homosexual Control	Lab Control
RBP[a]	4.3 + 2.1	7.2 ± 2.1	5.5 + 1.3
TIBC[b]	243 + 67	————	250–350
Albumin	3.2 + 0.6	————	3.5–5.2

[a]Retinol-binding protein.
[b]Total iron-binding capacity.

Source: Adapted from American Journal of Clinical Nutrition, Vol. 42, p. 1262, with permission of The American Society for Clinical Nutrition, Inc., © 1985.

priate therapy for hypokalemia and hypomagnesemia instituted.[60] Fluid status should be monitored continuously and may require restriction, as in patients with PCP who are receiving pentamidine, due to the nephrotoxic effects.[61] A temporary fluid restriction may be necessary during the hyponatremia that may accompany the administration of Septra. The hypoglycemia that commonly occurs during pentamidine treatment may require glucose infusion, frequent oral feedings, or continuous enteral feedings.[62]

Neutropenia may result from treatment with Septra and pentamidine due to bone marrow suppression. A low-microbial (neutropenic) diet may help to reduce pseudomonal contamination. Restricted foods include raw fruits, raw vegetables, salads, and unpasteurized milk products. Foods should be thoroughly cooked and should not be left out at room temperature, or below or above holding temperature, for long periods of time. Food not eaten within 30 to 45 minutes should be discarded.

Metabolic Requirements

The metabolic expenditure of immunodeficient patients is not known. Persons infected with HIV may be stressed due to opportunistic infections that result in higher basal energy needs. In many cases, poor appetite may prevent adequate intake. Basal energy expenditure can be estimated from the Harris-Benedict equation:[63]

males: 66 + (13.7 x actual body weight (kg)) + (5 times height (cm)) minus (6.8 times age (yr)) = basal energy expenditure in calories.

females: 655 + (9.6 times actual body weight (kg)) + (1.7 times height (cm)) minus (4.7 times age (yr)) = basal energy expenditure in calories.

Multiplying basal energy expenditure by an activity factor of approximately 1.2 and a stress factor of approximately 1.4 to 1.6 estimates total energy needs and may be used as a goal for nutrition support. The resulting number represents nonprotein calories, as the protein is assumed to be used for protein turnover and repletion. In addition, fever increases caloric requirements by a factor of 1.07 for each degree Fahrenheit over normal, or a 13 percent increase for each degree centigrade elevation over normal.

Protein requirements are usually high, secondary to the stress of the disease, and are estimated at 1.8–2.0 grams per kilogram, or calorie-to-nitrogen ratio of 150 to 1.0 for anabolism. The protein requirement can be determined by the following equation:[64]

Number of calories required ÷ 150 = grams of nitrogen.
This number × 6.25 grams protein per gram of nitrogen = total grams of protein.

During the early stages of the disease, when appetite is adequate, meeting these needs is easier. Calorie and protein intake deteriorate as the appetite diminishes during disease progression. Protein and calorie intake are often inadequate because of anorexia, taste alterations to protein foods, and nausea related to drug treatments for infection.

Adequate protein intake is especially important. Patients studied who met their caloric needs but had insufficient protein intake met their increased amino acid requirements by increased breakdown of somatic and visceral protein stores.[65] Animal protein has a higher biologic value than do grain and vegetable proteins, although vegetable proteins can be combined to provide a balance of essential amino acids in a vegetarian diet. However, because their appetites are often poor, AIDS patients may have difficulty obtaining adequate protein from a vegetarian diet unless it includes dairy products.

Diarrhea, vomiting, or fever increases losses of water and electrolytes, so fluid and electrolyte needs increase. Fluid status should be monitored and intake adjusted accordingly.

Enteral and Parenteral Nutrition

Many patients have functioning GI systems and tolerate oral feedings but may have difficulty eating enough to meet their increased metabolic needs. If GI function is adequate and the enteral route can be safely used, tube feedings may provide supplemental or total nutrition. Oral intake can be combined with tube feedings. For example, inadequate intake may be supplemented by enteral feedings only at night to encourage intake of foods during the day.

Low-volume diarrhea may be treated with a low-fiber, lactose-free, isotonic formula, along with antidiarrheal medications; pectin may help to decrease diarrhea by solidifying the stool.[66] If steatorrhea is present, as determined by a fecal fat test, a low-fat formula or one that contains medium chain triglycerides may be necessary. Each patient's tolerances and calorie, protein, and fluid needs should determine the appropriate enteral tube feeding formula.

TPN and parenteral hydration may be the only alternative when severe malabsorption with secretory diarrhea occurs, as in GI *Cryptosporidium* infections.[67] In addition, antispasmotic and antidiarrheal agents, along with antibiotics, may help to control the diarrhea.

Central-line TPN may maintain fluid and electrolyte balance, encourage bowel rest, allow the mucosal inflammation to resolve, and provide a short- or long-term alternative nutritional therapy. Problems with central-line TPN include high cost and risk of sepsis. Home parenteral nutrition may be employed, if appropriate. Peripheral parenteral nutrition (PPN) can be employed along with enteral or oral feedings to supplement intake.

A case study of TPN in HIV showed that an AIDS patient with KS, *Cryptosporidium* infection, fever spikes, intractable diarrhea of up to 12 liters/day, and possible malabsorption was able to maintain weight and visceral and somatic protein stores on TPN along with an oral intake of approximately 2,500 calories per day.[68] Though the patient lost weight on the 2,500-calorie oral diet alone, he was able to gain weight on oral intake supplemented with TPN.

ALTERNATIVE TREATMENTS

Individuals suffering from chronic or incurable illnesses may become desperate and turn to alternative nutritional practices without being fully aware of the possible risks involved. Providers should educate individuals with HIV at the time of diagnosis to help them improve their intake of food by selecting appropriate nutritional practices. Some popular diets or alternative nutritional treatments may be ineffective and sometimes harmful. In some cases, pursuit of unproven remedies may keep the HIV patient from obtaining more objectively evaluated and generally accepted therapies.

It is extremely important to evaluate critically studies on nutritional therapies to establish the validity, credibility, and significant effects of various practices. Questions may be directed to registered dietitians who can objectively evaluate the effectiveness and possible harmful effects of various nutrition-related regimens.

The following guidelines may be helpful in evaluating special diets or supplements. They should:

1. not contain substances in amounts that may be physically harmful
2. not completely replace health care that is generally accepted as effective
3. allow for an adequate calorie and protein intake along with a variety of foods
4. not incur unneccessary expense.

NOTES

1. R.K. Chandra, "Immunodeficiency in Undernutrition and Overnutrition," *Nutrition Reviews* 39, No. 6(1981):225–31.

2. M.E. Garcia, C. Collins, and P. Mansell, "The Acquired Immune Deficiency Syndrome: Nutritional Complications and Assessment of Body Weight Status," *Nutrition in Clinical Practice* 2 (1987):108–11.

3. Chandra, "Immunodeficiency in Undernutrition and Overnutrition."

4. W.T. Hughes et al., "Protein-Calorie Malnutrition: A Host Determinant for *Pneumocystis carinii* Infection," *American Journal of Diseases in Children* 128(1974):44–52.

5. G.W. Thorn et al., *Harrison's Principles of Internal Medicine*, 8th rev. ed. (New York: McGraw-Hill Book Co., 1977), p. 1669.

6. R.K. Chandra, "Nutrition, Immunity, and Infection: Present Knowledge and Future Directions," *Lancet* 8326 (March 26, 1983):688–91.

7. B.M. Dworkin et al., "Selenium Deficiency in the Acquired Immunodeficiency Syndrome," *Journal of Parenteral and Enteral Nutrition* 10(1986):405–07.

8. B.M. Dworkin et al., "Gastrointestinal Manifestations of the Acquired Immunodeficiency Syndrome: A Review of 22 Cases," *American Journal of Gastroenterology* 80(1985):774–78.

9. J. Scott Gillin et al., "Malabsorption and Mucosal Abnormalities of the Small Intestine in the Acquired Immunodeficiency Syndrome," *Annals of Internal Medicine* 102(1985):619–22.

10. R.K. Chandra, "Excessive Intake of Zinc Impairs Immune Responses," *Journal of the American Medical Association* 252(1984):1443–46.

11. Chandra, "Nutrition, Immunity, and Infection."

12. H.A. Schneider, C.E. Anderson, and D.B. Coursin, *Nutritional Support of Medical Practice*, 2d ed. (Philadelphia: Harper and Row, 1983), p. 443.

13. M.H. Malone, "Assessment of Nutritional Status in Patients with Acquired Immunodeficiency Syndrome (AIDS)" (Bethesda, Md.: National Institutes of Health).

14. Ibid.

15. D.P. Kotler, J. Wang, and R.N. Pierson, "Body Composition Studies in Patients with the Acquired Immunodeficiency Syndrome," *American Journal of Clinical Nutrition* 42(1985):1255–65.

16. Ibid.

17. Malone, "Assessment of Nutritional Status."

18. D.P. Kotler et al., "Enteropathy Associated with the Acquired Immunodeficiency Syndrome," *Annals of Internal Medicine* 101(1984):421–28.

19. Ibid.

20. Kotler, Wang, and Pierson, "Body Composition Studies."

21. Ibid.; and D.P. Kotler, "Why Study Nutrition in AIDS?" *Nutrition in Clinical Practice* 2 (American Society for Parenteral and Enteral Nutrition, 1987) pp. 94–95.

22. Candy Collins, "AIDS: Nutrition Interfaces," *Hospital Food and Nutrition Focus* 3, no. 12 (1987):1–7.

23. Garcia, Collins, and Mansell, "The Acquired Immune Deficiency Syndrome: Nutritional Complications."

24. American Hospital Formulary Services, *Drug Information '85* (American Society of Hospital Pharmacists, 1985), pp. 58–61, 70–71, 372–76; and Collins, "AIDS: Nutrition Interfaces."

25. Ibid.

26. U.S. Department of Health and Human Services (HHS), *Eating Hints: Recipes and Tips for Better Nutrition During Cancer Treatment* (Bethesda, Md.:National Cancer Institute, 1984), pp. 8–9.

27. Kotler et al., "Enteropathy."

28. Schneider, Anderson, and Coursin, *Nutritional Support of Medical Practice*, p. 444.

29. Catherine Belford Budd, "Nutritional Care of Patients with *Pneumocystis carinii* Pneumonia," *Nutritional Support Services* 2, no. 12 (1982):12–13.

30. HHS, *Eating Hints*, p. 5.

31. Jonathan Weber, "Gastrointestinal Disease in AIDS," *Clinics in Immunology and Allergy* 6, no. 3 (October 1986):519–41.

32. Dworkin et al., "Gastrointestinal Manifestations."

33. William C. Santangelo and Guenter J. Krejs, "Southwestern Internal Medicine Conference: Gastrointestinal Manifestations of the Acquired Immunodeficiency Syndrome," *American Journal of Medical Sciences* 292, no. 5 (1986):328–34.

34. Gillin et al., "Malabsorption and Mucosal Abnormalities."

35. Ibid.

36. Ibid., p. 619.

37. Kotler et al., "Enteropathy."

38. Robert R. Brinson, "Hypoalbuminemia, Diarrhea, and the Acquired Immunodeficiency Syndrome," *Annals of Internal Medicine* 102(1985):413.

39. Robert R. Brinson and Byron E. Kolts, "Hypoalbuminemia as an Indicator of Diarrheal Incidence in Critically Ill Patients," *Critical Care Medicine* 15, no.5 (1987):506–09.

40. Ibid.

41. HHS, *Eating Hints*, pp. 14–15.

42. Mark Krause and L. Kathleen Mahan, *Food, Nutrition, and Diet Therapy*, 7th ed. (Philadelphia: W. B. Saunders, 1984), p. 445.

43. Irwin H. Rosenberg, Noel W. Solomons, and Roberto E. Schneider, "Malabsorption Associated with Diarrhea and Intestinal Infections," *The American Journal of Clinical Nutrition* 30 (August 1977):1248–53.

44. Peggy O'Sullivan, Ruth A. Linke, and Sharron Dalton, "Evaluation of Body Weight and Nutritional Status Among AIDS Patients," *Journal of the American Dietetic Association* 85, no. 11 (November 1985):1483–84.

45. Ibid.

46. Kotler et al., "Enteropathy."

47. Malone, "Assessment of Nutritional Status."

48. Anne Grant, *Nutritional Assessment Guidelines* (Seattle, Wash.: Anne Grant, 1979), p. 10.

49. John P. Grant, "Nutritional Assessment in Clinical Practice," in *Nutrition in Clinical Practice* 1 (American Society for Parenteral and Enteral Nutrition, 1986), pp. 3–11.

50. Schneider, Anderson, and Coursin, *Nutritional Support of Medical Practice*, p. 136.

51. Malone, "Assessment of Nutritional Status."

52. Kotler, Wang, and Pierson, "Body Composition Studies," p. 1263.

53. Ibid.

54. Grant, *Nutritional Assessment Guidelines*, p. 37.

55. Ibid., p. 38.

56. Malone, "Assessment of Nutritional Status," and Kotler, Wang, and Pierson, "Body Composition Studies," p. 1263.

57. Kotler et al., "Enteropathy."

58. Malone, "Assessment of Nutritional Status."

59. Gordin, "Adverse Reactions," pp. 495–98; and American Hospital Formulary Services, *Drug Information '85*, pp. 372–76, 382–86.

60. Ibid., pp. 58–61.

61. Ibid., p. 386.

62. Ibid., pp. 382–86.

63. Krause and Mahan, *Food, Nutrition, and Diet Therapy*, p. 15.

64. Ibid., pp. 714–15.

65. Malone, "Assessment of Nutritional Status."

66. Krause and Mahan, *Food, Nutrition, and Diet Therapy*, p. 445.

67. Collins, "AIDS: Nutrition Interfaces," p. 5.

68. Terese L. Domaldo and Lourdes S. Natividad, "Nutritional Management of Patient with AIDS and Cryptosporidium Infection," *Nutritional Support Services* 6, no. 4(1986):30–31.

Appendix 16-A

Alternative Nutritional Therapies

AL 721

AL 721 is a lipid combination that has been shown to extract cholesterol from cellular membranes both in vitro and in vivo, thus increasing membrane fluidity and making it harder for the virus to attach to receptor sites.[1] Phosphatidylcholine (purified lecithin) is the active ingredient, acting synergistically with other lipids. All three ingredients are extracted from egg yolks. A study on normal elderly subjects, who have reduced lymphocyte proliferative capacity through aging, found this capacity restored with daily doses of 10-15 grams of AL 721.[2] The "home formula" consists of PC-55, a lecithin concentrate, sold in health food stores, which contains two of the three ingredients of AL 721. So far, there has been no research on the effectiveness of AL 721 workalikes. Most people tolerate up to 25 grams of commercial lecithin per day without side effects. Reactions to gradually increased doses include reduced appetite, vomiting, abdominal bloating, belching, and diarrhea with fatty stools.[3]

HERBAL REMEDIES

Claims have been made that herbs may regenerate the immune system.[4] Extracts from the herbs Astragalus membranaceous and Ligustrum lucidum showed immune restoration in vitro with cells from a small group of cancer patients.[5] Garlic is purported to have antiviral, anti-parasitic qualities. Using standards from traditional Chinese medicine, a study found garlic to be effective in treating cryptococcal meningitis in a small group of nonHIV patients in China.[6] Studies on the therapeutic uses of herbs are limited. An HIV patient who had been instructed to take three herbal medicine capsules before each meal experienced severe headaches, nausea, and a sense of disorientation shortly after starting

175

treatment. Trace amounts of heavy metals such as lead, cadmium, and beryllium were found in the capsules.[7] Other herbal medicines were also tested and found to have the same results. Lead is forbidden in food or drugs in any detectable amount.

COENZYME Q

Coenzyme Q ("CoQ") is produced by the body as a redox coenzyme of the respiratory chain, including the mechanisms of electron transfer and oxidative phosphorylation. These mechanisms, known as "bioenergetics," support life functions.

There is a high concentration of CoQ in the human myocardium. Administering CoQ to patients with cardiomyopathy resulted in improved CoQ blood levels and cardiac function.[8] No scientific studies have been done on its effectiveness in treating HIV but it is being sold in health food stores in pure form in capsules as an immune modulator. It is not approved as a prescription medicine. It may be legally sold over the counter, but without medical claims.

MACROBIOTIC DIET

The macrobiotic diet is based upon the Oriental philosophy that a balance of yin and yang, acid-forming and alkaline-forming foods, is necessary for a balanced body. The diet consists of 50-60 percent whole grains, and 25-30 percent vegetables along with miso soup, sea vegetables, beans, condiments, and occasionally seafood. Foods that are discouraged include all meat, eggs, dairy products, sugar, honey, large amounts of fruit, and foods that contain chemicals, or are highly processed.[9] This diet is being recommended to HIV patients based on testimonies of those who felt and looked better after following the macrobiotic diet. The diet is deficient in calories, protein, calcium, iron, and vitamin B12 which are an integral part of immune system function. Addition of milk products, eggs, or a vitamin B12 fortified soy milk will supply the missing B12 and protein. An iron supplement is recommended.

MEGADOSES OF VITAMINS AND MINERALS

Common supplements that are taken by immunosuppressed persons include: vitamins A, C, E, B12, Zinc, and selenium. These vitamins and minerals contribute to a proper functioning immune system, but excesses of some may cause serious side effects. High doses of the fat-soluble vitamins A and D can be toxic since they are stored in the body for a long time and metabolize slowly.[10]   Zinc intake of 10 to 20-fold over the RDA of 15 mg/day may cause impairment of lymphocyte and polymorphonuclear leukocyte (PMN) functions. Excessive intake of zinc may also result in vomiting, abdominal cramps, and diarrhea.[11] Vitamin C research has shown conflicting results in its effect on the immune system.[12-16] Although adequate vitamin C is necessary for some aspects of immune response,[17] more research is needed to determine the effectiveness of high doses of vitamin C in immunosuppressed patients.

YEAST-CONTROL DIETS

Yeast-control diets have been recommended to help control candida infections. Candidiasis is alleged to be a hypersensitivity syndrome (allergic reaction) caused by the *Candida albicans* organism. W. Crook, author of *The Yeast Connection*, cites a vast array of symptoms included in the syndrome and claims that yeast overgrowth of candidiasis can weaken the immune system further, leading to other infections and antibiotic treatment. This promotes the growth of more yeast, thereby feeding the vicious cycle. Foods to be avoided include sugar and sugar-containing foods, yeast and breads that contain yeast, alcoholic beverages, malt products, condiments, sauces, and vinegar-containing foods, processed and smoked meats, dried and candied fruits, leftovers that contain mold, canned, bottled or frozen juices, coffee and tea, melons, mushrooms, cheeses, packaged and processed foods, peanuts, vitamins and minerals (unless yeast-free and sugar-free), and antibiotics. The theory has been questioned by The Practice Standards Committee of the American College of Allergy and Immunology, which characterized it as "speculative and unproven." They stated that the diagnosis, laboratory tests, and special aspects of treatment should be considered experimental.[18]

DR. BERGER'S IMMUNE POWER DIET

Dr. S.M. Berger, in his book, claims that acute and chronic ill health, overweight, and a host of other problems "are caused by an immune hypersensitivity response to many of the foods we eat." According to Dr. Berger, the foods to which people are most sensitive are cow's milk products, wheat, corn, yeast, soy products, sugar and eggs. His menus are high in fruits and vegetables, low in fat and provide approximately 800-1200 calories, 60 grams of protein, and are low in calcium.[19] The inadequate energy intake, along with the foods restricted, may promote further malnutrition in patients whose nutritional status is already compromised by immunocompetence. The theories and diagnostic approaches promoted in this book are discounted by reputable immunologists.[20]

OTHER ALTERNATE THERAPIES

Other alternate therapies that remain unproven include:

1. Bee propolis as an antibiotic, used in treating thrush, fungal infections, and hairy leukoplakia.
2. Glandular enzymes, in freeze dried form, for cellular rejuvenation.
3. Amino acids cysteine and ornithine as immune boosters.
4. BHT, a food preservative, as an antiviral. It has promoted cancer in some animal experiments.
5. Glycyrrhizin (in licorice) is alleged to be an antiviral in large amounts. Large amounts over long-term use may result in high blood pressure, water retention and disturbances in electrolyte balance.
6. Blue-green manna is a single-cell algae that grows only in Klamath Lake in Oregon. It is purported to help rejuvenate the thymus gland and to stimulate the spleen and other factors of the immune system. It is also alleged to improve the assimilation of vitamins, so that smaller doses of vitamins may be taken.
7. Carrisyn, an aloe extract, as an immune stimulant.
8. Monolaurin, a monoglyceral ester of the fatty acid laurate, as an antimicrobial.

NOTES

1. M. Lyte and M. Shinitsky, "A Special Lipid Mixture for Membrane Fluidization," *Biochimica et Biophycica Acta* 812(1985):133–138.

2. P.S. Sarin et al., "Effects of a Novel Compound (AL 721) on HTLV-III Infectivity in Vitro," *New England Journal of Medicine* 313, no. 20 (1985):1289–1290.

3. P. Etienne, et al., "Clinical Effects of Choline in Alzheimer's Disease," *Lancet* 1 (1978):508–509.

4. Laurence Badgley, *Healing AIDS Naturally*, 1st ed. (San Bruno, CA: Human Energy Press, 1987):157.

5. M. Yan Sun, et al., "Immune Restoration and/or Augmentation of Local Graft Versus Host Reaction by Traditional Chinese Medicinal Herbs," *International Journal of Chinese Medicine* 1, no. 1 (1984):41–44.

6. "Garlic in Cryptococcal Meningitis: A Preliminary Report of 21 Cases," *Chinese Medical Journal* 93(1980):123–126.

7. Deidre A. Hill, "Trace Heavy Metals Found in AIDS Herbal Medicine Cure." Unpublished report.

8. P.H. Langsjoen, S. Vadhanavikit, and K. Folkers, "Response of Patients in Classes III and IV of Cardiomyopathy to Therapy in a Blind and Crossover Trial with Coenzyme Q-10," *Proceedings of the National Academy of Sciences USA*, vol. 82, no. 12 (1985):4240–4244.

9. Herman Aihara, *Basic Macrobiotics*. (Tokyo and New York: Japan Publ., 1985):30.

10. Schneider, *Nutritional Support*, 43.

11. R.K. Chandra, "Excessive Intake of Zinc Impairs Immune Responses," *Journal of the American Medical Association* 252 (1984):1443–46.

12. Robert F. Cathcart, "Vitamin C in the Treatment of Acquired Immune Deficiency," *Medical Hypothesis* 14 (1984):423–433.

13. E. Cameron and L. Pauling, *Cancer and Vitamin C* (Palo Alto, CA: Linus Pauling Institute of Science and Medicine, 1979).

14. William K. Yamanada, "Vitamin C and Cancer: How Convincing a Connection?" *Postgraduate Medicine* 8, no. 7 (1985):47–53.

15. J. Richardson, Vitamin C and Immunosuppression," *Medical Hypotheses* 21(1986):383–385.

16. J. Richardson, "Stress, Adrenals, and Vitamin C," *Medical Hypotheses* 17(1985):399–402.

17. Lourdes C. Corman, "Effects of Specific Nutrients on the Immune Response," *Medical Clinics of North America* 69, no. 4 (July 1985):759–789.

18. Executive Committee of the American Academy of Allergy and Immunology, "Candidiasis Hypersensitivity Syndrome," Position Statement, *Journal of Allergy and Clinical Immunology* 78, no. 2 (1986):271–272.

19. Cheryl L. Rock, "Popular and Fad Diets," *Nutrition and the M.D.*, 13, no. 4 (1987):1.

20. Ibid.

Chapter 17

Physical Medicine Management of HIV Patients

Mary Lou Galantino and Dale W. Spence

HIV patients are not typical physical medicine (PM) patients. They are frequently young and usually do not have a history of recent traumatic injury or surgery; thus they do not present with the usual primary disorders seen in PM. However, HIV patients do present with significant PM conditions stemming from HIV's overwhelming disease process. These conditions are not unique to PM, because HIV-spectrum disorders are typically multisystem diseases requiring close collaboration among various medical subspecialties.

The goals of PM for HIV patients are the same as those for any other PM patient: to relieve discomfort and restore function. Ultimately, the goal of PM for HIV-infected patients is to achieve and maintain the highest *quality* of life possible. For the HIV patient, compared with more traditional PM patients, these goals are more difficult to realize.

PM management of the HIV patient operates on the basic assumption that aggressive therapy techniques will restore function to varying degrees. Frequently restoration of normal function can either reduce or alleviate physical discomforts. The three PM conditions most commonly observed in HIV patients that may be treated by physical therapy are (1) nervous system disorders, (2) pain syndromes, and (3) a general category, reduced physical capacity.

NERVOUS SYSTEM DISORDERS

Nervous system disorders result from a variety of assaults from HIV disease, including CNS infections (e.g., toxoplasmosis), neoplasms, peripheral neuropathies, cerebral atrophy, and spinal cord syndromes associated with vacuolar myelopathic lesions. Specific CNS manifestations of the disease may include hemiplegia, paraplegia, loss of balance and coordination, and deficits in cognitive skills.

Generally, the primary PM treatment for most of the nervous system disorders associated with HIV is proprioceptive neuromuscular facilitation (PNF), involving repetitive practice of motor and cognitive activity. PNF techniques involve placing specific physical demands on the neuromuscular system to elicit a desired response. The emphasis is on the application of high resistance to the body segment throughout the range of joint motion using many combinations of movements. These motions simulate primitive movement patterns and also challenge postural and righting reflexes.[1] Additional therapeutic procedures include Bobath techniques, balance and coordination retraining, and developmental activities such as crawling, kneeling, and challenging positions. These techniques promote or hasten the response of the neuromuscular system through stimulation of the proprioceptive mechanisms. Frequently, central motor disorders are accompanied by pain. If so, a pain management program must provide effective analgesia and abolish splinting or guarding before neuromuscular facilitation procedures begin.

Toxoplasmosis

In toxoplasmosis, CT scan will reveal contrast enhancing lesions, which may result in hemiplegia, communication disorders because of receptive or expressive deficits, or both. The rehabilitation strategy for this condition includes (1) prevention of the commonly seen shoulder subluxation through use of a sling that positions the joint in a gravity-dependent position, (2) application of an appropriate orthotic device to compensate for foot drop, and (3) daily range of motion and therapeutic exercises incorporated into the rehabilitation program. Instructions to the patient's primary caregiver are an important responsibility of the physical therapist to ensure safe mobility and continued management of the patient at home.

Progressive Multifocal Leukoencephalopathy (PML)

PML is a chronic demyelinating CNS disease caused by the papovaviruses. CT scan of the PML patient often shows hypodense, nonenhancing lesions without mass confined to the brain's white matter regions. The cerebrospinal fluid (CSF) may show a slight elevation of protein, but CSF pleocytosis is rare. Patients with early PML may show asymmetric involvement of cerebral hemispheres with resultant hemiparesis, aphasia, dysarthria, and hemianopsia. Intellectual impairment has been noted in two-thirds of the cases.[2]

Physical therapy for patients with PML involves neurofacilitation techniques and gentle, persistent verbal cueing that is necessary for even simple activities of daily living. Their memory disturbance may be severe, requiring an extra effort on the part of the therapist. For example, exercises performed in front of a mirror may perceptually reorient the patient's body position and enhance body image. Cognitive retraining through the use of repetitive activities combined with verbal cueing may be effective.

Encephalitis, Meningitis

Several herpes viruses—CMV, herpes simplex, herpes zoster, and Epstein-Barr virus—have also been associated with CNS disease in HIV patients. CMV may be the primary cause of either encephalitis or meningitis and may be linked to subacute encephalitis. Herpes simplex II, either alone or with CMV, may cause progressive myelopathy.

HIV-CNS Infection

The ravages of HIV-CNS involvement are reflected in the neuropathology, which consists of (1) marked vacuolation accompanied by thinning of myelin sheaths and lipid-laden macrophages in the subcortical and spinal cord white matter, (2) lesions that are prominent in lateral and posterior columns and more extensive in the middle and lower thoracic regions, (3) lesions that affect the basal ganglia, thalamus, limbic system, and cerebellum, and (4) cortical atrophy.[3] Varying degrees of cognitive impairment can occur secondary to HIV-CNS involvement. These changes cause mild to severe neuropsychiatric complications such as delirium, dementia, and amnestic syndromes. Therefore, the physical therapist must have a working knowledge of HIV-CNS-related disease in order to provide optimal and timely assessment and intervention for each individual.

Ataxia

Ataxia is a frequent outcome of central motor disorders and may present a challenge for the patient who wishes to maintain maximum independence; therefore, gait training is essential. During ambulation, a lower-limb-loading technique involving the use of ankle weights that provide inertia against the characteristically exaggerated leg swing is more effective than gait training without limb loading. Again, neuromuscular facilitation is also indicated for the ataxia patient.

PAIN SYNDROMES

Pain syndromes are common among HIV patients, and the sources of pain may be multiple. As mentioned, various CNS degenerative disorders cause pain. Pain also may be related to rapid skeletal muscle atrophy that changes postural alignment, which in turn creates trigger points. The neurotoxic effects of antivirals and chemotherapies may produce peripheral neuropathies that are very painful and difficult to manage. Pain may also be associated with deafferentation pain syndromes secondary to viral infections such as herpes zoster, which can be a complication to HIV patients. Anxiety and depression may further complicate the management of the HIV patient in pain and require concomitant treatment for effective analgesia.

Pain management in HIV patients first requires an analysis of the cause of discomfort from among the many possibilities. A comprehensive and interdisciplinary approach to pain management is imperative. A pain management program may include the use of:

- transcutaneous electrical nerve stimulation (TENS)
- ultrasound
- laser
- myofascial release techniques
- hypnosis
- relaxation procedures
- visualization.

Biofeedback also may be used to enhance the patient's control of certain physiological processes that affect pain. Non-narcotic analgesics and psychotropic agents, which will act synergistically with these nonpharmacologic measures, may also be used as effective adjuvants in pain management.

An important aspect of pain management is focusing on posture and body awareness. This emphasis on the body and its alignment may reduce pain associated with the rapid musculoskeletal change observed in many patients. Myofascial release techniques are especially beneficial in pain management, particularly when the virus has invaded the CNS or the peripheral nervous system (HIV neuropathies) or when opportunistic infections have caused viral-related myelitis.

Low-energy laser systems have been used clinically to stimulate wound and fracture healing and to obtain analgesic effects. In Europe, low-power lasers (including helium-neon and gallium arsenide) have been used in PM programs since the 1970s. However, the use of low-energy laser radiation for human treatment is still considered experimental in this country. Some of the proposed benefits attributed to low-energy/cold laser include an increase in vascularization of healing tissue, collagen synthesis, a decrease in microorganisms, and pain reduction.[4] Therefore, with respect to wound healing (e.g., decubiti), low-energy laser can accelerate the healing process and is authorized for use with the patient's informed consent. Laser is a much more practicable treatment for superficial wounds than hydrotherapy, especially in light of the importance of infection control. Laser, in concert with other electrotherapeutic devices such as TENS, can be used for symptomatic relief and management of chronic, intractable pain or as an adjuvant for any pain treatment.

Trigger Points

A trigger point is a reactive point on the muscle that is usually tender to touch. Palpation will indicate tightness in a specific, localized region of the muscle. This condition may be caused by rapid changes in skeletal muscle as a result of accelerated muscle atrophy and concomitant changes in posture. All aforementioned modalities may be used to treat trigger points.

Peripheral Neuropathies

Peripheral neuropathies appear to be a persistent problem for the HIV patient. These neuropathies may be a result of either direct HIV infection to the nerves or side effects from various chemotherapeutic agents. The side effects resulting from chemotherapy, such as vincristine and bleomycin, include peripheral neuropathies that are predominantly distal symmetrical sensory neuropathies with painful parathesias and causalgias. The use of TENS at specific acupuncture points may diminish the pain associated with peripheral neuropathies. TENS electrode placement at acupuncture points BL60, GB34, LIV3, and K1 have been particularly effective in pain management of neuropathies in the lower extremity.

Herpes Zoster

Another common problem in HIV patients is the pain associated with herpes zoster, which may persist long after open lesions subside. When the disease is treated with an antiviral, acyclovir in concert with the use of TENS appears to be effective in pain control. The placement of TENS electrodes for optimum pain attenuation in this condition is to attach one electrode at the dorsal skin web between the first and second metacarpals and the other channel electrode at the bladder acupuncture meridian points above and below the dermatome of lesion involvement. An alternative electrode placement may be simply to bracket the shingles lesions.[5] Interestingly, several cases of erratic muscle fasciculations have occurred post-treatment with TENS. These muscle reactions to TENS treatment merit further neurophysiological investigation.

REDUCED FUNCTIONAL CAPACITY

The final disorder commonly affecting HIV patients in which physical therapy may intervene with some effectiveness is reduced physical capacity. Functional incapacity is usually manifested as substantial fatigue, including poor exercise response and muscle weakness.

The specific cause of such functional deficit has not been established but is probably the sum of several factors, including disruption of metabolic pathways resulting in negative energy balance, side effects of medication, deconditioning, psychogenic factors, and a variety of unidentified dysfunctional mechanisms associated with the disease process.

Exercise therapy has the potential to improve the patient's physical capacity for daily living. A satisfactory level of physical conditioning usually yields a greater sense of well-being and confidence to undertake physical challenges. If physical degeneration takes away such confidence, the quality of living diminishes. There-fore, HIV patients must be encouraged to continue a regular program of physical activity at home.

The general goal of physical activity is to achieve and maintain a level of endurance and strength suitable to manage daily living and work activities. Consistent with this goal, a home program of both endurance and resistance exercises is appropriate. In a home exercise program, the simplest and most effective endurance activity for the outpatient is walking. For the HIV inpatient, the bicycle ergometer is a suitable modality to maintain and improve car-diovascular endurance.

The intensity, duration, and frequency of walking should be based on the individual patient's exercise tolerance.[6] The physical therapist determines this level of tolerance in concert with other members of the medical team. For uncomplicated patients, the usual prescription for walking is to complete one and one-half miles in 22 to 23 minutes three to five times per week at an appropriate exercise target heart rate. Patients just beginning an exercise program should not attempt to achieve the preceding intensity and duration of exercise until they have undergone some adaptation of reduced exercise stress. In HIV patients, this may take several weeks or even months.

A significant number of HIV patients have presented with chronic resting tachycardia. Thus, the formulae for estimating exercise target heart rate simply based on age and a percentage of maximum heart rate may be inappropriate. A more suitable way of deriving an exercise target heart rate is first to determine the heart rate reserve, which is the difference between resting and maximum heart rate; multiply the heart rate reserve by a 60 percent stimulus factor; and add the resulting product back to the resting rate.[7] An example follows:

> Patient age = 30 Years
> Resting heart rate (RHR) = 115 BPM
> Estimated maximum heart rate (MHR) = (220 minus patient age) = 190 BPM
> Heart rate reserve (MHR minus RHR) = 75 BPM
>   times Stimulus factor (0.60) = 45 BPM
>   + RHR (115 BPM) = Target heart rate (160 BPM)

An estimate of maximum heart rate may be a major source of error in any formulation to ascertain target heart rate. A maximum stress test is the only accurate way to determine maximum heart rate, if the patient's status allows.

Even for uncomplicated patients, physical therapists should avoid the slavish use of a target heart rate in the first few weeks of exercise. Light exercise that elicits a response 15 percent less than the calculated target heart rate allows the patient to adapt gradually to exercise. Patients who present with cardiovascular complications should undergo exercise stress evaluation that establishes sign-symptom limiting levels of exercise intensity.

While the primary goal of exercise therapy is increased cardiovascular endurance to enhance the functional capacity of the HIV patient, improved muscle function is also an objective. Whether progressive resistance exercise reduces the rate of muscle atrophy commonly seen in the HIV patient has not been experimentally determined at this time. Investigation has shown that skeletal muscle of the chronic HIV patient improves in function as an outcome of resistance exercise training.[8]

Resistance training equipment that accommodates the patient's level of muscle function is the most suitable. Hydraulic, pneumatic, or electrical resistance machines can all produce accommodating resistance, in contrast to free weights or machines with weight stacks. However, accommodating resistance equipment often is not available to the outpatient. If not, conventional free weights or weight machines are acceptable. When using these conventional resistance training modalities, patients should observe the recommended load for progressive resistance exercise of 15 repetition-maximum poundage performed for one or two sets in a variety of exercises at a frequency of three times per week. Resistance exercises may be alternated with endurance activities on an every-other-day schedule.

ENERGY CONSERVATION

While exercise therapy involves energy expenditure, sometime in the course of the disease the focus of PM treatment may change to energy conservation. The

energy conservation techniques that should be employed with the severely debilitated HIV patient include (1) establishing priorities of daily activities, (2) pacing,
which involves performing a physical task in intervals, and (3) the technique of
diaphragmatic breathing.

Instruction in the various techniques of energy conservation is a major responsibility of the therapist. Arrangement of the living environment for efficiency, and
the use of assistive devices, contribute to energy conservation and enhance the
patient's ability to maintain independence. Patients must attempt physical activity
step-by-step, with frequent rest stops to conserve energy. The length of time spent
completing a physical task is not a consideration in the energy conservation
scheme. Pacing naturally extends the duration of the physical challenge, but the
patient usually does not experience the level of fatigue that frequently results from
performing a task continuously. By increasing ventilation volume through
diaphragmatic breathing, patients may manage various daily activities with
greater ease.

CONCLUSION

The neuromuscular complications and functional incapacity associated with
HIV infection and its treatments can seriously compromise the mobility of the
patient and create significant pain syndromes as well. When rendered in a
comprehensive program of medical care, PM as an integral component of medical
management has the potential to improve and maintain the quality of life for HIV
patients.

NOTES

1. M. Knott and D.E. Voss, *Proprioneuromuscular Facilitation: Patterns and Techniques*, 2nd ed.
(Hagerstown, Md.: Harper and Row, 1968), pp. 118–69.

2. R.M. Levy, D.E. Bredesen, and M.L. Rosenblum, "Neurological Manifestations of the Acquired
Immunodeficiency Syndrome (AIDS): Experience at UCSF and Review of the Literature," *Journal of
Neurosurgery* 62(1985):475.

3. R.W. Price, B.A. Navia, and E. Cho, "AIDS Encephalopathy," in *Proceedings of the National
Conference on AIDS* (Washington D.C., 1985), pp. 285–301.

4. L. Goldman, "Basic Reactions in Tissue," in L. Goldman, ed., *The Biomedical Laser: Technology
and Clinical Applications* (New York: Springer-Verlag, 1981), pp. 6–9; J.A. Kleinkort and
R.A. Foley, "Laser Acupuncture: Its Use in Physical Therapy," *American Journal of Acupuncture*
12(1984):51; and D.T. Yew, S.L. Lingwong, and Y. Chan, "Stimulating Effect of the Low Dose
Laser—A New Hypothesis," *Anatomica* 12(1982):131.

5. K. Lam, "Clinical Exchange—Effective Treatment of Herpes Zoster," *APTAN* 5 (1986).

6. American College of Sports Medicine, *Guidelines for Graded Exercise Testing and Exercise
Prescription*, 2nd ed. (Philadelphia: Lea & Febiger, 1980), pp. 45–48.

7. J.T. Karvonen, E. Kentala, and O. Mustala, ''The Effects of Training on Heart Rate, A Longitudinal Study,'' *Annales Medicinae Experimentalis et Biologiae Fenniae* 35(1957):305.

8. Mary Lou Galantino and Dale Spence, unpublished data (Institute for Immunological Disorders, 1987).

Chapter 18

Infection Control

Grace Lusby

AIDS infection control is not unique in its practical application. It differs only in the degree of fear, the perceived deadliness, and the social stigmas associated with the disease.

Studies have been conducted on over 3,000 health care workers (HCWs), many of whom were working with patients with AIDS prior to identification of HIV.[1] In 1,800 blood-contaminated incidents, only ten well-investigated cases of transmission appear to have occurred.[2] After the health care system has cared for more than 35,000 persons with AIDS, all cases of HIV transmission in health care have taken place in the context of "accidents":

- needle punctures with injection of blood
- vacutainer tube explosion because too much pressure was used to fill the tube
- HCWs working on blood equipment without the use of gloves
- prolonged contact with blood without the use of gloves.

The most effective infection precaution against AIDS in health care is the prevention of accidents.

Providing acute health care to HIV-positive people carries some risk of infection. However, the risk is quite low compared to that associated with Hepatitis B. AIDS must be kept in appropriate perspective with regard to Hepatitis B, CMV, and other blood-borne viruses, which also pose professional risk and significant risks to the caregiver's health.

Estimates of the number of asymptomatic HIV carriers vary widely, but it is clearly many times the number of reported cases. Because any person who enters a health care setting may be a carrier, uniform implementation of a system that includes basic infection precautions is essential. A number of hospitals have already implemented such a system,[3] usually referred to as "Body Substance

Precautions'' or ''Universal Precautions'' and recommended by the CDC in its AIDS Infection Control Guidelines.[4]

Rationale for a New System

The generally used diagnosis-related isolation systems fail to protect against unknown carriers because:

- causative agents are present prior to diagnosis
- clinically unrecognized infections may still be communicable (e.g., Hepatitis B carriers, CMV excreters)
- the system is designed for use only with "known" infected patients
- implementing precautions for the "known carrier" gives a false sense of security.

UNIVERSAL PRECAUTIONS

Universal precautions are based on risk of exposure to blood rather than on diagnosis. They are derived from current knowledge of disease transmission and effective infection precautions currently in use.[5] These precautions are generally simple and require more rigorous technique only under special conditions. They must be used with every patient, not just those thought to pose some risk.

1. Wash hands after contact with body substances, before clean or sterile invasive procedures, and before eating or preparing food.
2. Wear gloves for direct contact with body substances (pus, sputum, urine, feces, blood, saliva).
3. Wear a gown or moisture-repellent apron when spillage is expected on clothing.
4. Use masks and eye coverings when mucous membrane exposure is expected.
5. Wash exposed portions of body as soon as possible if unprotected contact occurs; also wash exposed clothing.
6. Promote ease in disposing of uncapped needles and sharps by locating and using disposal systems near usage areas.
7. Mask in the presence of known or suspected diseases spread by the respiratory route. When appropriate (e.g., chickenpox) exclude susceptible individuals.

8. *Implement and support an active health and safety program that investigates accidents and makes recommendations for changes in procedures, equipment, and education.*

A key to implementation of these precautions is for each department or specialty area to identify procedures or activities that increase the risk of exposure to blood or other body fluids. The department or area may then develop appropriate precautions and incorporate them into routine practice. As utilizing the precautions becomes habit, safe practice becomes easy.

When To Use Precautions

The following infection control precautions protect both the care provider and the patient by preventing their contact with blood or other body fluids. The precautions must be applied to all patients, regardless of diagnosis, in both the general care setting and specialty areas.

Handwashing

Most patient care activities of brief duration that involve no contact with blood or body secretions, such as taking a blood pressure or passing medications, do not require handwashing between contacts. Hands should be washed between more prolonged contacts and those that involve direct physical care. Hands should always be washed:

- before invasive procedures
- before eating, preparing food, or feeding patients
- before care of the severely immunocompromised patient
- after contact with blood or body substances
- after contact with equipment, linen, or trash contaminated with blood or body substances.

Gloves

Wearing gloves is not recommended for casual contact, such as giving a backrub or otherwise touching intact skin, nor are they needed for administration of medication, except rectal suppositories. They are required:

- for contact with blood and body substances, particularly visible amounts

  —for starting IVs
  —for drawing blood

—for changing chux, peripads, and dressings
—for surgical procedures
—for cleaning visible spills of body fluids

- in the presence of open, weeping lesions or chronic dermatitis on the hands of the care provider.

Gowns

Providers do not need to wear gowns for casual contact or for routine care such as passing medications. When gowns are required, a moisture-repellent nonsterile apron is often more appropriate unless surgical standards for patient protection require a sterile gown.

Gowns should be worn in the following situations:

- when splatter or heavy soiling is expected, e.g., when lifting a patient with draining wounds
- when splatter of blood or blood-contaminated secretions is expected, such as during bronchoscopy, certain surgical procedures, certain dental procedures, or vaginal deliveries.

Masks

In the absence of respiratorily spread diseases such as tuberculosis (TB), aerosols from ICU ventilators *do not* constitute a hazard and *do not* require masks. People with AIDS do not suffer more from colds than anyone else. Providers should wear masks:

- when a respiratorily spread disease is suspected (TB, meningococcal meningitis, etc.)
- when a patient undergoes a surgical or other invasive procedure
- when a procedure may splatter the mucous membranes of the mouth or nose of the caregiver (e.g., during bronchoscopy or vaginal deliveries).

Eye Covering

Use of an eye covering is recommended only for procedures during which splatter into the mucous membrane of the eye can be expected. Such procedures often include bronchoscopy and certain surgical, dental, and obstetrical procedures. Eye coverings are not required for fine, invisible, mist exposures, such as that produced by ventilators. The amount of infective organisms in such mist is low or absent and has not resulted in transmission of blood-borne diseases.

Sharps

Learning to dispose of needles without recapping, immediately after use, is one of the single most important measures a staff member can take to protect against needlestick injury. To make this possible, puncture-resistant containers, each with an accessible opening that does not impede disposal, should be located in areas where sharps are used. The containers should be located below eye level for good visibility and should be capped and discarded before the fill line is surpassed.

Specimens

Providers should wear gloves when drawing blood and when handling any specimen, regardless of source (blood, urine, sputum, feces). All specimen containers should be transported in bags that will not leak if the specimen is dropped or broken or if the container leaks.

In the clinical laboratory, any procedure that is likely to aerosolize blood should be reevaluated, and all specimens should be presumed infectious.[6]

Dietary

No special procedures are necessary.

Protective (Reverse) Isolation

People with AIDS are most seriously affected by diseases found everywhere in the environment and, in most cases, have previously been exposed to the diseases that will threaten their lives. Reverse isolation, as traditionally practiced, has largely been abandoned by hospitals except in cases of limited-duration immunosuppression. Patients with ongoing immunosuppression do not benefit from this practice.[7]

Room Assignment

Room assignment may be difficult because of the need to maintain confidentiality and, possibly, because of the patient's or family's desire for privacy. For infection control purposes, patients may be assigned to the same room if both roommates:

- practice good personal hygiene
- do not soil parts of the room outside their own space
- do not have a disease requiring a private room (e.g., TB, chickenpox).[8]

Resuscitation

Although there is no evidence that the AIDS virus, or any other disease, has been transmitted from patient to care provider, or provider to patient, through mouth-to-mouth resuscitation, a device such as an ambu bag or a one-way valve is recommended for the procedure.[9] The device protects the staff member against possible blood exposure if resuscitation is vigorous. A device also provides the margin of safety needed to calm the inner struggle between the desire to perform one's professional duty and the desire to avoid placing one's own life in jeopardy. It is important for the institution to make devices readily available in all patient care areas for use on *all* patients. There must be no deterrent to resuscitation when it is indicated.

Environmental Precautions

Decontamination of Equipment

Guidelines for decontamination of equipment are based on the degree of infection risk posed by any piece of equipment or environmental surface.[10] For example:

- Surgical instruments used on a sterile portion of the body must be sterilized so they are free of all living organisms.
- Instruments that will come in contact with mucous membranes or unsterile internal portions of the body require high-level viricidal and tuberculocidal disinfection.
- Environmental surfaces or equipment used in contact with intact skin require low-level disinfection, laundering by current methods, or cleaning to remove soilage with routine cleaners.

Products and methods to be used should be chosen in consultation with the hospital's infection control department or the CDC's guidelines.[11]

Trash Handling

Generally, infectious wastes are those that are hazardous if improperly handled because of their high volume, high concentration, or another characteristic. Not every bandage with a little blood, even if it has some infectious organisms, must be handled separately from other trash.[12] Final disposition of infective wastes is largely regulated by state laws; the hospital infection control committee and the local health department can provide appropriate guidance for specific areas.

To maintain a safe work environment and prevent accidents and environmental contamination, providers should:

- bag dressings and wet trash *before* placing them in holding containers
- contain broken glass separately
- schedule trash collection to prevent overflow
- use strong plastic liners that resist tearing during normal use.

Linen Handling

When the following procedures are used, linens from ''known'' infected patients do not need to be handled separately:

- Use a wash formula based on the type of linen being processed (e.g., sheets versus baby linen).
- Transport all soiled linen in impervious bags to prevent environmental contamination.
- In the laundry, separate the prewash sorting area from the clean area.
- Have laundry workers in the prewash area wear protective garments: gloves, gown, mask, and cap.
- Workers in the ''soiled'' laundry area should not work in the ''clean'' area on the same day.
- Develop a quality control program that includes infection control policies.

EMPLOYEE ISSUES

Parenteral or Mucous Membrane Exposures

The risk of acquiring HIV infection from a needlestick or mucous membrane splash is low compared with the risk of acquiring Hepatitis B infection.[13] When a worker was exposed to both AIDS and Hepatitis B in the same accidental exposure, Hepatitis B was transmitted, but AIDS was not.[14]

In developing a protocol for managing needlestick exposures to known and unknown cases of HIV infection, providers should consider:

- confidentiality of those tested for HIV antibody, both patient and employee (this point cannot be stressed enough)
- the use that will be made of the test result
- the cost-benefit ratio of having the results (Will the testing program increase or decrease anxiety? Will testing lead to a different action, and if so, what?)
- provision of counseling for employees
- protection of patients, employees, and the agency under existing laws.

If employees are to be tested, recommended intervals are as soon as possible after the exposure; at 6 weeks; and at 3, 6, and 12 months.[15]

Pregnant Employees

Pregnant employees are not known to be at increased risk; for infection to occur, the virus must still gain access to the body through blood or other body fluid. However, a woman who becomes infected during pregnancy carries a substantial risk of perinatal virus transmission. The pregnant employee does not need to use any special precautions beyond those used by other employees but should rigorously apply universal precautions with *all* patients.

Infection with CMV, which is excreted by many AIDS patients, can also threaten a fetus. In reality, most people who excrete CMV do so asymptomatically (3 percent of all healthy adults, up to 28 percent of all pregnant women, and up to 2.2 percent of all newborns).[16] Studies of care providers and CMV excreters have shown no increased risk when they engage in health care activities (over personal life risk) in which good handwashing is practiced.[17] Since patients often excrete CMV, the pregnant care provider should use good handwashing and gloving practices for contact with body secretions from all patients.

HIV-Positive Employees

To date, there is no evidence of HIV transmission to patients in the hospital.[18] Some precedent exists in the continued employment of health care providers who are Hepatitis B carriers.[19] The risk of Hepatitis B transmission by accidental blood exposure has been shown to be many times greater than the risk of HIV transmission.[20] Hepatitis B has been transmitted from care provider to patient when the recommended infection control precautions were not practiced. Therefore, all agencies and institutions must teach and reinforce good infection control practices.

The asymptomatic HIV-positive employee has not demonstrated immunosuppression by the development of opportunistic infection and should be able to function as usual without danger to self or others. However, since the first presenting sign of AIDS may be neurologic disease, supervisors should be alert to any changes in mental or physical ability in *all* employees.

Employees with AIDS

Many people with AIDS are not well enough to work. For those who are, the following points should be kept in mind:

- AIDS is a disability and must be treated as such under labor laws.
- ''Reasonable accommodation'' may mean altering work assignments; work assignments should be based on ability to perform, not diagnosis.
- The employer's obligation:

  —to protect the confidentiality of the employee with AIDS
  —to ensure that the employee with AIDS is able to perform assigned duties safely.

Fellow employees may be very nervous with a person known to have AIDS. Employers need to provide rap sessions where employees can discuss fears and facts about transmission can be made known. A continuing, equitable dialogue is important. (For discussion of education strategies, refer to Chapter 23.)

Administration's judgment that an employee with AIDS can safely work involves a case-by-case evaluation of the employee's ability to execute duties safely. Employees not caring for patients pose no risk in the workplace.[21] When an employee must perform invasive procedures, a hypothetical potential for viral transmission exists in cases of accident. Also, the rapidity with which physical and mental status may alter may be reason enough to monitor such an employee's ability to perform more closely than other employees.

Figure 18-1 provides a suggested algorithm for managing the employee with AIDS. The job that carries potential for transmission of HIV to patients is performing invasive procedures, especially those involving sharp instruments. The key points are the employee's ability to perform safely and protection of the employee from false accusations and harassment.

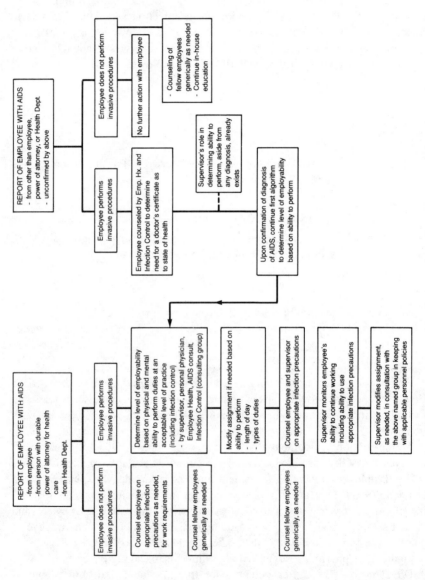

Figure 18-1 Algorithm for Management of an Employee with AIDS

NOTES

1. T.L. Kuhls et al., "A Prospective Cohort Study of the Occupational Risk of AIDS and AIDS-related Infections in Health Care Personnel [abstract]," *Clin Res* 34(1986):124A; Julie Gerberding et al., "Risk of Transmitting the Human Immunodeficiency Virus, Cytomegalovirus, and Hepatitis B Virus to Health Care Workers Exposed to Patients with AIDS and AIDS-related Conditions," *Journal of Infectious Diseases* 156(1987):1–8; and D.K. Henderson et al., "Risk of Nosocomial Infection with Human T-cell Lymphotropic Virus Type III/Lymphadenopathy-Associated Virus in a Large Cohort of Intensively Exposed Health Care Workers," *Annals of Internal Medicine* 104(1986):644–47.

2. U.S. Centers for Disease Control (CDC), "Update: Human Immunodeficiency Virus Infections in Health-Care Workers Exposed to Blood of Infected Patients," *Morbidity and Mortality Weekly Report (MMWR)* 36(1987):285–89.

3. P. Lynch et al., "Perspectives: Rethinking the Role of Isolation Practices in the Prevention of Nosocomial Infections," *Annals of Internal Medicine* 107(1987):243–46.

4. CDC, "Recommendation for Preventing Transmission of Infection with Human T-Lymphotropic Virus Type III/Lymphadenopathy-associated Virus in the Workplace," *MMWR* 34(1985):682–86, 691–95; and CDC, "Recommendations for Preventing Transmission of Infection with Human T-Lymphotropic Virus Type III/Lymphadenopathy-Associated Virus during Invasive Procedures," *MMWR* 35(1986):221–23.

5. J.S. Garner and M.S. Favero, "CDC Guidelines for Handwashing and Hospital Environmental Control, 1985: 1. Handwashing; 2. Cleaning, Disinfecting, and Sterilizing Patient-Care Equipment; 3. Microbiologic Sampling; 4. Infective Waste; 5. Housekeeping; 6. Laundry," *Infection Control* 7(1986):231–43; and J.S. Garner and B.P. Simmons, "CDC Guidelines for Isolation Precautions in Hospitals," CDC, *Guidelines for Prevention and Control of Nosocomial Infections*, HHS Publication no. (CDC) 83-8314, 1983.

6. CDC and National Institutes of Health, *Biosafety in Microbiological and Biomedical Laboratories*, HHS Publication no. (CDC) 84-8395, 1984.

7. Garner and Simmons, "CDC Guidelines for Isolation Precautions in Hospitals."

8. Ibid.

9. National Conference on CPR and ECC, "Standards and Guidelines for Cardiopulmonary Resuscitation and Emergency Cardiac Care: Disease Transmission and CPR Training and Safety in Training for and Providing CPR," *Journal of the American Medical Association* 255(1986):2926–28.

10. Garner and Favero, "CDC Guidelines for Handwashing and Hospital Environmental Control, 1985."

11. Ibid.

12. Ibid.

13. Gerberding et al., "Risk of Transmitting the Human Immunodeficiency Virus, Cytomegalovirus, and Hepatitis B Virus"; Gerberding et al., "Transmission of Hepatitis B without Transmission of AIDS by Accidental Needlestick," [letter], *New England Journal of Medicine* 312(1985):56; and David J. West, "The Risk of Hepatitis B Infection among Health Professionals in the United States: A Review," *American Journal of Medical Science* 287(1984):26–33.

14. Gerberding et al., "Transmission of Hepatitis B without Transmission of AIDS."

15. CDC, "Recommendation for Preventing Transmission of Infection."

16. California Morbidity Supplement no. 7, February 25, 1983; R.F. Pass et al., "Excretion of Cytomegalovirus in Mothers: Observations After Delivery of Congenitally Infected and Normal

Infants," *Journal of Infectious Diseases* 147(1982):1–6; and A.S. Benson, ed., *Control of Communicable Diseases in Man*, 14th ed., (American Public Health Assn., 1985).

17. Gerberding et al., "Risk of Transmitting the Human Immunodeficiency Virus, Cytomegalovirus, and Hepatitis B Virus"; and California Morbidity Supplement no. 7.

18. CDC, "Recommendations for Preventing Transmission of Infection with Human T-Lymphotropic Virus Type III/Lymphadenopathy-associated Virus in the Workplace." CDC, "Recommendations for Preventing Transmission of Infection with Human T-Lymphotropic Virus Type III/ Lymphadenopathy-associated Virus during Invasive Procedures."

19. W.W. Williams, "CDC, Guidelines for Infection Control in Hospital Personnel," in CDC, *Guidelines for Prevention and Control of Nosocomial Infections*.

20. West, "The Risk of Hepatitis B Infection among Health Professionals in the United States."

21. Ibid.

Part **III**

Care in the
Community

The importance of care in the community cannot be overemphasized. Almost since the beginning of the epidemic, many persons with AIDS/ARC have chosen to remain in their homes even during the acute phases of their illness. With the advent of AZT, AIDS and ARC have become chronic diseases for many persons, and most of their care will also be administered in the home or another community setting. Even among persons for whom AZT is ineffective, care in the home is still a first choice for many.

The San Francisco Bay Area has been the national leader in developing systems that make possible high-quality care in the home and community. Much of the leadership responsible for this development has come from nurses and other health care providers, strongly supported by community volunteers who participate actively in these endeavors.

This part begins with a discussion on discharge planning, which is a major focus for all care providers. Early in the San Francisco experience, the community began to develop networks and referral systems because difficulties in placement were evident from the very beginning. Two groups of providers who began to provide care in the home, and who have been instrumental in the development of an effective home care program, are the Public Health Nurses and the Visiting Nurses and Hospice of San Francisco. Their experiences are shared in the following chapters.

An important point is that development of liaisons with community volunteer groups is a critical factor in the success of the Bay Area's home care programs. These volunteers, who come from every segment of society, contribute countless hours in providing emotional support and helping with practical tasks in the home. The home care system could not function without them.

Chapter 19

Discharge Planning

Allison Moed and Anita Kline

Discharge planning for people with HIV infection is similar in many respects to that for patients with any other illness. The health care team must assess the individual's post-hospital situation with attention to the patient's medical, social, and emotional needs as well as the availability of help, both professional and nonprofessional, to meet these needs.

On the other hand, discharge planning for the AIDS patient is likely to present a number of special problems. To maintain the patient's quality of life, providers must elicit and consider the patient's wishes. The goals are to maintain optimal health and independence as long as possible and to minimize the length and frequency of hospitalizations. Early and meticulous discharge planning is vital to ensuring that patients can live their remaining days or years in a fulfilling manner.

For the PWA, hospitalization is never a step toward complete recovery. Plans for the future must, to one degree or another, reflect an understanding that patients will at some point probably become unable to care for themselves. One of the many consequences of this situation is the severe limitation on patients' ability to pay for life's necessities and for services they need because of loss of employment and health insurance benefits.

Nor are existing community agencies always able or willing to provide their services to PWAs. Fear of contagion as well as prejudice and ignorance about homosexuality and IV drug use have adversely affected the availability of suitable housing, home care, and chronic care facilities for PWAs in virtually every area of the country. Even when agencies have been willing to help, they are often unable to modify their programs to meet the special needs of AIDS patients. For the most part, funding on the federal, state, and local levels has not been sufficient to encourage the development of appropriate resources.

In addition, the manifestations of HIV and its associated opportunistic infections, which have a diverse and erratic impact on the post-hospital course, can complicate the discharge plan. Because the progression of the illness and each patient's response to infection and treatment are so difficult to predict, devising a plan that addresses the many contingencies involved in each particular case can be challenging. In addition to needing special medical considerations, the PWA is likely to present a unique profile of psychosocial needs, as described in Chapter 8. For these reasons, individualization, flexibility, and creativity in planning are imperative.

To facilitate a pertinent and appropriate discharge plan that addresses the needs expressed by the patient and loved ones, the nurse must develop a relationship of trust and acceptance, especially with those individuals who might have had few or negative experiences with health care providers because of their youth, life style, or racial background. Planning for Black and Hispanic people with AIDS should be culturally sensitive. Whenever possible, nurses should make special referrals to ethnically oriented agencies in the community. HIV-infected women and children pose an additional challenge for the discharge planner, especially in relation to appropriate housing facilities. (Special considerations for these populations are described in Part I.)

ROLE OF THE NURSE

To address these complex psychosocial problems, even communities outside the major metropolitan areas where HIV has hit hardest are educating the population about AIDS and developing resources. The hospital-based nurse can play a part in this work through the discharge planning process. The nurse's job is to identify and assess the needs of the HIV-infected individual and coordinate the services of the personnel and agencies that can meet these needs, always remembering that the goal is to enhance the patient's well-being and independence. For optimal results, the nurse should work as a member of an interdisciplinary team in the inpatient setting that coordinates its work with the relevant agencies and significant others in the patient's environment. The team's job is to orchestrate a wide variety of community services along a continuum of care, based on the dictates of the individual patient's wishes and stage of illness.

STAGES OF HIV INFECTION

Symptomatic HIV infection usually manifests in distinct stages. The early phase is marked by one or more bouts of acute infection, between which the person feels relatively well. During the middle phase the infections become chronically debilitating, and in the end stage the person nears death and is actively dying. An understanding of where the patient falls on this continuum and what issues typically arise during that phase can help a nurse who is assessing a patient to anticipate discharge needs.

The Acute Phase

In the acute phase, the patient is often hospitalized for an opportunistic infection requiring short-term treatment, such as PCP, from which the patient usually makes a good recovery. This treatment may well be the first time the person has been hospitalized for an HIV-related problem and possibly the first time the person has been diagnosed with full-blown AIDS. Under these circumstances, discharge concerns often focus on the specific issues of finances, housing, education, the patient's support network, outpatient treatment, and emotional issues.

Finances

The first concern is most often finances, including health insurance. As early as possible during the initial hospitalization, the nurse must thoroughly assess the patient's financial status and health insurance benefits. Is the person employed? Will the person be able to return to work? Are there emergency financial needs, such as rent, to be taken care of even before discharge? What will the source of payment be for ongoing medical needs, such as medications?

A social worker must be involved at an early date to assist the patient in negotiating the often confusing maze of assistance programs. In addition to any employer sick leave or state disability benefits for which the person may be eligible, federal government regulations stipulate that a confirmed AIDS diagnosis is presumptive evidence of medical eligibility for Social Security disability payments. In most states, indigent patients with AIDS also qualify for payment of some or all of their medical expenses under the federal Medicaid program. Patients with private medical insurance who must terminate their employment should be counseled regarding the value of continuing their coverage on a private-pay basis. A plan that reimburses for home care is most desirable.

In addition, the patient should be referred to AIDS service organizations if they exist in the area. Social workers associated with these agencies can ensure that the patient has access to services, such as food banks or bus passes, that might be available to them at reduced cost.

Housing

Many AIDS/ARC patients present with an unstable or nonexistent housing situation, either because of a drug-using life style or because the effects of HIV-related conditions have made employment impossible. Does the patient have a home? If so, is it a healthy environment? Will it continue to be affordable? Are there other housing options that the patient might exercise in the future?

A desire to maintain a "positive attitude" may make patients reluctant to look ahead to the day when their current housing is financially or medically unsuitable. Social workers and discharge planners should encourage the patient to discuss housing with family and friends and to explore such programs as the shared low-cost residences for PWAs that private or public agencies have established in some cities.

Education

Education is a key component of the discharge plan in this initial stage to prevent premature return to the hospital or continued transmission of the disease. Knowing what to expect can reduce the anxiety of the patient and significant others.

Immediately upon diagnosis, the nurse must assess the knowledge deficits of the patient and key caretakers and develop a teaching plan. Do patients understand the diagnosis, treatment, and prognosis? Do patients need help explaining them to family and friends? Are patients familiar with the expected progress of the illness? Do patients know what signs and symptoms should prompt a visit or call to a care provider? Is everyone clear about measures to prevent transmission of the virus in the home setting and about safe sexual practices and safe needle use? Are patients familiar with the care and operation of equipment, such as a central IV line or oxygen, that will be used in the home? Do patients know the nature of medications to be taken, their dosage schedule, and their side effects?

The nurse is responsible for becoming familiar with all components of the educational plan and for achieving a level of comfort in discussing sensitive issues, such as sexual practices, with the patient and significant others, as described in Chapter 25. Because a high level of anxiety usually accompanies the initial diagnosis, and because this anxiety is likely to interfere with the learning process, frequent repetitions of educational concerns are desirable. The nurse should provide the patient with illustrated brochures and printed materials that reinforce key points. The patient may require outpatient referrals to a visiting nurse from the public health department or a private agency to continue the educational process.

Support Network

An important step in discharge planning is to identify key caregivers in the patient's environment as early as possible. Their role will become vital in ensuring that the patient can remain at home as the illness progresses. Who is willing to provide support? How extensive and stable is the network of family and friends? How available are they to the patient?

Churches and other organizations in some cities are recruiting and training volunteers to help AIDS patients at home with more physically exerting tasks such as shopping, laundry, and light housekeeping. The patient should be informed of programs like these as well as of services for the disabled, such as transportation to medical appointments and books on tape for the blind, that might be available to PWAs.

Outpatient Treatment

Patients may have scant need for outpatient treatment at this time. However, the nurse should arrange for ongoing monitoring of the patient's condition and ability to function in the home environment. Wherever possible, outpatient care providers should become acquainted with the patient before discharge to facilitate follow-up and continuity of care. Will the patient be followed by a private physician or appropriate clinic? Is there a dentist willing to provide care? Are there skilled nursing needs, such as administration of IV drugs, that will continue at home?

Many visiting nurse and home care agencies have been able to incorporate AIDS patients into their regular caseloads, while others have established specialized programs. Nurses involved in discharge planning should know the capabilities and admissions requirements of various home care agencies in their community. The nurse should be prepared to refer the patient to physicians and other health care professionals with experience in caring for PWAs.

Emotional Issues

Often the patient and loved ones do not experience the emotional impact of the life-threatening diagnosis of AIDS until after the first hospitalization. What feelings have the patient and significant others expressed during the hospitalization? Was the diagnosis a shock to the patient? To family and friends? Is there a history of psychiatric illness or substance abuse? If a drug user, is the individual interested in treatment?

Peer support groups in which PWAs or their family members can talk with others who are facing the same problems may be available. Patients who require individual therapy or spiritual counseling should be referred to therapists and clergymen in the community who are familiar with the emotional issues endemic to AIDS. Patients with more serious psychiatric problems, such as a history of suicide attempts, should always be evaluated for outpatient treatment, preferably by someone experienced in distinguishing emotional disorders from the organic brain syndromes often seen in AIDS patients. Likewise, people who have abused alcohol or drugs should be taught about such subjects as safe needle use and be referred to treatment programs, if they desire. (See Chapter 4 for further discussion of substance abuse.)

The Chronic Phase

In the second or chronic stage of AIDS, the need for frequent hospitalizations often increases as the patient's ability to fight off opportunistic infections declines. The patient's energy level, mental status, and general ability to perform activities of daily living often progressively deteriorate. During this stage, a new set of discharge planning questions is likely to arise.

Home Care

Evaluating the effect of the progression of the illness on the patient's and caregivers' ability to function in the home environment is important in the chronic phase. In many cases, this phase is the point at which the patient is becoming too debilitated to perform some or all activities of daily living. Perhaps a meals-on-wheels program is sufficient; perhaps a few hours of daily attendant care is required while a caretaker is at work. The patient who is incontinent or in danger of falling may need a home care nurse. In some cases, patients in this stage of illness require 24-hour nursing care or supervision because they are bedbound or demented. Under these conditions, the patient may not be able to return home, and a board-and-care home or chronic care facility that admits PWAs must be located.

Housing

For patients who live alone, the chronic phase may well be the time they decide to move in with roommates or family members to increase access to practical and emotional support. This phase is also an important time to assess the ability of those who are already involved with the patient to give the care needed, as significant others may not be emotionally or practically capable of providing the assistance the patient needs at this stage. Perhaps supplementing their attention with volunteer help or attendant care will enable them to continue to care for the patient at home.

Legal Issues

Legal questions associated with the end of life often arise at this time, and nurses should encourage patients and families to discuss them. In most cases it is advisable to consult a lawyer about the execution of documents such as a will or a "living will" or to designate someone to speak for the patient about health care or financial matters if the patient becomes unable to do so. Clear documentation of a patient's desires regarding such issues as mechanical life support can greatly enhance the quality of life and lessen the anxiety of loved ones when they are confronted with difficult treatment decisions during the last months and weeks of life.

Emotional Issues

Counseling during the chronic phase is likely to focus on helping the patient and significant others to move from the psychological stages of denial and anger to a place of acceptance. The PWA may be fearful of becoming a "burden" to loved ones. Caretakers, on the other hand, may need encouragement to take care of their own needs and to accept "outside" help, at least for respite.

Terminal Phase

In the terminal phase the individual is actually dying, and the prognosis is framed in terms of weeks or days rather than months. Patients are likely to be hospitalized for an exacerbation of chronic problems for which no further treatment is possible or desired. Under these conditions, discharge usually centers on placement, disposition of remains, and emotional issues.

Placement

Depending on physical manifestations, hospice care in the home may be possible through the combined efforts of a home care agency, family, and friends. When the support network or financial constraints do not allow this, or when the patient feels more secure with 24-hour professional help, placement in a residential hospice or skilled nursing facility is preferable to staying in the acute care setting.

Unfortunately, the level of care described above is still not available to PWAs in many areas of the country. If this is the case, the patient must be made aware that "comfort care" without aggressive treatment is an option even in the acute care setting.

Disposition of Remains

During the terminal phase it is often helpful to inquire about funeral arrangements and other decisions to be made following death. Such inquiries can help identify the patient's wishes and the individual designated to carry them out, and can minimize disagreements among family members and friends.

Emotional Issues

A common theme for both patients and loved ones during this stage is the willingness to "let go." Counseling from a social worker experienced in issues of death and dying can show people that "acceptance" does not mean relinquishing hope. For many people, the grieving process begins even before death. Bereavement support groups, which may or may not be AIDS-identified, are available in many communities and are a helpful referral for some who have lost a loved one to AIDS.

CONCLUSION

In the early days of the AIDS epidemic, the paucity of needed services and facilities in the community meant that patients were likely to languish in the acute hospital setting for weeks or even months after their acute care needs were resolved. In a worse scenario, patients who had no home or referral for follow-up care were discharged, setting the stage for a quick return to the hospital and another lengthy hospitalization. Either case diminished the quality of the HIV-infected individual's life and incurred costs of millions of health care dollars on the local and national levels.

The development of volunteer networks, hospice programs, and other AIDS-specialized resources has changed the situation dramatically in many cities. The nurse involved in discharge planning in the hospital can play an important role in assuring the continuation of this trend by actively encouraging the involvement of community-based agencies in the inpatient discharge planning process. Nurses can foster the development of needed services by inviting representatives of pertinent agencies, such as home hospices and skilled or chronic nursing facilities, into the hospital to open dialogue about correlating patient needs with available resources. Informal liaisons with church groups or other agencies or facilities that can provide volunteer practical or emotional support are desirable. Nurses should inform themselves about AIDS organizations in nearby metropolitan areas that can provide referrals for patient services.

Early discharge planning for the HIV-infected patient in any stage is of paramount importance. After identifying the stated wishes of the individual and significant others, the nurse can assess the patient's ability to perform activities of daily living, the suitability of the home environment, and the availability of services needed. The patient and loved ones need time to adjust to changes in life style necessitated by the progress of the disease, and frequently the scarcity of home care resources or chronic care facilities for people with AIDS results in waiting lists. Early planning is necessary to ensure that individualized, comprehensive care is available on discharge.

REFERENCES

Coleman, D.A. "How to Care for an AIDS Patient." *RN* 49, no. 7 (July 1986):16–21.

DeHovityz, J.A. "Planning for the AIDS Epidemic: Public Health Control Measures and the Provision of Patient Care." *Journal of Community Health* 11, no. 45 (Winter 1986):215–17.

Feuer, L.C. "Discharge Planning: Home Caregivers Need Your Support, Too." *Nursing Management* 18, no. 4 (April 1987):58–159.

Levine, A.; Quick, B.; and Yanez, L. "The Uneven Odds." *U.S. News and World Report*, August 17, 1987, pp. 31–32.

Moed, Allison. "Discharge Planning for Persons with AIDS." In *The Person with AIDS: Nursing Perspectives*, edited by J. Durham and F. Cohen. New York: Springer, 1987, pp. 150–60.

Schietinger, Helen. "A Home Care Plan for AIDS." *American Journal of Nursing* 86, no. 9 (September 1986):1021–28.

Scitovsky, M.A. and Ricke, D.P. "Estimates of the Direct and Indirect Costs of Acquired Immunodeficiency Syndrome in the United States, 1985, 1986, and 1991." *Public Health Reports* 102, no. 1 (January–February 1987):5–17.

Chapter 20

AIDS Nursing Care in the Home

Dena Dickinson, Christina M. F. Clark, and
Maria J. Gonzales Swafford

Community nursing is a significant factor in the lives of persons affected by HIV. Health care needs extend beyond hospital and clinic visits; complex issues arise at home and in the community. The physical and psychosocial impact of HIV-related illness is frequently compounded by loss of job, insurance, and support systems. Nurses working in the PWA's home must comprehensively assess all of the client's needs.

Nursing care delivered in the community assists clients in maintaining an optimum level of health and functioning throughout the course of illness. Preserving both quality of life and client autonomy is an important component in the provision of care. This goal is often better accomplished in the home environment, which is more conducive to maintenance of relationships with family, friends, lovers, and others. The home allows more normalcy by preserving some connection with support systems and providing a greater opportunity for personal autonomy. Home care also reduces the cost of health care and the utilization of resources severely taxed by the AIDS epidemic.

The complexity of the care these clients require distinguishes it from care of clients with other illnesses. Financial, psychosocial, and housing problems compound the situation, and the severity and unpredictability of the disease accentuate clients' needs. Changes in status occur rapidly; all body systems may become affected. There may be many acute, life-threatening episodes during the progression of the disease. Clients usually have concurrent infections for which they are being treated, and nursing needs become more complex with the onset of each new problem. Aggressive medical treatments promote recovery from many of the opportunistic infections and reduction of disease symptoms. (For further discussion of medical treatment, see Chapter 14.)

ROLES OF NURSES IN THE HOME

Risk reduction and disease prevention comprise the primary approach to the HIV epidemic. Many individuals do not know they are among the over 1 million

HIV-infected persons and that they may be carriers. Therefore, nurses, including public health nurses (PHNs), must take an active part in educating all populations, not just those identified as high risk, regarding high-risk behaviors, modes of transmission, and actions that prevent the spread of HIV.

Several nurses, often with overlapping roles, may care for patients in the home. PHNs, home care nurses, and hospice nurses provide basic nursing functions:

- assessment
- monitoring
- teaching
- counseling
- case management
- implementation of prescribed treatment
- referral.

Home care and hospice agency involvement usually requires reimbursement, the source of which varies greatly among states and individuals.

PHNs provide services to individuals, families, and the community. They may intervene at any point along the continuum of illness, from the time an individual is at risk for infection through the terminal phase of the disease. An epidemiological approach focuses on education and prevention, but PHNs are also involved in long-term monitoring and case management. The nurse may be the primary advocate for the client in the health and social services. Often clients live alone and cannot carry out ADLs to provide for their own needs. PHNs help them arrange for necessary supports and community resources.

Home care nursing becomes involved as the client needs skilled treatment at home. The challenge of providing home care to people with HIV-related illnesses lies in the rollercoaster nature of the disease, in which periods of apparent health alternate with exacerbation. The varied and multiple physical and psychosocial issues involved make each case unique. Often problems do not respond to standard treatments, and the nurse must rely on a mixture of skills, knowledge, creativity, and compassion. The client may require wound care for lesions or decubiti, IV therapy for fluid replacement or medications, and pain or symptom management. Clients may also require a home health aide to assist with personal care, a physical therapist to assist in adapting to functional limitations, or both.

Hospice nursing begins during the terminal phase of the disease. The issue of death not only surfaces at this stage but must be confronted from the onset of illness. (For a discussion of hospice care, see Chapters 21 and 27.)

NURSING PROCESS

The nursing process must be individualized to each client. A thorough assessment that encompasses physical condition, psychosocial concerns, environmental factors, and financial concerns is critical. Information about disease status is obtained through the health history:

- perception of illness
- symptoms of opportunistic infections
- medication regimen
- alternative therapies
- allergies
- diet and hydration
- activity level and functional limitations
- sexuality
- substance use
- identification of psychosocial issues.

Self-care capabilities and availability of support systems are also essential pieces of information. The home environment must also be assessed early:

- living conditions
- availability of cooking and laundry facilities
- accessibility of stores and transportation
- hindrances to activities
- potential sources of infection or injury.

Examining an HIV-infected client involves the same assessment skills and professional judgment as examining any other client. However, the physical examination of the HIV-infected client is often more extensive because of the greater potential for problems resulting from acute opportunistic infections. All systems are assessed at intake, which allows the case manager to establish a data base and generate the nursing diagnoses. On subsequent visits, the examination is tailored to the client's needs but must routinely cover the following areas, which are prone to opportunistic infections: eyes, mouth, lungs, groin and rectum, skin, GI tract, as well as neurologic and mental status.

Nursing Care Plan

The nursing care plan (see Appendix 20-A) is contingent on the client's perception of the disease, the baseline assessment data, and the goals for care.

Family, friends, and caregivers should participate in development of the care plan, since the client's cognitive function may be impaired. Family members may be able to provide information the client is unable to recall and also indicate their availability to assist with care at home. Collaboration with the physician, clinic, and other health care providers is essential in designing a plan that meets the client's many needs. Care planning also provides an excellent opportunity to help clients strengthen their capacity to make decisions regarding care and treatment, to cope with the stress of illness and loss, and to prevent or manage crises while maintaining maximum autonomy.

Nursing diagnoses should focus on the actual problems experienced by the client and family. The magnitude of the problems faced by clients with HIV infection makes it unworkable to cover all possibilities here. Some possible nursing diagnoses include:

- impaired gas exchange
- alteration in GI function
- alteration in temperature regulation
- circulation impairment
- impairment of skin integrity
- alteration in mental status
- inadequate financial, housing, or health resources.

Family, friends, and volunteers frequently assist in providing personal care, maintaining the household, and monitoring the patient's status. Establishing a care plan that includes such support can be valuable to the nurse, the client, and the caregiver. (For an example of this type of care plan, refer to Appendix 20-B.)

Nursing Interventions

Nursing interventions depend on the problems identified. Education and instruction are appropriate nursing actions for virtually all clients. By understanding disease progression, characteristics of conditions, and symptoms of opportunistic infections, the client and family can monitor and identify problems. Education about medications and treatment regimens is necessary to increase clients' compliance and ability to make decisions. Information on self-care techniques and use of community resources helps clients maintain their independence. Education about nutrition, dietary supplements, and food preparation is also necessary, as is advice on symptom management. Instruction should be culturally sensitive and include support of beliefs and preferences related to diet and other aspects of health.

Counseling is essential because clients are coping with continuing physical and emotional changes, many of which threaten life style, body image, self-esteem, and self-sufficiency. (For further discussion of these issues, see Chapter 8.)

Psychosocial problems may be complicated by organic mental disorders, including delirium and dementia caused by HIV, opportunistic infections, drug use, or a combination. The nurse contributes to a differential diagnosis of the condition to determine the cause and appropriate treatment. Thus the nurse should evaluate the onset of mental status changes and their relation to drug use and identify cognitive, affective, or physical signs and symptoms of neurological involvement that can provide valuable information for all care providers. The nurse may play an important role in monitoring the client for these changes, as well as in helping to provide a structured and supportive environment. Consistent surroundings, routine schedules, and familiarity of objects and people aid in the management of dementia. Medications that depress the CNS should be minimized and drug interactions closely evaluated.

Confusion and disorientation are initial signs of neurological involvement that may progress to headaches, focal motor deficits, and seizures followed by coma and death. Memory loss, impaired concentration, apathy, agitation, ataxia, and tremors are other signs of the early stages of AIDS dementia or other problems such as CNS lymphomas, toxoplasmosis, or progressive multifocal leukoencephalopathy. Individuals may be referred to the physician for medical or psychiatric evaluation, diagnosis, and treatment. The nurse should counsel families to aid them in understanding the changes.

Case Management

Case management is a primary role of PHNs and home care nurses. The services clients require evolve from the complex needs that manifest throughout HIV infection. The AIDS or ARC client usually experiences profound weakness and fatigue and cannot cope with the many problems they face. When clients can no longer work and lose income sources, they may also lose health insurance and often need assistance in establishing continuing medical management. To conserve money, some clients may not buy sufficient food or heat their homes. Some lose their housing because of cost or conflict with roommates and may thus require assistance in relocating. With disease progression, clients require help with housekeeping chores, grocery shopping, laundering clothes, and meal preparation. The nurse helps establish and coordinate the many different services needed, which can involve referring the client to several agencies and organizations and supervising support services.

Monitoring

Monitoring of medications, symptom management, and disease progression is an important ongoing nursing function. Clients may need medisets, calendars, or other orientation aids to use as memory devices for compliance with medications and treatments. Some patients self-medicate or modify prescribed doses in an attempt to relieve symptoms. Many medications have significant side effects and interactions that must be monitored. Nurses should also consider nontraditional treatments when evaluating the effects and interactions of medications.

Nurses should monitor symptoms and alter interventions as required. Alternative methods, such as visualization, relaxation techniques, diversional activities, and massage, often enhance traditional interventions. Neurological status and other systems affected by infections must be frequently reassessed because change can occur precipitously. The nurse must communicate any changes in status and problems to the clinician for timely intervention.

Treatments and Physical Care

Home care nurses routinely provide treatments and physical care based on standard nursing practice and specific medical orders. Wound care may be necessary for ulcerated KS lesions, herpes lesions, and other sites of skin breakdown. Oxygen administration may be prescribed for respiratory compromise. The client may need physical, speech, and occupational therapies. Central IV lines are placed for the administration of medications, TPN, or both, as described in Chapter 15.

Evaluation and Referral

The final phase of the nursing process is evaluation and referral, if required. Evaluating the care plan and disease progression is an ongoing process, and nurses must frequently modify plans to meet changing conditions and needs. Care also involves a significant number of referrals, although limited community resources may pose difficulties in arranging for necessary services. Collaboration with other health care and social services is critical. Creative thinking and coordination of efforts, the hallmarks of community nursing, are particularly needed with HIV clients.

INFECTION CONTROL IN THE HOME

Infection control techniques based on scientific principles and good standard practices (as described in Chapter 18) should guide precautions in the home.

Excessive measures are unnecessary and can contribute to the client's psycho-social disturbance. There has been no documented case of AIDS being transmitted by casual contact in homes where PWAs share kitchens, dishes, and bathrooms with others. The virus is controlled by basic hygienic practices; liquid soap and paper towels limit reservoirs of bacteria.

Normal household cleaning prevents the growth of organisms that might cause illness in the immunosuppressed individual. Spills of blood, body fluid, or excretions should be cleaned with soapy water and then disinfected with a dilute (10 percent) solution of household bleach, which kills the virus. Body fluids may be flushed in the regular sewer system. Items soiled with blood or body fluids should be discarded in sealed plastic bags and removed by the usual garbage disposal service, and trash cans should be lined with plastic bags that prevent leakage. Basic, routine household cleaning is indicated.

PWAs benefit greatly from keeping pets but should not clean up after them. If no one else is available, the client should be cautioned to use gloves when cleaning bird cages (because of the risk of psittacosis), cat litter boxes (because of the risk of toxoplasmosis), and tropical fish tanks (because of the risk of mycobacterium). Other regional organisms may warrant special caution.

As noted in Chapter 18, needles should not be recapped, bent, or broken after use but placed directly into a puncture-resistant container such as a large coffee can that is covered and stored in a safe place when not in use. The container should be disposed of according to agency policy. Some agencies advocate sealing the container with tape before regular disposal; others direct clients to bake the container at 400°F for 30 minutes (which melts syringes to prevent reuse) and then to dispose of the sealed container in regular trash; still others suggest returning containers to a central location for disposal. The guiding principle should be preventing exposure to contaminated supplies.

Because AIDS is a devastating disease, families and health care workers fear for their safety. Education about transmission and precautions is essential to allay some of the fears. The nurse can assist caregivers by being a role model in following infection control guidelines while also demonstrating closeness and warmth by openly showing affection by touching clients, who may feel "untouchable." The nurse thus sets an example for other caregivers about the safety of such contact.

CONCLUSION

The course of HIV-related illness may fluctuate in its presentation and severity of symptoms. It may be short or protracted. The nurse must set priorities for plans according to the stage of the disease and adjust visit schedules accordingly. Visits may be lengthy when clients have multiple problems and concerns. More frequent and shorter visits may be more productive to conserve the client's energy and ensure knowledge retention. Due to the overwhelming problems associated with AIDS, it is useful for home care agencies to provide on-call services to reduce client and caregiver anxiety as well as to assist in symptom management or death.

The comprehensive and devastating nature of the disease requires the attention of many people. A multidisciplinary approach is ideal but not always feasible. The importance of early involvement and coordinated services by health care professionals, other agencies, and personal support systems cannot be overemphasized. Care requires close communication between the nurse and the physician to provide appropriate and effective interventions. The nurse can play an important part in assisting the client to make decisions about approaches to therapy (aggressive versus palliative) and death (home versus hospital). The roles of community health nurses can be essential in permitting the person with HIV-related illnesses to stay at home rather than be confined to a hospital. The experience, training, compassion, and professional focus of these nurses permit them to provide a central role in dealing with this profound challenge.

REFERENCES

Acevedo, J. "Understanding ARC: The Broader Spectrum of AIDS." *Focus: A Review of AIDS Research* 1, no. 3 (February 1986).

Bernstein, P.H., Parker-Martin, J., and Franks, P. "Aid for AIDS: United Way Funds AIDS Care in Houston." *Caring* 5, no. 6 (June 1986):47–52.

Brammer, M.L. *The Helping Relationship.* Englewood Cliffs, N.J.: Prentice-Hall, Inc., 1979, pp. 67–76.

Bryant, J.K. "Home Care of the Client with AIDS." *Journal of Community Health Nursing* 3, no. 2 (1986):69–74.

Budd, Cathie. "Nutritional Care of Patients with *Pneumocystis carinii* Pneumonia." *Nutritional Support Services* 2, no. 12 (December 1982):12–13.

Carr, G. and Gee, G. "AIDS and AIDS-Related Conditions: Screening for Populations at Risk." *Nurse Practitioner* 11, no. 10 (October 1986):25–48.

DeVita, V., Hellman, S., and Rosenberg, S. *AIDS Etiology, Diagnosis, Treatment, and Prevention.* Philadelphia: J.B. Lippincott, 1985.

DiClemente, R. and Boyer, C. "Ethnic and Racial Misconceptions about AIDS." *Focus: A Review of AIDS Research* 2, no. 3 (February 1987).

Gonda, R. and Ruark, J. *Dying Dignified: The Health Professional's Guide to Care.* Menlo Park, Calif.: Addison-Wesley, 1984.

Hughes, A.M., Parker-Martin, J., and Franks, P. *AIDS Home Care and Hospice Manual.* San Francisco AIDS Home Care and Hospice Program, 1987.

Lieberman, J. *Home Health Care and AIDS.* Unpublished manuscript, June 1987.

Lusby, E., Parker-Martin, J., and Schietinger, H. "Infection Control at Home: A Guide for Caregivers to Follow." *American Journal of Hospice Care* (March/April 1986):12–22.

Mandel, Jeff. "The Psychosocial Challenges of AIDS and ARC." *Focus: A Review of AIDS Research* 1, no. 2 (January 1985).

Mills, S. "Attitudes and Trends: Public Perception of AIDS." *Focus: A Review of AIDS Research* 2, no. 1 (December 1986).

Namir, S. "Treatment Issues Concerning Persons with AIDS." In *What To Do about AIDS*, edited by L. McKusick. Berkeley: University of California Press, 1986, pp. 87–94.

Navia, B. A., Jordan, B.D., and Price, R.W. "The AIDS Dementia Complex." *Annuals of Neurology* 19, no. 6 (June 1986):517–35.

Parker-Martin, J. "Challenges in Caring for the Person with AIDS at Home." *Caring* 5, no. 6 (June 1986):12–22.

Schietinger, H. "A Home Care Plan for AIDS." *American Journal of Nursing* 86, no. 9 (September 1986):1021–28.

Swafford, M. "Caregiver-In-Home Careplan." Unpublished manuscript, January 1986.

Webster, M. "Are AIDS Patients Getting Good Nursing Care?" *Nursing Life*, January/February 1987, pp. 48–53.

Wolcott, C.L. "Neuropsychiatric Syndrome in AIDS and AIDS-Related Illnesses." In *What to Do about AIDS*, pp. 32–44.

Wright, L., and Leahey, M. *Nurses' and Families' Guide to Family Assessment and Intervention*. Philadelphia: F.A. Davis, 1984.

Appendix 20-A

Home Nursing Care Plan

Date _____

Nurse _____
Patient _____

Problem/Etiology	Assessment	Nursing Action
Impaired gas exchange related to:	Respiratory rate, breath sounds, vital signs	Teach energy conservation techniques
P. carinii pneumonia	Cough—dry vs. productive	Teach pursed lip breathing, deep breath and cough
Bacterial pneumonia	Green-yellow sputum w/bacterial pneumonia	Decrease aggravating factors: anxiety, environmental
Pulmonary KS	Percussion/auscultation	Increase fluids to thin secretions
CMV pneumonitis	Dull + rales w/pneumonia	Give oxygen therapy per orders
Tuberculosis	Dull + crackles w/pulmonary KS	Instruct re: recognition of S/S infection; pulmonary care regime; use of medications, O_2
MAI	Clear w/PCP	Give medications as prescribed by physician for cough and control of pulmonary secretions
Anemia	Cool extremities, pallor, cyanosis	Refer for immediate evaluation of acute distress or unanticipated worsening condition
	Anxiety, irritability	
	Activity tolerance	

Source: Maria Gonzales Swafford.

224

Alteration in GI function related to:	*Nausea and Vomiting* belching	If vomiting, give no food/fluid × 1–2 hours, then gradual intake of ice chips; sips of ginger ale, clear fluids; progress as tolerated
Cryptococcal meningitis	Weight, changes	Teach relaxation and breathing techniques
Cryptosporidiosis	Fluid and electrolyte imbalance	Give antiemetics as prescribed and administer 30 minutes ac
CMV		Provide frequent oral care
MAI		Give appealing meals, food supplements
Adrenal insufficiency		Increase fluids as tolerated
Medication or radiation		Limit dietary fiber, hold supplements, e.g., Ensure
KS in GI tract		
Malabsorption	*Diarrhea*—frequency, quantity	Increase fluids to maintain/replace balance
Narcotics	Poor skin turgor	Encourage potassium-rich foods (give list)
Diet	Dehydration and electrolyte imbalance	Give prescribed antidiarrheals—may need around the clock
Inactivity	Hypokalemia—fatigue, weakness, anorexia, hypoactive reflexes	Alternating meds (e.g., Lomotil and Immodium) may increase effect; Metamucil may help regulate
	Abdominal pain and cramping	Give meticulous perirectal skin care using skin barriers
		Discuss use of incontinence appliances, e.g., fecal incontinence bags, adult diapers, pads
		Identify precipitating factors and treat if possible
		Instruct re: monitoring for constipation/impaction

continues

Problem/Etiology	Assessment	Nursing Action
GI function (cont.)	Constipation	Increase dietary fiber and fluids Give stool softeners routinely Give laxatives and enemas as prescribed
Alteration in temperature regulation related to: Viral and bacterial infection Medication induced, e.g., AZT, amphotericin HIV infection primary UTI	Temperature–persistent vs. intermittent Effective meds or other treatments	Monitor temperature T > 101.5°F, assess for acute infection Encourage fluids as tolerated Give tepid sponge baths prn Bathe and change linen as needed Determine if patient desires to pursue aggressive treatment Obtain specimen for culture and sensitivity as ordered Medicate w/antipyretics as needed
Circulation impairment, edema related to: KS lesions obstructing lymphatic or venous system Dehydration Malnutrition	Degree of swelling—measure, pitting Pain, numbness, tingling Ulceration, skin breakdown Dehydration Skin care practices Pulses, skin temperature	Instruct re: skin/foot care Massage gently with oil/lotion to prevent skin breakdown Avoid use of strong soaps on skin Elevate extremities Use support stockings in initial stages, scrotal support Facial edema—elevate HOB, cool compresses to eyes

		Assess for difficulty swallowing or breathing
		Refer for immediate evaluation if indicated
Impairment of skin integrity related to:	Thorough assessment for any skin lesions or breakdown, size, characteristics, odor	Encourage position change and mobility as tolerated.
KS lesions	Determine current treatment/medications being used and compliance	Instruct re: skin care techniques, hygiene, recognition to new pathology, use of medications and treatments.
Herpes—genital or oral		Soak feet and hands in warm water and apply isopropyl alcohol to prevent fungal infections; dry thoroughly
Molluscum contagiosum		
Fungal infections		
Bacterial infections		
Immobility/decubiti		
Abscesses		
Dehydration		
Incontinence		
Pruritis	Kaposi's sarcoma	Observe size and report to MD for consideration of chemo/radiation. Usually no care unless draining
Seborrheic dermatitis	Purplish lesions that do not blanch	Cleanse w/soap and H_2O, pat dry, leave open to air
Candida		For draining wounds:
		Betadine soaked gauze, BID
		Vaseline gauze wrap, BID
		Vigilon or protective dressings
		Carbol—Fuchsin solution (Castellani paint)—paint on lesions qd to dry lesions and prevent breakdown. Lower extremities' lesions only

continues

Problem/Etiology	Assessment	Nursing Action
Skin integrity (cont.)	Candida (oral) Vary from scant white coating on the tongue to clumps of white curdlike material that cannot be removed by scraping	Use vigorous mouth care—brush teeth 2–3×/day Use toothettes or gauze on gloved finger to clean tongue and buccal mucosa Oral rinse: H_2O_2 ½-strength solution or salt and baking soda solution rinse
	Candida (skin/perineal) Erythematous patches and geographic configurations or dry, flaky, reddened skin	Wash with nonirritating soap, dry with blow dryer 2–4×/day, apply antifungal creams
	Rashes/generalized pruritis	Cleanse skin with soap and water, dry thoroughly Apply lotions or creams as prescribed For itching without rash, recommend Cetaphil-Phenol-Menthol lotion and apply prn
	Dermatitis Involves scalp, face, beard	Use steroidal creams and soap bars as prescribed Use Eucerin cream to decrease scaling and flaking Use Seborex or other dandruff shampoo 3×/week

Decubiti
Reddened or excoriated areas over pressure points

Prevent! Use gel or foam pads, air mattress, eggcrate mattress, electric air beds, overhead trapeze, bed cradle
Instruct client and caregiver re: frequent position change and skin care
Keep skin clean and dry. Use condom catheter and fecal incontinence bags to prevent skin irritation and breakdown
Use massage with lotions, oils, creams to stimulate circulation
Apply skin barriers to prevent skin breakdown, e.g., Duoderm, Tegaderm, Opsite

Herpes—types 1 and 2, oral and genital and surrounding skin

Wear gloves when caring for lesions and rashes
Wash lesions w/soap and H_2O, air dry, dress with dry gauze
Perirectal lesions—give sitz baths and analgesics to relieve discomfort
Oral lesions—apply Mylanta or other chalky solution topically, honey held in mouth as soothing agent
Vigorous mouth care—brushing teeth 2–3 ×/day, use toothettes or gauze on gloved finger to clean

continues

Problem/Etiology	Assessment	Nursing Action
Alteration in mental status related to: Primary HIV brain involvement Opportunistic infections *Toxoplasma gondii* Cryptococcus Cytomegalovirus Varicella-zoster virus *Candida albicans* KS CNS lesions Progressive multifocal leukoencephalopathy Iatrogenic drug induced Depression/affective disorder Substance abuse	History of changes in mental status, sensory function, motor function, behavioral patterns, seizure activity Subjective findings: impaired concentration, apathy, dull headaches, photophobias, tingling sensations in extremities, change in eye sight or hearing, unsteady gait, or loss of memory, drowsy, depression Objective findings: Cognitive—memory loss, mental slowing, confusion. Behavioral—apathy, withdrawal, agitation, hallucination, personality change, impulsivity, delusional thinking Motor—progressive loss of balance or coordination, paresis, facial palsy, difficulty swallowing, tremors, decreasing muscle tone, nuccal rigidity Drug/medication side effects or interactions Safety hazards re: to level of functioning Ability for self care, availability of supports/caretakers	Assist to develop systematic plan for medication and treatment program regimen with use of mediset and daily monitoring by caregiver Modify home environment for safety and convenience Remind family that changes are often more difficult for them to see than for the patient to experience Instruct re: management of seizure activity, monitoring of neuro/mental status, methods to react to strong emotional responses *Orientation*—use of clocks and calendars, night lights, written daily schedule of routine, appointments *Memory aids*—mediset for medications, alarm med boxes, telephone answering machines, tape cassettes for messages *Structured environment*—Keep uncluttered and consistent without major changes, use sign posts to help client find way around house, keep familiar objects around client, have caregiver provide assistance with ADLs and ensure safety

Communication—respond in calm manner, repeat information, give client only one thing to do at a time, avoid arguing, explain behavioral changes to family members and involve them in plan of care

Medications—Teach family/caregiver to care for central line if present for treatments, teach about signs of adverse reaction to drugs, administer antipsychotics, antianxiety agents, and other medications as prescribed

Assist with long-term care planning and placement if necessary

Inadequate financial, housing, and health resources related to:
Loss of employment
Loss of health insurance
Displacement

Determine financial, health, and housing needs
Discuss client's personal perception of problems and needs
Assess psycho/emotional response to situation
Determine eligibility for available assistance programs

Inform client/caregiver about various types of governmental disability programs (eg., SSI, SSA, state disability)
Inform about community food resources
Advocate for and assist to obtain services
Refer to available community resources
If medical provider not established, provide information and referral sources of knowledgeable medical services
Evaluate success in obtaining services/funds, to which client is entitled
Refer to social worker for further assistance in obtaining services if needed

Appendix 20-B

Caregiver/Aide
Patient Care Plan

Date _____

PT. NAME _____
RN _____
SW _____

Problem	What to do about it	Call RN if:	Charting
Generalized weakness, fatigue	1. Assist with personal hygiene, linen change, laundry, light shopping and housekeeping, bathing 2. Monitor and assist with ambulation 3. Encourage slow, steady movements and repositioning 4. Encourage spacing of activities, providing adequate rest periods 5. Encourage use of cane or walker if appropriate 6. Encourage frequent repositioning to alleviate pressure on skin	Weakness increases	Daily activity and tolerance

Source: Maria Gonzales.

Problem	Interventions		
Shortness of breath	7. Provide daily massage with lotion to stimulate circulation and prevent bedsores 8. Assist up to chair three times/day for meals 1. Allow adequate time for activities with rest periods 2. Space activities according to energy level 3. Monitor use of oxygen if ordered; clean equipment three times/week 4. Prop with pillows to sitting position if in bed	Any increase in SOB or respiratory distress	Tolerance to activity Presence of SOB; use of O$_2$ Cough
Loss of appetite; rapid weight loss (nutrition and hydration)	1. Assist with meal preparation 2. Encourage small, frequent meals and high protein, high-calorie snacks vs. three large meals 3. Encourage use of nutritional supplements, i.e., Ensure (may be made into delicious shakes mixed with fresh fruits, ice cream, protein powder, brandy, etc.) 4. Encourage fluids to hydrate and filter body 5. Encourage oral care to stimulate appetite and prevent thrush. Do three to four times a day, especially after meals and before bed/sleep 6. Apply Vaseline or other lip balm to dry lips	Persistent lack of appetite Oral sores	Appetite Presence of mouth sores
Pain	1. Offer massage, heating pad, soothing music, rest, visual imagery, meditation, deep breathing 2. Encourage to take medicine for pain as directed by RN or MD	Increase in pain or pain not relieved by medication	Presence of pain, location, and how and when relieved

continues

Problem	What to do about it	Call RN if:	Charting
Nausea &/or Vomiting	1. Encourage to take medication for nausea when no longer vomiting, or encourage to take it at least ½ hour before meals 2. Encourage deep, slow breathing when nauseated 3. Encourage use of Antacids 4. Offer popsicles, ice chips, ginger ale, sips tea, broth, flat 7-Up, dry toast, crackers as tolerated 5. Encourage fluids, i.e., Gatorade, when tolerated, to replace those lost in vomiting	Uncontrolled nausea and/or vomiting	Presence of nausea and/or vomiting, duration, and when/how relieved
Diarrhea	1. Encourage to take medication for diarrhea after each loose stool as directed by RN/MD 2. Keep skin *very* clean; wash with mild soap and water; dry with blow-dryer if skin is broken, and apply lotion, creams, oil, Desitin. Do not use talcum powder. 3. Avoid spicy foods, caffeine, and Ensure, as they may increase diarrhea 4. Encourage fluids such as Gatorade, broths, etc., in small amounts 5. Use bland, soft foods such as rice, banana flakes, applesauce	Uncontrolled diarrhea Red or broken skin around anus or buttocks	Number of stools and consistency of stool
Constipation	1. Encourage fluids; water, juices 2. Encourage mobility as tolerated 3. Use fresh fruits and vegetables whenever possible for meals and snacks	No bowel movement for three days or more	Lack of bowel movements

		Report	Record
	4. Use of stool softener or laxative as directed by RN/MD		
Bedsores (*prevent them!*)	1. Give daily skin massage to promote and improve circulation. Pay special attention to areas over bony prominences 2. Encourage changing position often to prevent pressure which leads to breakdown 3. Keep dry and clean if incontinent 4. Eggcrate on bed (ask RN to get one) 5. Apply heel and elbow protectors if bedridden 6. Apply Duoderm to bony areas such as coccyx and cover with Tegaderm to increase wearing time 7. Assist RN with wound care to open bedsores (RN will instruct you on wound care on individual basis)	Report reddened areas/bedsores	Condition of skin Size of reddened areas
Genital or Rectal Herpes	1. Wear gloves when caring for lesions or during rectal and genital care 2. Cleanse lesions with warm soapy water, rinse and pat dry or dry with blow-dryer 3. Do not use toilet paper on lesions as abrades; use soft cloth or Tucks/Wet Ones 4. Apply Zovirax cream to lesions after BMs and three times/daily	Increase in lesions Drainage or bleeding	Status of lesions

continues

Problem	What to do about it	Call RN if:	Charting
Depression	1. Be a good listener and stay in your hearts 2. Encourage person to verbalize his/her feelings 3. Offer support, encouragement, praise, feedback, humor, diversion 4. Take on walks or for rides to park, lunch, etc. if condition allows 5. Bring a surprise or a pet to stroke WEAR A SMILE. SHOW YOUR LOVE AND CARING!	Talks of suicide	Mood
Blindness	1. Do not change environment 2. Orient to surroundings often 3. Assist with feeding, or cut food and orient to placement of foods on plate 4. Do not leave hot foods, plates, liquids with person if unattended 5. If feed, do slowly and tell of approaching spoonful and what it is 6. Do not speak louder than normal. Hearing may not be affected 7. Assist with all activities of daily living and ambulation with safety in mind at all times 8. Do not leave unattended if smoking	Complains of eye pain	

| Altered mental status
Confusion
Disorientation
Combativeness
Hallucinations
Personality changes | 1. Reassure person of your presence, especially at night, to alleviate fears
2. Don't argue with their logic
3. Don't make complex, multistep demands
4. Post signs to bathroom, kitchen, bedroom
5. Keep a large clock and calendar on the wall
6. Don't change the environment
7. Reorient to time, place, person as needed when confused
8. Explain changes to family and involve them in the plan of care | Increase in confusion or other mental status changes that are new to person
Questions regarding care of person with altered mental status | Mental status |

Chapter 21

The Hospice Approach to Care

Robin Candace and Margaret Walter

HISTORY OF HOSPICE AS A PHILOSOPHY OF CARE

The hospice concept of caring for the dying is not new. Sandol Stoddard chronicles a history dating back 2,000 years.[1] The modern idea of hospice has its roots in medieval Europe, where numerous way stations emerged as places of respite for weary travelers. In the mid-1800s Mary Aikenhead founded an order of nuns, the Sisters of Charity, who opened what is considered the first modern hospice in Dublin, Ireland, and devoted themselves to the care of the terminally ill. The facility was called "hospes," from the French word meaning both guest and host. Mary Aikenhead eventually traveled to London, where she founded St. Joseph's Hospice.

In 1948 a nurse–social worker named Cicely Saunders was working at St. Joseph's. She was given a grant toward establishing her own hospice by a Jewish immigrant from the Warsaw Ghetto, who wanted only to be "a window in your home," a small contributor to this important work.[2] Ms. Saunders subsequently attended medical school and founded St. Christopher's Hospice in London.

It was during this period that the hospice movement, a system of comprehensive care for the dying based on their physical, psychological, and spiritual needs, was born. Dr. Saunders pioneered pain and symptom management, and St. Christopher's became a proving ground for many of the tenets of hospice care.

Many people can be credited with helping to develop a philosophy of care for the dying. Twenty years ago Dr. Elizabeth Kubler-Ross came to this country to continue her work with the terminally ill. When she asked physicians for the names of dying patients to interview she was told repeatedly, "there are no dying patients here." In the introduction to *Death: The Final Stage of Growth*, she encourages us to accept that "death does not have to be a catastrophic, destructive thing; indeed it can be viewed as one of the most constructive, positive and creative elements of culture and life."[3] She recognized that the dying are our teachers and that their lesson is not necessarily about death and dying but rather about life and living.

In this country hospice has evolved mainly as a system of home-based care. In 1978 the National Hospice Organization was established to promote the hospice concept of providing support and care for persons in the last phases of disease so that they can live as fully as possible.[4] The National Hospice Organization's *1986 Guide to the Nation's Hospices* lists almost 1,500 hospices, representing all 50 states.[5]

THE GOAL OF HOSPICE CARE

The goal of hospice care is to enable persons who are dying to function optimally, in spite of the devastating effects of their physical condition, by preventing pain and other symptoms, anticipating and minimizing the side effects of drugs and fatigue, and allowing control and independent decision making by the patient and "family" of caregivers.

Ideally, the person dying and those providing care experience the death in a positive manner. The literature offers many examples of people who have died peacefully, with dignity and awareness. Hospice is a means of facilitating this transition by providing an environment of openness and permission for whatever the outcome may be.

It is important for hospice workers to examine their own feelings and attitudes about death. When people are confronted by the dying process, it is normal to have feelings of helplessness, anger, and sadness. Caregivers have their own ideas about what a "good" death would be, but these may not match those of the patient.[6] A posture of openness and tolerance is preferable.

Sometimes there may not be anything to "do" for a person who is dying. What may be most helpful at these times is to demonstrate a way of being that is calm, thoughtful, and compassionate, without pity but with a willingness to be available for whatever is needed.

The goal of hospice is that all persons involved perceive the situation as manageable, without emergencies, with staff available to respond to needs as they arise. Often persons with terminal diagnoses identify their greatest fears as suffering and abandonment; hospice care attempts to address these fears.

COMPONENTS OF THE HOSPICE APPROACH

Hospice care uses a multidisciplinary approach to assist clients and their caregivers through the dying process. Programs vary greatly in form and in the range of services provided. Some are staffed completely by volunteers and run with little or no funding. These hospice programs may not consider themselves to be part of the traditional health care system.[7] On the other end of the continuum are programs that bill Medicare or other insurance, have a majority of paid staff, and provide a pool of volunteers as one of many services.

Following is a comprehensive listing of the services ideally provided for clients with AIDS/ARC by a fee-based professional hospice in a large community with a large client base. All of these services may not be appropriate in every community. Each community and hospice program must take stock of its own resources and determine which services it can provide to meet the needs of that community most effectively. Specific components of the hospice approach include:

- pain and symptom management
- emotional support to patient and family
- multidisciplinary team
- pastoral and spiritual care
- bereavement counseling
- 24-hour on-call nurse/counselor
- staff support.

Pain and Symptom Management

The hospice approach emphasizes quality of life. As such, control of pain and other unpleasant symptoms is a primary goal. For PWAs, pain may be less of a primary problem than are nausea, vomiting, and diarrhea. The focus of care is to control these symptoms and allow the patient to be as comfortable as possible while still being alert and able to interact with loved ones.

Emotional Support

Emotional pain may equal or surpass physical pain in causing discomfort and inability to function. The hospice approach emphasizes emotional support for clients and their partners, families, and friends as they face the issues of illness, dying, and death. Not everyone wishes to discuss these issues, and the hospice team must respect that decision and provide emotional support on other levels. For many persons, however, the willingness of team members to discuss death and the dying process frankly and openly is a relief. It enables them to ask questions, work through fears, and prepare for the coming events in a more realistic way. Talking about what is really happening may also enable the patient and loved ones to make a closer emotional connection.

Multidisciplinary Team

The hospice approach utilizes a multidisciplinary team to provide coordinated holistic care, as shown in Figure 21-1. Members of this team usually include:

- a registered nurse (RN) case manager
- a medical social worker (MSW)
- one or more home health aides, homemakers, or vocational nurses
- volunteers
- a medical consultant.

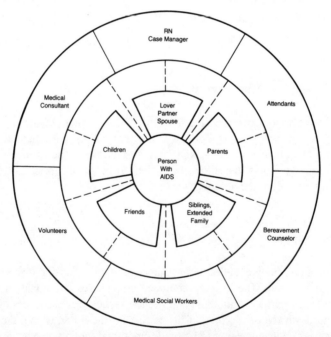

Figure 21-1 Lines of communication are direct from the hospice team to and from the patient as well as to and from the family support network. The hospice approach to care makes care to the family equally as important as care to the patient. The definition of family in hospice care is not limited to blood relations. It includes all close relationships.

Based on the specific needs of the client, the team may also include:

- rehabilitation therapists
- a nutrition consultant
- a pharmacist
- an IV nurse.

Specific to the needs of persons with HIV infection, a program may utilize consultants in two additional areas:

- a clinical psychologist, psychiatrist, or psychiatric social worker
- a substance abuse counselor.

RN Case Manager

The RN coordinates and manages direct patient care and the hospice team. On the initial visit, the RN makes an assessment, as described in Chapters 10 and 20. In addition, the RN:

- discusses disease prognosis and treatment goals with the patient's primary physician and determines if these goals are compatible with those of the patient and family
- serves as an advocate by assisting the patient and family to obtain the information necessary to make appropriate decisions
- provides physical care when needed
- supervises caregivers, hospice attendants, and volunteers
- educates the patient, caregivers, and hospice team in the areas of pain management, symptom control, and infection control precautions.

After completing the assessment, the RN institutes hospice services as needed. The hospice team holds conferences to discuss goals and to formulate an individualized plan of care that enables clients to live their lives as independently and fully as possible. Initial goals are regularly revised in response to new developments in the patient's condition.[8]

When the goals of the patient, family system, physician, or hospice team conflict, the RN must maintain communication with all members of this complex group and, jointly with the MSW, set up family meetings or arrange other interventions to clarify needs and set realistic mutual goals.

Medical Social Worker

The MSW conducts a mental status evaluation as one of the first steps in assessing the functioning and goals of the patient and family system. Further assessments by the MSW cover financial and environmental needs, availability of support systems, and legal needs, such as the existence of a will and delegated powers of attorney for health and finances.

In addition to these more concrete areas, the MSW assesses the emotional needs of clients and their support persons—how they have responded to the knowledge of illness and approaching death and how they are coping with this knowledge.

Based on this assessment, the MSW informs and counsels the patient and caregivers, and facilitates communication among the patient, family system, physician, and hospice team. Information is provided on community resources, especially public benefits and how to obtain them. If the patient and caregivers are unable to negotiate these systems, the MSW may intervene and advocate on the patient's behalf.

The MSW also counsels the client and caregivers to facilitate coping and assists them in planning for the future, especially in relation to legal and financial arrangements. As physical care becomes more demanding, the MSW assists the caregivers as they assess whether they can care for the patient without overstressing themselves and helps them set appropriate limits. If the patient and caregivers are ready, the MSW discusses funeral arrangements and assists with setting up a plan. Functions of the RN and MSW sometimes overlap.

Attendants: Home Health Aides and Vocational Nurses

A majority of PWAs who need home care or hospice services also need some level of attendant care, ranging from homemaking tasks to sophisticated nursing procedures. Members of the hospice team who provide attendant care may be:

- noncertified attendants, who provide basic homemaking services
- certified nursing assistants (CNAs) or home health aides (HHAs), who provide personal care as well as homemaking
- licensed vocational or practical nurses (LVNs, LPNs), who administer medications or tube feedings, change dressings, etc.

All providers of attendant services are valuable and necessary members of the team. They provide an ongoing assessment of the patient's physical condition and the family system's ability to cope that may be difficult for an RN or MSW, who visits the patient intermittently, to obtain. Attendants are paid much less than the value of the services they provide. As a home care and hospice manual states,

"The intensive needs for support and supervision for these caregivers cannot be overemphasized, as they are truly the front line providers."[9]

Volunteers

Volunteers, who often provide services otherwise unavailable because of financial restrictions, are vital to any hospice program. They assist in the office, help with fund raising, and provide direct patient care services, including homemaking, transportation, and grief counseling. Still others possess skills in special areas, such as massage therapy. Hospice programs train volunteers in the hospice philosophy, sensitivity to the needs of dying patients, and methods of dealing with their own feelings about death and dying. Support groups for volunteers and maintenance of good communication with the hospice team are essential for a successful ongoing volunteer pool.

Medical Consultation

When a hospice team sees a client, the treatment plan and orders for nursing and other services continue to come from the primary physician. In addition, the hospice team has a medical director/consultant who has expertise in pain and symptom management for the terminally ill and who advocates the hospice approach. This physician attends patient care conferences, provides staff inservice education, and is invaluable as an advocate for hospice within the medical community.

PRN Members of the Hospice Team

Physical, Occupational, and Speech Therapies. Rehabilitation therapies can often help meet the hospice goal of improved quality of life at all times. Physical therapy can help with equipment needs, assist patients with mobility, and teach caregivers how to move the patient easily and safely. (For more information, refer to Chapter 17.) Occupational therapy assists with ADL training or muscle reeducation after neurologic damage or onset of blindness. Speech therapy can assist in maintaining communication between the patient and caregivers and is especially helpful in cases of aphasia.

Nutrition Consultant. If a patient suffers from weight loss, poor appetite, chronic diarrhea, or nausea and vomiting, a nutritionist provides expertise in how to improve the patient's oral calorie and protein intake. If a patient needs TPN or tube feedings, a nutritionist may also be of assistance in determining the correct balance of nutrients. (See Chapter 16 for further discussion of the role of the nutritionist.)

Pharmacist. Patients who are taking many medications or are experiencing symptoms that are difficult to explain may need a pharmacist consult. The pharmacist can help to determine whether symptoms are side effects of one medication or the result of the interaction of several medications and suggest a more appropriate dosage or medication.

IV Therapy. IV therapy is used rarely in the traditional hospice setting since aggressive therapy is usually not pursued. If IV therapy is used, it is most often for hydration or pain control. The latter is infrequent when patients take appropriate oral medications.

For persons with AIDS/ARC, IV therapy may be a larger part of the overall hospice program. Opportunistic infections occur and recur frequently, and although treatment for them may be considered aggressive, it in no way alters the progression of the underlying disease. (For discussion of IV therapy, see Chapter 15.)

Psychiatric Services: Clinical Psychologist, Psychiatrist, or Psychiatric Social Worker. People with a terminal illness often experience a reactive depression. If they have a history of mental illness, the reactive depression may trigger it or make it worse. Such persons may need ongoing counseling. In persons with HIV infection, in which dementia is a major problem, differentiating between reactive depression, endogenous depression, and dementia may require additional expertise. If correctly diagnosed, depression may respond to antidepressant therapy. Correct diagnosis also assists caregivers in understanding and coping with erratic behavior and in continuing to provide support.

Substance Abuse Services. Persons with AIDS/ARC may also have a history of substance abuse and may exhibit drug-seeking behavior by asking for more or stronger medication. (See Chapter 4 for more information.) In addition to offering counseling and treatment to clients, a substance abuse consultant can educate and support staff who deal with persons having these additional problems.

Pastoral and Spiritual Care

In the broadest sense, all members of the multidisciplinary team try to extend spiritual care to the person suffering from a terminal illness. Clients may also seek out a member of the clergy or other spiritual healer. Inclusion of this practitioner in the team, if desired, can increase the client's ability to make decisions about accepting further aggressive treatment, making funeral arrangements, and other matters.

Bereavement Counseling

Survivors often need help in the grieving process, which can come from a bereavement counselor or bereavement volunteers who have completed a specialized training program. A hospice client's survivors may have access to these services for up to a year after their loved one has died.

When PWAs die, the same psychosocial factors that enter into provision of care complicate the grieving process for survivors. Lovers and friends may also have HIV infection or fear that they will develop the disease. Parents or families may have withheld support because they feared contagion or because of prejudice. These and related issues, plus the natural grief at the death of a loved one, make the grieving process more difficult.

Twenty-Four-Hour On-Call

A nurse or counselor who is available by phone or for home visits 24 hours a day is an important component of hospice. Crises often happen in the middle of the night or on weekends when normal support systems are least accessible. The 24-hour on-call nurse or counselor provides a connection to a support system as well as direct emotional support. If the patient dies in the night, the on-call person gives practical support by advising the partner or family how to proceed.

Staff Support

Support services for all members of the hospice team are necessary to retain staff and volunteers in the face of the emotional stress involved in assisting persons through the dying process. Burnout is a common problem for all health care professionals, but it can be an even more serious one for hospice staff. Patient care conferences are supportive of care planning, but hospice staff members need additional support services. Support groups may benefit from professional counselors acting as facilitators, and single-discipline meetings may be useful so staff can discuss discipline-specific problems and support. Support groups for non-professional staff and volunteers are equally necessary.

Supervisors' acknowledgment of the stressful nature of the job and flexibility in responding to that knowledge are invaluable in helping staff feel good about their work. Frequent inservice education programs are also helpful. Finally, good lines of communication among all staff members, supervisory through volunteer, reduce the stress level, help create trust, and help the team function better.

HOSPICE REIMBURSEMENT

The Medicare Hospice Benefit

In the fall of 1982 Congress passed the Tax Equity and Fiscal Responsibility Act (TEFRA). This complex piece of legislation contained a model for providing eligible Medicare beneficiaries with hospice care. In 1984 agencies certified by the Health Care Financing Administration (HCFA) began to provide hospice care under this model.

The usual age of eligibility for Medicare is 65, but a younger person who has been disabled for over two years may qualify for benefits. Medicare beneficiaries are eligible for the hospice benefit if they have a prognosis of six months or less and if they consent to cessation of curative treatment. The benefit covers a total of 210 days of Medicare-paid home hospice care. Patients may choose to revoke the benefit at any time (if they choose to resume treatment, for instance) and may reelect it at a later date. Revoking and reinstating the benefit may cause the patient to lose some of the days of care.

Medicare pays the hospice provider a flat daily rate for each day the patient receives the benefit, and this payment must cover all expenses related to the terminal illness, including medications and durable medical equipment. The hospice provider may not discharge the patient based on either the difficulty or the cost of care. If the patient continues to need hospice care beyond 210 days, the hospice program must continue to provide hospice level care, but reimbursement reverts to regular Medicare.

The hospice home care benefit requires the hospice program, which must have a medical director, to provide direct core patient care services, including intermittent nursing, social work, and counseling. Other services, including rehabilitation, attendant care, pastoral, pharmacy, and private duty nursing, may be contracted.

Non-hospital-based hospices are required to have beds available in an inpatient unit. Hospitalization for disease progression or for pain and symptom control that is not manageable at home may not represent more than 20 percent of the total patient days on the benefit. In addition, inpatient respite care to relieve the primary caregiver may not exceed 15 days total, in 5-day segments.

Private Insurance

Private insurance coverage of home care and hospice is erratic. Some policies have good home care benefits, some have none, and others have home care provisions that are unusable. For example, if a patient needs ongoing homemaker care four hours a day, the policy may provide RN services only in eight-hour shifts, for a total of 20 shifts.

One home care provider believes that, if possible, the hospice–home care approach to the insurance company should avoid discussion of specific benefits. Even if the patient does not have a specified hospice or home care benefit, it may be possible to negotiate reimbursement. The focus of discussion must be the cost savings for the insurance company that result from paying for home care at a lower cost in lieu of covering hospitalization at a higher cost. This approach is particularly effective with companies that have individual case management programs. Some companies without individual case management programs will also negotiate, but usually only on a supervisory level.[10]

Medicaid Hospice and Home Care Reimbursement

Each state has different Medicaid regulations for reimbursement of hospice care. Local Medicaid offices can supply accurate information for the state in question.

TRADITIONAL HOME CARE AND HOSPICE COMPARED WITH AIDS HOME CARE AND HOSPICE

While home care has long been recognized as a practical and economical means of reducing the number of hospital inpatient days, today's climate of cost containment has made an even stronger case for home-based care.[11] Reimbursers often require that covered services be skilled and provided by professional clinicians, and expect services to be time limited and task oriented, with resulting improvement.

Unlike that of home care, the focus of hospice care is palliative rather than restorative or curative. Because of the structure of the Medicare hospice benefit, which provides payment of a certain amount per day for a limited time, strict lines have been drawn between home care and hospice in fee-based hospice agencies. This division has influenced thinking about which patients are appropriate for hospice care.

Criteria of Eligibility

Two main criteria for eligibility for hospice programs are (1) a life expectancy of less than six months and (2) cessation of any curative treatment. Because of the differences between the "traditional" hospice client's situation and that of the person with HIV infection, these criteria may need to be reevaluated for their appropriateness for the person with AIDS/ARC.

Persons with AIDS or ARC constitute a population of terminally ill people who are, in the majority, *not* eligible for Medicare because of their youth and the relatively short course of the disease. (Thirteen months is the average life expectancy after diagnosis.) Reimbursement of medical costs for these patients often comes from private insurance or Medicaid.

Medicaid regulations that provide a specific hospice benefit have been passed only recently and have been instituted in only a few states. Some individual insurance plans have a hospice benefit, but many do not. Therefore, reimbursement in most cases comes from home care provisions.

Hospice and home care do not meet everyone's needs. Many PWAs, however, prefer to be at home, as they find the constant tension and impersonal atmosphere of the institution unsettling. Other PWAs find that they primarily need the emotional support and focus on comfort and palliative care provided by a hospice team, whether or not they choose to pursue treatment as well.[12]

At this writing there is no cure for AIDS. Treatments for the opportunistic diseases often provide only a respite from symptoms. The disease continues to progress, in an often rapid but unpredictable fashion. Physicians reluctant to give a prognosis of only six months have often faced the reality of a patient's demise within one month.

Traditionally, hospice programs have defined termination of aggressive curative therapy as one admission criterion. Because PWAs frequently undergo aggressive therapies against opportunistic diseases, these patients may on the surface seem inappropriate for hospice care. However, since the results of these therapies are basically palliative, this assumption needs to be reevaluated.[13]

Three patient groups who may have an interest in hospice are:

1. acute care patients who are receiving aggressive therapy and have cure or long survival as an achievable goal
2. transitional patients whose course of disease cannot be significantly changed by treatment but who still have goals beyond the immediate
3. hospice-appropriate patients whose goals and treatment are strictly palliative and immediate.[14]

From a Medicare-based economic standpoint, hospice programs cannot afford to take in patients in the first two groups.[15] However, many PWAs may fit into the transitional group. Exclusion of this group based on economic grounds needs to be reexamined in light of (1) primary funding sources other than Medicare, (2) the reality that therapy provided to persons with AIDS is mainly palliative, and (3) the unpredictability and rapid progression of the disease in the majority of cases.

Another criterion for hospice admission has been the availability of a primary caregiver. Because of the nature of the disease, persons with AIDS/ARC have often been rejected by friends and family who would normally provide primary caretaking. For hospice programs to reject candidates because they have no primary caregiver seems to contradict the basic aims of hospice.

Psychosocial Differences

A person facing death experiences intense grief. The hospice team must be prepared to assist the patient in the grieving process in spite of the difficult emotions engendered by issues of contagion, death at a young age, and society's negative judgments towards sexuality, homosexuality, and drug abuse. To support the patient and family, members of the hospice team must respond to their own emotions concerning these issues and not add to the judgmental attitudes the dying person faces. These issues make emotional support by and for the hospice team more necessary and more demanding than the support needed by many traditional hospice patients. (For a complete discussion of the psychosocial issues surrounding HIV infection, refer to Chapter 9.)

Finally, hospice services have usually been provided by young and middle-aged people to their elders. In the case of clients with AIDS, hospice staff are usually in the same age group and life stages as their clients. Watching the deaths of growing numbers of people with whom staff members can identify in terms of age and goals can have a strong impact on staff morale. Seeing families in which both parents and several children are dying, or seeing the consecutive deaths of persons who have been the partners and caretakers of patients who have died previously, can have a devastating effect on providers. Staff support services are mandatory.

AN ALTERNATIVE

This century has seen unparalleled progress in the field of medical technology, with the focus on prolonging life. Now we are faced with a catastrophic disease and years of research before a cure is found. The anticipated mortality rate is staggering. Because of its focus on treatment and cure, the hospital is not always the ideal environment in which to die. Indeed, given the number of available hospital beds and high inpatient costs, dying in the hospital may not be realistic.

Hospice offers an alternative. The belief that death is a part of life—a natural, inevitable consequence of living—enables an approach whereby persons may choose to die at home surrounded by the people and things familiar to their lives. The hospice team, guided by the patient and caregivers, assists in creating a plan of care based on pain and symptom management and emotional support that promotes quality of life throughout the dying process.

Hospice has emerged as a legitimate alternative. The continued rapid growth of the hospice movement will ensure that this service can be available for those who choose it.

Coming Home Hospice

Coming Home Hospice is a residential hospice in San Francisco operating on the board and care pattern. When it became clear that the community needed a facility that could provide AIDS patients with housing and 24-hour care outside of the hospital setting, plans for Coming Home Hospice were set in motion. It is funded by a combination of voluntary donations, patient fees for room and board, grants, and third party payer fees. The Catholic Parish of Our Most Holy Redeemer granted a 17-year lease on a vacant convent building for this facility.

Coming Home Hospice provides a homelike setting in which 15 persons with terminal illness can receive necessary care and yet not have to experience the alienation of a hospital. Coming Home does not discriminate against those who do not have AIDS or ARC; it is open to any person suffering from a terminal illness who meets the eligibility criteria. Persons who are eligible to move into Coming Home Hospice are those who (1) have a medical prognosis of six months or less; (2) need 24-hour attendant care because of dementia, physical deterioration, or both and are unable to get this care in their own home; and (3) have an ongoing need for intermittent skilled nursing care. Residents receive all services of Hospice of San Francisco as if still in their own homes.

Each room at Coming Home Hospice has its own hospital bed, sink, and TV. Beyond that, the resemblance to a hospital fades. The dining room is bright and airy, and residents may choose to eat there or in their rooms. A beautiful common room with stained glass windows is open to residents and families. Small pets are allowed and enjoyed.

Each resident and family brings its own spirit and imprint. Brightly covered afghans crocheted by our volunteers often meet the eye. Teddy bears of all types are residents also, and some teddies even have name tags that identify them as ''Hospice Bear,'' members of the team.

Coming Home Hospice is one example of a hospice and community response to the AIDS crisis.

A Personal Experience

Andrew lay in bed without moving, as usual. His eyes were glassy and unfocused. He rarely responded to my questions and comments, and when he did he mumbled so softly I could barely hear him. He was close to death, within the week, I thought, but not yet actively dying. I don't know what made me ask him. I was new to this job of caring for people who were dying and I felt very unsure of myself. But something in his eyes, in his feel, made me ask him.

"Are you worrying about dying, Andrew?"

His eyes focused on me, there was a flicker in them, and he nodded slightly.

"Do you want me to talk to you about what it will be like?"

Again the flicker, the nod. He was definitely paying attention. I sat down and held his hand.

"It's not going to hurt you," I said. "It will be like going to sleep. . . ."

I don't really remember all I said to him. I encouraged him that if he felt ready to die, it was okay to let go. I didn't talk very long. It was a one-sided conversation, but he was with me, listening. . . .

It was time for me to go home, Friday afternoon at 4:30, and I'd had a long week. I told him I was going to go.

He grasped my hand.

"Don't go," he said softly.

Oh, I felt conflicting feelings. Part of me wanted to get out of there fast and just forget Andrew for the weekend. But, poor guy, he couldn't forget.

"Andrew, you want me to just sit here with you for awhile?"

He squeezed my hand and held on. I looked at my watch.

"Andrew, I really can't stay for very long. But I'll stay for a little bit, okay?"

He closed his eyes. His arm relaxed and his hand slipped out of mine to rest against my knee. I held it there. When I left a little while later, he let me go without a protest. Somehow his eyes seemed more peaceful.

Monday morning I called to ask how he was. He had died Saturday. I was so glad I had stayed.

NOTES

1. Sandol Stoddard, *The Hospice Movement: A Better Way of Caring for the Dying* (New York: Random House, 1978).

2. Richard Lammerton, *Care of the Dying* (New York: Penguin Press, 1973), p. 19.

3. Elisabeth Kubler-Ross, *Death: The Final Stage of Growth* (Englewood Cliffs, N.J.: Prentice Hall, 1975), p. 2.

4. National Hospice Organization, "Standards of A Program of Care" (McLean, Va.: National Hospice Organization, 1979).

5. National Hospice Organization, *1986 Guide to the Nation's Hospices* (Arlington, Va.: National Hospice Organization, 1986).

6. Benita Martocchio, "Agendas for Quality of Life," *The Hospice Journal* 2, no. 1 (Spring 1986):11–20.

7. Carol J. Sheehan, "Hospice: A Program for All Who Are Dying?" *The American Journal of Hospice Care* 3, no. 1 (July/August 1986):8–14.

8. Patricia E. Green, "The Pivotal Role of the Nurse in Hospice Care," *Cancer Journal for Clinicians* 34, no. 4 (July/August 1984):204–05.

9. Ann Hughes, Jeannee Parker Martin, and Pat Franks, *AIDS Home Care and Hospice Manual* (Visiting Nurses' Association of San Francisco, AIDS Home Care and Hospice Program, 1987), p. 42.

10. Steven Zembo, VNA Home Care, private conversation, June 23, 1987; and Zembo, "Insurance Negotiation," in Hughes, Martin, and Franks, *AIDS Home Care and Hospice Manual*, pp. 159–69.

11. Leora Paradis, et al., "Home Health Agencies and Hospices: Stronger Together or Alone," *Nursing and Health Care* 8, no. 3 (March 1987):167–71.

12. Jeannee Parker Martin, "Ensuring Quality of Hospice Care for the Person with AIDS," *QRB* 12, no. 10 (1986):353–58.

13. Ibid.

14. Andrew B. Adams, "Dilemmas of Hospice: A Critical Look at Its Problems," *Cancer Journal for Clinicians* 34, no. 4 (July/August 1984):183–90.

15. Ibid.

REFERENCES

Beresford, Larry. "Summary of the Hospice Medicare Benefit." Hospice of San Francisco, 1984.

Bryant, Jerri Kennicott. "Home Care of the Client with AIDS." *Journal of Community Heath Nursing* 3, no. 2 (1986):69–74.

Graves, Edmund J., and Moien, Mary. "Hospitalizations for AIDS, United States 1984–85." *American Journal of Public Health* 77, no. 6 (1987):729–30.

Health Care Financing Administration. "Department of Health and Human Services Rules and Regulations: Medicare Program and Hospice Care." *Federal Register* 48, no. 43 (1983):56008–35.

_____. *Hospice Benefits Under Medicare*. Publication HCFA-02154. Washington, D.C.: U.S. Government Printing Office, 1984.

Jackson, Pauline, and Goldman, Carol. "AIDS: Caring for Your Patient at Home." *The Canadian Nurse* 82, no. 3 (March 1986):18–22.

Lack, Sylvia, and Buckingham, Robert. *First American Hospice: Three Years of Home Care*. New Haven, Conn.: Hospice Inc., 1978.

Larson, Patricia J. "Cancer Nurses' Perceptions of Caring." *Cancer Nursing* 2 (1986):86–91.

Levine, Stephen. *Who Dies: An Investigation of Conscious Living and Conscious Dying*. New York: Doubleday Anchor Press, 1982.

MacDonald, Neil. "The Hospice Movement: An Oncologist's Viewpoint." *Cancer Journal for Clinicians* 34, no. 4 (1984):178–82.

Martin, J.P. "The AIDS Home Care and Hospice Program: A Multidisciplinary Approach to Caring for Persons with AIDS." *American Journal of Hospice Care* 3, no. 2 (March/April 1986):35–37.

National Hospice Organization. *1984 Guide to the Nation's Hospices*. Arlington, Va.: National Hospice Organization, 1984.

———. "Standards of a Program of Care." McLean, Va.: National Hospice Organization, 1979.

Petrosino, Barbara M. "Research Challenges in Hospice Nursing." *The Hospice Journal* 2, no. 1 (Spring 1986):2–8.

Saunders, Cicely. *The Management of Terminal Disease*. London: Edward Arnold Ltd., 1971.

Schofferman, Jerome. "Medicine and the Psychology of Treating the Terminally Ill." In *What To Do About AIDS*, edited by L. McKusick. Berkeley: University of California Press, 1986.

Sheehan, Carol J., and Raush, P. Gregory. "Analysis of the Medicare/Hospice Program: Rural Applications." *Home Health Care Nurse* 2, no. 5 (September/October 1984):38–40.

Schietinger, Helen. "A Home Care Plan for AIDS." *American Journal of Nursing* 86, no. 9 (September 1986):1021–28.

Vachon, M.L.S. "Myths and Realities in Palliative Hospice Care." *The Hospice Journal* 2, no. 1 (Spring 1986):63–77.

Part IV

Staff Education and Support

Administering care to persons with HIV infection is often very rewarding for staff, but it can also be draining. Helping develop support systems to minimize the drain on health care workers is everyone's responsibility and offers a continuing challenge to all levels of staff. For example, although administrators assume overall responsibility for staff support, it is often the staff nurse who counsels the concerned housekeeper and the nutritionist who listens to the fears of the food service worker. The feelings and fears of these staff members are most often related to contagion, homosexuality, and perhaps drug abuse, sexuality, and death. These issues must be addressed before staff members can listen to and understand the facts. Obviously, any health care workers who are to counsel others must first deal with their own attitudes and feelings. Self-awareness, which has been stressed repeatedly throughout this book, remains a central theme in Part IV.

The first steps in staff support are (1) understanding staff reactions to the epidemic and then (2) developing and implementing strategies to maximize staff's ability to handle these reactions constructively. The first three chapters in this part discuss techniques that will assist in that endeavor, including an innovative approach to staff education and a discussion of techniques for increased self-awareness. One educational strategy that has proven very effective is to include one or more persons with HIV infection as program speakers. Additionally, PWAs can provide valuable insight for program planners and are often willing to participate actively in program planning.

Finally, because ethical and legal questions often cause concern among staff, the last chapter in Part IV identifies and addresses some of the common issues.

Chapter 22

Understanding and Working with the Emotional Reactions of Staff

Shellie Hatfield and Joan Dunkel

OVERVIEW OF THE EPIDEMIC

Epidemics—widespread, of uncertain etiology, and incurable—are not new in the history of mankind. The plagues of the Middle Ages, in overall numbers, were the most devastating epidemics in recorded history. The most recent epidemic before HIV infection was the outbreak of polio in the 1930s and 1940s, which killed and crippled large numbers of young people. Nor is it new that helpers treat and comfort the afflicted; that there is minimal treatment available and much comfort needed is also a familiar feature.

Several aspects of the epidemic of HIV infection, however, make it different from others. It has developed at a time in the history of medicine and science when a series of scientific breakthroughs has brought health care workers to the point of believing that science and technology can make all good things possible. Care providers have had to relearn the fact that their limitations are still with them, and most health care workers find it difficult to accept that they have only a little more to offer than did those who worked during the plagues of the Middle Ages.

A second distinguishing feature of the HIV epidemic is the expectation in the industrialized nations of almost unlimited health care resources. The proposition that what medical and biological science can't prevent or cure will receive unlimited treatment from the health care community is not economically feasible; without the thousands of hours of volunteer care, particularly from the gay and lesbian community, the diminishing resources allocated for health care in America would be grossly depleted.

A third feature, reflective of today's lifestyle, is the rapidity with which the HIV virus has spread around the world. While there is less infection in some areas, nowhere is there freedom from the fear of exposure. HIV infection is an epidemic of global proportions.

THE HEALTH CARE PROVIDER

Persons who become health care workers bring to their work a set of commonly shared characteristics that have contributed to what can be called the medical culture.[1] A 1979 study of health care providers, primarily nurses and social workers, working in the intensive care unit (ICU) identified their most common psychological features and described how they served either an adaptive or maladaptive function for the worker. Since ICU staff have always worked with catastrophic illnesses, the application of this profile to health workers in the HIV epidemic is a useful one. The four features identified are (1) high performance expectations, (2) professional omnipotence, (3) need to control, and (4) need to "save."

High Performance Expectations

Health care workers as a group are ambitious and hardworking, aspiring to a perfection in their performance that will result in a successful outcome. These expectations for performance and outcome may be unrealistic, but health care workers often achieve what appears impossible, both in professional advancement and in the success rate of treating patients. The adaptive part of high performance expectation is high achievement, which reinforces an even higher level of self-expectation.

Conversely, when goals for achievement are unrealistic and are not reached, the inevitable loss of self-esteem causes depression, lack of job satisfaction, and contributes to what is well known as burnout. Workers depressed by their performance must reevaluate their performance goals and, if necessary, establish new goals that are more consistent with the realistically possible.

Omnipotence

References to miracles in the health care community have been common in the last 15 to 20 years: the "miracle baby," the "miracle drug," the "miracle case." The usual state of affairs is to expect a miracle, and more and more health care workers believe in their own omnipotence, or power as makers of miracles.

The sense of omnipotence is necessary and adaptive for people who work with catastrophic illness. Without it, few would venture "where angels fear to tread" and thus save lives that would have otherwise been lost. From this sense evolves a perseverance and hope, even in the face of the most hopeless cases, that is often rewarded with outstanding success. The belief in professional omnipotence is maladaptive when the worker's ability to tolerate or cope with failure is impaired or when failure is defined as anything less than cure.

Control

The need to be in control of difficult work situations is both a real requirement of work with catastrophic illness and a psychological defense against being overwhelmed or immobilized by feelings such as fear, grief, and anger. In controlling the work situation, health care workers assume responsibility, are reliable, and strive for excellence in patient care. Crises may bring out personal capabilities previously unknown to the health care worker; an alert, clearheadedness when making life and death decisions on the spot is not an unusual response: everything is under control!

The need for control is maladaptive when the control defends against normal emotions or responds to the unconscious threat of unresolved dependency needs. These situations may bring out a rigidity in the health care worker that can create problems in patient care as well as stress for the worker who defends against feelings. Particularly, control can become maladaptive when the person receiving the health care is an alert, independent person who does not want to accept the dependent, controlled role of patient.

Saving

Rescue or savior fantasies are common among health care workers, most of whom derive great satisfaction from helping make someone's life free from disease and pain. The identity of helping or being a helper provides much of the worker's sense of self-worth. One of the reciprocities in health care is the patient's wish to get well, followed by actual improvement; this act justifies and makes worthwhile the long, hard hours of patient care.

But when the patient does not want to be rescued and, in fact, focuses on self-destructive behavior such as a drug habit, what is the effect on health care workers? Sometimes they may continue to save anyway; in that instance the saving meets the needs of the worker rather than those of the patient. Again, this primarily adaptive psychological feature of work in health care can, under certain circumstances, become maladaptive.

In addition to the four characteristics of health care providers that may make work difficult in the HIV epidemic, we have identified individual emotional reactions in our work with health care workers.[2]

Fear of the Unknown

Much about AIDS remains unknown to many people, including some health care workers:

- the cause of the disease
- the means of transmission

- methods to alter its course
- the population at risk.

The "population," in this case most often gay men or IV drug abusers, as exemplified by one person, can easily become the "other," and the empathic process that is central to the helping relationship may either not develop easily or not develop at all. Detachment, which can give the worker the appearance of objectivity, replaces the process of empathy and objectivity. The patient who remains an unknown runs a greater risk of being the recipient of both conscious and unconscious countertransference, a term most commonly used in psychiatry that refers to "those conscious, preconscious, and unconscious responses and feelings of the health care worker that can be both a problem and a valuable therapeutic and diagnostic tool."[3] To prevent countertransference, learning about AIDS and homosexuality and personalizing the person who has AIDS becomes particularly important for health care workers.

Fear of Contagion

The fear that AIDS can somehow be transmitted through the air or through contact with the skin has been a common misconception since the syndrome was identified as infectious. Although it is known that AIDS is transmitted only by blood and body fluids, many health care providers remain fearful, particularly of passing contamination on to family and friends. They question whether enough is known to say that contagion by proximity is impossible. The infection control recommendations described in Chapter 18 represent a reasonable, well-thought-out plan for control of AIDS and its associated infections. However, from time to time the fear of contagion may accelerate into panic.

Fear of Dying and Death

Separate from the fear of the unknown and the fear of contagion, but linked to both, is the fear of death and of the person who is dying—as if death, too, might be transmissible. This dynamic is not uncommon, particularly among health care providers, who place such a high priority on "beating" death. Working with a dying person challenges unresolved feelings about one's own mortality. An individual death is considered in relation to oneself, or one denies the existence of death by denying the personhood of the dying person. The untimely death of a young person can exacerbate the intrapersonal conflict surrounding mortality.

Fear of Homosexuality

Although only ego-dystonic homosexuality is included in the *Diagnostic and Statistical Manual of Mental Disorders*, the standard psychiatric text for diagnosis and classification of disease, it is incorrect to suggest that all members of the lay and professional communities now accept homosexuality as "normal." It is also naive to assume that health care providers, despite their values of respecting the uniqueness of each individual, are immune to homophobia.

The psychological "ghettoization" of homosexuals results in the following:

1. developmental delay for some homosexuals who do not have the opportunity to master intimacy in their teens and early 20s
2. internalization of the dominant group's perception of gay people so that both gays and straights can be homophobic
3. fear of homophobia by those who view themselves as liberal or liberated
4. unresolved homosexual feelings in straight health care providers, which may be reactivated by gay patients.

Overidentification

Inherent in the empathic process is the ability to feel with the patient, and, therefore, identification is a necessary part of the helping relationship. Overidentification occurs when a worker loses the ability to return to an objective stance. This loss of objectivity can result in the worker's investing unrealistic amounts of time and energy in the patient, fusing personal needs and professional responsibilities and, in extreme cases, generating symptom formation. The homosexual health care provider may identify most sensitively with PWAs and thus may be particularly vulnerable to overidentification. Recent studies in this area, however, have shown no significant differences between gay and straight providers.[4]

Anger

The worker may be angry because of feelings of helplessness, fear, and guilt, which result in blaming the victim. Anger can be an unconscious attempt to punish, leading to irrational, explosive, and unpredictable behavior on the part of the worker. Anger that distances the worker from the patient is a form of self-preservation and serves to protect the worker from experiencing the pain of loss and death. This natural resistance to death, which the PWA can experience as anger, can consciously or unconsciously provoke the patient to decrease the number of contacts with the worker. It is then easy for the worker to rationalize the decreased contacts as patient-initiated. Such countertransference blocks empathy and prevents the provider from being emotionally available to the patient. The worker successfully avoids grief and, therefore, is "saved" for patients who have a chance of survival. Staff education and support must address this kind of reaction, since it is critical for the worker to be available, reliable, empathic, and able to respond emotionally to the patient, particularly during times of regression.

Anger that strikes out against the political and moralistic tones of the epidemic is misdirected. The worker can use the patient as a tool to gratify a sense of wanting to get back at society for discriminating against minority groups. As the worker pursues this larger cause and begins unconsciously viewing the patient as a means to a political end, objectivity is lost and the worker ceases to see the individual as unique. This kind of countertransference anger may be more prominent for the homosexual worker, women, and the minority worker whose own sense of oppression is activated in the course of working with PWAs.

THE HEALTH CARE WORKER IN TROUBLE

Clearly, providing health care for people infected with the HIV virus can be problematic for health care workers; those whose self-esteem is dependent on curing, who define success as curing, or whose job satisfaction is derived from saving lives may be particularly at risk for burnout. The stress on the rigid, controlling worker may become unbearable when feelings remain unexpressed and unresolved for a long period of time. The traumas are ongoing and cumulative and result in severe stress disorders not unlike the post-traumatic stress syndrome.[5]

Working through a traumatic event normally involves a series of emotions, defenses, thoughts, and more emotions. Emotions typically include sadness, anger, shock, and fear, very quickly followed by a feeling of disbelief or denial of the event. Thought disturbances are not uncommon, and the person may obsess over the event, as well as engage in magical or "as if" thinking. If a terminally ill patient dies while a nurse is on break, the nurse may briefly and irrationally think that the patient would not have died had the break not been taken; as if, by magic, the patient had not been terminally ill and the nurse's presence made the difference between the patient's life and death. (What complicates this situation is that there is often truth in this feeling!)[6] These normal responses to trauma are usually of short duration, and, with or without help, the worker accepts and integrates reality. Resolution of the response is necessary so that the worker can free physical and psychological energies to go on with life.[7]

Trauma, as experienced by health care workers in the AIDS epidemic, occurs almost daily. Trauma can be defined as any event that interferes with the worker's sense of homeostasis. Death is a traumatizing event, but so is a Code Blue or the initial diagnosis of an untreatable illness. Symptoms such as wasting and disfigurement can be traumatic for health care workers who care about the people they are treating. Pain and suffering, odors, the "dirty work" of caring for people, and the hospital environment itself can all contribute to trauma.

The pathological trauma response occurs when health care workers care for patients at an almost assembly-line pace and do not have time to deal with their own responses to a traumatic event, or when workers do not allow themselves time, using a busy schedule as a defense against normal working-through. What follows is a panic or exhaustion reaction to the repressed emotional responses and an escalation of the avoidance measures. It is not unusual at this point for health care workers to resort to drugs, increased frantic activity, emotional withdrawal from professional and personal involvement, or a combination of these measures. Without resolution, the possible responses to stress expand to include psychosomatic symptoms such as sleeplessness, gastritis, or increased vulnerability to infection. Characterological changes may also occur.

The potential for trouble for the health care worker in the AIDS epidemic is great. The sources lie in part in the characteristics of the worker, the daily traumas associated with provision of health care, and the range of emotional reactions to the work. At times, these reactions may be mild, while at other times they can escalate to near-panic level for either the individual worker or groups of workers. The following list of danger signs of burnout serves as a helpful inventory for those working in the AIDS epidemic:

- chronic exhaustion
- nightmares
- psychosomatic pains
- physical weakness
- vulnerability to illness
- avoidance of patients
- deterioration of relationships with other staff members
- tensions in home life.[8]

TREATMENT OF STAFF

The treatment of staff is a critical part of clinical care in the AIDS epidemic and is central to the health care professional's survival.

A Personal Philosophy of Care

Staff who choose to work with persons with the HIV virus have special sensitivities that make them both valuable and vulnerable to the demands of the dying. HIV patients typically present with tremendous needs for reassurance and psychological security. Staff must be encouraged to adopt a philosophy of care that allows them to function effectively while meeting these regressive needs.

The notion of "taking care of oneself" is a valuable one in countering stresses inherent in "people work."[9] This self-care includes setting limits and realistic goals, taking things less personally, having a life of one's own, and creating variety in one's work schedule.[10] Staff need to develop a *balance* when working with patients with HIV virus. First, staff must balance taking their work seriously and being able to look at themselves and the situation with humor and levity. Second, they must balance their professional and personal lives, and clear boundaries must exist between job and home, especially when someone in a staff member's personal life dies of AIDS and boundaries appear blurred. Third, staff must attain a balance between identification and overidentification, and between empathizing and not losing objectivity. Last, staff must strike a balance between meeting the patient's need for safety and respecting their own need for safety, including psychological safety and protection against the risks of infection.

Attempting to achieve this balance may produce a great deal of guilt and ambivalence, as most staff feel uncomfortable respecting and honoring their own needs for comfort and safety. A recent study at The Medical Center at the University of California, San Francisco, found that health providers do *not* comply with infection control practices and, in fact, underprotect themselves in favor of providing humane care.[11] This tendency may reflect staff's great ambivalence and struggle to achieve a satisfactory balance. Because this process produces so much anxiety, emotional reactions and countertransference issues that surface should be managed immediately. Common countertransference issues are fear, anger, guilt, and overidentification.[12] Staff should retain an open mind to their own personal issues, both to know themselves and to continue to use self-awareness and introspection to monitor personal reactions in all caretaking exchanges.[13]

A philosophy of care for staff helps protect their professional role and mitigates the influence of emotional reactions on providing care.

FACILITATING STAFF'S GRIEF WORK

When a patient dies, a staff member may not have the luxury of stopping to mourn, especially if several patients are dying at once, which may be the case for staff working primarily with AIDS. Numerous tasks associated with death may need to be attended to:

- contacting family members
- making funeral arrangements
- completing required paperwork
- preparing a death certificate
- asking about wills, autopsy, and next of kin

- preparing the body
- clearing the room.

What happens psychologically to the staff person? What does the health care worker do with the fact that his or her unconscious has just registered a loss? Often the staff person is encouraged to carry on, despite the fact that death marks the end of a relationship probably characterized by intense attachment and personal involvement. A staff person may have too many other patients waiting to stop and take stock of internal changes.

Not all deaths constitute losses for a staff person; the sense of loss depends on the special meaning of the relationship for the deceased and the bereaved.[14] Nevertheless, the problem comes when staff *do* feel a loss with its accompanying emotional reactions and *the loss is not recognized*. "If grief is not expressed at the time of a loss, the feelings can hang on for years."[15] This has implications for the individual's personal future and current working life because problems inevitably arise when grief is avoided.

Problems that may be seen immediately are:

- exhaustion
- reduced sense of accomplishment
- numbness
- withdrawal
- apathy
- illness
- depersonalization.

When depersonalization pervades the personal life, the staff member may need professional help. With repeated exposure to death, a staff member can ultimately appear to be suffering from trauma, not unlike the trauma of combat fatigue during war.

Normal and Pathological Responses to Loss

Staff must be educated about what can happen to them and about what constitutes a loss for them. They must be taught (1) how to recognize, understand, and diagnose the range of responses to loss and (2) how to facilitate the expression of grief.

The range of responses to loss include:

- normal grief
- anticipatory grief
- inhibited, delayed, and absent grief
- chronic grief
- depression
- hypochondriasis
- development of medical symptomatology and illness
- psychophysiological reactions (sweating, palpitations)
- acting out (sociopathic or promiscuous behavior)
- specific neurotic and psychotic states.[16]

These reactions can occur in combination or alone. It is not always easy to distinguish a normal grief reaction from other reactions, but staff must be trained to detect these responses in themselves and in their colleagues.

Staff Strategies for Facilitating Expression of Grief

The expression of grief is easiest when the loss is recognized and shared. Professional help is not necessary if a staff permits this expression and is sensitive to the issue. Individuals must recognize their own feelings and express them without shame, and all members of the health care team, including nursing administration and physicians, must not only tolerate but approve this expression of grief. Permission to cry and otherwise express grief should be granted. The staff person may need a break in the routine or may be unable to care for other HIV patients immediately. Staff's perspective can be expected to return to normal if they are helped to "feel" and provided with external support and validation. The staff person in mourning must be taken seriously.

A variety of techniques can help facilitate staff grieving. Creative rituals and rites of mourning may be helpful to the entire team. Rather than attendance at all funeral services, rituals can include socialization outside of work, for example, potlucks or dances. One staff group gathers to set off numerous helium balloons symbolizing a letting go of patients lost. Another technique, the use of humor, can be therapeutic and quite healing for staff; it serves to release tension when exposure to death and morbidity is constant. The team jokes with patients using humor to relax new patients. One staff group has organized a kazoo band that marches from room to room entertaining the patients.[17] Finally, death and dying rounds is an academic technique that uses the team approach to evaluate how care was delivered to a deceased patient. Although primarily an analytical tool, it can be a cathartic experience for staff who wish to bring closure to patients who have passed away.

Combating Hopelessness

Providing clinical care to patients with HIV virus can be discouraging. Although the rewards are deep, there is no known cure. The death rate is staggering, and treatment efforts are primarily palliative.

Patients easily lose hope, and so can staff. Conveying hopelessness and helplessness to patients can be deadly, leading to patient depression, withdrawal, and possibly death.[18] One way staff can support their patients' quest for hope is to alleviate their own feelings of hopelessness and inadequacy by learning methods to employ with patients that emphasize gaining control and personal power. One way of combating hopelessness is to develop the belief that one has control over parts of one's life, or the perception of control, at least.[19]

A first step in combating hopelessness is for staff to recognize that patients can act to improve their chances of psychological survival. Staff must be able to delineate to patients which situations are beyond control and which lie within control. Information about one's situation is highly valuable and facilitates the ability to cope, even if one is helpless to effect any change.[20] The tasks that lie within patient and staff control are in the area of coping, including learning how to:

- cope with diagnosis and problems in living
- solve problems effectively
- use relaxation to reduce anxiety
- alter cognitive beliefs and attitudes that are detrimental to psychological adjustment.

When staff feel confident that they can help patients cope, they are less likely to feel hopeless and ineffectual themselves.

A useful model for teaching coping skills to patients is based on an investigation of cancer patients in which screening and intervention were offered to offset problems in coping, despite poor prognosis.[21] Staff undergo cognitive skills training and in turn instruct their patients. Patients are taught how to confront and clarify the problems they associate with their disease. They are taught the actual process of problem solving and instructed to find solutions to their own difficulties. Patients are also taught how to relax when anxious as well as how to recognize thought processes that may be harmful to adjustment. Patients feel more hopeful when they are helped to take steps on their own, and the entire staff can feel hopeful when working together on a concrete task that they believe effects psychological adjustment and well-being.

Another study found that men with HIV virus who believed that the cause of their illness lay within themselves had little hope about their future and health, resulting in hopelessness and helplessness.[22] These men were found to be at great psychological risk.[23] It may follow that staff who maintain beliefs about disease causation may unconsciously project hopelessness or blame patients for their illness, thus contributing to distress. It is important for staff to examine their own beliefs about disease etiology and blaming patients so they do not inflict attitudes that jeopardize patients' emotional well-being and sense of hope. Hopelessness is likely to result when staff and patients alike maintain such attitudes toward illness; both then feel powerless to make any changes. Powerlessness is the cause of hopelessness and despair.

Relaxation

Relaxation is a self-management tool that staff can learn and use to offset the stresses associated with clinical care. Staff have reported feelings ranging from mild nervousness to full-blown panic in response to AIDS, particularly staff outside the California and New York areas.

Relaxation techniques can be combined with anxiety management training, imagery, cognitive restructuring, and systematic desensitization to help staff deal with general and specific fears. Preferably, relaxation should be taught to staff in small groups in which individuals can practice together.

Progressive relaxation and deep breathing exercises are recommended to teach relaxation. Progressive muscle relaxation is effective in the treatment of anxiety, hypertension, insomnia, and headaches due to stress.[24] These disorders are frequently reported by staff under a high level of strain.

Anxiety Management Training

Anxiety management training (AMT) is appropriate for staff working in the AIDS epidemic.[25] Staff are helped to visualize themselves when they are anxious or fearful and taught to relax while imagining themselves in the situation. Common clinical situations that cause staff anxiety or fear are drawing blood, doing a physical, and suctioning. Staff are taught to substitute a relaxed response in these situations to gain self-control. They are then encouraged to use further imagery to practice seeing themselves without fear (looking calm, confident, and poised) and to develop other ego-enhancing images. They are encouraged to develop their own special cue word to use outside the experimental setting so they can signal the relaxation response to themselves while in a real situation. Staff are also asked to practice regularly. AMT is helpful for staff with low-level anxiety and free-floating anxiety.

Cognitive Restructuring

Cognitive thinking includes beliefs, attitudes, and perceptions. Cognitive restructuring, used in treating depression and anxiety, can also be applied to staff working in the AIDS epidemic. Cognitive appraisal plays a major role in determining the intensity of arousal in stressful situations; therefore, it is important to help staff isolate their own perceptions, thoughts, or beliefs that may be exacerbating or distorting an existing clinical situation.[26] In cognitive restructuring, staff are taught to identify maladaptive thinking, such as self-defeating statements, statements of panic, statements of hysteria, or negative beliefs or attitudes, and replace them with more rational modes of thinking. They are instructed to relax and discover for themselves any thought pattern contributing to anxiety or worry and then taught to utilize new thoughts and attitudes, to "stop thoughts," and to appraise situations in new ways in order to reduce the intensity of anxiety and fear. An example is a nurse who discovered she had a recording running in her mind saying, "I know I can catch AIDS if I get too close." This obsessive thought generated massive anxiety every time she cared for a patient. She was able to modify her anxiety by replacing this self-defeating thought with a more constructive thought. The new thought reinforced the idea that there was *no* risk of infection by proximity. Once she rehearsed this in her mind, she was able to react without hysteria. Cognitive restructuring is a helpful technique for moderate to severe levels of anxiety that are directly related to a staff member's cognitive thinking. This technique is also helpful for staff who harbor attitudes about how patients get the disease and blame patients for their disease.

Systematic Desensitization

Systematic desensitization can help staff who are suffering specific anxiety reactions, phobic reactions, or avoidant behavior.[27] It is similar to anxiety management training, but it is used in more specific situations. Staff are taught to recall the anxiety-producing images that result in avoidance or panic, to experience the anxiety, and to see the images while relaxed. They are taught to develop a hierarchy of images that they visualize successively while in the relaxed state, beginning with the least upsetting image and working up to the most upsetting image. Through this process, an individual can learn new conditioned responses and can transfer the anxiety-free state to the real-life situation.

Creating Staff Support Groups

Support groups are an effective way for staff to share concerns and discuss feelings and fears that arise during the course of patient care. The groups are voluntary and offer a nonthreatening atmosphere in which staff members can safely explore feelings. Support groups can be offered at the work setting, but preferably take place outside the workplace in a relaxed environment. The emphasis must always be on validating staff members' feelings, no matter how irrational or illogical they sound. Even the most sophisticated and well-trained staff may have troubling or conflicting feelings that they need to talk out. The primary focus of the support group is work-related issues, not resolution of personal problems. This does not mean that personal issues cannot be discussed, but the goal of the group is primarily problem solving in relation to the job.

Administrative backing is essential for the group's success. Compensatory time off while participating increases the likelihood that staff will attend, particularly those who are reluctant to attend but who may need the group the most. Administrative backing also gives an important message to staff about their value and worth to the institution.

An outside facilitator, or ideally cofacilitators, are advisable. Some suggestions for facilitators are:

- chaplain
- social worker
- psychiatric clinical nurse specialist
- psychologist
- psychiatrist.

An excellent combination is the team approach offered by a social worker and an infection control practitioner. Staff's emotional needs are best served when both the technical and emotional aspects of the AIDS epidemic can be addressed simultaneously.

RECOMMENDATIONS FOR INSTITUTIONAL MODIFICATIONS IN TREATING STAFF

We encourage adoption of the following recommendations, which are directed to organizations and institutions that employ staff working in the AIDS epidemic. Institutions need to:

1. Sanction compensatory time off and promote mental health leave.
2. Encourage professionals to seek support.
3. Offer time, pay, or both for professional development outside work.
4. Encourage a multidisciplinary team approach.
5. Be flexible in resource allocation:

    a. Allow caseloads to be balanced with a variety of patients.
    b. Allow staff to switch individual cases with other staff if necessary.
    c. Allow staff to alternate work assignments (administrative time, lab time, paperwork, research, publishing, supervising) when pressure of direct care is too extreme.
    d. Allow "time out" or intermittent breaks during the work day, particularly to deal with grief.
    e. Limit "on-call" time while off duty.

6. Screen staff carefully during the interview process to screen out caregivers who might be at high risk for burnout.[28]
7. Alert new employees during the interview to stresses associated with care and the risk for burnout.
8. Offer regular employee training programs to sensitize staff to problems and teach coping strategies.
9. Encourage two-way communication between administration and line staff, with an emphasis on feedback. Administrators need to demonstrate their support of staff.
10. Encourage staff participation in decision making and determination of policies for care.
11. Offer professional, confidential help to employees, and families of employees, through employee assistance programs or existing social work or mental health departments.
12. Conduct regular staff surveys to assess job satisfaction and to find out if any institutional practice is placing limits or additional strain on contact with patients.
13. Ensure that employees are regularly and frequently evaluated to detect and prevent burnout and that they have "pre-burnout checkups." Check for signs, symptoms and attitudes of burnout and trauma during evaluation.
14. Consider investing in an on-site wellness program, perhaps including exercise, nutrition, stress reduction, and smoking cessation.

CONCLUSION

Several remaining areas of staff education and support require further understanding and exploration. The question remains, for example, how to help the worried families of health care workers in the epidemic. Concern is also emerging for the health care workers in the prison systems, who may feel isolated from their professional colleagues. Another issue that must be addressed is the response of the minority communities to the White health care worker. There is evidence that preexisting racial problems, plus the political aspects of the AIDS epidemic, may intensify the issues of trust between the minority person at risk for the HIV virus and the predominantly White health care system.[29] (For further discussion of these issues, see Chapter 3.)

The educational curriculum in most professional training schools includes very little, if anything at all, about health care workers' emotional reactions to their work and ways they can help themselves. A course on self-care, introduced early in the training of health care workers, would be a proactive measure to assist future staff in working with their emotional reactions to the serious illness, including the AIDS epidemic.

Finally, we have referred briefly to the vast numbers of volunteers who, thus far in the epidemic, have given their time and skills to work alongside health care workers. Questions arise regarding how long volunteer support will continue, how to ensure the continuation of volunteer support, and what the impact would be of decreased volunteer support on those in the trenches.

Understanding and working with the emotional reactions of staff in the AIDS epidemic is a complex task and an extremely important part of clinical care for the person with HIV virus. With further advances in practice, a systematic approach to helping staff will eventually become an integral and routine part of patient care.

NOTES

1. Stuart J. Eisendrach and Joan Dunkel, "Psychological Issues in Intensive Care Unit Staff," *Heart and Lung* 8, no. 4 (July–August, 1979):751–58.

2. Joan Dunkel and Shellie Hatfield, "Countertransference Issues in Working with Persons with AIDS," *Social Work* 32, no. 2 (March–April 1986):114–19.

3. Ibid., p. 115.

4. Mark Gates, "Attitudes of Professionals and Volunteers Who Work with People with AIDS," Graduate Student Research Project, School of Social Welfare, University of California, Berkeley, 1986.

5. Mardi Horowitz, *Stress Response Syndrome* (New York: Jason Aronson, Inc., 1986).

6. William Horstman and Leon McKusick, "The Impact of AIDS on the Physician," in *What To Do about AIDS*, ed. Leon McKusick (Berkeley: University of California Press, 1986).

7. The work of John Bowlby, congruent with our experience, indicates that complete resolution of traumas is not a realistic expectation. See John Bowlby, *Attachment and Loss: Vol. III, Loss, Sadness and Depression* (New York: Basic Books, Inc., New York, 1980). Rather, a reasonable working-through and putting-aside of the event seems to occur. However, with each new event, traumatic stress responses become reactivated, accounting for the cumulative effects, including flat affect, irritability, and immobilization, which can occur.

8. Christine Maslach, "Toward Understanding of Burn-out," Paper presented at conference, Burnout in the Acute Care Setting, University of California, San Francisco, November 1977.

9. Christine Maslach. *Burn-out—The Cost of Caring* (Englewood Cliffs, N.J.: Prentice-Hall, 1982).

10. Gerald Koocher, "Adjustment and Coping Strategies among the Caretakers of Cancer Patients," *Social Work in Health Care* 5, no. 2 (Winter 1979):145–50.

11. J.L. Gerberding et al, "Risk of Transmitting HIV, Hepatitis-B Virus, and CMV to Health Care Workers," *Journal of Infectious Diseases*, 156 (1987):1–8.

12. Dunkel and Hatfield, "Countertransference Issues."

13. Maslach, *Burn-out*.

14. D. Peretz, "Reaction to Loss," in *Loss and Grief: Psychological Management in Medical Practice*, ed. Schoenberg et al. (New York: Columbia University Press, 1970), pp. 20–30.

15. Ibid.

16. Ibid.

17. Koocher, "Adjustment and Coping Strategies," p. 145.

18. Jeff Mandel, "Affective Reactions to a Diagnosis of AIDS or ARC in Gay Men" (Ph.D. diss., Wright Institute, 1985).

19. Martin Seligman, *Helplessness: On Depression, Development, and Death* (San Francisco: W.H. Freeman and Co., 1975).

20. Ibid.

21. Avery Weisman, Harry Sobel, and William Worden, *Psychosocial Screening and Intervention with Cancer Patients* (Boston: Harvard Medical School, Department of Psychiatry, Massachusetts General Hospital, Project Omega, 1980).

22. J.M. Moulton, "Adjustment to a Diagnosis of Acquired Immune Deficiency Syndrome and Related Conditions: A Cognitive and Behavioral Perspective" (Ph.D. diss., California School of Professional Psychology, 1985).

23. Ibid.

24. Edmond Jacobson, *Progressive Relaxation* (University of Chicago Press, 1938).

25. Richard Suinn, "Anxiety Management Training for General Anxiety," in Suinn and Richard Wiegel, *The Innovative Psychological Therapies: Critical and Creative Incidents* (New York: Harper and Row, 1978).

26. A. Ellis, "Rational Emotive Therapy," *Counseling Psychologist*, January 1977.

27. S. Wolpe, *The Practice of Behavior Therapy* (New York: Pergamon Press, 1973).

28. Maslach (*Burn-out*, pp. 56–70) describes the demographic characteristics and personality traits that make a person vulnerable to the risks of burnout. This description may be useful in developing a screening tool for employees most at risk for the burnout syndrome.

29. Calu Lester, "AIDS in the Minority Communities" (Presentation at Colloquium, University of California, Berkeley, School of Social Welfare, March 1987).

REFERENCES

Borland, James. "Burn-out among Workers and Administrators." *Health and Social Work* (1981):73–80.

Carpenter, P., and Morrow, G. "Clinical Care of Cancer Patients: Close Interpersonal Encounters of the Difficult Kind." *Journal of Psychosocial Oncology* 3, no. 4 (Winter 1986):86.

Feifel, H. *The Meaning of Death*. New York: McGraw-Hill Book Co., 1965.

Krieger, Nancy, and Appleman, Rose. *The Politics of AIDS*. Oakland, Calif.: Frontline Pamphlets, The Institute of Social and Economic Studies, 1986.

Paine, W.S. "Burn-out Stress Syndrome in the 1980's." In *Job Stress: Research Theory*. Beverly Hills: Sage Publications, 1982.

Tolman, Richard, and Sheldon, Rose. "Coping with Stress, A Multimodal Approach." *Social Work* 30, no. 2 (March–April 1985):151–60.

Chapter 23

Staff Education:
Nurses and Others

Helen Schietinger and Pat McCarthy

The AIDS epidemic has created unnecessary panic among those health care workers who have only their fears and misconceptions on which to base decisions about caring for PWAs. Among care providers who have gone beyond their fears and now routinely care for people with the disease, the epidemic has presented another challenge, that of working with people whose physical and emotional needs tax even the most well-equipped health care systems.

Staff education needs range from basic information about transmission for health care workers who are not yet caring for PWAs to complete information about the physical and psychosocial sequelae of the disease syndrome for those who are providing direct care. Even more fundamental is the need for thorough education of all health care workers regarding the institution of universal blood and body fluid precautions (described in Chapter 18).

For the purposes of this chapter, the term "health care workers" encompasses professional direct care providers (e.g., nurses and physicians), nonprofessional direct care providers (e.g., aides and orderlies), and indirect care providers (e.g., housekeeping, clerical, and dietary staff). No health care workers are immune to fear of AIDS. All are susceptible to potential exposure to HIV-infected blood, and all need AIDS education tailored to their job responsibilities.

The continuing overflow crowds at AIDS conferences demonstrate an awareness on the part of many health care workers that they need to be informed about AIDS, that they lack confidence in their patient care skills, and that they have insufficient information. Accounts have surfaced of nurses and physicians who refuse to care for identified PWAs and of others who do not use appropriate infection control precautions with any of their patients. Despite this situation, some administrators still refuse to provide inservice time for employees to be educated about AIDS.

INEFFECTIVE STRATEGIES FOR STAFF EDUCATION

A frequent response of institutions to the idea of educating staff about AIDS is to decide that it is not necessary because one's own institution has no AIDS patients. Then the first patient is admitted or, more commonly, the first patient is worked up for AIDS, leaving staff aware that they have just been caring for someone who may have AIDS and that they took no special precautions. Staff act out their ensuing panic and hysteria on the patient, whose confidentiality becomes their last concern. The staff's reaction in the aftermath of the first AIDS patient is the impetus for education. However, attempting to respond to the aroused fear and hysteria is not an effective way to impart information.

The most common strategy for providing AIDS education to staff is to develop a workshop in which a series of invited speakers lecture on AIDS. The institution devotes a great deal of time and effort to this one-time event; limited resources may prevent the workshop from being repeated. This approach has several problems. First, a single event cannot begin to address the ongoing needs of staff. Second, if the workshop is voluntary, only staff who are already aware of and concerned about AIDS usually attend, and those who are most afraid or hostile to the idea of caring for PWAs do not attend. On the other hand, if the workshop is mandatory, staff who are already mistrustful of the institution's motivations in asking them to care for people with AIDS may not trust the information provided. Third, inviting outside experts makes the institution appear unable to respond to the questions and needs of staff once the workshop is over. Finally, the traditional lecture format is an ineffective way of teaching about a disease with such a highly charged emotional impact.

PRINCIPLES OF ADULT LEARNING

The emotional climate surrounding the subject of AIDS requires the institution to address the feelings and fears of staff before they will be receptive to information. Often intellectual-sounding questions and concerns about AIDS are based in deep-seated fears, and no amount of logic can dissuade people from their understanding of the "facts." AIDS inservices and workshops, therefore, must use the most sensitive and creative approaches possible. The body of knowledge regarding adult learning provides us with a framework.

The field of adult learning is predicated on the assumption that adults learn for different reasons and in different ways than children do. The fact that adults are responsible for their own lives underlies this assumption. The following principles of adult learning can be used as guidelines for effective AIDS education for health care workers:

1. *Adults are self-directed.* Any education must begin with determining their particular needs and facilitating the meeting of those needs. **Therefore**: Any plan for AIDS education must begin with a needs assessment, which may be conducted informally by talking to a few staff members prior to planning a class, or by developing a simple questionnaire for staff to complete. The needs assessment might even be the first activity of the class, with participants asked to list their concerns and questions about AIDS. The presentation must then address the identified needs, even if doing so means changing the objectives and planned content of the class.

2. *Adults take personally the mistakes they make.* They must maintain their self-esteem if learning is to take place. **Therefore**: The learning climate must be safe and supportive. The facilitator must establish an environment in which staff can share their fears and concerns without fear of reprisal or judgment and in which their ideas are respected and heard. The facilitator can model nonjudgmental listening and ensure that participants respect each other's opinions. In planning a class, the facilitator should consider issues such as which levels of staff will feel comfortable in a class together.

3. *Adults are motivated to learn not because they want to acquire abstract knowledge but because they need information to apply to a certain situation or to solve a problem.* **Therefore**: Information must be directed at resolving concerns about HIV infection that relate to staff's personal lives and work situations. The material must be relevant to them and should not be only information the instructor perceives as important for them to know.

4. *Adults have a wealth of life experiences to draw upon that enhance the learning process.* The educator can assume that the learners have a relevant base of expertise and knowledge on which to build and can fill in the gaps rather than provide an entire body of information for the learners to absorb. **Therefore**: The instructor is most effective as a facilitator rather than a lecturer. The role of facilitator involves asking participants to share what they already know about AIDS and conducting learning activities that enable the participants to incorporate new information with previous knowledge. For example, if the staff are direct care providers, they can compare patient care problems of PWAs with the problems experienced by persons with other diagnoses. By building upon existing skills, the facilitator can increase staff's confidence in their ability to care for PWAs.

5. *Adults must be active participants rather than passive listeners to achieve optimum learning.* **Therefore**: Engaging staff in an active process in which they react to, grapple with, and challenge AIDS information is more productive than simply spoonfeeding them information. For example, if the learners are nurses or physicians, the facilitator might list the means of transmission of HIV and then ask the participants to develop infection control guidelines based on this information. Potentially, the group may

develop unreasonable guidelines, requiring the facilitator to correct the conclusions. However, even the process of explaining the correct guidelines is a more valuable learning experience than a lecture.

Some additional considerations evolve out of the principles of adult learning: (1) class should begin with disclosure and discussion of concerns and fears, and separation of irrational fears from reasonable fears; (2) content should be limited to what staff need rather than overwhelming them with information; (3) the facilitator should provide staff with names of local resources and materials so that they have access to additional information if they need it; and (4) the workshop should demystify the processes of care and infection control. For an initial class on AIDS, staff need basic information; the most important aspects may be sharing concerns and fears and dispelling myths.

EFFECTIVE STRATEGIES FOR STAFF EDUCATION

As the AIDS epidemic continues, a systematic approach to AIDS education is necessary in every health care setting. One of the most important factors in providing AIDS education for staff is administrative support. A well-developed training plan includes regularly scheduled inservices for all staff, on work time. An identified AIDS resource person or persons should be available to staff on an ongoing basis; this person may be the infection control practitioner, or, in a large setting with many AIDS patients, a nurse may hold the position of AIDS coordinator. Other indications of administrative support that reinforce staff education are (1) straightforward policies regarding the care of people with HIV infection and AIDS; (2) provision of appropriate supplies for universal infection control measures; and (3) an AIDS task force of representatives from various disciplines and departments to address problems or questions and to coordinate uniform implementation of policies.

The planning of staff education should utilize the respected leadership of each level of staff. Staff needs can be assessed by polling these people or asking them to poll other staff. If a labor organization represents staff, it is helpful to incorporate a labor representative or shop steward in the planning of the program. In a hospital setting, department heads should be trained before the staff in each department. An effective method for planning inservices is to target homogeneous groups of health care workers—emergency room staff, floor nurses, aides and orderlies, dietary workers, and others. The presentation can then be tailored to the occupational needs and concerns of each group, and workers can ask questions and discuss concerns among their peers without the possibility of being embarrassed by superiors, subordinates, or people with more or less medical knowledge.

Inservices presented in small, informal settings provide an opportunity for staff participation. The avoidance of rigid lecture formats that separate the audience from the presenter also promotes group discussion. It is more important for staff to have their individual questions about AIDS answered than to hear a preestablished body of information.

Planning a series of classes effectively reaches more staff than holding one session. Word-of-mouth descriptions of the first class attract people to the next one; people who were not working the day of the first presentation have another opportunity to attend. Asking supervisors to cover for staff or to provide relief staff gives more people an opportunity to attend. Incorporating AIDS education into the orientation for new personnel ensures uniform implementation of policies. These measures convey the message that learning about AIDS is essential for all staff.

TRAIN THE TRAINER MODEL

The recommended training plan can obviously be very labor intensive for the staff educator, who usually has many other responsibilities in addition to AIDS education. Preparing trainers within the institution who then teach staff about AIDS is a very efficient and cost-effective method of implementing a systematic educational program. The California Nurses Association (CNA) AIDS Education and Training Project has developed such a program, based on adult learning principles.

In the CNA AIDS Train the Trainer Program, trainers are given preliminary reading and learning activities about AIDS so that the two-day training session can focus on teaching strategies rather than on basic AIDS information. The training coordinator who conducts the training serves as a role model by (1) facilitating learning activities that establish an effective climate for learning; (2) encouraging exploration of personal feelings and values about AIDS, sexuality, death and dying, and cross-cultural issues; and (3) conveying AIDS information using various media techniques and group discussion and participation. The training coordinator also discusses the educational theory underlying these activities. The trainers then practice implementing learning activities founded on these adult learning principles. In the last activity in the two-day session, the trainers prepare a lesson plan designed for the specific health care workers they expect to teach in their health care setting. The training coordinator is available for technical assistance and feedback in the months following the training program; trainers thus have support as they teach their own classes.

One approach to systematic AIDS education is to establish several trainers within a single health care setting (for example, a person in each department and on each nursing unit). This approach makes ongoing AIDS education readily available to staff. Ideally, these trainers have the backup of a training coordinator to keep them updated, provide technical assistance, and answer their questions.

SUMMARY

In the years ahead, the AIDS epidemic will place increasing demands on health care staff. All levels of staff must be able to care compassionately and safely for people with HIV infection. However, the fear engendered by the word AIDS can be a serious deterrent to effective care.

Adult learning principles are the foundation for effective teaching that reduces fear and enhances knowledge. A train the trainer approach gives health care providers immediate access to AIDS expertise rather than having it imported from outside their institution or department. Given the burden of the increasing number of AIDS cases, ongoing education of all health care workers is the only means of maintaining an effective health care system.

Chapter 24

Dealing with Issues of Sexuality

Angie Lewis

Drugs, sex, and death. These themes make AIDS one of the most sensational topics of our times. The idea of talking with patients and families in detail about any of these topics makes many staff members uncomfortable. Using sexuality as the example, we can learn to help ourselves and our colleagues address these and other sensitive topics.

Although sexuality may have been mentioned during our education, it is a topic that our profession and our society choose to ignore. AIDS health teaching demands that we overcome our personal embarrassment so we may discuss prevention in the explicit terms our clients understand while still maintaining a sense of personal comfort.

THE P-LI-SS-IT MODEL

P-LI-SS-IT stands for permission, limited information, specific suggestion, and intensive therapy.[1] Although it is a model developed for use in sex counseling, the first two levels apply to our dealings with clients with AIDS.

Often, all we need to offer our clients is permission, which we can do in a variety of ways. Offering to modify family visiting rules to include a patient's significant other is an obvious expression of permission, while having AIDS literature clearly visible in the setting is more subtle but still likely to be interpreted positively.

Limited information is also a useful concept in AIDS prevention education. We need to assess each client, learn about life style and risk behaviors, and provide information that is relevant for the client's situation.

283

SETTING A CLIMATE

As a staff member or administrator, you affect the tone of your environment by the permission you give, or fail to give. What messages do clients and colleagues receive about sexuality in general and homosexuality in particular? Begin your assessment of the climate by considering the following questions:

- Have you ever attended or suggested the presentation of an inservice program specifically related to sexuality?
- When was the last time you initiated a discussion of sexuality in a professional situation?
- If colleagues bring up the subject of sexuality, are they encouraged, either verbally and nonverbally, to elaborate on their comments?
- Are colleagues who are gay men or lesbians included in unit or departmental activities?
- If an open homosexual or lesbian is admitted as a patient, how do staff handle questions and negative comments? What visiting policies apply to the individual's partner?

These are a few of many applicable questions. Reflect on your specific situation—what questions should you be considering?

We all give messages through what we actually say and through the topics we discuss and are willing to have discussed, but in addition we give nonverbal messages. The way we respond to topics with our body language is readily observable. Our thoughts and attitudes may also be reflected by things as simple as the books on our shelves, the buttons stuck on our bulletin boards, and the posters on our walls.

CONSIDERING OUR VOCABULARY

One of the first hurdles for many of us is learning to understand and use words that have meaning for clients. When we discuss sex, most of us are more comfortable with medical or technical terminology than with common language. As long as the client understands and is comfortable with the words we use, our terminology isn't a problem, but for patients who are familiar only with street talk, medical language is ineffective and inappropriate. For these patients we need to learn to say "screw" or "fuck" instead of intercourse or coitus.

Regardless of the specific situation, we will probably need to learn some new vocabulary when we initiate AIDS prevention education or begin to integrate discussions of sexuality into our practice. One way to begin is to gather several people together and make a list of all the sexuality-related words the group can think of, along with their definitions. At the next staff meeting pass out the list of words (without definitions), then have each person in turn read a word and give a definition. Before you begin, make it clear that participation is voluntary but highly encouraged. For this technique to be effective, the group leader obviously needs to create an atmosphere of trust and good humor. Just hearing and saying the words gives a message of permission and opens the door for further discussion of how we can make ourselves more comfortable.

CONFRONTING OUR HOMOPHOBIA

Homophobia, as discussed in Chapter 2, is an attitude held by many health care workers, including gay men and lesbians. Before you can effectively care for gay men with HIV infection, you must honestly confront both your attitudes and your feelings.

Gay HIV patients have clearly indicated both the support they feel when homosexual or lesbian staff members come out to them and their desire for them to do so. However, it can't, or won't, happen often if these staff members recognize homophobia among their colleagues. You can help create an atmosphere of acceptance by asking yourself:

- What specifically bothers you about homosexuality?
- How deep-seated are these feelings?
- What behavior of your family or friends may contribute to your attitude?
- Do your feelings seem reasonable to you? If not, do you want to change them?

The straight care provider has probably never before considered these questions, and all who answer them will gain increased self-awareness.

Continue your exploration by considering the assumptions you make about homosexuality. These may include ideas such as:

- Homosexuals suffer from gender confusion and really want to be the opposite sex.
- Homosexuals lead unhappy lives.
- Homosexuals want to be heterosexual.
- Homosexuals have chosen to be that way and could really be straight if they desired.

None of these statements is true. Be aware of your stereotypes; don't force them on others.

Compare your assumptions with your experiences with gay men and lesbians who have been patients, colleagues, family, or friends. What is the reality for those individuals? If your first thought is that you have never known a gay man or lesbian, stop and think again. That is quite unlikely given that homosexuality is the most common sexual variant in the United States, estimated by many to be practiced by 10 percent of the population.

Learn more, not just about "homosexuality," but about the people who are living the experience. Doing the exercises in this chapter is a beginning, as is working with the gay men who have HIV infection. Begin to do some reading of gay literature to increase your familiarity with the community and its vocabulary. If you have colleagues or acquaintances whom you believe are closeted gay men or lesbians, don't confront them with the fact they have spent tremendous energy trying to hide. Rather, in general conversation, perhaps when talking about HIV and the people who have it, indicate your support for an alternative life style. Show your willingness to be a friend by being genuinely interested in their lives away from work, including their personal relationships.

Beginning to deal with HIV and homosexuality raises not only general issues of sexuality, but perhaps more personal issues. Some individuals may experience particular difficulty, especially if they have secret fears that they might really be gay. Sex researchers have identified a seven-point scale related to sexuality, with exclusive heterosexuality on one end, exclusive homosexuality on the other, and five additional points on the scale in between reflecting a variety of behavior patterns.[2] Notably, few persons fall on one end of the scale or the other; the point on the continuum where each of us falls varies throughout our lifetimes.

For the care provider who is a gay man or lesbian, the appearance of a homosexual with HIV infection may be very threatening. The patient is labeled on the basis of his diagnosis and, regardless of the energy previously expended on being "in the closet," he no longer has that option. Gay or lesbian providers are confronted with the homophobia of colleagues and the institution. If they have not previously chosen disclosure, they may be tremendously fearful of being "discovered" if they give too much attention to the patient. The gay male provider is probably also dealing with feelings of personal vulnerability. In addition to the work situation, these providers may also be handling stress related to the loss of friends or a lover.

Your acceptance and caring can make a major contribution toward helping these individuals provide the support desired by patients.

NOTES

1. Jack S. Annon, *Behavioral Treatment of Sexual Problems: Brief Therapy* (Hagerstown, Md.: Harper and Row, 1976).

2. A. Kinsey et al., *Sexual Behavior in the Human Male* (Philadelphia: W.B. Saunders, 1948).

Chapter **25**

Ethical and Legal Issues in the AIDS Epidemic

Barbara A. Koenig

Since its recognition in 1981, the AIDS epidemic has posed a serious challenge to society as a whole and to health care professionals in particular. The challenge to health workers is clear: how can we respond to this new and deadly disease with compassion, understanding, and skill? Any illness requires skillful and knowledgeable management. AIDS, in addition, presents an array of ethical and legal dilemmas of profound scope. Finding solutions to these dilemmas is proving to be as daunting as finding answers to the remaining scientific questions about HIV infection. A New York physician whose residency training coincided with the initial years of the epidemic described learning the ethics of AIDS as her most perplexing task. In reflecting on her experiences she wrote, " . . . for all the dizzying medical difficulties of the disease, its ethical difficulties were even greater."[1]

A host of questions accompany the daily care of patients with AIDS, ranging from how best to protect the patient's confidentiality to how best to make decisions about specific medical and nursing interventions. The dilemmas of AIDS are felt most intensely by individual clinicians, but the impact of the ethical questions extends beyond the hospital through society as a whole. After briefly mentioning the challenges to society as a whole, this chapter will focus on the ethical and legal issues confronted by nurses in the clinical care of persons with AIDS. Three key problem areas will be covered: (1) ethical decisions about life-sustaining treatment, (2) confidentiality and HIV antibody tests, and (3) the nurse's obligation to provide care.

On a societal level, the challenge of AIDS mirrors the threats posed by great epidemics of the past. A recurring question is how best to balance individual rights and liberties against the need to protect the health of the public as a whole.[2] The

Note: The author wishes to thank Marsha Fowler for a thoughtful review of an earlier version of this chapter.

balance has swung both ways, although in the past procedures such as quarantine by definition subordinated the rights of individuals to the larger goals of protecting the public health. When asked to make determinations about the extent of constitutional liberties in the face of a communicable disease threat, courts " . . . have found the balance between health and liberty difficult to strike."[3]

The special character of AIDS, particularly the fear and hysteria the disease has engendered, makes our public responses to the disease problematic. Although AIDS is certainly a serious public health threat, "the furor aroused by AIDS has gone far beyond the actual danger it poses."[4] Our cultural reactions to AIDS have been shaped by the unique epidemiological features of the disease, particularly its association with sexuality, especially homosexuality, and socially "deviant" activities, such as IV drug use. Those afflicted with AIDS must bear the burden of social stigma as well as life-threatening illness.

The fear of AIDS, plus its association with "sin," creates a climate in which PWAs are seen as deserving punishment rather than treatment. Discrimination against those exposed to the AIDS virus or manifesting the disease is a significant danger, in spite of legislative efforts in some cities to prevent such occurrences. Patients and HIV antibody-positive individuals have lost jobs, been denied insurance, and occasionally been denied medical care. Legislation requiring mandatory screening of low-risk populations, such as marriage license applicants, has been passed[5] despite almost unanimous scientific opinion that such policies are not effective in disease control.[6] In addition to being ineffective, many of these screening programs would fail an ethical analysis.[7]

Repressive governmental responses to sexually transmitted diseases are not new. It is a little-known fact that prostitutes were subject to quarantine, detention, and internment during World War I as a way of controlling sexually transmitted diseases. Thirty thousand prostitutes were incarcerated in an effort to control the spread of venereal disease.[8] This dramatic example of the abuse of individual liberties under the guise of controlling communicable disease reveals our collective cultural hysteria about sexually transmitted illness. The case also illustrates that abuses of individual liberty do not in themselves guarantee success. Rates of venereal disease increased dramatically during World War I in spite of these restrictive measures.[9]

In our society the courts and the legal arena provide the setting in which to argue the inherent conflicts between public health policies and individual rights. As suggested above, the issues are complex and the answers far from straightforward. "AIDS poses the most profound issues of constitutional law and public health since the Supreme Court approved compulsory immunization in 1905."[10] Litigation in the courts and debate in legislative bodies will proliferate on these issues.

How can the epidemic be contained by effective public health measures that minimize the potential discrimination and actual harm to the individual rights of those affected? Nurses, as health professionals, have an obligation to engage in the ensuing national debate about AIDS health policy issues in an informed manner.[11] They must be knowledgeable about the nature of the debate and the consequences of various solutions, recognizing that some of the proposed "solutions" are responses to the fear and hysteria generated by the disease and, as such, are unlikely to be effective.

CLINICAL DECISION MAKING IN AIDS TREATMENT

Ethical issues in the clinical care of AIDS patients are not unlike those arising in the care of any patient suffering from a life-threatening disease.[12] Since AIDS has so far proven to have no apparent cure—and since therapies like AZT that affect the course of the disease are new—providers must make decisions almost constantly about what constitutes appropriate therapy. Many of these decisions are in the area of medical care, for example, decisions about whether a patient would benefit from renal dialysis or therapy in ICU. Other decisions are in the realm of nursing care, for example, in pain management or symptom control. Some patients may want supportive care only, and others may wish to take every possible treatment option, including participation in research protocols.

Patient Autonomy in Decision Making

In ethics, a consensus has developed over the last 15 years that making decisions about what constitutes appropriate therapy is the right of the patient. The courts have supported this position; patients who are legally competent may execute their right. In cooperation with the provider of care, who is obligated to provide realistic information about available options, it is the patient who determines what kind of care is desired.[13] Patients may wish to exercise control over all aspects of their care, from basic comfort measures to the most invasive medical tests and procedures.

In AIDS care, the ethical goal of respect for patient autonomy is complicated by many factors. Certain clinical features of the disease may impair the decision-making capacity of persons with AIDS or ARC. A significant percentage of patients experience dementia or psychiatric problems caused by primary brain infection with HIV. Mental abilities may also be compromised by other infections of the CNS or metabolic imbalance caused by anoxia or other disease processes. For any number of reasons, patients may be physically unable to participate in decision making at the moment decisions need to be made.

Even when patients maintain decision-making capacity, other problems may impede their participation in treatment decisions. Research has shown, for example, that patients may have unrealistic ideas about the benefits of treatment. In one study AIDS patients—homosexual men in this case—significantly overestimated the odds of surviving intensive care treatment for PCP.[14] Thus their ability to give truly informed consent to therapy was limited by a lack of realistic knowledge of how successful treatment might be.

Respecting the autonomy of patients may be especially difficult in certain populations of AIDS clients. Some patients, such as IV drug users and prostitutes, have socially disapproved life styles. Discomfort or lack of familiarity with these groups of patients may cause health professionals to devalue their choices. For example, it may be difficult to respect a patient's decision to continue living in one room in a dilapidated residence hotel rather than be cared for in a specialized AIDS inpatient hospice. Medical and nursing paternalism may favor a more middle-class setting at the expense of patients' wishes. Respecting autonomy may be a challenging goal to carry out. Too frequently patient autonomy is respected only when patient preferences match those of their care providers.

Advance Directives for Health Care Decisions

It is vitally important for all patients, but particularly for AIDS patients, to document their wishes about life-sustaining therapy as early as reasonably possible in the course of their illness, preferably before they are admitted to the hospital during a crisis. There are a number of legal methods for documenting patient wishes about life-sustaining treatment, often called advance directives. Legislative efforts in a number of states allow patients a specific legal say in future medical decisions about their care.

The California Natural Death Act, passed by the legislature in 1976, was the first U.S. effort to allow patients a voice in decisions about care at the end of life; legislation in other states quickly followed.[15] In a document commonly called a "living will," a patient specifies desires about treatment before becoming seriously ill and losing the capacity to participate in medical decisions. A number of problems are associated with living wills, specifically, the difficulty of imagining ahead of time all the different kinds of decisions that a health care team might face. Also, most living will legislation limits the document to patients who are in the final stages of a terminal illness, and then only to medical care that is "futile."[16] Some legislation mandates a waiting period before providers can respect patients' wishes.

Although a living will is preferable to no guidance at all, a better legal document is a "durable power of attorney for health care" (DPAHC). This document allows patients to indicate preferences for treatment and to select a surrogate decision maker for health care providers to consult when patients are unable to make decisions for themselves. The existence of a surrogate decision maker familiar with the desires and values of the patient is more useful than the limited guidance provided by a living will. Proxy decision makers must make decisions in accord with what patients would have wished if able to decide themselves. Surrogates may not go against the known wishes of patients. In addition, under a DPAHC a person may refuse any medical or nursing intervention. The DPAHC is not biased toward limiting treatment, and signers may stipulate exactly which treatments they desire. Both kinds of advance directives protect health professionals from legal repercussions (or professional disciplinary actions) for following the patient's preferences about therapy.

Many states have specific DPAHC statutes. In states without a specific DPAHC statute for health care, at least two court rulings have suggested that physicians may respect an adult patient's written advance directive about medical treatment without fear of adverse legal consequences.[17]

The DPAHC may be a particularly useful document for gay men with AIDS or ARC. Although not a strict legal requirement, the tradition in most medical decision making calls for consulting the immediate family of an incompetent patient about decisions to withhold or withdraw therapy.[18] Since a gay man may be part of a ''nontraditional'' family, he might wish to specify, in advance, exactly who should be consulted about these decisions. The DPAHC allows a friend, or other nonfamily member, to be the designated surrogate decision maker. The PWA may then discuss his wishes at length with the proxy, who then explains the patient's desires to health care providers if the patient becomes unable to make decisions directly.

Nurses, because of their extensive daily contact with patients, are uniquely suited to assist patients with executing advance directives. Because nurses possess direct knowledge of the likely clinical outcomes of AIDS (e.g., the possible need to make decisions about intubation and intensive care for PCP), they can help patients clarify their wishes. Nurses show respect for patients' autonomy by making sure that the appropriate legal documents are available. Many agencies providing services for AIDS patients routinely offer assistance with legal issues such as the DPAHC, financial matters, and wills.

Offers to provide this type of information and attempts to gain knowledge about a patient's wishes must be handled sensitively. For example, it is generally inappropriate to ask a patient about a do-not-resuscitate order during an admitting interview. Providers must undertake these emotionally charged discussions with the utmost care and skill, counteracting legitimate patient fear of abandonment with a positive commitment to supportive care. In spite of a widespread belief on the part of health professionals that information on advance directives harms patients, research reveals that patients are often anxious to discuss these matters and await an appropriate opening from their health care providers.[19] Nonetheless, some patients may refuse to participate in such discussions, and providers should respect consistently stated refusal. The California DPAHC statute (Civil Code

Sections 2410–43) specifically states that patients cannot be required to execute an advance directive as a condition for receiving health care.

In actual practice health professionals must care for many patients without either the capacity for decision making or specific advance directives. In these situations useful guidelines are available in several recent documents.[20] When knowledge of the patient's wishes is unobtainable and no surrogate decision maker is available, health professionals must make decisions, in conjunction with family and friends if possible, based on the presumed "best interests" of the patient. When conflicts cannot be resolved at the bedside, practitioners might benefit from consulting their institution's ethics committee, a forum for ethical discussion and debate found in increasing numbers of hospitals. Courts should be asked to resolve clinical problems only as a last resort. Many recent cases have affirmed the basic principle that decisions to limit treatment do not require judicial review in most situations.

USE OF HIV ANTIBODY TESTS

Since 1984, when testing blood for past infection with HIV became a technical reality, the many ethical and legal implications of screening programs have become apparent. Handling information about HIV antibody status presents vexing problems for health professionals interested in respecting the confidentiality of their patients as well as their obligations to society to prevent the spread of a fatal, transmissible disease. The questions raised are predominantly social and political. They present a major challenge to our political democracy to construct public health policies that effectively prevent the spread of HIV infection while minimizing the risk of discrimination against individuals who may be tested.

Nurses have an obligation to understand the complexities of HIV antibody screening for two reasons. First, they may be able to play an important role in educating the public about HIV infection and screening programs. This urgent need is demonstrated by a 1987 news report of a family with three sons with hemophilia, all HIV antibody–positive, whose Florida home was fire-bombed because of fear that the children could infect others if they attended school. Because of the public's highly emotional reaction to AIDS, patients are at great risk if screening programs are not handled appropriately. Nurses must guard against clients' being subjected to "the double jeopardy of lethal disease and social oppression."[21] Second, nurses must understand how best to manage information about HIV antibody status in their places of employment.

Guarding Patient Confidentiality

Protecting the confidentiality of clients—either hospitalized patients or potential participants in a screening program—is a major ethical obligation of all health professionals, supported by the Code for Nurses.[22] Respecting patients' rights to keep information about their health status private is a necessity in maintaining the sense of trust on which a productive patient-caregiver relationship rests. Patients cannot disclose important and relevant information if they believe confidentiality will be routinely breached.

Central to this discussion is the idea that the ultimate goal of HIV testing programs must be to prevent the spread of HIV infection and thus protect the health of the public as a whole. This longstanding and laudable public health goal must be balanced against potential risks to the rights of individuals to keep potentially damaging information about their health status confidential. However, an ethical dilemma results from the conflict between two principles: respecting confidentiality and protecting the public as a whole.

The Limitation of Screening Programs

The goal of respecting confidentiality is especially pertinent because of the many potential risks to individuals participating in screening programs. The major risk is unfair discrimination and stigmatization based on an uncertain probability of contracting AIDS or of being identified as a member of a "high-risk" group. Although the exact numbers remain unknown, some HIV-positive individuals may remain disease free. An irreducible rate of false positive tests, a technical and scientific problem of great import, also limits the usefulness of screening programs. Many problems with screening programs arise because the tests used were originally devised to screen donated blood, not to test individuals. Hence, HIV antibody tests like the ELISA (enzyme-linked immunosorbent assay) have a very high sensitivity. Blood banks want to eliminate all contaminated blood, and false positives are not a serious problem. Discarding some virus-free blood is a small cost for eliminating contaminated blood from the general supply. However, this approach presents serious difficulties in screening a population of low-risk individuals because of a small, but unavoidable, incidence of false positive test results. Assuming an ideal testing situation, with all positive tests confirmed with a second test, a minimum of one out of three positive results will be false positives and the number of false results is likely to be much higher if screening becomes routine.[23] The number of false positives may, in fact, be much higher than the number of true positive individuals identified. Considering the enormous implications of a positive test, the goals of the screening program must be urgent and realistic to justify subjecting individuals to the risk of false positive results. Even if mandatory screening programs could be made highly effective, it is doubtful that their ultimate utility would outweigh the high likelihood of harm to those participating.[24]

Legal Issues

Respecting confidentiality, a legal requirement in virtually all circumstances, derives from the basic right to privacy set forth in the U.S. Constitution.[25] Medical information may be disclosed only with the permission of the person involved. Exceptions include situations in which reporting a disease to health officials is required by law, as in cases of AIDS and many other communicable diseases. Although the large number of people with access to a hospitalized patient's medical record may greatly reduce the likelihood of confidentiality, it is a goal toward which to strive. Some AIDS patients may wish to have information about their diagnosis disclosed in order to obtain disability or other benefits. But others, especially those with HIV infection but no disease, may not.

California (and a small number of other states) has passed specific laws that regulate the handling of information obtained from HIV antibody tests. The California law (Health and Safety Code 199.20 et seq.) is particularly stringent, creating some difficulties for health professionals along with protections for individual clients. California law stipulates that individuals can be tested for HIV only with their specific written consent and that they must be advised of the implications of permitting the test. Furthermore, test results can be disclosed to any third party only with the patient's written authorization. The one exception to the requirement of written consent is tests conducted within the system of alternative test sites, where testing is completely anonymous. Effective January 1988, the Health and Safety Code is being modified so that the physician or surgeon who orders an HIV test may (but is not required to) disclose the patient's positive test results to a person believed to be the patient's spouse. The physician is protected from criminal or civil liability for the disclosure. Also, with the test subject's written consent, the county health officer is permitted to alert the sexual partners of a seropositive test subject, as well as persons with whom the subject has shared a hypodermic needle.

Because of legal requirements to maintain confidentiality about HIV antibody status, the question arises where and how to store information obtained in testing. For example, should the laboratory results be placed routinely in a patient's medical record? Because of California's strict law, some hospitals maintain all test results in a controlled, centralized location, accessible only to those with a clear need to know. Since requirements vary considerably from state to state, decisions about handling HIV antibody test results must incorporate local regulations. The ethically based goal of respect for patient confidentiality is, however, independent of legal requirements.

Duty to Third Parties

The ethical obligation to maintain strict patient confidentiality (supported in most instances by a legal duty as well) may create conflicts. A nurse caring for an

HIV-infected client also has ethical obligations to others, such as the sexual partners of a client who may not know the client's antibody status. What is the nurse's obligation if the client persistently refuses to inform a spouse? Similarly, a nurse involved in discharge planning for an HIV-positive infant being placed in foster care may feel a conflict between an ethical obligation to notify the prospective foster parents about the child's test results and the strict requirements of the law, which may prohibit such disclosure. In states lacking stringent statutes governing testing and disclosing information about HIV, the issues may be slightly different, but the ethical obligation of the health professional to maintain confidentiality remains.

In some situations the nurse may decide that the ethical obligations to warn a third party override the requirement to respect confidentiality. These instances are likely to be rare. For a nurse to make this decision, the danger to the third party must be real, significant, and immediate. For example, a sexual partner of an HIV-positive individual faces real risks, whereas a coworker with casual contact faces no risk of infection. There is also legal precedent for arguing that the health professional's duty to respect a patient's confidentiality may be abrogated in the face of real and significant danger to a third party. In the *Tarosoff* case a California court found that a psychotherapist erred by respecting a patient's confidentiality in failing to warn a third party who was murdered by a patient, who had previously revealed this plan to the therapist.[26] However, the exact legal ramifications of warning, or failing to warn, third parties remain unclear. A nurse making the ethical assessment that an obligation to a third party exists must be prepared to accept possible legal consequences of performing an act that might violate specific laws about disclosing HIV antibody status. In general, few exceptions to the tradition of respecting confidentiality should be tolerated.

THE NURSE'S RESPONSIBILITY: DUTY VERSUS FEAR

The fear created by an infectious, fatal disease presents another, very different ethical dilemma for all providers of care: can an individual nurse balance the risk of acquiring AIDS with the professional obligation to treat all patients, whatever the cause of their sickness? Do nurses have a moral duty to provide care for patients with AIDS?

Early in the epidemic reports were heard of nurses (as well as other health professionals) who refused to care for PWAs and even resigned positions to avoid contact with the disease.[27] Research during this period documented significant levels of fear among nurses.[28] Health professionals were not alone in their fear; they reflected a growing concern in the community at large, fostered by news reports of a ''gay plague'' and other strident descriptions of a mysterious and deadly disease in our midst. Concern (but not hysteria) was justified in the first years of the epidemic before the viral agent was identified and when the exact means of transmission was poorly understood. Especially for nurses trained in the post–World War II antibiotic era, concerns about the dangers posed by patients seemed new and unexpected.

Risk versus Fear

The low risk of occupational transmission of HIV infection is now well established. Risk of acquiring the virus in casual patient contact is negligible.[29] However, the risk to health care workers is not zero. As of November 1987, 12 health care workers were documented to have been infected with HIV in the course of their duties.[30] Most of the infections are the result of accidental needlestick injuries. The likelihood of seroconversion following such an accident has been calculated as 0.13 to 0.39 percent, a very low rate.[31]

Given the deadly nature of the disease, it is not surprising that fear continues. Fear, especially fear of contagion, is not totally subject to rational control. Irrational fear of a contagious disease, not a new phenomenon, reflects basic cultural concerns about danger, pollution, and purity. Fear of AIDS has been intensified by the social stigma of those groups of people, primarily gay men and IV drug users, who, through chance, experienced the first waves of the epidemic. The stigma of these groups became part of the ''meaning'' of AIDS in American society. Sexually transmitted diseases have historically been the source of enormous stigma. The mere association of illness and sexuality seems sufficient to confer stigma on the unwitting disease carrier; that the sexual acts are often homosexual merely intensifies the stigmatization. Health professionals are not immune to these cultural preconceptions. Research with practicing physicians and medical students suggests these groups have negative attitudes toward homosexuals and PWAs.[32]

Like perceptions of fear, perceptions of risk are, at least in part, socially and culturally patterned.[33] The world contains innumerable risks, only a few of which become the cause of conscious concern. Hepatitis presents greater health risks for nurses, but the social contamination associated with AIDS has made the fear of this disease predominant and has emphasized its risks.

Nurses must recognize the potential confusion between the stigma of AIDS and perceptions of risk. Understanding this confusion may help nurses in dealing with the issue of fear. Health professionals are not immune to the general social hysteria surrounding AIDS, but they are in a better position to counteract stereotypical responses through (1) understanding the cultural sources of stigma leading to fear and (2) having the facts about the poor transmissibility of HIV readily at hand.

Research on medical residents suggests that level of fear lessens with ''exposure'' to patients with AIDS.[34] Although greater experience with AIDS patients is not a magic vaccine that immunizes staff against fear, it does force practitioners to deal with individuals rather than with stereotypes. Perhaps the fear of AIDS is greatest in the abstract; when the disease is manifest in a real patient, fear may lessen.

Legal Issues in Refusing To Provide Care

Returning to the original question, can a nurse refuse an assignment to an AIDS patient? Legally, the issue for a nurse who is an employee of a health care organization is quite straightforward. Nurses can be disciplined for failure to carry out patient assignments.[35] An assignment to an AIDS patient therefore cannot be refused. There is an important exception to this general rule: if the employee genuinely believes that proper infection control guidelines are not being followed in the institution, the employee has a legal right, under the federal Occupational Health and Safety Act, to complain about potentially unsafe working conditions without jeopardy. A nurse may not be legally dismissed for refusing to work under unsafe conditions.[36] Nurses working in blood banks were reportedly discouraged (and disciplined) for wearing latex gloves when drawing blood, an infection control practice almost universally recommended as a means of preventing the spread of HIV.[37] It is highly unlikely that the courts would uphold the dismissal of a nurse in this situation. However, if the institution is following (and enforcing) proper and up-to-date infection control guidelines (see Chapter 18), the nurse-employee risks being disciplined for failure to care for AIDS patients.

An Ethical Obligation To Provide Care

The ethical issues in refusing to provide care are more complex, based on conflict between two fundamental ethical principles: altruism and self-interest. In ethics problems frequently arise, or begin to be perceived, when two or more important duties or goals are in opposition. Health professionals have a social obligation to put the patient's needs above their own, yet there is no absolute obligation to do so at risk of serious personal harm.

One way of examining the problem is to look to the existing ethical judgments of the nursing profession for guidance. The American Nurses' Association (ANA) Code for Nurses clearly states that the nurse has an obligation to provide services "unrestricted by considerations of social or economic status, personal attributes, or the nature of health problems."[38] More recently, the ANA addressed the issue of AIDS specifically. The 1987 House of Delegates reaffirmed the commitment of the nursing profession to provide care regardless of the severity of the patient's illness.[39] The ANA Ethics Committee "Statement Regarding Risk versus

Responsibility in Providing Nursing Care'' (reprinted as Appendix 25-A) concludes that service to the sick is an ethical ''ideal'' and that there are limits to the amount of actual risk an individual nurse is obligated to take. The statement describes criteria meant to aid individuals in deciding what actions to take.

Given that the actual risk to nurses appears to be low, the moral tradition of nursing supports a strong obligation to provide care for patients with AIDS. Certainly prejudice is an inadequate justification for denying care to any patient. The ANA statement resolutely supports the position that care should be delivered without consideration of the patient's personal attributes, socioeconomic status, or the nature of the health problem.

To meet the ethical obligation of providing care, the nurse has a responsibility to overcome fear through accurate information about the transmission of HIV and a thorough understanding of the best means to prevent occupational exposure. Nurses must also understand the sources of both fear and prejudice. Part of this burden must be borne by nursing administration, which has the obligation to provide education and information on infection control and to enforce guidelines carefully so that individual nurses do not have to feel awkward about protecting themselves. Nonetheless, in rare situations, risk to the nurse may exceed benefit to the patient. In these situations the individual nurse must decide. Foresight might prevent some of these moral difficulties. For example, providing resuscitation devices at each patient's bedside obviates the moral dilemma of whether or not to provide mouth-to-mouth resuscitation if a patient has an unexpected cardiopulmonary arrest.

JUSTICE: THE ETHICAL CHALLENGE OF AIDS

This discussion of the issues surrounding the clinical care of AIDS patients— including clinical decisions to limit treatment, handling HIV antibody status, and the health professional's obligation to provide care—in no way exhausts the ethical and legal dilemmas this epidemic presents. For example, there remain the ethical or legal issues of conducting research in AIDS, including the ethical complexities of drug testing and vaccine development.[40] Undoubtedly, ethical issues will continue to be at the forefront of debate about AIDS. These issues will not resolve but intensify as the epidemic continues and hundreds of thousands already infected with HIV throughout the world become ill.

No discussion of the ethical issues in AIDS can be complete without mention of the fundamental questions of justice and fairness that the epidemic raises.[41] The individual nurse feels the financial impact of AIDS most directly while witnessing the impoverishment of patients as insurance benefits run out, or seeing the large percentage of patients with no health insurance. But most financial decisions about AIDS are made beyond the confines of clinical settings. National debate about what constitutes a fair and just allocation of resources for AIDS has been spurred by estimates that U.S. government spending on AIDS will reach $10 billion to $15 billion by 1991.[42]

Recent appropriations have increased significantly after an initial failure on the part of the government, particularly at the federal level, to respond quickly to the epidemic. However, deciding how to use available resources is in itself quite complex and politically sensitive. How much should be allocated to basic research, how much to educational efforts to contain the epidemic, and how much to direct patient care? Dollars spent on patient care must then be further divided among hospital services and community-based care. A nursing voice in striking this balance is critical if long-term care is to keep an adequate share of available resources. And how much money should be allocated to AIDS? The epidemic is devastating and frightening. But the allocation of health dollars must take into account other diseases, many of which, such as cancer and heart disease, touch vastly more people than AIDS is projected to affect, even accepting the highest estimates of its likely spread.

Economic constraints will increasingly be felt in clinical settings as well as debated by health policy experts. An undesirable confusion may cloud the overlap of ethics and economics. As the financial burdens of the epidemic deepen, it is crucial not to allow the motivation of cost savings to muddy how health care professionals make decisions about life-sustaining treatment, such as providing intensive care, for individual patients. Well-reasoned ethical decisions to limit treatment—those based on clearly stated patient preferences or on the medical futility of a proposed action—should not be confused with decisions based on a need to conserve scarce resources.[43] Furthermore, making choices about just allocation of resources should not become the burden of individual nurses or physicians working at the bedside but must be clear public choices based on well-informed and open debate.

Although media reports about AIDS have produced the misconception that it is a peculiarly American disease, its ravages are by no means limited to the United States. Do our responsibilities extend beyond our own borders? The situation in central Africa, where as many as 10 percent of some urban populations may already be infected with HIV, is critical. What is our obligation to contribute to international work, for example, by the World Health Organization?

CONCLUSION

In the clinical setting nurses bear specific ethical responsibilities, among them the duty to help abate the fear of AIDS through education of staff and clients alike. Nurses also must strive to respect the confidentiality of individual clients to the greatest degree possible, making exceptions only when there is clear danger of harm to others. And finally, nurses must respect individual autonomy by honoring the patient's wishes about treatment and actively assisting patients in documenting their desires.

In our society ethics can rarely be separated from political considerations. To be truly effective, nurses must enter the political dialogue about AIDS, since it is in this arena that the ethical issues will be debated and specific laws formulated.[44] Two areas are crucial to the debate. First, adequate resources must be devoted to the epidemic and distributed in a just fashion.[45] Second, as the debate continues on public health policies that attempt to control the spread of AIDS, it is vital to remember that coercive policies prompted by the fear that AIDS generates may have symbolic effectiveness only. Nurses have a responsibility to design effective voluntary policies to avoid the imposition of coercive policies (like mandatory screening programs) that have the potential for enormous harm.[46] The history of this generation of health professionals will be measured by how it reacts to this tragic new disease called AIDS.[47]

NOTES

1. A. Zuger, "AIDS on the Wards: A Residency in Medical Ethics," *Hastings Center Report* 17, no. 3 (1987):17.

2. E.J. Juengst and B.A. Koenig, *The Meaning of AIDS: Implications for Science, Clinical Ethics, and Public Health Policy* (New York: Praeger, in press).

3. D.J. Merritt, "The Constitutional Balance between Health and Liberty," *Hastings Center Report*, 16, no. 6 (Suppl.) (1986):9.

4. L. Eisenberg, "The Genesis of Fear: AIDS and the Public's Response to Science," *Law, Medicine, and Health Care* 14 (1986):245.

5. D. Johnson, "Broad Laws on AIDS Signed in Illinois," *New York Times*, September 22, 1987.

6. L.O. Gostin, W.J. Curran, and M.E. Clark, "The Case Against Compulsory Case Finding in Controlling AIDS —Testing, Screening, and Reporting," *American Journal of Law and Medicine* 12 (1987):7–53; and A.R. Moss, "Coercive and Voluntary Policies in the AIDS Epidemic" (Paper presented at the Society for Health and Human Values National Meeting, San Francisco, Calif., April 1986). (Also in Juengst and Koenig, *The Meaning of AIDS*.)

7. R. Bayer, C. Levine, and S.M. Wolf, "HIV Antibody Screening: An Ethical Framework for Evaluating Proposed Programs," *Journal of the American Medical Association* 256 (1986):1768–74.

8. A.M. Brandt, "AIDS: From Social History to Social Policy," *Law, Medicine, and Health Care* 14 (1986):231–42.

9. Ibid.

10. M. Mills, C.B. Wofsy, and J. Mills, "The Acquired Immunodeficiency Syndrome: Infection Control and Public Health Law," *New England Journal of Medicine* 314 (1986):931.

11. F.E. McLaughlin, "Political, Ethical and Legal Issues Involving Persons with AIDS and Care-givers" (California Nurses' Association, unpublished report, 1987).

12. N. Milliken and R. Greenblatt, "Ethical Issues of the AIDS Epidemic," in *Medical Ethics: A Guide for Health Care Practitioners*, ed. D. Thomasma and J. Monagle, (Rockville, Md.: Aspen Publishers, 1988).

13. M.D.M. Fowler, "Withholding or Withdrawing Life-Sustaining Treatment," *California Nurse* 83 (June 1987):16; and President's Commission for the Study of Ethical Problems in Medicine and Biomedical and Behavioral Research, "Making Health Care Decisions: The Ethical and Legal Implications of Informed Consent in the Patient-Practitioner Relationship" (Washington, D.C.: U.S. Government Printing Office, 1982).

14. R. Steinbrook et al., "Preferences of Homosexual Men with AIDS for Life-Sustaining Treatment," *New England Journal of Medicine* 314 (1986):457–60.

15. A.R. Jonsen, "Dying Right in California: The Natural Death Act," *Clinical Research* 26(1978):55–60.

16. R. Steinbrook and B. Lo, "Decision Making for Incompetent Patients by Designated Proxy: California's New Law," *New England Journal of Medicine* 310 (1984):1598–1601.

17. L.J. Nelson, "Law, Ethics and Advance Directives Regarding the Medical Care of AIDS Patients" (Paper presented at the Society for Health and Human Values National Meeting, San Francisco, Calif., April 1986) (Also in Juengst and Koenig, *The Meaning of AIDS.*)

18. J. Areen, "The Legal Status of Consent Obtained from Families of Adult Patients to Withhold or Withdraw Treatment," *Journal of the American Medical Association* 258 (1987):229–35.

19. Steinbrook et al., "Preferences of Homosexual Men with AIDS for Life-Sustaining Treatment."

20. Hastings Center, "Guidelines on the Termination of Life-Sustaining Treatment and the Care of the Dying" (Briarcliff Manor, N.Y.: The Hastings Center, 1987); and President's Commission for the Study of Ethical Problems in Medicine and Biomedical and Behavioral Research, "Deciding to Forgo Life-Sustaining Treatment" (Washington, D.C.: U.S. Government Printing Office, 1983).

21. Brandt, "AIDS: From Social History to Social Policy."

22. S.J. Smith, "AIDS: Ethical Duties of Nurses," in *Ethics: Principles and Issues* (San Francisco: California Nurses' Association, 1985), pp. 28–29.

23. K.B. Meyer and S.G. Pauker, "Screening for HIV: Can We Afford the False Positive Rate?" *New England Journal of Medicine* 317 (1987):238–41.

24. Gostin, Curran, and Clark, "The Case against Compulsory Case Finding."

25. H. Creighton, "Legal Aspects of AIDS—Part I," *Nursing Management* 17 (November 1986):14–16.

26. W.J. Winslade, "AIDS and the Duty to Warn Others" (Paper presented at the Society for Health and Human Values National Meeting, San Francisco, Calif., April 1986). (Also in Juengst and Koenig, *The Meaning of AIDS.*)

27. "Two RNs Refuse to Treat AIDS Patient, Resign," *San Francisco Examiner*, June 12, 1983.

28. M. Blumenfield et al., "Survey of Attitudes of Nurses Working with AIDS Patients," *General Hospital Psychiatry* 9 (1987):58–63.

29. E. McCray et al., "Occupational Risk of the Acquired Immunodeficiency Syndrome among Health Care Workers, *New England Journal of Medicine* 314 (1986):1127–32.

30. J. Gerberding, "Occupational Infection: A Worry That Won't Go Away," *AIDSFILE* 2, no. 4 (November 1987):5–6.

31. G.H. Friedland and R.S. Klein, "Transmission of the Human Immunodeficiency Virus," *New England Journal of Medicine*, 317 (1987):1125–35.

32. J. A. Kelly et al., "Stigmatization of AIDS Patients by Physicians," *American Journal of Public Health*, 77 (1987):789–91; and Kelly et al., "Medical Students' Attitudes toward AIDS and Homosexual Patients," *Journal of Medical Education* 62 (1987):549–56.

33. R. Lessor and K. Jurich, "Ideology and Politics in the Control of Contagion: The Social Organization of AIDS Care," in *The Social Dimensions of AIDS: Method and Theory*, ed. D.A. Feldman and T.M. Johnson (New York: Praeger, 1986), pp. 256–59.

34. B.A. Koenig and M. Cooke, "Physician Response to a New, Lethal, and Presumably Infectious Disease: AIDS and Medical Residents in San Francisco" (Paper presented at the Society for Health and Human Values National Meeting, San Francisco, Calif., April 1986). (Also in Juengst and Koenig, *The Meaning of AIDS.*)

35. H. Creighton, "Legal Aspects of AIDS—Part II," *Nursing Management* 17 (December 1986):14–16.

36. Ibid.

37. E. Herscher, "Blood Banks Reportedly Ban Protective Gloves," *San Francisco Chronicle*, November 18, 1987.

38. Smith, "AIDS: Ethical Duties of Nurses," in *Ethics: Principles and Issues.*

39. P. McCarthy, *American Nurse*, 1987, p. 1.

40. R. Purtilo, J. Sonnabend, and D.T. Purtilo, "Confidentiality, Informed Consent and Untoward Social Consequences in Research on a 'New Killer Disease' (AIDS)," *Clinical Research* 31 (1983):462–72; and J.D. Durham, "The Ethical Dimensions of AIDS," in *The Person with AIDS: Nursing Perspectives*, ed. J.D. Durham and F.L. Cohen (New York: Springer, 1987) pp. 229–52.

41. A.R. Jonsen, M. Cooke, and B.A. Koenig, "AIDS and Ethics," *Issues in Science and Technology* 2 (1986):56–65.

42. J.K. Iglehart, "Financing the Struggle against AIDS," *New England Journal of Medicine* 317 (1987):180–84.

43. M.L. Brown, "AIDS and Ethics: Concerns and Considerations," *Oncology Nursing Forum* 14 (1987):69–73; and Fowler, "Withholding or Withdrawing Life-Sustaining Treatment."

44. McLaughlin, "Political, Ethical and Legal Issues."

45. Durham, "The Ethical Dimensions of AIDS."

46. Moss, "Coercive and Voluntary Policies."

47. Iglehart, "Financing the Struggle against AIDS."

Appendix 25-A

Statement Regarding Risk versus Responsibility in Providing Nursing Care*

This statement, developed by the Committee on Ethics of the American Nurses' Association, examines the question, At what point does it cease to be a nurse's duty to undergo risk for the benefit of the patient? That question is particularly relevant for nurses caring for patients afflicted with communicable or infectious diseases such as typhoid, tuberculosis, plague, Hansen's disease, influenza, Hepatitis B, Legionnaires' disease, cytomegalovirus, and AIDS (acquired immune deficiency syndrome). Not only must nursing care be readily available to individuals afflicted with communicable or infectious diseases, but also nurses must be advised on the risk and the responsibilities they face in providing care to those individuals. Accepting personal risk which exceeds the limits of duty is not morally obligatory; it is a moral option.

According to the Code for Nurses, nurses may morally refuse to participate in care, but only on the grounds of either patient advocacy or moral objection to a specific type of intervention. Nursing is resolute in its perspective that care should be delivered without prejudice, and it makes no allowance for use of the patient's personal attributes or socioeconomic status or the nature of the health problem as grounds for discrimination.

The first statement of the Code for Nurses says, "The nurse provides services with respect for human dignity and the uniqueness of the client, unrestricted by considerations of social or economic status, personal attributes, or the nature of the health problems." Here, the code is addressing the issue of nondiscrimination in the allocation of nursing resources (a question of justice and fairness).

Historically, nurses have given care to those in need, even at risk to their own health, life, or limb. Indeed, the *Suggested Code* of 1926 proclaims that "the most precious possession of this profession is the ideal of service, extending even to the

---

*This statement was developed by the American Nurses' Association Committee on Ethics, November 1986. It is reprinted with permission of ANA.

sacrifice of life itself. . . ." Nursing history is replete with examples of nurses who have knowingly incurred great risk in order to care for those in need of nursing or to contribute to the advancement of health science. Contemporary nurses, too, knowingly place themselves in jeopardy when giving care on the battlefield, in places of squalor and poor sanitation at home and abroad, in situations of natural or manmade disaster, and to those with communicable or infectious diseases.

As the *Suggested Code* of 1926 recognizes, the ideal of service is, in fact, an ideal. There are limits to the personal risk of harm the nurse can be expected to accept as a moral duty. The profession does not and cannot demand the sacrifice of the nurse's well-being, physical, emotional, or otherwise, or the nurse's life for the benefit of the patient.

For assistance in resolving the question of risk versus responsibility, nurses must turn to the field of ethics for guidance. In ethics, the differentiation between benefiting another as a moral duty and benefiting another as a moral option is found in four fundamental criteria. As applied to nursing, they are as follows:

1. The patient is at significant risk of harm, loss, or damage if the nurse does not assist.
2. The nurse's intervention or care is directly relevant to preventing harm.
3. The nurse's care will probably prevent harm, loss, or damage to the patient.
4. The benefit the patient will gain outweighs any harm the nurse might incur and does not present more than minimal risk to the health care provider.

Nursing, as nursing, creates a special relationship between nurse and patient, with special duties for the nurse. The nurse is not a "stranger" and thus is not at liberty to walk away from those in need of nursing assistance. The nurse is obliged to care for those in need of nursing when all four of the criteria are met.

For example, in most instances, it would be considered morally obligatory for a nurse to give care to an AIDS patient. If the nurse is immunosuppressed, however, it could be reasonably argued that the nurse is not morally obligated to care for that patient on the grounds that the fourth criterion, the most crucial, has not been met. Apart from the issue of personal risk to the nurse, it must be mentioned that it is incumbent upon the hospital or agency administration to provide adequate safeguards, such as equipment and enforcement of procedures, for the protection of nursing staff.

Nursing is a caring, patient advocacy profession. Because of nursing's long history of standing ready to assist the ill and the vulnerable in society, society has come to rely on nursing and to expect that it will rise to the health demands of virtually any occasion. In a sense, this reciprocity is crucial to the life of the profession. All must know that care will be given when needed and that it will not be arbitrarily, prejudicially, or capriciously denied.

Yet, there are limits to the moral obligation of the individual nurse to benefit patients. Beneficence stands as a moral duty in those situations where the four criteria can be met. When not all of the criteria can be met, the individual nurse must evaluate the situation according to the criteria and choose whether or not to go beyond the requirement of duty.

Part V

The Community Provider Experience

From the earliest days of the AIDS epidemic, nurses have assumed a strong leadership role both in their institutions and their communities. For example, the first meeting of the KS Foundation, which later evolved into the San Francisco AIDS Foundation, was held in a school gymnasium and was organized and led by health care providers, including a nurse, a hospital administrator, and a physician, working with two or three community organizers. The realization of the need for community action and commitment of time and energy to that end often evolves from the obvious needs of clients, which commonly include community support services as well as preventive education.

Recognizing the fact that out of necessity or out of choice nurses and other providers must often take the initiative in program development, within both institutions and communities, the first three chapters in the final unit of this book describe the experiences of nurses in three different communities. The final chapter discusses techniques that have been successful for program development in a variety of settings.

I encourage you to assume a proactive attitude in relation to AIDS. Rather than simply waiting to see what will happen in your institution and your community, you should take the initiative and become a leader who works with others to create a positive approach to the challenges that lie ahead.

Chapter 26

The Approach of One Community Hospital

Marilyn S. Rodgers, Elaine M. Peterman, Patsy J. Oliver,
Julia A. DeLisser, and Terri J. Brown

In the fall of 1983, a three-month-old baby with a diagnosis of "failure to thrive" was admitted to El Camino Hospital, a 470-bed full-service community hospital in Mountain View, California. After two weeks of treatment and a subsequent diagnosis of PCP and thrush, the baby was transferred to a nearby university hospital. The baby's condition continued unchanged and the cause of its immunodeficiency undiagnosed. A diagnosis of AIDS came much later.

During the winter of 1983, a young man was admitted to the hospital. He presented with a severe case of interstitial pneumonia, which did not respond to treatment. As this young man was seriously ill, he was placed on isolation precautions. He was admitted to the ICU by the third day of hospitalization, intubated, and placed on a respirator. The infection control coordinator, a nurse, provided the ICU staff with information and support. The hospital guidelines, which covered basic blood and body fluid precautions, were reviewed in detail with all staff. The infection control coordinator provided one-to-one education, group inservices, and emotional support to the staff. The young man was well cared for but was eventually transferred to a university hospital, where he later died.

These two admissions raised many issues, questions, and concerns for the nursing staff, medical staff, and administration of El Camino Hospital:

- What exactly was known about this disease called AIDS?
- How many people would it affect in the community that El Camino served?
- How many patients should El Camino expect to receive with this disease?
- Could a community hospital care for such patients, or should they be immediately transferred to a teaching center?

El Camino is located 35 miles south of San Francisco and 20 miles north of San Jose, in the middle of the Silicon Valley. The hospital, which has a reputation for innovation and high-quality patient care, enjoys close ties to the community for which it provides a variety of health care services.

In the early 1980s, staff at El Camino began reading articles about a mysterious disease called AIDS. Initially it was something of an intellectual curiosity, a subject only for casual professional discussion. The whole phenomenon seemed somehow remote—something that would not directly affect the lives of staff or patients at El Camino. After all, weren't most PWAs either homosexuals or IV drug users who lived in San Francisco or New York? Wouldn't people diagnosed with AIDS be treated and cared for by the large teaching centers with specialty units? Right? Wrong!

The realization that PWAs could and should be treated and cared for in community hospitals like El Camino came slowly. PWAs, like persons with other diseases, wanted to remain in their own communities, whenever possible, rather than being forced to travel to, or be hospitalized in, another city, even if it was less than 30 miles away. PWAs, like other community residents, wanted to be treated by physicians they knew, in hospitals close to home, where they could be close to friends and loved ones.

No one knew the numbers of people that AIDS would affect. Projections of an AIDS epidemic appeared much later. In retrospect, had El Camino been aware of what was about to happen, the hospital would have initiated an aggressive plan to provide a whole new patient service.

POLICY DEVELOPMENT

El Camino Hospital is decentralized and follows a philosophy of participative management. Organizational systems utilize task forces or committees for planning, solving problems, gathering information, and developing draft documents for policy, guidelines, or protocol. Multidisciplinary task forces, including representatives from staff support departments and administration, facilitate input from staff who are most affected by or concerned about a problem or issue.

Policy development for El Camino on AIDS/ARC began in earnest with the admission of the second diagnosed patient, which prompted assembly of a task force composed of:

- representatives of the medical staff
- the Infection Control coordinator
- the nurse manager of the ICU
- representatives from Human Support and Nursing Administration.

The purpose of this task force or ad hoc committee was to review the second case and determine the implications of caring for this person. The initial outcome was a draft of guidelines for management that incorporated the psychosocial needs of the patient, family, and significant other along with the physical care component. These guidelines were designed to accompany another set, already in place, that were for blood-borne infections.

ACQUIRING INFORMATION AND IDENTIFYING RESOURCES

Information from CDC was the basis for developing guidelines for patient care and staff procedures. In the San Francisco Bay Area, San Francisco General Hospital (SFGH) provided valuable information and leadership on all issues of patient care. Formal and informal networking among professional colleagues also proved invaluable. SFGH; University of California, San Francisco; and the California Nurses' Association provided ongoing education in the form of lectures and workshops.

When El Camino began to care for patients with AIDS/ARC, the need for a coordinated hospital effort became evident, and the hospital identified key people to take responsibility for developing policy and providing leadership, education, and emotional support. These people, chosen for their interest and commitment to the issues and as a result of their professional roles, were:

- the assistant administrator for Nursing
- the Infection Control coordinator
- the director of Human Support
- medical staff representatives from the Infection Control Committee.

Assistant Administrator for Nursing

The assistant administrator for Nursing was responsible for planning and carrying out the best possible care for all patients, including those with AIDS/ARC. She was responsible for policy development and for the education and support of staff. She also acted as a conduit of information between administration and staff, facilitated administration's preparation for the acute care needs of patients, and supported and promoted involvement and leadership in the community.

Infection Control Coordinator

While assuming primary responsibility for the education of hospital staff in the area of AIDS/ARC, the Infection Control coordinator was also involved in the development of policies and protocols. She ensured that the most current information was available for staff, oversaw the development of guidelines based on time-honored principles of infection control to protect staff while ensuring the best possible care for patients, and facilitated the purchase of supplies and equipment that provide for a safe working environment. Along with education, the infection control coordinator provided emotional support for staff.

Director of Human Support

The director of Human Support's major focus was emotional support for patients, families, and staff—both emotional and educational support to patients with AIDS/ARC while they are hospitalized and postdischarge support to patients, families, and significant others. The director assisted in the education of staff and was also involved in community education.

Medical Staff Representatives

El Camino was fortunate to have several physicians, including the chairman of the Infection Control Committee, who were interested and knowledgeable about AIDS/ARC. These physicians served as leaders for hospital staff as well as for their physician colleagues. They assisted in education and policy development and were involved in the development of the hospital multidisciplinary committee on AIDS.

With the second admission, one issue the hospital needed to address was whether to have a unit identified as the "AIDS Nursing Unit." While the decision was made not to dedicate a unit specifically to the care of AIDS/ARC patients, a medical unit, 6East, seemed to be a logical place to care for many of these patients.

6East

As it became apparent that El Camino would be caring for patients with AIDS/ARC, the nursing managers of 6East met and agreed that patients who needed less intensive care should be admitted to the 31-bed medical unit. It has a unique physical arrangement in that 8 of the 11 private rooms are designed specifically for isolating patients. Each room has a "clean sink," private bathroom with shower, special containers for laundry and trash, and double-door pass-through cupboards.

Patients admitted to these rooms generally fall into one of two categories: (1) immunosuppression, due to such conditions as burns, chemotherapy, or a compromised or debilitated state; or (2) infection, such as tuberculosis, hepatitis, or a draining wound. As people with AIDS/ARC are both immunosuppressed and potentially infective, 6East became the logical unit to care for this patient group.

The nursing staff of 6East knew the principles of caring for infected and immunosuppressed patients and were sensitive to their patients' feelings of isolation. Furthermore, these nurses were particularly skilled in caring for patients with life-threatening and terminal illnesses. It was determined that the staff needed education specifically related to AIDS/ARC. All of the key people—Infection Control coordinator, director of Human Support, assistant administrator for Nursing, and medical staff—were involved in supporting 6East. That support began in preparation for the first patient and has continued in varying degrees with each subsequent patient.

The Infection Control coordinator met with staff several times for both formal and informal educational sessions. She shared current information about the disease process and emphasized how health care workers could protect themselves while providing compassionate, high-quality patient care. It is imperative in any setting that staff's questions and concerns be addressed immediately. Three of the most frequently questions asked were:

- "How can I protect myself and other patients on the unit?"
- "How is the disease transmitted?"
- "Is there a risk that I might carry this virus home to my family?"

Guidelines pertaining to isolation equipment and handling specimens, laundry, and wastes were developed or revised following CDC recommendations. Over time, several issues surrounding equipment, supplies, and safety of the environment arose and were dealt with successfully. Staff were encouraged to protect themselves by wearing gloves, made available to each nurse, whenever they anticipated coming in contact with the blood or body fluids of any patient. Goggles were provided in areas where nurses might be at risk for having blood or body fluids splatter in their face or eyes. Disposable ambubags were placed in every patient's room or in a convenient location for staff. Needle safety, and the issue of recapping versus not recapping, became a major concern, and El Camino reviewed and piloted many possible products and procedures. The hospital decided to place a hard plastic container in each patient's room, into which needles would be placed uncapped. These measures reassured the staff of 6East, and of the hospital, that El Camino was concerned about their safety and welfare while they and the hospital cared for patients.

Another important component of providing a safe environment for staff without compromising patient care was the decision *not* to mandate that all health care workers care for patients with AIDS/ARC. By allowing freedom of choice while providing education and support, the nursing staff came to view caring for these patients as a challenge—an opportunity for professional growth—rather than as a threat. Nurses have always cared for people in need, regardless of the disease, and these nurses were no exception. Nurses have also traditionally been role models for other health care workers, from housekeepers to medical staff. Once guidelines were in place, nurses role-modeled appropriate infection control principles and incorporated safe care into their practices. Nurses from 6East became resources for their colleagues on other nursing units and in the community.

Staff Education

Two key contributors to quality care for patients with AIDS/ARC were staff education and staff support. Staff education is an ongoing process that has taken many forms at El Camino: one-to-one sessions, small groups of fewer than 15 people, and large groups or forums of up to 250 people. Education has been provided hospitalwide and by individual nursing units or departments. One exposure to the information is not enough; staff need updates at least every six months.

The Infection Control coordinator, with assistance from key medical staff, took primary responsibility for staff education. Beginning in 1982, inservices were held for staff on diseases for which staff should take precautionary measures. Initially, information on AIDS was included with information on Hepatitis B and Creutzfeldt-Jacob disease. In 1984 education efforts concentrated on AIDS/ARC. Later, educational events were particularly meaningful and successful if they were presented when new or controversial information was published in journals or appeared on television. Health care workers, like the public, receive much of their information from TV. Unfortunately, much of this information has in the past been sketchy, erroneous, or misunderstood.

Staff Support

An important component of each educational experience was staff support. Each educational event included ample time for questions from participants, with particular attention to emotional or controversial issues, as described in Chapter 23.

In 1984, following the admission of the second suspected AIDS patient, many staff voiced concerns. It was soon evident that many were anxious, fearful, and lacking in knowledge and understanding of the disease. Direct caregivers— nurses, therapists, and physicians—voiced the same concerns about exposure. Spouses of these direct caregivers were also concerned. Education helped alleviate these fears, but a supportive environment also encouraged staff to verbalize feelings that often do not come out initially. Such feelings, which are not easy to express, may be a factor in a staff member's hesitancy to care for a PWA.

The philosophy at El Camino has been not to force any nurse or caregiver to care for PWAs as long as patient care is not compromised. The hospital has honored individual preferences. Through education and strong support by the key people identified as experts, fears and anxieties precipitating an unwillingness to provide care have been minimal. At El Camino, when caregivers have refused or indicated they may refuse to care for an AIDS patient or a patient with another disease or condition, the process has been first to determine the cause for the refusal. If the caregivers have reasons for their refusal, such as pregnancy, they have been accepted as complying with the guidelines. If there appear to be no valid reasons for refusal, uncovering the possible barriers or causes has helped give clearer direction to education and support.

To assist with ongoing education, El Camino utilized the concept of resource nurses, direct caregivers who have been given the opportunity and responsibility to develop a body of knowledge about a disease entity or expertise for a targeted group of patients. For instance, resource nurses were identified for parenteral nutrition, diabetes, gerontology, and ostomy. These nurses have been sources of information for patients and families and for their nurse colleagues. In addition, the infection control coordinator established infection control resource nurses several years ago to develop experts on infectious diseases. The group includes at least one representative from each clinical nursing unit. These resource nurses have assisted in providing information to their peers on AIDS/ARC as well as on any other disease process warranting infection control measures. At this writing the chairman of the AIDS committee was considering the development of a physician resource group, with physician members representing the various specialties.

AIDS Committee

The establishment of the AIDS committee and the development of clear guidelines have also provided support for staff. In early 1985 the AIDS task force, a multidisciplinary subgroup of the Infection Control Committee, was formed. The new task force had strong leadership from a physician (an infectious disease specialist) and equally strong membership from Nursing and the Human Support departments. The infection control coordinator was an active member. The purpose of the task force was to study issues and questions and to recommend policy or guidelines to the hospital and medical staff. In 1986 the AIDS task force became an official committee—the AIDS Committee, under the auspices of the medical staff. The multidisciplinary committee meets monthly. A discussion of ethical issues became a regularly scheduled agenda item. The formation of the committee has provided the hospital with a recognized vehicle for addressing issues regarding AIDS. There are three subcommittees to the AIDS committee: one on hospital policy and guidelines, a second on education, and a third on community resources. Work generated by the AIDS committee has resulted in the following policies and guidelines:

- Guidelines for management of AIDS/ARC patients (revised)
- Guidelines for staff exposure
- Guidelines on HIV testing
- Personnel guidelines for AIDS in the workforce—assisting employees with life-threatening illnesses.

The AIDS committee, which has played a key role in education efforts for staff, addressed patient education and support as well. During the last half of 1984, staff became more concerned with the psychological care of patients and their significant others. When the task force on AIDS was formed, the development of an AIDS team approach for patients was the first order of business. When a patient was identified, the team, which included the infection control nurse, the patient's nurse or a representative from Nursing, the patient's physician, and a representative from Human Support, would work together for the welfare of the patient. The patient and significant other were followed by Human Support unless the patient refused, and educational materials were given to both patients and their significant others as requested. Additionally, the committee has begun to educate the community in a variety of settings.

TASK FORCE ON COMMUNITY RESOURCES

One issue identified in the summer of 1986 was concern over the availability of community resources for PWAs who did not require, or who no longer needed, acute care. These concerns led to the formation of the task force on community resources.

Articles appearing in the literature indicated that PWAs often were unable to leave the acute care hospital even when they no longer needed acute care. Lack of financial resources, lack of appropriate insurance coverage, fear of AIDS by people in the community, and lack of appropriate facilities were a few of the problems cited.

El Camino Hospital was interested in obtaining information about resources available to PWAs within the county. Apparently, before 1986 no skilled nursing facility (SNF) in the county had accepted a PWA. One objective was thus to determine what factors prevented admission of a PWA to a SNF and what action the hospital might take to overcome these factors. Several key community people were invited to attend a luncheon meeting held in the hospital in January 1987. People attending included:

- the executive director of ARIS (a support service for PWAs in Santa Clara County, fashioned after the Shanti Project in San Francisco)
- the public health nurse responsible for coordinating the county's AIDS project
- an administrator from a local skilled nursing facility
- a director of nursing from a second skilled nursing facility
- representatives from two home health agencies.

Also in attendance, representing El Camino, were:

- the chairman of the AIDS Committee
- a second interested physician on staff at El Camino
- the assistant administrator for Nursing
- the Infection Control coordinator
- the AIDS resource nurse in the Continuing Care Department (Discharge Planning).

The purpose of this meeting, which was chaired by the AIDS resource nurse, was to determine resources available and barriers to the resources, especially in regard to SNFs. One conclusion was that a second meeting was needed and that a high priority was AIDS education for health care workers outside the acute care hospital, especially health care workers employed in skilled nursing facilities.

At the second meeting attendance increased by four new members:

- a physician from another acute care facility that had a large number of PWAs needing intermediate or SNF care
- a director of a home IV company
- a director of Nursing from a third SNF
- an assistant manager of an independent employee assistance program.

The statement of purpose for the committee was finalized to read that the committee was to identify barriers within the community that prevented the appropriate post-hospital placement of PWAs. Further, the committee's purpose was to determine and implement, when possible, a means of overcoming the barriers.

The status and success of El Camino's educational program was also discussed. Three nurses from El Camino who had attended the Train the Trainer program (see Chapter 23) gave nine educational presentations at the three SNFs represented on the committee, each attended by over 50 licensed and nonlicensed health care personnel. The committee has continued to meet, and membership has increased with each meeting. Participants agree that one of the greatest benefits has been the opportunity to open channels of communication and to learn from one another the particular guidelines and restraints under which each agency works.

El Camino Hospital believes that establishing a committee on community resources is one strategy a community hospital can use to identify ways to eliminate barriers to community resources for post-hospitalized PWAs. The hospital has kept statistics on actual and projected numbers of PWAs to enable El Camino to anticipate the need for community resources and, it is hoped, implement necessary changes, or influence necessary changes, before the number of patients far exceeds those resources.

AIDS IN THE WORKPLACE

Another way El Camino has begun to take a leadership role in the community it serves is by providing education and resources for information on AIDS in the workplace.

El Camino is both a provider of care and an employer. As an employer, El Camino has instituted educational efforts and support for managers and staff on AIDS in the workplace. El Camino, anticipating that eventually one of its employees will become a PWA, has prepared policies and guidelines. The questions have just begun, many with no apparent answers:

- How many health care providers will contract the disease?
- Who will pay for their treatment—insurance companies, federal government, no one?
- Will Workmen's Compensation pay for their care?
- Will employees be required to prove the illness was work related?
- Will employees be required to prove they utilized good infection control principles—wore gloves and other appropriate clothing, used appropriate technique in disposing of needles, and so forth?
- What resources will be available—emotional, physical, financial, employment, housing, etc.?

To begin a dialogue on these issues, El Camino first held workshops for its own managers. Local community groups and industries then began to request courses and information. El Camino has tapped its established networks for information on AIDS, including contracts with local industries for courses on preventive health maintenance, assistance for employees through contracts with El Camino's employee assistance programs, and a health newsletter mailed to chief executive officers of local businesses. Workshops have also been presented to the general public. Special attention was given to hospital auxilians, whose members often serve as community liaisons.

El Camino Hospital must attempt to look into the future of the AIDS epidemic and predict how many patients the community will need to care for during the next several years. Additional community resources are critical, particularly in the areas of alternative housing and less acute care facilities. All health care systems will face ever-increasing financial considerations. Legal and ethical issues will present increasing challenges. El Camino will continue to address AIDS in its own setting as well as provide education and support in the community. Community hospitals can, and should, be leaders in the area of AIDS.

Chapter 27

Developing Community-Based AIDS Services

Frances Blasque and Elissa Chandler

AIDS is a complex medical, psychological, and social disease. From diagnosis to death, the patient and family have a variety of needs that challenge social service, mental health, and medical care providers in the hospital, clinic, or home care setting. The development and implementation of effective community-based AIDS services requires a coordinated team approach composed of multiple disciplines that provide a continuum of services.

In the late 1970s the hospice movement began an organized community response to the limits of the traditional health care system on meeting the needs of the terminally ill. Pioneering the concept of "case management," hospice focuses on the patient and family as the unit of care and multiple disciplines participate in a cooperative team effort. (For an in-depth discussion of hospice care, see Chapter 21.)

A community-based hospice program serves as a model for a possible solution to the "AIDS care crisis." The impact of AIDS is so extensive that effective responses must involve an organized community effort of patients, families, caregivers, and volunteers. As a compassionate and cost-effective approach, hospice may also be considered an appropriate option for caring for the terminally ill AIDS patient in the home care setting.

DEVELOPMENT OF HOSPITAL SERVICES

In the San Francisco Bay Area in the early 1980s, many PWAs without financial resources or private medical coverage turned to San Francisco General Hospital for medical treatment. The impetus for development of AIDS services in Alameda County, a large county close to San Francisco, developed when the county's first AIDS death occurred. The person who died was a well-known county employee who was diagnosed at Kaiser Hospital in Oakland, but since neither the county nor

Kaiser was prepared to meet his needs, he was transferred to the Kaiser Hospital in San Francisco. As a result of this episode, an administrator at Fairmont Hospital, located in Alameda County, began to plan for the development of comprehensive AIDS services.

Fairmont Hospital has served PWAs since the early 1980s. As the number of PWAs continued to rise and their specific needs became evident, community members lobbied for an AIDS ward. Community fund raisers were held to furnish a ward with bedside phones, TVs, planters, plants, and other amenities.

As services evolved, it rapidly became clear that both patients and hospital staff needed additional support. Patients needed emotional and practical support in addition to that provided by the hospital staff. Hospital staff needed additional ongoing education and emotional support. Staff and volunteers from a local community-based service, the Pacific Center's AIDS Project (PCAP), offered some of these services and support in the form of education, patient advocacy, group and individual emotional support for patients and families, and problem solving for staff. In 1984 a staff member was appointed advocate for inpatients, with the job of connecting inpatients with community-based services and working to develop new services.

In spring of 1986 Fairmont Hospital fulfilled the requirement of a minimum of seven patients on the ward at one time and officially opened an AIDS ward.

Attendant Referral Registry

The Center for Independent Living, located in Alameda County, is a living situation for individuals with physical limitations. These persons, who are encouraged to live as normal a life as possible, are assisted by attendants who are paid to help with activities of daily living. In 1985 Fairmont developed an attendant referral registry for PWAs, modeled after the center's attendant registry. Attendants assist PWAs with meal preparation, light housework, grocery shopping, errands, and showers. This added service allows patients to be discharged sooner and to resume more normal activities as soon as possible. Attendant services became the key to keeping PWAs at home for as long as possible, if not indefinitely, and also gave clients the option of dying at home with dignity and among friends.

COMMUNITY INTERFACE

The patient advocate at Fairmont had the pioneering task of locating needed community services, most of which were not involved in provision of AIDS services, convincing them to include PWAs as clients, developing a system of service integration, and resolving problems. Community services began to be identified and eligibility requirements established.

Established Community Support

In the local community, some persons were interested in providing direct services to PWAs in the hospital, while others wished to assist in fund raising. Hospital volunteers ran errands for patients, gave rides to family members, shopped, and provided companionship. Emotional support volunteers came from religious organizations and from PCAP. Each organization was responsible for educating and supervising its volunteers. The group providing financial assistance, composed of community business persons, evolved as the East Bay Assistance Fund. It was instrumental in gathering cases of food, paper articles (i.e., chux and diapers), clothing, a microwave oven, and miscellaneous goods, as well as in providing emergency services such as plumbing, housecleaning, and yard work.

Pacific Center AIDS Project

During the early 1980s, community-based services for PWAs were based in PCAP, which, in addition to services already noted, also offered benefits counseling and peer counseling. Community members were planning other services with county officials, but no other formal or official service center was designated until the Fairmont Ward was opened in 1986.

Patients still in the hospital were put in contact with PCAP and matched with a volunteer peer counselor. When it came time for patients to be discharged from the hospital, additional needs and wants evolved and had to be addressed. Patients going home usually lived alone and were too weak to take care of basic daily needs. For example, after spending three weeks in the hospital, Danny was excited and felt pretty good to be going home. When he opened the front door to his house, it was stuffy and dark. Quickly, he opened the curtains and windows to let in light and fresh air and was out of breath. After resting a bit, he went to the kitchen for something to drink. He had forgotten that he had been sick for a while before going into the hospital. There was no food in the house, dishes were stacked high in the sink, and his bed had not been changed. The store was about two blocks away— he'd just rest a while and then walk, as usual. Within a week, Danny was back in the hospital, where he stayed for two more weeks with dehydration and high temperatures. In this situation, Danny needed some assistance with:

- meal preparation
- housework

- laundry
- linen changing
- shopping
- transportation to and from his doctor's appointments.

While some persons do go home to live with someone willing to assist with these activities, the task can, and often does, become too much for just one person. And, in the case of a person living alone, friends, neighbors, and family members may not be available when assistance is needed. Attendant services, as described earlier in this chapter, and practical support volunteers began to fill this need.

Practical Support Volunteers

Practical support volunteer (PSV) services evolved out of a need to assist clients with practical tasks such as filling out forms, paying monthly bills, running errands, and accompanying a newly discharged patient home. PSVs also help out during the interim when paid services are pending due to delay in allocation of funds. Attendant services and PSVs are the backbone of service delivery to PWAs in Alameda County.

Postdischarge Facilities

Some persons had no home to go to upon discharge. Board and care facilities did not accept PWAs, nursing homes could not accept persons with a contagious disease, and housing was not available in the county. If family or friends could not accommodate a PWA, the individual usually remained in a community hospital indefinitely.

Fairmont referred patients being discharged and in need of skilled care at home to home health care agencies, whose services could include infusion therapy, nursing care, home health aides, and limited chore provider services. Some private insurance policies cover home health care services, but not an attendant or chore provider. A letter from the patient's physician, stating the daily costs for hospital versus home care and the cost effectiveness of the insurance company's paying for attendant or chore provider services in lieu of hospitalization, has usually received a positive response.

Patients at the terminal stage of AIDS have had the option of requesting hospice services. One reason for the too-few requests for this service may be that clients have not been aware of services, have not been emotionally prepared for hospice, or both. Another is that too few people, including service providers, know enough about hospice to make an appropriate referral. Future planning should include education about hospice services for staff, volunteers, and other service providers.

SECURING SERVICES

The process of securing services for a person with little or no income begins with applications to social service agencies. In California, these may include any or most of the following, depending on eligibility requirements:

- State Disability Insurance (SDI)
- Social Security Disability (SSD)
- Supplemental Security Income (SSI)
- Medi-Cal
- Medicare
- In-Home Supportive Services (IHSS)
- County Medical Services (medically indigent adult, or MIA)
- General Assistance (GA)
- Food stamps.

Diagnosis plays a large part in benefit eligibility. For example, Jerry has ARC, diagnosed about a year ago, at which time he applied for SSI. Four months later the application was denied. Jerry has made an appeal but does not think he will qualify the next time either. To qualify, he needs a real diagnosis: AIDS. The impact on a person who has been denied services based on no diagnosis can be devastating. "I wonder if I'm making this up and nobody is telling me?" "How much longer can I go on like this?" "How am I going to live?"

Financial assistance for PWAs, on the other hand, has been available through the existing system, but in the past clients were often dead before they received the first check. For example, it took at least six months before SSI benefits began. IHSS, which pays for attendant services, could not begin until a person was eligible for SSI benefits, so these services were delayed unless the person had personal financial resources. On occasion, friends would take up a collection or the East Bay AIDS Fund would assist with a one-time payment of $300 for some attendant services, but in reality the money was usually needed for rent and utilities.

As social service agencies processed more applications, listened to community input, and realized the urgency of the need, they began to look for ways to expedite the process. As a result, application for financial assistance now begins before a person is discharged from the hospital. Sometimes a patient is sent home with forms that can be filled out later and hand-carried to the agencies. These efforts have been successful, and PWAs now receive services in half the time it once took.

CASE MANAGEMENT

As services in Alameda County evolved, the need for coordination of client services grew. A case management model developed and was officially implemented to ensure coordination of services and continuity of care.

The In-Home Service's case management program has been in operation too short a time to make a just and comprehensive evaluation. However, the consensus is that a "Hospice AIDS Team" approach should be *the* delivery system for in-home services.

AIDS AND HOSPICE

As an alternative model of health care delivery, an interdisciplinary home hospice program responds to the effects of AIDS on the patient, family, and community. While the hospice team is multidisciplinary, the Community Hospice of the East Bay assigns a specific nurse–social worker team to each AIDS patient. Home hospice services in conjunction with community-based AIDS services have been found to dramatically reduce AIDS-related health care costs.

Several important points to remember about provision of hospice services are:

- "Family" in hospice is a term that, in addition to biological family, includes same-sex partners, friends, and children.
- Fear of transmission of the AIDS virus may have a detrimental effect on the already physically and emotionally vulnerable person with AIDS.
- Homophobia and fear of transmission of AIDS are often most effectively confronted by a nurse–social worker visit.

Development of an AIDS Community-Based Hospice Program

Efforts to develop a community-based hospice program must be preceded by an extensive education and organizing campaign. Education about all aspects of AIDS and about the concept of and services provided by hospice is an essential community-organizing tool. Documentation of the numbers of AIDS cases, the limits of existing services, and the cost effectiveness of home hospice care compared with the high cost of acute hospitalization strengthen the educational, planning, and fund-raising efforts.

Planning forums should involve all interested persons, including, but not limited to:

- staff and volunteers of agencies working with PWAs
- hospital administrators
- hospice staff
- nurses
- social workers
- physicians
- public health officials
- clergy
- business people
- members of the gay, Black, and Latin communities.

Effective fund-raising strategies stress identification, recruitment, and expansion of a core group of organizational and financial supporters. Trained volunteers can effectively carry out much of the fund raising. In areas with large AIDS populations, operational funds may be obtained by submitting grant proposals to corporations and foundations. Obtaining grants may also be feasible in other areas if corporations or foundations with an interest in funding AIDS-related service projects, hospice programs, or both can be identified. Other possible sources of funding include governmental agencies, service clubs, churches, insurance companies, and local businesses. Establishing contact with existing hospice programs in the community or other social service agencies may provide leads on important sources and strategies for long-term funding.

Communities should carefully examine state and federal regulations for hospice licensure when planning hospice services. Medicare and Medicaid hospice licensure, hospice accreditation by the Joint Commission on Accreditation of Hospitals, or home health agency certification may be desirable for insurance reimbursement, governmental funding, or both.

DEVELOPING COMMUNITY SERVICES

Some of the many aspects of care to consider when developing community services are:

- medical concerns
- education
- financial concerns
- psychological concerns
- home care/hospice

- food
- social services
- clothing
- legal services
- shelter
- client input
- minority advocates.

The following suggestions were useful in program development:

- Check to see if stores are willing to donate canned foods.
- Look into resource persons or centers in the local community, such as resource centers for the disabled, senior citizens' organizations, church groups, the American Cancer Society, the Red Cross, gay and/or lesbian resources, and women's centers.
- Check with established programs that have dealt with similar problems in the local area or another part of the country. (See Appendix B.)
- See whether community meal delivery services will extend their services to PWAs (for example, Home for Jewish Parents has a home meal service in Alameda County that serves PWAs).

REFERENCES

Beresford, L. *Hospice Creative Contracting and Case Management of the Terminally Ill, Final Public Report and Manual*. May 1, 1987.

Hutzen, H.S. "A Community Approach to AIDS through Hospice." *American Journal of Hospice Care* 3 (March–April 1986):17–23.

Martin, J.P. "The AIDS Home Care and Hospice Program: AIDS Multidisciplinary Approach to Caring for Persons with AIDS." *American Journal of Hospice Care* 3 (March–April 1986):35–37.

Scitovsky, M.A.; Cline, Mary; and Lee, Phillip R. "Medical Care Costs of Patients with AIDS in San Francisco." *Journal of the American Medical Association* 256 (December 1986):3103–06.

Weiss, A., and Chandler, E. "AIDS and Hospice." Presentation to the World Public Health Association Conference, Mexico City, March 1987.

Chapter 28

Establishment of a Program To Care for Infants with AIDS

Marsha Lose and Tolbert McCarroll

In response to the need to provide nourishing home care for infants and young children with the AIDS virus, a model program was established by the Starcross Community in Sonoma County, California. When the Community began its project, it adopted the name "Morning Glory" from the writings of a 19th-century Japanese poet, Issa. One little daughter, Sato, brought Issa a special joy. She fell victim to smallpox before she was two. Issa wrote that Sato died as the morning glories faded in the noon heat.

> *. . . withering away like some untainted blossom ravished by the sudden onslaught of mud and rain.*
> *As the morning glories were just closing their flowers, she closed her eyes forever.*
> *On hot summer days the morning glories close up early. The short-ness of their blooming time does not diminish their beauty.*

The Community worked closely with a medical support team. The practical procedures were established in consultation with the personnel at Santa Rosa's Community Hospital. Part I of this chapter was written by Brother Tolbert "Toby" McCarroll of the Starcross Community. Part II was written by Marsha Lose, the infection control nurse at Community Hospital.

PART I: THE HOME PERSPECTIVE

Responding to a Need

The problem of providing home care for infants and young children with the AIDS virus did not become known outside a few eastern cities until early 1986. At that time reports were made to Congress and appeared in the national media about 200 infants with AIDS, 100 of whom were abandoned and needlessly living in hospitals. An undetermined number of infants testing antibody-positive but without symptoms were unable to be placed in normal foster care. Within a short time projections began to appear indicating that, like other aspects of the AIDS plague, the number of babies with the AIDS virus would dramatically increase within a short time. By the summer of 1987, projections were that in 1992 as many as 7,000 infants would have AIDS and an undetermined but staggering number of infants with the virus would need home care. Because there is no medical justification for warehousing these infants in hospitals, the need for alternatives became increasingly apparent. In New York City the hospital cost was $700 to $900 a day. Of greater significance, the children were being deprived of the nurturing necessary for the development of any child.

We at Starcross were troubled by the reports. Our small community of lay Catholics has been caring for children with special needs as a licensed foster home since 1972. We live on a farm in northern California's Sonoma County (Annapolis, CA 95412) and have access to the medical facilities in Santa Rosa and San Francisco. Our liberal community is independent of church control but enjoys a friendly relationship with church authorities. We raise Christmas trees and make wreaths as a means of support.

By fall 1986 we determined that there was definitely a need. We established a support team that included physicians and nurses specializing in AIDS, pediatrics, and infectious disease control, underwent preliminary training, and announced our intention to our immediate neighbors.

Providing a Stable Home: Opposition and Support

A surprising amount of media attention was directed to the Morning Glory project, even before the first baby was placed with us. It became obvious that we had an opportunity, because of the national and international attention, to serve as a model for similar projects in other areas. Our plan was to furnish a stable home environment for up to four infants and to provide a support system for other homes in the northern California area caring for babies with the virus.

There was some local opposition from neighbors, but also some strong support. The most difficult opposition came from the social service system, for which this was a new problem. There was overreaction on the part of some social workers who did not have a solid understanding of the methods through which the AIDS virus is communicated. However, with the assistance of local public health officials, this situation corrected itself, and within 10 months we had a constructive and cooperative relationship with the social service system. There were difficulties from other government sources; a minor official referred to these infants as "little rattlesnakes"; threats were made that garbage from Starcross would not be allowed in county dumps; concerns were voiced by local firefighters as to whether they could safely respond to fire or medical emergencies. The intervention of public health officials, politicians, and the media combined to remove these obstacles.

Initially there was some concern that all families willing to provide a permanent home for an infant with the virus would be subjected to the same difficulties. But within a short time it became obvious that we were breaking new ground; as a result of the resolution of our conflicts, other families would not have to face these problems.

A Baby with the AIDS Virus Has the Needs of Any Infant

The central theme of our program is that the babies should not be defined as medical problems. In the early months we consistently encountered an attitude that a baby with the virus was a sick baby. It was difficult to communicate, even to some members of the medical and social work professions, that babies with the virus are capable of living an entirely normal existence for most of their lives. On the other hand, we sadly realized that the environment around the baby had an enormous influence on how the baby reacted.

The first baby at Starcross, known as "Melissa," came to make her home with us in January 1987. When Melissa was born she was eight weeks premature and weighed 3.35 pounds. There was a positive toxicology screen for opiates and cocaine. She had been swaddled during narcotic withdrawal. A carrier of the AIDS virus, the mother had no prenatal care and was unable to cope with the daily needs of her baby.

To thrive, a child must be bonded with at least one other individual. Sister Julian "Julie" De Rossi became the person Melissa knew would always be with her. A psychologist tested Melissa in the hospital when she was four months old. Her report described Melissa as "a frantic, desperate little infant, constantly sucking on her hand or her wrist" and showing "no real response to a human face, preferring to look at objects or simply avoid eye contact. She did not smile or brighten for a toy, person, or stimulation." In addition she was weak and lacking in motor skills—"very poor head control, reduced movements in her legs."

Two weeks later, Melissa moved to Starcross. By coincidence, when she was almost seven months old the same psychologist examined Melissa in a routine checkup at another hospital. She was found to be coming along well in all areas. Her physical skills were now developing. Most important, Melissa "has a lovely social response, smiling at her own reflection, enjoying frolic play, and responding to social stimulation." The psychologist found that Melissa was "functioning at her corrected age in all areas of development." The summary stated:

The positive changes in her physical strength and, more dramatically, in her social development are exciting to observe. . . . It is clear that Sister Julie and Melissa are developing a significant, reciprocal nurturing relationship and that this relationship accounts for a major portion of the improvements I observed today. It is such a pleasure to see a sad, closed-off little infant changing into a more normal, alert child able to trust and take pleasure in her environment.

During the period of time between the two reports there were no special activities for Melissa, only the normal nurturing expected in the home care of any infant.

There is, in the beginning, a need to focus on stimulating a baby coming from any institutional setting. It is important never to postpone any opportunity for human contact. The practice at Starcross is to celebrate every stage of a child's development, such as learning to turn over or to play with leaves and holding half-a-birthday parties at six months of age.

Becoming Advocates for Children with AIDS

In 1986 we and our growing support associates were primarily arguing for a stable home environment as opposed to care in a medical facility. In 1987 there was little continuing support for the medical facility model. The child with the AIDS virus was increasingly being portrayed by the media as a fundamentally healthy child. Instead of the medical model, a "shelter/temporary foster home/hospice" model was being suggested. In this situation the child would be taken from the hospital as soon as possible to a shelter for a few months, then placed in a specially trained foster home until the occurrence of terminal illness, at which time the child would be transferred to a hospice. We and our friends undertook to speak out whenever possible against this "shelter/temporary foster home/hospice" model.

Our model of "stable home care" corresponds to the recommendations of the Surgeon General's *Workshop on Children with HIV Infection and Their Families* (April 6–8, 1987). The central issue for the specialized work group was "bonding." The first preference is for the children to remain with their families with extensive support. When this is not possible, the best alternative is "individual" foster families with increased funding and support. In addition there is a need for "innovative nurturing homes for *small* numbers" of children where caregivers "will bond with and care for the children and, if possible, their parents." Obviously, neither the medical facility model of care nor the "shelter/temporary foster care/hospice" plan provides the bonding that is essential to both the physical and emotional well-being of the child.

One of the difficulties in some states is an ordinarily commendable public policy toward the reunification of children who are dependent wards of the court and their parents. To effect this reunification courts often require that there be no permanent planning for 12 to 18 months. As laudable as this policy is, it is a serious obstacle to providing a stable environment and to the possibility of developing a significant relationship with an adult for a child who may have a life expectancy of approximately three years.

The ultimate right of any child is not to die among strangers.

Profiles of Babies with the AIDS Virus

We receive inquiries in a broad spectrum of situations. One abandoned five-month-old baby in a hospital on the East Coast had never been visited by his mother and had no name. This child was adopted by a local family, which seemed more appropriate than moving him across country. Dr. Elizabeth Kubler-Ross has sponsored an organization on the East Coast for adopting babies with the AIDS virus. Another inquiry was on behalf of a single mother dying with AIDS and expected to live only a few days. Her three-year-old daughter had the virus. The mother's family would not accept responsibility for the child. In this case it was obviously better to work toward a solution that would leave the child with family members whom she had known, rather than placing her among strangers. A similar situation concerned a four-year-old boy who was dying from AIDS. He contracted the disease from blood transfusions as a result of leukemia. The mother had reached a point where she could not cope with the increasing demands of his medical condition. In this situation providing her with respite and other home support, nursing, and practical assistance enabled her to care for her child in the remaining months of his life.

There are obviously many unique situations concerning a baby with the AIDS virus. However, in a typical situation the baby is born of an IV drug user, who may very well have been a prostitute or former prostitute, and who is herself increasingly sick as a result of the virus she carries. It is not accurate to assume that the mother has no interest in the child. The experience at Starcross has been that it is important for the health of both the mother and the child that the mother be involved, to the extent possible, with those providing the child with a stable home. Sometimes it is difficult for a mother to participate in court proceedings that she feels judge her as a ''bad mother.'' Despite superficial callous appearances, the mothers of babies with AIDS often have a deep sense of guilt. Sometimes they find it impossible to go into a hospital because they believe people are looking at them and accusing them of killing their babies. At such times it is important for the person providing a home for the baby to keep the mother advised of the child's condition. The mother's fear of condemnation should not blind caregivers to her deep concern for her baby.

Babies coming into foster care are normally dependent wards of a county social service department. Every effort should be made to guarantee that a child will not be moved from home to home. Stability can sometimes be accomplished through permanent foster home placement or, with the cooperation of the mother, guardianship or adoption.

Primary Medical Support

There is a need to have a strong relationship with a primary care physician, who at times has to be an advocate for the best interest of the child in relation to a larger medical system. Hard decisions may have to be made about whether it is better for a child to die in familiar surroundings or to continue extraordinary medical procedures.

One of the most important friends to a family providing care for a baby with the AIDS virus is an infection control nurse, or a specially trained pediatric or public health nurse, who visits and provides in-home training and establishes a simple procedure from which there are never exceptions.

PART II: THE HEALTH CARE PERSPECTIVE

An Expanded Role for the Infection Control Nurse

The call came in the summer of 1986. "We've decided to start a program to care for infants with AIDS. We've heard you are knowledgeable about AIDS and could be a resource person for our program. Could you please help us?"

The role of the infection control nurse (ICN) in small hospitals is multidimensional: educator, consultant, coordinator, resource person, investigator, epidemiologist, and role model. My particular job description states that I am a consultant and educator to staff, patients, and the community, a function supported by our hospital's mission statement.

When the request for assistance came, most of the usual AIDS questions and problems relating to care of the adult patient were settled within the hospital. The staff was comfortable with the patients and the disease. There was recognition that someday patients with an HIV-related disease would appear in one of our maternal/child departments, if it hadn't already happened in an undiagnosed patient. If Starcross's Morning Glory Project proceeded, our hospital would most likely provide health care to these infants. This request stimulated efforts to develop programs within the hospital as well as the local community to care for infants, children, and mothers with AIDS.

In light of the above, and because I always love a challenge, my response was, "I'd love to help!" And then my apprehension began. The following is an account of some of the trials, tribulations, frustrations, satisfactions, and genuine joy encountered.

Background

Sonoma County, nestled between the Pacific Ocean and the beautiful wine country 40 miles north of San Francisco, has one of the highest per capita AIDS rates in California. Many of the "children of the sixties" have migrated to Sonoma County's rural areas rather than maintain city life. Included in these numbers are "yuppies," as well as gay and bisexual men. In addition, Guerneville, the Russian River resort area, is known for its gay hospitality. Sonoma County has its share of persons who are in the groups at highest risk for AIDS.

Community Hospital is a 175-bed hospital noted for maternal/child programs and its family practice residency, which is affiliated with The Medical Center at the University of California, San Francisco. The hospital admitted its first patient with AIDS in January 1983 and since then has been actively involved in the care and treatment of persons with AIDS in Sonoma County.

Development of new policies and procedures in small hospitals is sometimes difficult. Policy development is usually based on standards of practice from other hospitals, guidelines from recognized organizations like the CDC, reports in the medical literature, or applicable laws. Many times a problem presents itself to us before a solution, guidelines, or legislation is available. There is no standard of practice to follow, and we must "blaze new trails." On the other hand, sometimes the situation is to our advantage. Because we are smaller and fewer people are involved, communication between key individuals, departments, or committees, as well as decisions, can happen faster than in a larger university hospital setting. If we had blazed new trails with other AIDS problems, we certainly could do it again.

Getting Started and Getting Help

The first step was to gather support and to get help. A health care team was identified, including a pediatrician, a physician–AIDS expert, and most important, three well-qualified, caring, and interested pediatric nurses. Because we had no experience with children with AIDS (California had a total of 20 reported pediatric cases at that time), we began to ask ourselves questions and tried to anticipate the future:

- Who are our regional medical resources for children with AIDS?
- Is there a standard of practice for home care?
- How sick are these children?
- Can we appropriately provide medical care to this isolated community? (Annapolis is located in the northernmost section of the county 60 miles of winding roads above our location.)
- How long do children with AIDS live?
- What specific precautions must we take that are different from those taken with adults?
- What do the children eat? Are there feeding problems?
- What is the children's level of growth and development?
- What is their level of activity? Should we expect a child in bed, crawling, walking?
- How many children with AIDS are there? Where are they?
- What procedures should we expect to be performing?

We began to review the literature and find resources. We tried to identify organizations and hospitals with experience in dealing with children and made calls to potential resources in San Francisco and New York. Assistance was found in New York, where the majority of infants with AIDS lived. A New York day care center was especially helpful in giving us the information we needed most, a picture of everyday living.

Resources were also identified within the county government systems:

- Public Health Department
- Sanitation Department
- Fire Department
- Social Service
- County Counsel.

It was important to educate key individuals, including the Board of Supervisors. Attorneys in the County Counsel's office were invaluable in their support.

Going Public

In September 1986, Starcross made a public announcement to inform the county and the community of its plans to establish a program to care for infants with AIDS

. . . and then rumors started in the town of Annapolis. To provide information and answer questions, a concerned and very supportive citizen group called a town meeting in October. A medical team composed of a local physician, a pediatrician, a pediatric nurse, and myself were the educators. Starcross staff were there to answer questions about their plans. Most of the town attended. There were general questions about AIDS, as well as specific questions about the effect on the community, the schools, and the public's health.

- Will these children go to school?
- Is AIDS transmitted by coughing, sneezing, or through the air?
- How do you know those answers are true?
- What about mosquitoes?
- What about the water supply?
- How do we know information won't change tomorrow?

One of the most interesting questions was, "Where are they going when they die?" Brother Toby smiled and responded, "Why, to heaven, of course." The real question was, "I hope you do not expect to use the community cemetery, or if they are buried at Starcross, will that contaminate the soil or the water supply?"

All in all, the townspeople's questions were good ones. One person even disclosed that one of her family members had AIDS. The local doctor shared that the local clinic had already treated cases of AIDS. Direct questions to the Starcross staff helped to quell the rumors. Information about how AIDS is transmitted decreased fear and anxiety, and most of the neighbors became more tolerant and supportive.

Home Care: Formulating Infection Control Policies

Educating the Starcross staff was a pleasure. They were already AIDS-knowledgeable. Initially, they needed advice on how to cope with everyday infection control problems: how to wash the dishes, do the laundry, and establish general decontamination procedures, like keeping bleach available. The biggest policy decisions related to diapers—how to dispose of them and whether gloves needed to be worn with each diaper change. Hospital policies are often different from home care policies. Personnel, time, equipment, level of education, and, of course, cost, are major variables.

Gloves

Caring for a child in the hospital, the nurse wears gloves to change diapers. But in checking with other centers, mothers and caregivers of children at home didn't necessarily wear them for every diaper change if they had no open cuts. Diapers, in most situations, can be changed in a way that avoids contamination with body fluids. The question was settled with observation of the hands of the caregivers; hands that pull weeds, milk cows, braid wreaths, chop wood, and have numerous nicks, cuts, and rough edges. The policy was established that caregivers would wear gloves when changing diapers.

Diapers

How would we dispose of them, especially in light of the concerns expressed by refuse disposal personnel? Studies were not available to tell us the level of infectivity in stool or urine. Most authorities suggested that virus could be present, but probably in very small quantities, and precautions should be taken when coming in contact with any body secretion. One alternative was cloth diapers, which could be adequately disinfected by machine washing with bleach. However, this would increase the water and septic system usage as well as staff's time requirements.

Disposable diapers would be easier, but what about the refuse disposal site? In California, infectious waste laws regulate hospitals and clinics that generate more than 100 kilograms of infectious waste per month. Starcross would not fall into this category, but the community was concerned about the public's health. A call to the Public Health Department's sanitarian indicated approval of the procedure to dispose of diapers in landfill if stool is first flushed into a sanitary sewer or septic system and the diapers are adequately contained in impervious bags during transport. Disposable diapers could be safely and legally disposed of via landfill.

Masks and Caps

After Melissa arrived, the Starcross staff asked for a box of masks and caps. This was an unusual request, which in normal situations raises the hair on the back of any infection control nurse's neck. Caps and masks are *not* necessary in general care of persons with AIDS. Their use usually indicates the person's lack of knowledge about the disease's mode of transmission. Masks are used to prevent airborne transmission. Caps are necessary for hair control, not infection control. But there was a simple explanation. Occasionally a caregiver or a visitor had a cold, and a mask was needed to protect Melissa. The caps? Melissa had a problem with spitting up and an occasional emesis. Caregivers who were cuddling became tired of washing their hair so often, so they wore the caps!

Nursing Care

The Starcross staff also needed help with everyday nursing procedures like assessment of growth and development, feeding techniques, and observations of signs and symptoms of wellness and illness. Three pediatric nurses from the hospital were extremely helpful in providing information and support. They made home visits for education and support.

The Hospital: Formulating New Infection Control Techniques

If Starcross was to have infants, they would require medical care. Policies and procedures were necessary, and staff needed education.

Policies and Procedures

No specific changes in isolation procedures were necessary for the Pediatrics Unit. The majority of children admitted had some type of infectious disease, and the staff was very familiar with isolation techniques. However, development of procedures in the maternity department was slower. The problem was not how to specifically "isolate" mothers with HIV disease delivering infants but how to formulate and implement policies for protection of staff from every patient.

As policies were being formulated, the pediatric nurses prepared and presented educational programs to the maternal/child staff. Nursing administration provided support by emphasizing the importance of this project and making the programs mandatory for all staff.

In the meantime, the hospital infection committee, public health department, and other advisory committees began to promote prevention of perinatal AIDS by educating, testing, and screening women in risk groups before pregnancy.

The hospital Infection Committee, after much thought and discussion, adopted the policy of Universal Body Substance Precautions. We have asked nurses to do more screening for infectious diseases. "Have you had hepatitis, herpes? Do you have any risk factors for AIDS?" The most obvious answer from the patient has been "What are the risk factors?" This has been a perfect opportunity for more patient education. This concept is difficult to implement in some maternal-child areas. (For further information, see Chapter 12.)

Preparation for Other New Procedures

- "Where do we get the Salk vaccine? Do we have it? How do we administer it?"
- "Gamma globulin therapy—what's that?"
- "What will we do if we have chickenpox on Pediatrics at the same time we have a child with AIDS?"

We began to anticipate these potential problems, gather resources, and prepare action plans.

HINDSIGHT

One aspect that was neglected was preparation and education of staff in the private physician's office. The hospital had experience with AIDS, and staff were educated, sensitized, and comfortable. We spent much time anticipating the care of the hospitalized child, or the child and mother in labor and delivery, but we completely forgot about the health care workers providing well-child care in a private pediatric practice. The lack of planning was obvious from comments and suggestions by the pediatric office staff that they might refuse to care for infants if they were seen in the office or that they might quit working in the office altogether. Additional concerns were raised about the other patients in the office and the effect publicity would have on this extremely busy office practice.

With these considerations, the physicians were hesitant to see the children in the office until educational programs and group policies could be formulated. In the meantime, alternative care was provided. The office staff attended classes and had the opportunity for questions and answers.

CONCLUSION

Lack of knowledge about AIDS fosters fear. The infection control nurse can provide the knowledge and has the resources to pave the way for programs to deal with AIDS in the community as well as the hospital. Working with the people at Starcross—Brother Toby, Sister Marti, Sister Julie, and especially Melissa—has given me a tremendous amount of pleasure. It has allowed me to expand my role: as educator; consultant; coordinator; and resource person to staff, to the people of the community and county, patients, the general public, other county departments, and even the media.

So far in Community Hospital we've seen a child with AIDS only in our outpatient setting. We haven't delivered an infant with AIDS, nor have we admitted a child with AIDS, but we're prepared. Melissa finally arrived at Starcross. What a beautiful baby! When she comes to the hospital (so far, just to visit), I feel a tremendous amount of joy, personal as well as professional, in watching staff members cooing, cuddling, and babbling with her. She is treated as a person, not a disease. [Note: In 1987 a second and third baby arrived at Starcross, and Community Hospital delivered its first known HIV-positive mother.]

As a member of the Starcross Community has written, ''For some time to come there will be morning-glory babies in the world. Even though they may not live long, each of them will have a beauty and a right to play with kittens and sunbeams, to hear the songs of the birds and the wind, to smile, to laugh and to be loved as a unique and indispensable part of the story of creation.''

Chapter *29*

AIDS Resource Development

Isabel Auerbach and Lyn Paleo

The process of developing a coordinated program of core AIDS education and services is the same in both rural and urban areas. In presenting this model of resource development, we hope to encourage health officials, nurses, and others to develop their own local comprehensive plan for addressing the full range of issues associated with AIDS. The methodology, techniques, and perspective in this chapter come out of a particular set of circumstances and experiences in rural northern California. Readers should examine their own situations and adapt our model as necessary.

HISTORICAL PERSPECTIVE

The Northern California Services Department was established in 1984, when less than a third of the 45 counties in northern California had reported a case of AIDS among residents and the disease was perceived as San Francisco's problem. However, AIDS knows no geographic boundaries. Callers on the northern California toll-free AIDS Hotline, operated by the San Francisco AIDS Foundation (SFAF), reported that people with AIDS symptoms were being turned away from emergency rooms and forced to travel to San Francisco for diagnosis and treatment. They were leaving families, friends, and communities in northern California to establish residence in San Francisco because only there could they get adequate care. Most rural communities were struggling financially to provide basic public health services such as public health nursing and indigent care. Health and human service providers in these communities were unprepared to serve a new group of clients.

SFAF thus established the Northern California Services Department, partly funded by a grant from the California State Department of Health Services, to address systematically the need to develop a full range of services in rural and suburban communities. The department contained two components: program assistance and direct education.

In the few counties with existing AIDS programs, department staff served as consultants to enable these programs to gear up their services quickly and provide extensive information and updates on:

- prevention
- learning techniques and models
- conference and seminar development
- educational materials and syllabi
- research and clinical information
- organizing methods
- volunteer management
- techniques for working with the media
- other related issues.

This service, called program assistance, provided agency staff with a continuous source of consultation on virtually any programmatic issue. Further, beginning agencies were encouraged to consult with each other in a cooperative, rather than competitive, model.

The second component of the Northern California Services Department was direct education. In counties with no funded AIDS program, the staff worked closely with health officials to encourage health department staff to take an increasingly active role in coordinating the development of services. The staff educated and trained people at risk, health and human service providers, and the general public. Much of the work was responsive in detail, that is, conferences and seminars were geared to particular groups on request. However, the overall program was planned to ensure that prevention programs were established and that people at the core of the service delivery system received information and education about AIDS.

During the first three years of the Northern California Services Department's operation, 13 AIDS programs came into existence in the 11-county area it serves. The department was sufficiently successful for the California State Department of Health Services to withdraw funds on the basis of completed work. Program consulting in the formative stages had helped programs reach a stage at which they no longer needed outside assistance for continued development.

PROVISION OF AIDS SERVICES

From the experience of the Northern California Services Department, we have assembled a working model of the steps necessary for a county with no local services to develop a full spectrum of medical, support, and educational services. Medical services include:

- treating reported cases
- identifying and treating unreported cases
- screening
- providing outpatient and inpatient hospital services
- providing extended and intermediate care services
- providing home health and hospice services.

Support and social services include emotional and practical support for daily living, emergency and long-term housing, mental health services, social services case management, and legal services. Educational services consist of programs to decrease unwarranted fear about casual contagion, to produce behavioral change among people at risk, and to educate professionals.

In hard-hit urban areas, providing this full range of services has proven difficult, especially in the fields of extended and intermediate care and emergency housing. Professionals in hard-pressed localities with limited resources may look at this services list and throw up their hands. Yet many rural and suburban counties in California have developed plans, in a relatively short period, to supply a significant core of this comprehensive list of services.

Assessment

An AIDS response plan begins with an assessment of:

- existing local AIDS services (if any)
- existing services that may be adapted or expanded
- people, agencies, or institutions interested in taking a leadership role in service development
- regional assistance available.

The California Conference of Local Health Officers recommends that such a plan contain an assessment of the current incidence of infection and disease and projections of the increase of infection in the community, to be presented to the governing body of the jurisdiction and reviewed by local advisory committees, local providers, and representatives of high-risk groups.

Regional Task Force

A regional task force on AIDS can most effectively deal with these overall assessment tasks. Such a group can formulate a plan, ascertain priorities, and serve as an ongoing forum in which AIDS issues can legitimately be discussed. Task force members can support and encourage each other in emotional as well as practical ways by sharing information, skills, and contacts. As resources and activities develop, the task force acts as a central coordinating body among various groups with different views and priorities.

Purpose

If the task force determines its purpose and limitations early on and reassesses them periodically, it stands in an excellent position to become the vital entity within the community for discussion of and recommendations on AIDS activities. Task forces should avoid trying to be all things to all people. As its primary purpose, a task force may take on:

- education of health and human service providers
- fund raising
- public policy formation
- media relations activities
- housing
- education of the general public and people at risk
- formation of support groups targeted to different AIDS issues.

When a voluntary committee attempts to take on all of these activities, a frantic energy ensues for a few months, and then member after member drops away in frustration and defeat. Work may be accomplished during this frenetic period, but it has shallow roots. Much of what the group has set out to do remains incomplete and, worse, members sense defeat and perhaps are reluctant to join future AIDS efforts. Committee members should focus on examining the needs and resources available rather than attempting to do everything themselves.

Membership

A number of functionaries and groups should be represented on a task force. Often representatives of the health department form the core. Other health and human service providers, including, but not limited to, physicians, nurses, blood bank representatives, and mental health workers, should be invited and encouraged to participate, as should representatives of high-incidence groups such as gay and bisexual men, hemophiliacs, and drug users. Programs targeting these populations have proven more effective if members of the groups participate in planning. If suitable members are unavailable or are unwilling to serve publicly, service providers targeting these groups are helpful in representing their interests. PWAs and their friends or families are appropriate task force members, for they know firsthand the gaps in services. Task forces should encompass all community groups: women, Third World people, parents, businesses, nonprofit groups, and others. The more people who have input into a community plan, the more committed the community will be to it. A task force may meet as a large group at monthly, bimonthly, or quarterly intervals, with committees working between these meetings.

Professional Involvement

The task force should initially work with five specific professional groups to ensure that core services are available. These groups are:

- hospice and home health staff
- hospital personnel
- law enforcement and emergency response personnel
- public health, sexually transmitted disease (STD), and family planning clinic nurses and staff
- IV treatment program staff and other mental health professionals.

Hospice Staff. Starting with hospice or home health staff and working backward on the continuum of services may be practical. Many people with AIDS go to a city with established services for diagnosis and initial treatment and then return home. They may receive the first service in their own county during the final stages of their illness when they are too weak to travel.

The first barrier to address before the task force can provide an adequate training program for hospice and home health staff and volunteers is the extreme limitations on the resources available to many of these programs. Administrators may be unwilling to support an AIDS program that would drain limited funds. Staff and volunteers may be too few to provide the service. Other barriers are attitudinal. Staff and volunteers are accustomed to dealing with familiar diseases in older patients residing in traditional family settings and to training family members to care for the patients. They may be concerned about coming into contact with the disease or about caring for younger people in groups, such as gay men or IV drug users, that are new to them.

Creativity and persistence will overcome these barriers. The program administrator can be reminded that in many communities members of the gay community have provided voluntary attendant care and daily living support to PWAs; staff need to learn how to attract and use this new pool of volunteers. Other people may also be recruited, not because they specifically want to do hospice volunteer work, but because they want to contribute to the fight against the epidemic.

Staff and volunteers can be prepared to deal with the specific needs of PWAs. However, before a training program is established, the task force should examine patient needs and identify and overcome potential barriers through meetings with administrators and key staff.

Other problems arise in rural settings, and they, too, can be solved creatively. In an effective volunteer-based home health program in one isolated area, providing services entailed not only caring for patients but also caring for a client's goats and chickens. And since back roads make for extremely long and arduous travel, the care plan included an additional volunteer who brought in the goats and chickens of the volunteer who was providing attendant care.

Hospital Personnel. The second group to receive training should be hospital personnel, starting with hospital administrators, whose organizational support is essential. Administrators are especially concerned about the cost of care and reimbursement rates. They are often eager to facilitate and support the process of establishing outpatient services and home support services when they learn the direct relationship between this support and reduced costs. Administrators may also be strong advocates for appropriate legislative lobbying.

Infection control coordinators are often key personnel to involve in hospital and community education. They, in collaboration with the nurse training coordinator, plan inservice training sessions for other hospital nurses. (For further discussion of staff training, refer to Chapter 23.)

Law Enforcement and Emergency Response Personnel. Law enforcement and emergency response personnel should receive written infection control procedures and attend seminars on the procedures in the early stages of the program. Law enforcement officials from the area, or from another community accustomed to dealing with AIDS, should serve as trainers along with a health educator or health department official. Personnel often are extremely concerned about transporting accident victims who might be gay or drug users, isolating jail inmates who might be infected, and arresting people known to have AIDS. Law enforcement officers have been known to state that they favor bringing in "Sam Colt" to solve the AIDS problem while making the sign of a gun with their fingers. Again, per-sistence as well as education can change these attitudes. The value of humor should not be underestimated—for instance, acting out an officer standing over an accident victim and trying to decide if the person looks like a gay person or like a drug user.

Trainers should always expect professional behavior from participants. Good policy and protocol are essential to protect officers from infection and to protect the civil rights of citizens; meetings between key law enforcement and health department personnel should establish the medical base for recommended protocol. Department-issue gloves and respiration-assist masks should be supplied in conjunction with training on their appropriate use.

Public Health Staff. The fourth core group for the task force to involve is public health staff, who are at the heart of planning and implementing services. In particular, PHNs, family planning staff, and STD clinic staff benefit from information about screening, symptoms, transmission, and patient education. In many areas of the country, screening programs are already operative.

Mental Health Professionals. Last, the task force must educate and establish programs for professionals dealing with IV drug use and other mental health problems. Generally, drug treatment providers, rather than drug users themselves, must advocate for services for this group. Administrators should develop policies to ensure that clients receive information on AIDS upon intake even if they are not then accepted for treatment, that AIDS is discussed extensively as a part of treatment, and that people are not turned away from treatment because they have AIDS. Staff can then implement a program to increase awareness through brochures and posters, followed by educational events to promote individual acknowledgment of risk.

While the intention of treatment programs is to stop the use of drugs, some clients continue their use for long periods of time. The strategy for these clients may be to obtain a commitment to a small change in behavior (such as sharing needles with fewer people, or sharing less frequently), then to increase the commitment (for example, cleaning needles between uses), and to develop strategies that maintain these commitments (such as having the bleach in the same room with the needle before using the needle). Staff should encourage drug users in treatment to talk about prevention with friends who are not in treatment. This informal networking may at some point be extended to a street outreach program for people not in treatment. (For further information, refer to Chapter 4.)

Finally, mental health and social workers should meet among themselves, arrange to attend seminars on the psychosocial issues of AIDS, and examine the ways in which they can and will change their programs. Mental health workers need to be prepared to deal with crisis issues such as the shock of being diagnosed and grief over loss of loved ones. Their practice should also incorporate methods to address the stress of clients living in fear of contracting AIDS.

Gay Community Involvement

Concurrently with educating health providers, a program for AIDS resource development must make efforts to work within the gay community. A nonjudgmental approach that recognizes the importance of community norms is most helpful. The basic goals of a prevention program in the gay community are a social climate that supports safe sex, skills development in interpersonal communication, and easy access to condoms. The basic steps of education are to:

- increase knowledge about AIDS
- change community attitudes toward prevention (particularly toward use of condoms)
- change the behaviors of individuals
- extend the program by encouraging people to become volunteers in local AIDS services.

Local community sites where gay men gather, such as bars or resorts, can be keystones in changing the social climate. Bartenders in rural and urban gay communities can play a vital role in this work since they are already seen as free counselors at the heart of the community. They may need to be reminded of their special position, for they may feel that discussing AIDS is bad for business. Several areas in the country have had success with "Bartenders against AIDS" programs in which bartenders receive basic information, referral resources, and condoms to give patrons. A trained bartender is especially effective in the reinforcement of appropriate behavior at the exact time when practicing the behavior may be most difficult—when people are inebriated.

Further, once bartenders support the idea of AIDS education, prevention workshops may be held at bars. Developing a clear, consistent message that is not moralistic is essential. Workshops on transmission, antibody testing, and in-home infection control precautions may make up one series of workshops; another series may focus on eroticizing safe sex. Afterward, a number of gay men educated through these prevention efforts may be recruited as volunteers in providing education, emotional support, or home attendant care.

Service Coordination

Once initial work in the five core areas and in the gay community is underway, coordination of service delivery becomes crucial. The following model has been found most effective:

- The health department has a planned response that includes professional education and screening clinics.
- A community-based agency works closely with the health department to provide fear reduction and prevention education to the community.

- A task force coordinates the effects of all related health and human service providers.
- Minority service agencies perform specific outreach and education programs.

In this configuration, the components reap mutual benefits. Health department programs can assist nonprofit agencies in gaining credibility. Nonprofit agencies can effectively perform tasks that may be difficult for health departments, especially tasks that may arouse community controversy or that require trust from groups traditionally suspicious of health officials. Task forces can bring in all concerned community members so that no group feels disenfranchised from a comprehensive response plan. Minority service agencies can provide relevant information to other providers and receive training from them.

Legislative Issues

Any of the components in the model may take on the task of educating local and state health policy makers and legislators about AIDS issues and assisting and urging officials to establish appropriate policies on antibody testing, the schools, the workplace, and AIDS-related discrimination. If the state has a good antibody policy that ensures anonymity, voluntary testing, and thorough pre- and post-test counseling, the locality need only endorse it.

School and workplace policies can be similar because the basic issue is usually an unjustified fear of casual contagion. In both cases, the focus needs to shift to individuals and their socialization and medical needs. A clear policy on non-discrimination in these areas as well as in housing, insurance, and medical confidentiality helps to set a community tone of openness to education about AIDS and support for AIDS services.

CONCLUSION

The model presented here is broad enough to include all necessary components of AIDS education and resource development. It also suggests clear priorities for services when community resources are limited. Having seen this model work in different areas and under different conditions, we know it is effective and encourage others to adapt and use it.

1987 Revision of Case Definition for AIDS for Surveillance Purposes*

For national reporting, a case of AIDS is defined as an illness characterized by one or more of the following "indicator" diseases, depending on the status of laboratory evidence of HIV infection, as shown below.

I. Without Laboratory Evidence Regarding HIV Infection

If laboratory tests for HIV were not performed or gave inconclusive results (*See* Appendix I) and the patient had no other cause of immunodeficiency listed in Section I.A below, then any disease listed in Section I.B indicates AIDS if it was diagnosed by a definitive method (*See* Appendix II).

A. Causes of immunodeficiency that disqualify diseases as indicators of AIDS in the absence of laboratory evidence for HIV infection

1. high-dose or long-term systemic corticosteroid therapy or other immunosuppressive/cytotoxic therapy ≤3 months before the onset of the indicator disease
2. any of the following diseases diagnosed ≤3 months after diagnosis of the indicator disease: Hodgkin's disease, non-Hodgkin's lymphoma (other than primary brain lymphoma), lymphocytic leukemia, multiple myeloma, any other cancer of lymphoreticular or histiocytic tissue, or angioimmunoblastic lymphadenopathy
3. a genetic (congenital) immunodeficiency syndrome or an acquired immunodeficiency syndrome atypical of HIV infection, such as one involving hypogammaglobulinemia

B. Indicator diseases diagnosed definitively (*See* Appendix II)

1. candidiasis of the esophagus, trachea, bronchi, or lungs
2. cryptococcosis, extrapulmonary

---

*Reprinted from *Morbidity and Mortality Weekly Review,* Vol. 36, Supp. No. 1S, 4S–7S and 10S–14S, U.S. Centers for Disease Control, August 14, 1987.

3. cryptosporidiosis with diarrhea persisting >1 month
4. cytomegalovirus disease of an organ other than liver, spleen, or lymph nodes in a patient >1 month of age
5. herpes simplex virus infection causing a mucocutaneous ulcer that persists longer than 1 month; or bronchitis, pneumonitis, or esophagitis for any duration affecting a patient >1 month of age
6. Kaposi's sarcoma affecting a patient <60 years of age
7. lymphoma of the brain (primary) affecting a patient <60 years of age
8. lymphoid interstitial pneumonia and/or pulmonary lymphoid hyperplasia (LIP/PLH complex) affecting a child <13 years of age
9. *Mycobacterium avium* complex or *M. kansasii* disease, disseminated (at a site other than or in addition to lungs, skin, or cervical or hilar lymph nodes)
10. *Pneumocystis carinii* pneumonia
11. progressive multifocal leukoencephalopathy
12. toxoplasmosis of the brain affecting a patient >1 month of age

II. With Laboratory Evidence for HIV Infection

Regardless of the presence of other causes of immunodeficiency (I.A), in the presence of laboratory evidence for HIV infection (*See* Appendix I), any disease listed above (I.B) or below (II.A or II.B) indicates a diagnosis of AIDS.

A. Indicator diseases diagnosed definitively (*See* Appendix II)

1. bacterial infections, multiple or recurrent (any combination of at least two within a 2-year period), of the following types affecting a child <13 years of age:
   septicemia, pneumonia, meningitis, bone or joint infection, or abscess of an internal organ or body cavity (excluding otitis media or superficial skin or mucosal abscesses), caused by *Haemophilus, Streptococcus* (including pneumococcus), or other pyogenic bacteria
2. coccidioidomycosis, disseminated (at a site other than or in addition to lungs or cervical or hilar lymph nodes)
3. HIV encephalopathy (also called "HIV dementia," "AIDS dementia," or "subacute encephalitis due to HIV") (*See* Appendix II for description)
4. histoplasmosis, disseminated (at a site other than or in addition to lungs or cervical or hilar lymph nodes)
5. isosporiasis with diarrhea persisting >1 month
6. Kaposi's sarcoma at any age
7. lymphoma of the brain (primary) at any age
8. other non-Hodgkin's lymphoma of B-cell or unknown immunologic phenotype and the following histologic types:

a. small noncleaved lymphoma (either Burkitt or non-Burkitt type) (*See* Appendix IV for equivalent terms and numeric codes used in the *International Classification of Diseases,* Ninth Revision, Clinical Modification)

b. immunoblastic sarcoma (equivalent to any of the following, although not necessarily all in combination: immunoblastic lymphoma, large-cell lymphoma, diffuse histiocytic lymphoma, diffuse undifferentiated lymphoma, or high-grade lymphoma)

Note: Lymphomas are not included here if they are of T-cell immunologic phenotype or their histologic type is not described or is described as "lymphocytic," "lymphoblastic," "small cleaved," or "plasmacytoid lymphocytic"

9. any mycobacterial disease caused by mycobacteria other than *M. tuberculosis,* disseminated (at a site other than or in addition to lungs, skin, or cervical or hilar lymph nodes)

10. disease caused by *M. tuberculosis,* extrapulmonary (involving at least one site outside the lungs, regardless of whether there is concurrent pulmonary involvement)

11. *Salmonella* (nontyphoid) septicemia, recurrent

12. HIV wasting syndrome (emaciation, "slim disease") (*See* Appendix II for description)

B. Indicator diseases diagnosed presumptively (by a method other than those in Appendix II)

Note: Given the seriousness of diseases indicative of AIDS, it is generally important to diagnose them definitively, especially when therapy that would be used may have serious side effects or when definitive diagnosis is needed for eligibility for antiretroviral therapy. Nonetheless, in some situations, a patient's condition will not permit the performance of definitive tests. In other situations, accepted clinical practice may be to diagnose presumptively based on the presence of characteristic clinical and laboratory abnormalities. Guidelines for presumptive diagnoses are suggested in Appendix III.

1. candidiasis of the esophagus

2. cytomegalovirus retinitis with loss of vision

3. Kaposi's sarcoma

4. lymphoid interstitial pneumonia and/or pulmonary lymphoid hyperplasia (LIP/PLH) complex) affecting a child <13 years of age

5. mycobacterial disease (acid-fast bacilli with species not identified by culture), disseminated (involving at least one site other than or in addition to lungs, skin, or cervical or hilar lymph nodes)

6. *Pneumocystis carinii* pneumonia
7. toxoplasmosis of the brain affecting a patient >1 month of age

III. With Laboratory Evidence Against HIV Infection

With laboratory test results negative for HIV infection (*See* Appendix I), a diagnosis of AIDS for surveillance purposes is ruled out *unless*:

A. all the other causes of immunodeficiency listed above in Section I.A are excluded; **AND**
B. the patient has had either:
1. *Pneumocystis carinii* pneumonia diagnosed by a definitive method (*See* Appendix II); **OR**
2. a. any of the other diseases indicative of AIDS listed above in Section I.B diagnosed by a definitive method (*See* Appendix II); **AND**
   b. a T-helper/inducer (CD4) lymphocyte count <400/mm^3.

COMMENTARY

The surveillance of severe disease associated with HIV infection remains an essential, though not the only, indicator of the course of the HIV epidemic. The number of AIDS cases and the relative distribution of cases by demographic, geographic, and behavioral risk variables are the oldest indices of the epidemic, which began in 1981 and for which data are available retrospectively back to 1978. The original surveillance case definition, based on then-available knowledge, provided useful epidemiologic data on severe HIV disease.[1] To ensure a reasonable predictive value for underlying immunodeficiency caused by what was then an unknown agent, the indicators of AIDS in the old case definition were restricted to particular opportunistic diseases diagnosed by reliable methods in patients without specific known causes of immunodeficiency. After HIV was discovered to be the cause of AIDS, however, and highly sensitive and specific HIV-antibody tests became available, the spectrum of manifestations of HIV infection became better defined, and classification systems for HIV infection were developed.[2-5] It became apparent that some progressive, seriously disabling, and even fatal conditions (e.g., encephalopathy, wasting syndrome) affecting a substantial number of HIV-infected patients were not subject to epidemiologic surveillance, as they were not included in the AIDS case definition. For reporting purposes, the revision adds to the definition most of those severe non-infectious, non-cancerous HIV-associated conditions that are categorized in the CDC clinical classification systems for HIV infection among adults and children.[4,5]

Another limitation of the old definition was that AIDS-indicative diseases are diagnosed presumptively (i.e., without confirmation by methods required by the old definition) in 10%–15% of patients diagnosed with such diseases; thus, an appreciable proportion of AIDS cases were missed for reporting purposes.[6,7] This proportion may be increasing, which would compromise the old case definition's usefulness as a tool for monitoring trends. The revised case definition permits the reporting of these clinically diagnosed cases as long as there is laboratory evidence of HIV infection.

The effectiveness of the revision will depend on how extensively HIV-antibody tests are used. Approximately one third of AIDS patients in the United States have been from New York City and San Francisco, where, since 1985, < 7% have been reported with HIV-antibody test results, compared with > 60% in other areas. The impact of the revision on the reported numbers of AIDS cases will also depend on the proportion of AIDS patients in whom indicator diseases are diagnosed presumptively rather than definitively. The use of presumptive diagnostic criteria varies geographically, being more common in certain rural areas and in urban areas with many indigent AIDS patients.

To avoid confusion about what should be reported to health departments, the term "AIDS" should refer only to conditions meeting the surveillance definition. This definition is intended only to provide consistent statistical data for public health purposes. Clinicians will not rely on this definition alone to diagnose serious disease caused by HIV infection in individual patients because there may be additional information that would lead to a more accurate diagnosis. For example, patients who are not reportable under the definition because they have either a negative HIV-antibody test or, in the presence of HIV antibody, an opportunistic disease not listed in the definition as an indicator of AIDS nonetheless may be diagnosed as having serious HIV disease on consideration of other clinical or laboratory characteristics of HIV infection or a history of exposure to HIV.

Conversely, the AIDS surveillance definition may rarely misclassify other patients as having serious HIV disease if they have no HIV-antibody test but have an AIDS-indicative disease with a background incidence unrelated to HIV infection, such as cryptococcal meningitis.

The diagnostic criteria accepted by the AIDS surveillance case definition should not be interpreted as the standard of good medical practice. Presumptive diagnoses are accepted in the definition because not to count them would be to ignore substantial morbidity resulting from HIV infection. Likewise, the definition accepts a reactive screening test for HIV antibody without confirmation by a supplemental test because a repeatedly reactive screening test result, in combination with an indicator disease, is highly indicative of true HIV disease. For national surveillance purposes, the tiny proportion of possibly false-positive screening tests in persons with AIDS-indicative diseases is of little consequence. For the individual patient, however, a correct diagnosis is critically important. The use of supplemental tests is, therefore, strongly endorsed. An increase in the diagnostic use of HIV-antibody tests could improve both the quality of medical care and the function of the new case definition, as well as assist in providing counselling to prevent transmission of HIV.

REFERENCES

1. World Health Organization. Acquired immunodeficiency syndrome (AIDS): WHO/CDC case definition for AIDS. *WHO Wkly Epidemiol Rec* 1986;61:69–72.

2. Haverkos HW, Gottlieb MS, Killen JY, Edelman R. Classification of HTLV-III/LAV-related diseases [Letter]. *J Infect Dis* 1985;152:1095.

3. Redfield RR, Wright DC, Tramont EC. The Walter Reed staging classification of HTLV-III infection. *N Engl J Med* 1986;314:131–2.

4. CDC. Classification system for human T-lymphotropic virus type III/lymphadenopathy-associated virus infections. *MMWR* 1986;35:334–9.

5. CDC. Classification system for human immunodeficiency virus (HIV) infection in children under 13 years of age. *MMWR* 1987;36:225–30,235.

6. Hardy AM, Starcher ET, Morgan WM, et al. Review of death certificates to assess completeness of AIDS case reporting. *Pub Hlth Rep* 1987;102(4):386–91.

7. Starcher ET, Biel JK, Rivera-Castano R, Day JM, Hopkins SG, Miller JW. The impact of presumptively diagnosed opportunistic infections and cancers on national reporting of AIDS [Abstract]. Washington, DC: III International Conference on AIDS, June 1-5, 1987.

APPENDIX I: LABORATORY EVIDENCE FOR OR AGAINST HIV INFECTION

1. For Infection
   When a patient has disease consistent with AIDS:
   a. a serum specimen from a patient ≥15 months of age, or from a child <15 months of age whose mother is not thought to have had HIV infection during the child's perinatal period, that is repeatedly reactive for HIV antibody by a screening test (e.g., enzyme-linked immunosorbent assay [ELISA]), as long as subsequent HIV-antibody tests (e.g., Western blot, immunofluorescence assay), if done, are positive; **OR**
   b. a serum specimen from a child <15 months of age, whose mother is thought to have had HIV infection during the child's perinatal period, that is repeatedly reactive for HIV antibody by a screening test (e.g., ELISA), plus increased serum immunoglobulin levels and at least one of the following abnormal immunologic test results: reduced absolute lymphocyte count, depressed CD4 (T-helper) lymphocyte count, or decreased CD4/CD8 (helper/suppressor) ratio, as long as subsequent antibody tests (e.g., Western blot, immunofluorescence assay), if done, are positive; **OR**
   c. a positive test for HIV serum antigen; **OR**

d. a positive HIV culture confirmed by both reverse transcriptase detection and a specific HIV-antigen test or in situ hybridization using a nucleic acid probe; **OR**

e. a positive result on any other highly specific test for HIV (e.g., nucleic acid probe of peripheral blood lymphocytes).

2. Against Infection

A nonreactive screening test for serum antibody to HIV (e.g., ELISA) without a reactive or positive result on any other test for HIV infection (e.g., antibody, antigen, culture), if done.

3. Inconclusive (Neither For nor Against Infection)

a. a repeatedly reactive screening test for serum antibody to HIV (e.g., ELISA) followed by a negative or inconclusive supplemental test (e.g., Western blot, immunofluorescence assay) without a positive HIV culture or serum antigen test, if done; **OR**

b. a serum specimen from a child <15 months of age, whose mother is thought to have had HIV infection during the child's perinatal period, that is repeatedly reactive for HIV antibody by a screening test, even if positive by a supplemental test, without additional evidence for immunodeficiency as described above (in 1.b) and without a positive HIV culture or serum antigen test, if done.

APPENDIX II: DEFINITIVE DIAGNOSTIC METHODS FOR DISEASES INDICATIVE OF AIDS

Diseases   **Definitive Diagnostic Methods**

cryptosporidiosis
cytomegalovirus
isosporiasis
Kaposi's sarcoma
lymphoma
lymphoid pneumonia
  or hyperplasia   } microscopy (histology or cytology).
Pneumocystis carinii
  pneumonia
progressive multifocal
  leukoencephalopathy
toxoplasmosis

Diseases	Presumptive Diagnostic Criteria
candidiasis	gross inspection by endoscopy or autopsy or by microscopy (histology or cytology) on a specimen obtained directly from the tissues affected (including scrapings from the mucosal surface), not from a culture.
coccidioidomycosis cryptococcosis herpes simplex virus histoplasmosis	microscopy (histology or cytology), culture, or detection of antigen in a specimen obtained directly from the tissues affected or a fluid from those tissues.
tuberculosis other mycobacteriosis salmonellosis other bacterial infection	culture.
HIV encephalopathy* (dementia)	clinical findings of disabling cognitive and/or motor dysfunction interfering with occupation or activities of daily living, or loss of behavioral developmental milestones affecting a child, progressing over weeks to months, in the absence of a concurrent illness or condition other than HIV infection that could explain the findings. Methods to rule out such concurrent illnesses and conditions must include cerebrospinal fluid examination and either brain imaging (computed tomography or magnetic resonance) or autopsy.
HIV wasting syndrome*	findings of profound involuntary weight loss >10% of baseline body weight plus either chronic diarrhea (at least two loose stools per day for ≥30 days) or chronic weakness and documented fever (for ≥30 days, intermittent or constant) in the absence of a concurrent illness or condition other than HIV infection that could explain the findings (e.g., cancer, tuberculosis, cryptosporidiosis, or other specific enteritis).

*For HIV encephalopathy and HIV wasting syndrome, the methods of diagnosis described here are not truly definitive, but are sufficiently rigorous for surveillance purposes.

APPENDIX III: SUGGESTED GUIDELINES FOR PRESUMPTIVE DIAGNOSIS OF DISEASES INDICATIVE OF AIDS

Diseases	Presumptive Diagnostic Criteria
candidiasis of esophagus	a. recent onset of retrosternal pain on swallowing; **AND** b. oral candidiasis diagnosed by the gross appearance of white patches or plaques on an erythematous base or by the microscopic appearance of fungal mycelial filaments in an uncultured specimen scraped from the oral mucosa.
cytomegalovirus retinitis	a characteristic appearance on serial ophthalmoscopic examinations (e.g., discrete patches of retinal whitening with distinct borders, spreading in a centrifugal manner, following blood vessels, progressing over several months, frequently associated with retinal vasculitis, hemorrhage, and necrosis). Resolution of active disease leaves retinal scarring and atrophy with retinal pigment epithelial mottling.
mycobacteriosis	microscopy of a specimen from stool or normally sterile body fluids or tissue from a site other than lungs, skin, or cervical or hilar lymph nodes, showing acid-fast bacilli of a species not identified by culture.
Kaposi's sarcoma	a characteristic gross appearance of an erythematous or violaceous plaque-like lesion on skin or mucous membrane. (**Note:** Presumptive diagnosis of Kaposi's sarcoma should not be made by clinicians who have seen few cases of it.)
lymphoid interstitial pneumonia	bilateral reticulonodular interstitial pulmonary infiltrates present on chest X ray for ≥ 2 months with no pathogen identified and no response to antibiotic treatment.

Diseases	Presumptive Diagnostic Criteria

Pneumocystis carinii pneumonia

a. a history of dyspnea on exertion or nonproductive cough of recent onset (within the past 3 months); **AND**

b. chest X-ray evidence of diffuse bilateral interstitial infiltrates or gallium scan evidence of diffuse bilateral pulmonary disease; **AND**

c. arterial blood gas analysis showing an arterial pO_2 of <70 mm Hg or a low respiratory diffusing capacity (<80% of predicted values) or an increase in the alveolar-arterial oxygen tension gradient; **AND**

d. no evidence of a bacterial pneumonia.

toxoplasmosis of the brain

a. recent onset of a focal neurologic abnormality consistent with intracranial disease or a reduced level of consciousness; **AND**

b. brain imaging evidence of a lesion having a mass effect (on computed tomography or nuclear magnetic resonance) or the radiographic appearance of which is enhanced by injection of contrast medium; **AND**

c. serum antibody to toxoplasmosis or successful response to therapy for toxoplasmosis.

Guidelines for Reducing Risk through Safer Sex*

Reducing risk for AIDS may mean making changes in sexual practices, but it does not mean denying the sexual part of one's life. The safer sex guidelines below are recommended to all persons in groups at higher risk regardless of the results of the AIDS antibody test, because of unknown or inaccurate antibody status of one's partner and because of the risk of other sexually transmitted diseases. Sexual practices are classified into four categories: NO RISK, LOW RISK, MODERATE RISK, and HIGH RISK.

NO RISK

Most of these activities involve only skin-to-skin contact, thereby avoiding exposure to blood, semen, and vaginal secretions. This assumes there are no breaks in the skin.

- social kissing (dry)
- body massage, hugging
- body to body rubbing (frottage)
- light S & M (without bruising or bleeding)
- using one's own sex toys
- mutual masturbation (male or external female). Care should be taken to avoid exposing the partners to ejaculate or vaginal secretions. Seminal, vaginal, and salivary fluids should not be used as lubricants.

---

*Reprinted from *Medical Evaluation of Human Immunodeficiency Virus Infection* by J.M. Campbell, pp. 16–18, with permission of Bay Area Physicians for Human Rights, © 1987.

LOW RISK

In these activities small amounts of certain body fluids might be exchanged or the protective barrier might break, causing some risk.

Anal or Vaginal Intercourse with Condom

Studies have shown that HIV does not penetrate the condom in simulated intercourse.[1] Risk is incurred if the condom breaks or if semen spills into the rectum or vagina. The risk is further reduced if one withdraws before climax.

Fellatio Interruptus (Sucking, Stopping before Climax)[2]

Preejaculate fluid may contain HIV.[3] Saliva or other natural barriers in the mouth may inactivate virus in preejaculate fluid. Saliva may contain HIV in low concentration.[4] The insertive partner should warn the receptive partner before climax to prevent exposure to a large volume of semen. If mouth or genital sores are present, risk is increased. Likewise, action which causes mouth or genital injury will increase risk.

Fellatio with Condom (Sucking with Condom)

Since HIV cannot penetrate an intact condom, risk in this practice is very low unless breakage occurs.

Mouth-to-Mouth Kissing (French Kissing, Wet Kissing)

Studies have shown that HIV is present in saliva in such low concentration that salivary exchange is unlikely to transmit the virus.[5] Risk is increased if sores in the mouth or bleeding gums are present.

Oral-Vaginal or Oral-Anal Contact with Protective Barrier (e.g., a latex dam, obtainable through a dental supply house)

Do not reuse latex barrier because sides of barrier may be reversed inadvertently.

Manual-Anal Contact with Glove (Fisting with Glove)

If the glove does not break, virus transmission should not occur. However, significant trauma can still be inflicted on the rectal tissues, leading to other medical problems, such as hemorrhage and bowel perforation.

Manual-Vaginal Contact with Glove (Internal)

If the glove does not break, virus transmission should not occur.

MODERATE RISK

These activities involve tissue trauma and/or exchange of body fluids which may transmit HIV or other sexually transmitted disease.

Fellatio (Sucking to Climax)[6]

Semen may contain high concentrations of HIV and, if absorbed through open sores in the mouth or digestive tract, could pose risk.

Oral-Anal Contact (Rimming)

HIV may be contained in blood-contaminated feces or in the anal-rectal lining. This practice also poses high risk of transmission of parasites or other gastrointestinal infections.

Cunnilingus (Oral-Vaginal Contact)

Vaginal secretions and menstrual blood have been shown to harbor HIV, thereby causing risk to the oral partner if open lesions are present in the mouth or digestive tract.[7]

Manual-Rectal Contact (Fisting)

Studies have indicated a direct association between fisting and HIV infection for both partners.[8] This association may be due to concurrent use of recreational drugs, bleeding, prefisting semen exposure, or anal intercourse with ejaculation.

Sharing Sex Toys

Ingestion of Urine

HIV has not been shown to be transmitted via urine; however, other immunosuppressive agents or infections may be transmitted in this manner.

HIGH RISK

These activities have been shown to transmit HIV.

Receptive Anal Intercourse without Condom

All studies imply that this activity carries the highest risk of transmitting HIV.[9] The rectal lining is thinner than that of the vagina or the mouth, thereby permitting ready absorption of virus from semen or preejaculate fluid into the bloodstream. One laboratory study suggests that the virus may enter by direct contact with rectal lining cells without any bleeding.[10]

Insertive Anal Intercourse without Condom

Studies suggest that men who participate only in this activity are at less risk of being infected than their partners who are rectally receptive; however, the risk is still significant.[11] It carries a high risk of infection with other sexually transmitted diseases.

Vaginal Intercourse without Condom

This practice has been implicated in heterosexual transmission of HIV for both the male and female. Some studies suggest that risk of transmission is greater in the male-to-female direction; others suggest an equal risk.[12]

GENERAL FACTORS

Since sexual compatibility is important, it is best to discuss your concerns about health before becoming sexual with a new partner. If you or your partner are a member of a group at higher risk and you both have tested negative for the AIDS antibody, it is still advisable to practice low risk sex. If the antibody status of either you or your partner is unknown or positive, you should practice no risk or low risk sex, depending on the degree of risk you wish to take.

Monogamy in itself does not ensure safety unless both partners are known to be HIV antibody–negative after six months of mutual monogamy. It is safer to have no risk activity with several partners than high risk activity with one who might be infected.

Sex in groups may expose you to risks carried over from encounters with others in the group. Adherence to only no risk practices is advised in group situations.

Cleanliness is important in disease prevention. Showering with one's partner before sex can be erotic as well as cleansing and also affords the opportunity to find problems beforehand. Another shower after sex is advisable. Douching can increase the risk for Hepatitis B and presumably HIV by disrupting the protective mucus of the bowel or vagina.

Some studies suggest that certain recreational drugs may suppress immune system function.[13] However, there are no studies indicating direct correlation between AIDS and recreational drugs except when IV needles are shared and when the use of drugs leads to impaired judgment and reduced inhibitions, resulting in high risk activity. Perception of pain may also be diminished, leading to trauma and increased risk of exposure to HIV.

Recommendations include adequate rest, good nutrition, physical exercise, reduction of stress and the avoidance of excess alcohol, tobacco, and drugs. Practice safer and responsible sexual activities.

Taking care of one's body and general health should be recommended.

These guidelines are intended to help prevent transmission of the virus, to arm us against the fear generated by it, and to remind us of the importance to our general well-being of healthy sexual expression.

NOTES

1. Marcus Conant et al., "Condoms Prevent Transmission of AIDS-Associated Retrovirus," *Journal of the American Medical Association (JAMA)*, 255 (1986):1706.

2. M.T. Schecter et al., "Can HTLV-III Be Transmitted Orally?" *Lancet* 1 (1986):379; D. Lyman et al., "Minimal Risk of Transmission of ARV Infection by Oral Genital Contact," *JAMA* 255 (1987):1703; W. Winkelstein et al., "Sexual Practices and Risk of Infection by the Human Immunodeficiency Virus," *JAMA* 257 (1987):321–25; and L.A. Kingsley et al., "Risk Factors for Seroconversion to Human Immunodeficiency Virus Among Male Homosexuals. Results from the Multicenter AIDS Cohort Study," *Lancet* 1 (1987):345–48.

3. M.S. Borzy and A.A. Kiessling, "Reverse Transcriptase Activity in Seminal Fluid from Patients with AIDS and from a Normal Heterosexual Male (Abstract) (T-5 Poster, International Conference on AIDS, Atlanta, Ga., April 1985).

4. P.N. Fultz, "Components of Saliva Inactivate Human Immunodeficiency Virus," *Lancet* 2 (1986):1215; D.W. Archibald et al., "Antibodies to HTLV-III in Saliva of AIDS Patients and in Persons at Risk for AIDS," *Blood* 67 (1986):831–34; D.D. Ho et al., "Infrequency of Isolation of HTLV-III Virus From Saliva in AIDS," *New England Journal of Medicine* 313 (1985):1606; and J.E. Groopman et al., "HTLV-III in Saliva of People with AIDS-Related Complex and Healthy Homosexual Men at Risk for AIDS," *Science* 226 (1984):447.

5. Ibid.; Fultz, "Components of Saliva"; Archibald et al., "Antibodies to HTLV-III in Saliva"; and Ho et al., "Infrequency of Isolation of HTLV-III Virus."

6. Schechter et al., "Can HTLV-III Be Transmitted Orally?"; Lyman et al., "Minimal Risk of Transmission of ARV Infection"; Winkelstein et al., "Sexual Practices and Risk of Infection"; and Kingsley et al., "Risk Factors for Seroconversion."

7. M.W. Vogt and D.J. Witt, "Isolation of HTLV-III/LAV from Cervical Secretions of Women at Risk for AIDS," *Lancet* 1 (1986):525–26; and C.B. Wofsy, L.B. Hauer, and J.A. Levy, "Isolation of ARV from Genital Secretions of Women with Antibodies to the Virus," *Lancet* 1 (1986):527–28.

8. M.F. Rogers et al., "National Case-Control Study of Kaposi's Sarcoma and *Pneumocystis carinii* Pneumonia in Homosexual Men," *Annals of Internal Medicine* 99 (1983):145–58.

9. R. Detels et al., "Relation Between Sexual Practices and T Cell Subsets in Homosexually Active Men," *Lancet* 1 (1983):609–11; J.E. Groopman et al., "Seroepidemiology of HTLV-III Among Homosexual Men with AIDS or Generalized Lymphadenopathy and Among Asymptomatic Controls in Boston," *Annals of Internal Medicine* 102 (1985):334–37; Winkelstein et al., "Sexual Practices and Risk of Infection"; and Kingsley et al., "Risk Factors for Seroconversion."

10. A. Adachi et al., "Productive, Persistent Infection of Human Colorectal Cell Lines with Human Immunodeficiency Virus," *Journal of Virology* 61 (1987):209–13.

11. Schechter et al., "Can HTLV-III Be Transmitted Orally?"; Lyman et al., "Minimal Risk of Transmission of ARV Infection"; Winkelstein et al., "Sexual Practices and Risk of Infection"; and Kingsley et al., "Risk Factors for Seroconversion."

12. C. Harris, C.B. Small, and R.S. Klein, "Immunodeficiency in Female Sexual Partners of Men with AIDS," *New England Journal of Medicine* 308 (1983):1181–84; P. Piot, "AIDS in a Heterosexual Population in Zaire," *Lancet* 2 (1984):65–69; R.R. Redfield et al., "Frequent Transmission of HTLV-III Among Spouses of Patients with AIDS-related Complex and AIDS," *JAMA* 253 (1985):1571–74; and M.A. Fischl et al., "Evaluation of Heterosexual Partners, Children, and Household Contacts of Adults with AIDS," *JAMA* 257 (1987):640–44.

13. Rogers et al., "National Case-Control Study"; and G.R. Newell et al., "Volatile Nitrites: Use and Adverse Effects Related to the Current Epidemic of AIDS," *American Journal of Medicine* 78 (1985):811–16.

Useful Resources

The number of educational resources, audiovisual materials, and organizations related to AIDS has grown exponentially since the recognition of the epidemic; organizations alone number over 500. The following list represents just a small portion of those that may be of interest.

To become acquainted with the resources in a particular community, individuals should begin to develop networks with other care providers, community organizations, and PWAs. If unable to locate an organization, any of the following can be contacted for referral:

- National AIDS Network, 1012 14th Street, N.W., Suite 601, Washington, DC 20005; (202) 347-0390.
- National Gay Task Force AIDS Information Hotline, (800) 221-7044; in New York, (212) 807-6016.
- Public Health Service AIDS Hotline, (800) 342-2437.
- National AIDS Hotline, (800) 342-7514.
- San Francisco AIDS Foundation (SFAF), P.O. Box 6182, San Francisco, CA 94101-6182; (415) 863-AIDS.
- Gay Men's Health Crisis, P.O. Box 274, 132 West 24th Street, New York, NY 10011, (212) 807-7035.
- AIDS Project Los Angeles, 1362 Santa Monica Boulevard, Los Angeles, CA 90046; (213) 871-AIDS.
- Health Education Resource Organization (HERO), 101 West Read Street, Suite 819, Baltimore, MD 21201; (301) 685-1180.

EDUCATIONAL AND INFORMATIONAL RESOURCES

- *AIDS EDUCATOR:* SFAF, P.O. Box 6182, San Francisco, CA 94101-6182. Call (415) 861-3397 to order materials only; for technical or program assistance, call (415) 863-4376.

This publication, a 19-page catalog listing a wide range of AIDS educational brochures, videos, manuals, booklets, and posters, is available free of charge.

- *AIDSFILE:* AIDSFILE, San Francisco General Hospital, Ward 84, 995 Potrero Avenue, San Francisco, CA 94110.

  AIDSFILE is a free quarterly newsletter for physicians that focuses on disease manifestations and medical management.

- American Red Cross: Contact your local chapter or the AIDS Education Office, 1730 D Street, N.W., Washington, DC 20006; (202) 737-8300.

- Centers for Disease Control, Still Picture Archives, 1600 Clifton Road, N.E. Still Picture Archives, D.T.S., T.L.P.O., Altanta, GA 30333; (404) 639-1388.

  The CDC produces epidemiological and surveillance slides that are available without charge.

- *FOCUS, A Guide to AIDS Research:* University of California, San Francisco, AIDS Health Project, Box 0884, San Francisco, CA 94143-0884.

  This is a four-page monthly publication presenting AIDS research information relevant to health care and service providers. It costs $36 a year for U.S. residents and $48 for international residents. Make checks payable to "U.C. Regents."

- National Coalition of Gay Sexually Transmitted Disease Services (NCGSTDS): c/o Mark Behar, P.O. Box 239, Milwaukee, WI 53201; (414) 277-7671.

  This organization publishes an excellent newsletter, *Sexual Health Report* (four to six issues a year) that includes a great deal of AIDS information, reprints from *Morbidity and Mortality Weekly Report*, and updates on community action.

- Train the Trainer Program: For further information on this program, contact the California Nurses' Association, 1855 Folsom Street, Suite 670, San Francisco, CA 94103; (415) 864-4141.

- Shanti Training: Shanti Project, 525 Howard Street, San Francisco, CA 94105; (415) 777-CARE.

  Shanti training is a 40-hour program designed to train the layperson to provide support for PWAs. The program is available on videotape.

- *Morbidity and Mortality Weekly Report (MMWR):* Centers for Disease Control.

  Subscriptions are available through the Massachusetts Medical Society, C.S.P.O. Box 9120, Waltham, MA 02254-9120.

VIDEOTAPES

- "AIDS: A Nurse's Responsibility" (1985): Double Vision Video, 401 S Street, Sacramento, CA 95814; (916) 448-8220.

An instructional program produced by the California Nurses' Association detailing hospital care, discharge planning, and home health needs of people with AIDS, this package includes a 30-minute videotape and a leader's workbook written by nurses. It is appropriate for all health care providers.

- "AIDS: Care Beyond the Hospital" (1985): SFAF.

  This program is the videotape version of a slide presentation specifically designed as a teaching tool for health care providers who are or will be working with PWAs in the home. The 45-minute Case Management version is directed to health professionals, while the 30-minute Attendant Care version outlines basic home hygiene techniques.

- "AIDS and the Health Care Provider": Advanced Imaging, Inc., c/o Care Video Productions, P.O. Box 45132, Cleveland, OH 44145; (216) 835-5872.

  Health care professionals and coworkers discuss the cause, transmission, and prevention of AIDS. In addition to showing practical control measures, the videotape goes beyond the concern of the health care worker to the innermost thoughts of the PWA. The program was produced in cooperation with Yale–New Haven Hospital, Connecticut.

- "Beyond Fear" (1986): Free rental from local Red Cross chapters.

  This videotape consists of a series of three 20-minute segments: "The Virus"; "The Individual"; and "The Community." Designed for the public and health professionals, topics include epidemiology, transmission, risk reduction, screening, the need for education, and discrimination issues. The program also includes interviews with a woman with AIDS, another with ARC, and a family with AIDS.

ORGANIZATIONS

- AIDS Health Services Program and AIDS Resource Program, 1326 Third Avenue, San Francisco, CA 94143-0936, (415) 476-6430.

- AIDS Health Project, Box 0884, San Francisco, CA 94143-0884; (415) 476-6430.

- American Association of Physicians for Human Rights, P.O. Box 14366, San Francisco, CA 94114; (415) 558-9353.

- National Association of People with AIDS (NAPA), 2025 I Street N.W., Washington, DC 20006; (202) 429-2856.

- Minority Task Force on AIDS, c/o New York City Council of Churches, 475 Riverside Drive, Room 456, New York, NY 10115; (212) 749-1214.

- Mothers of AIDS Patients (MAP), c/o Barbara Peabody, 3403 E Street, San Diego, CA 92012; (619) 234-3432.

USEFUL REFERENCES

Faltz, Barbara, and Rinaldi, Joanna. *AIDS and Substance Abuse: A Training Manual for Health Care Professionals*. San Francisco: AIDS Health Project, 1987.

McIlvenna, Ted, ed. *The Complete Guide to Safe Sex*. San Francisco: The Institute for Advanced Study of Human Sexuality, 1987.

Shelp, Earl E.; Sunderland, Ronald H.; and Mansell, Peter. *AIDS: Personal Stories in Pastoral Perspective*. New York: The Pilgrim Press, 1986.

Index

Note: Page numbers in italics indicate material found in figures, exhibits, and tables.